Lecture Notes in Computer Science   1005

Springer
Berlin
Heidelberg
New York
Barcelona
Budapest
Hong Kong
London
Milan
Paris
Santa Clara
Singapore
Tokyo

Jacky Estublier (Ed.)

Software Configuration Management

ICSE SCM-4 and SCM-5 Workshops
Selected Papers

 Springer

Series Editors

Gerhard Goos
Universität Karlsruhe
Vincenz-Priessnitz-Straße 3, D-76128 Karlsruhe, Germany

Juris Hartmanis
Department of Computer Science, Cornell University
4130 Upson Hall, Ithaca, NY 14853, USA

Jan van Leeuwen
Department of Computer Science,Utrecht University
Padualaan 14, 3584 CH Utrecht, The Netherlands

Volume Editor

Jacky Estublier
LGI LSR, BP 53
F-38041 Grenoble Cedex 09, France
Jacky.Estublier@imag.fr

Cataloging-in-Publication data applied for

Die Deutsche Bibliothek - CIP-Einheitsaufnahme

Software configuration management : selected papers / ICSE
SCM-4 and SCM-5 Workshops. Jacky Estublier (ed.). - Berlin ;
Heidelberg ; New York ; Barcelona ; Budapest ; Hong Kong ;
London ; Milan ; Paris ; Tokyo : Springer, 1995
  (Lecture notes in computer science ; Vol. 1005)
  ISBN 3-540-60578-9
NE: Estublier, Jacky [Hrsg.]; International Conference on Software
  Engineering <15, 1993, Baltimore, Md.>; SCM <4, 1993, Baltimore,
  Md.>; GT

CR Subject Classification (1991): D.2, K.6

ISBN 3-540-60578-9 Springer-Verlag Berlin Heidelberg New York

© Springer-Verlag Berlin Heidelberg 1995
Printed in Germany

Typesetting: Camera-ready by author
SPIN 10487149   06/3142 – 5 4 3 2 1 0   Printed on acid-free paper

Preface

This workshop is the fifth in a series. The previous workshops were held in Grassau (Germany, 1988), Princeton (USA, 1990), Trondheim (Norway, 1991), and Baltimore (USA, 1993). The goal in this workshop series is to merge the work of researchers and practitioners in an attempt to discuss and establish concepts and techniques, and to gather experiences in the field of Software Configuration Management.

The proceedings for the Baltimore workshop (SCM-4) were never published, which is why this issue begins with 4 papers selected among the best presented at Baltimore.

The SCM-5 workshop attendance was restricted to 35 persons, selected on the basis of the quality of a paper or position paper. From the 35 selected papers, only 18 are published in this volume. Attendance split up nicely: 13 persons from university, 13 from industry, and 9 'in between'. This is a perfect ratio for Software Engineering. 16 persons were SCM designers or researchers, 12 SCM developers, 4 involved in development, and 4 users.

This workshop was held at a point in time where the second generation SCM systems are becoming widely available, and when it is increasingly understood that SCM is mandatory in today's software engineering. It is required by a number of standards (ISO) and constantly flagged as the major tool for controlling software production (SEI, CMM...). As a consequence, the SCM market is booming, attracting attention from researchers, industrialists, and vendors.

Whatever the reason, this workshop was one of the best in the series, with a clear increase in interest. It was remarkable for the balance between university and industry and for the presence of major vendors and research groups. Throughout these two days, rich and vivid interchanges took place, making this workshop appreciated by attendants.

This workshop also showed a shift in focus. The traditional topics 'versioning' and 'rebuilding' were not very much discussed, while new topics like process modelling support, distribution, and evaluation were discussed at length.

The new SCM generation did not sterilize the field, but instead raised the level of expectation and identified new challenges. The SCM field is still attracting the attention of both researchers and practitioners, and should remain for the years to come a major Software Engineering research and development domain.

Thanks to the committee who helped me to set up this event, and the ICSE team for the tremendous work done in organizing the whole week.

September 1995

Jacky Estublier, Chair
(LGI, France)

Programme Committee

Reidar Conradi (NTH, Norway)
Susan Dart (Continuus, USA)
Stu Feldman (Bell Core, USA)
Michel Lacroix (EC Belgium)

Table of Contents

An Overview of the CAPITL Software Development Environment *

Paul Adams[1] and Marvin Solomon[2]

[1] Grammatech, Inc., Ithaca, NY, USA (adams@grammatech.com)
[2] Computer Sciences Department, 1210 W. Dayton St., Madison, WI 53706–1685,
USA (solomon@cs.wisc.edu)

Abstract. The CAPITL programming environment is comprised of a
shared, object-oriented, versioned database, an embedded logic-based
data-manipulation language, and a graphical user interface. With each
software object the database stores a rich set of attributes that describe its syntax, intended semantics, and relationship to other objects.
CAPITL is implemented in POL, a data model and deductive query language with elements of persistent, object-oriented and logic-based programming languages. POL is implemented in and tightly coupled with
C++.
A request for a derived object consists of a partial description of its
attributes. A planner written in POL searches the database for tools and
sources that can be combined to create an object meeting the description.
Since tools are stored in the database like other objects, plans that create
tools as well as intermediate inputs are possible. A builder, also written
in POL, executes plans to materialize software products. The builder
verifies that existing objects are current, minimally re-applying tools as
sources, tools, or system descriptions change.
After an overview of the database and the POL programming system, we
outline CAPITL's logic-based approach to system modelling, illustrating
it with two examples. We conclude with a status report and an outline
of future directions.

1 Introduction

Large software systems are hard to build and maintain. The sheer number of
components involved make the management, coordination, and storage of the
components difficult. Because of the malleable nature of software, components
are constantly changing. Change is not limited to source text; attributes of the
source files, relationships among them, tools used to process them, and even
architectures of whole subsystems change as bugs are fixed, new functionality is
added, and components are re-organized. Maintaining invariants in an evolving
system is a critical task for any support system [41, 48, 50].

---

* This work was supported in part by the Defense Advanced Research Projects Agency
under ARPA Order No. 8856 (monitored by the Office of Naval Research under
contract N00014-92-J-1937).

The CAPITL [3] project at the University of Wisconsin has been investigating a logic-based approach to software configuration management [42]. The basic thesis of our approach is that if all objects in the environment carry with them sufficiently detailed descriptions, desired software products can be described declaratively and the system can infer the process necessary to build them. To test these ideas, we have constructed a environment that tightly integrates a logic-based language with a versioned, object-oriented database. By tightly coupling the database with both an imperative object-oriented language and a declarative language, CAPITL gets the best of both worlds: declarative queries and specifications, and object-oriented extensibility and state encapsulation. This paper describes the main components of the environment and outlines how they support maintenance of large software systems.

CAPITL was designed with four principles in mind.

- **Uniformity.** All objects are represented and described in a common language.
- **Locality.** The information that describes an object and its relationships with other objects is directly associated with that object.
- **Extensibility.** New types of objects, new descriptive properties, and new relationships can be added easily.
- **Flexibility.** Policies for access control and modification to objects can be specified rather than such policies being "wired in."

CAPITL consists of three main components: a shared, versioned database, a graphical user interface, and a fully embedded logic-based data-manipulation language. The CAPITL database records all aspects of software construction: source files, documentation, sub-systems, system descriptions, tools, executables, and configurations. The form and function of each database object, as well as its relation to other objects, is described in detail by attributes stored with it. Support for efficient maintenance of multiple versions of the database is built in. A compatibility feature allows existing Unix tools to manipulate CAPITL objects as if they were Unix files.

The database is accessible via an interactive browser/editor based on the X Window System [45] and the InterViews graphical toolkit [34]. CAPITL's browser can navigate the version history of the database and the links between objects. It also provides facilities for the display and manual update of objects.

Most of the features of CAPITL are implemented in POL [3], a data model and deductive query language synthesized from elements of persistent, object-oriented, and logic-based programming languages. POL is tightly integrated with the database (all database objects are POL terms) and with a general-purpose host language (C++). The database uses the Exodus toolkit [11] to provide low-level concurrency control, error recovery, and network access. POL includes a logic-based programming language called Congress, which also servers as a query and update language.

---

[3] Computer Aided Programming In The Large

CAPITL uses Congress as the basis for a tool that automatically builds and maintains derived objects. An architect of a software system describes tools and policies using Congress as a specification language. A program written in Congress accepts declarative specifications of desired products and deduces plans to locate or construct them. CAPITL thus provides a platform supporting application-specific notions of consistency and correctness.

The remainder of this paper is organized as follows. Section 2 describes the POL data model, the embedded language Congress, and the interface between Congress, C++, and the database. The use of the database to store software objects is explored in Section 3. Section 4 explains how CAPITL is used for software configuration management (SCM). Section 5 illustrates these ideas with two concrete examples. Section 6 discusses related work. We close with a status report and future plans.

2 POL

POL (Persistent Objects with Logic) is a mixture of three styles of programming language: object-oriented, logic-based, and persistent. Each style has features that make solving certain problems easier: Object-oriented languages encapsulate state and behavior and support extension by inheritance; logic programming languages allow programmers to concentrate on describing *what* a solution is rather than *how* to find it; persistent programming languages relieve the programmer of the burden of saving and restoring data. By combining features from all three domains, POL provides an environment in which application programmers can take advantage of the particular style that best suits the problem at hand.

POL derives its object-oriented features from C++ (§ 2.2), persistence from the Exodus database toolkit (§ 2.3), and logic-based features from Congress – a derivative of Prolog (§ 2.4). POL integrates these components with a shared data model and a two-way embedding of Congress in C++ and C++ in Congress. The remainder of this section describes the data model, the three components, and the interfaces between them.

2.1 Term Space

As in Prolog and LISP, POL uses one data structure for both programs and data. A *term space* is a directed graph with labelled nodes and arcs. The label associated with a node is called its *functor*[4] and the label associated with an arc is called its *selector*. No two arcs leaving the same node may have the same selector. A *term* is the subgraph of the term space reachable from a node, called the *root* of the term. We occasionally identify a term with its root node, when the meaning is clear from context. For example, the "functor of a term" means the functor of its root node.

---

[4] This unfortunate choice of terminology is inherited from Prolog.

POL is "identity-based": Two nodes with identical contents are nonetheless considered to be distinct. Nodes are explicitly created, and updates to a node do not change the node's identity. In this way POL differs from "value-based" Prolog and relational databases, and more closely resembles so-called "object-oriented" databases.

POL supports multiple versions of the term space called *worlds*, and uses an algorithm devised by Driscol *et. al.* [16] that supports efficient "checkpointing" of the entire term space. POL has operations to save the current term space as a world, and to reset its state to any previously saved world. A checkpoint operation does not copy the entire term space, but only an amount of data proportional to the changes made since the previous checkpoint.

2.2 C++

C++ is a strongly typed object-oriented language derived from C. C++ classes encapsulate both data and operations on that data. C++ allows multiple inheritance and supports information hiding via explicit public/private declarations. Subclasses can override methods of their super-class as well as add new data fields and operations.

C++ classes are used in POL to provide a concrete realization of term space nodes and arcs. Data structures used to represent nodes come in a variety of flavors. Leaf nodes (nodes with no outgoing arcs) are classified according to the data types of their functors: integers, real numbers, printable strings, byte strings (arbitrary binary data) or "variables." (Variables are explained in Section 2.4.) An internal node contains a functor (which must be a printable string) and a table of references to other nodes indexed by distinct printable strings. Internal nodes are similar to C structs, Pascal records, SNOBOL tables, and AWK associative arrays. Unlike structs or records, the number and names of "fields" may vary dynamically, and their contents are restricted to be non-null pointers to nodes. C++ subclass derivation is used to add additional behavior and restrictions to classes of internal nodes. We shall return to this point in Section 3.

2.3 Exodus

Exodus [11] is a toolkit for creating custom database systems. POL uses two components of Exodus, a low-level storage subsystem and a persistent programming language. The Exodus Storage Manager provides efficient access to an arbitrary-sized persistent chunk of uninterpreted data called a "storage object" through a unique identifier called an "OID." The Storage Manager supports concurrency control through two-phase locking, and a simple transaction facility with full recovery from hardware and software failures. The E programming language [43] is an extension of C++ that supports persistent data – data that retains its state between runs of a program. E syntax extends C++ with a "db" version of each primitive type and type constructor (e.g. `dbint`, `dbclass{ ... }`, etc.). Instances of a db type can be allocated from a persistent heap. The E runtime support library ensures that persistent data structures are securely stored on disk at the end of a transaction, and are fetched on demand (whenever a pointer to one is dereferenced). POL implements the term space with persistent data structures.

Throughout this paper, all references to the C++ programming language should be understood as referring to the E dialect of C++.

2.4 Congress

Congress may be described as a logic programming language, a deductive database query language, an embedded query language, or a library of classes for convenient database access, depending on one's point of view. Since Congress is implemented as a library of classes, any C++ program can use Congress as a "higher level" alternative to or enhancement of the raw C++ term interface.

As a logic-programming language, Congress is a dialect of LOGIN [5], an extension of Prolog that supports cyclic terms. It provides transparent persistence, and has an identity-based rather than value-based semantics. The following paragraphs briefly describe the syntax and semantics of Congress. The reader who is familiar with logic programming may skim this section.

Congress programs are built from terms in the POL term space. A *program* is a set of *procedures*, a procedure is a sequence of *clauses*, and a clause is a sequence of terms. In particular, a clause consists of a single term called its *head* and a sequence of zero or more additional terms called its *body*. The *predicate* of a clause is the functor of the root node of its head term. A procedure is a sequence of clauses with a common predicate, referred to as the *name* of the procedure. A program is a set of procedures with distinct names.

The operational behavior of Congress is defined by the same recursive backtracking search as in Prolog. A *goal* (or "query") consists of a term. It is "called" ("evaluated," "proved") by searching the procedure named by its functor for a clause whose head "matches" the goal. If a matching clause is found, each term in its body is called in turn. If no matching clause can be found, the interpreter backs up by undoing all of its actions since the last "choice point" (the point at which a clause was chosen to match against a goal) and attempts another match. The process continues either until all goals and subgoals have been proven, in which case the original call "succeeds," or until all alternatives have been exhausted, in which case it "fails".

The heart of this process is the definition of "matching" between terms, called *unification*[5] Congress uses a variant of unification that supports cyclic terms [5]. The goal of unification is to determine if two terms are isomorphic, or can be made isomorphic by substituting terms for variables. Two terms unify if their roots match (have the same functor) and corresponding successors (recursively) unify. That is, if both roots have arcs with the same selector leaving them, the nodes reached by these arcs must also unify. As mentioned in § 2.2, some nodes are designated as *variables*; a variable matches any node. A side effect of a

---

[5] Background material on unification can be found in many logic programming texts and in an excellent survey by Knight [28].

successful unification is an equivalence relation that records which nodes were matched. The evaluation of a call adds a *copy* of a clause to the term space and identifies nodes matched as a result of unifying its head with the query. The terms of the body are called in this extended term space.

Congress has a character-string *expression language* that may be used to enter or print programs or fragments of programs, or to enter queries from the keyboard. A term t may be denoted $f(s_1 => t_1, ..., s_n => t_n)$, where f is its functor, $s_1, ..., s_n$ are the selectors of the arcs with f as their tail, and $t_1, ..., t_n$ are textual representations of the terms at the heads of the corresponding arcs. A variable is denoted "@". A *tag* (an alphanumeric string starting with a capital letter) is used to indicate shared subtrees or cycles. For example, the term

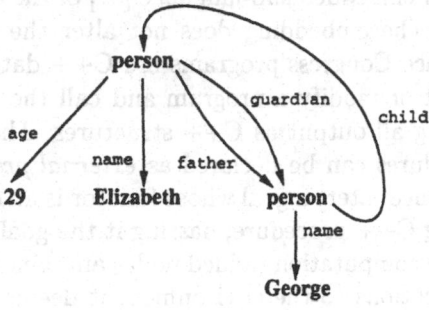

may be denoted[6]

```
F:person(
    name=>      "Elizabeth",
    age=>       29,
    father=>    G:person( name => "George", child => F ),
    guardian=> G
).
```

The expression language denotes a clause with head t_0 and body $t_1, ..., t_n$ as "$t_0 : - t_1, ..., t_n$." The expression language also includes "syntactic sugar" for representing common infix operators such as +, *, -, /, and for Prolog style lists. For example, the expression [a, b | Tail] denotes the same term as the expression cons(car => a, cdr => cons(car => b, cdr => Tail)). A missing selector implies an edge labelled with an integer and occurrences of @ can be omitted in most cases. For example, f(a,X) is the same as f(1=>a, 2=>X:@).

With these abbreviations, the Congress expression language becomes a strict superset of Prolog. It extends Prolog in two important ways. First, the successors of a node are indicated by keyword rather than positional notation. This extension helps avoid programming errors[7]. For example, the Congress expression employee(age=>25,salary=>30) is less confusing than the corresponding

---

[6] A functor that contains non-alphanumeric characters or starts with an upper-case letter must be quoted.

[7] It also has a rather subtle effect on the definition of unification. See the LOGIN paper [5] for details.

Prolog expression `employee(25,30)`. Second, while Prolog terms are trees (except for identification of multiple occurrences of the same variable), Congress allows arbitrary graphs, including cycles. Variables serve two purposes in Prolog: They represent "wild cards" for pattern matching and they indicate sharing. The expression language of Congress uses the functor "@" for the first purpose and tags for the second.

2.5 Embedding

The coupling between C++ and Congress is a two-way embedding: Each language appears to be an embedded sub-language [37] of the other. Each language retains its own style. The embedding does not alter the syntax or semantics of either language. Since Congress programs are C++ data structures, a C++ program can construct or modify a program and call the Congress interpreter to execute it, capturing all output as C++ structures. The embedding is bidirectional: C++ procedures can be declared as *external predicates* in Congress. When the interpreter encounters a goal whose functor is an external predicate, it calls the corresponding C++ procedure, passing it the goal and a description of the current state of the computation (added nodes and bindings). The procedure may make any modifications to the environment it deems appropriate (for example, adding bindings) and return either a success or failure indication. During backtracking, the interpreter may call the procedure again, asking whether it can succeed in other ways. In short, an external predicate is any C++ procedure that follows the protocol of a Congress procedure.

External predicates have proven extremely useful. They are used to implement all of the built-in predicates usually found in Prolog implementations, such as arithmetic operations, as well as other functions that are awkward or impossible to implement directly in Congress, such as file system access or invocation of other programs. The Congress interpreter is itself an external predicate so Congress programs can invoke the interpreter recursively.

3 CAPITL Object-base

CAPITL uses the persistent term space of POL to build an object-oriented database (or *object-base* for short). All the entities used during the process of software development – source files, derived binaries, documentation, executable tools, and descriptions of subsystems – reside in the object-base. Properties attached to each object describe it and its relationship to other objects. The object-base is organized into a tree-structured naming hierarchy similar to a Unix file system (§ 3.1). The object-base can be accessed interactively, from programs written in C++ or Congress, or through a Unix compatibility feature (§ 3.3). In the last case, an extension to Unix path-name syntax provides access to versions of the term space.

3.1 Objects

The fundamental entity in the CAPITL database is the *object*. An object is a "heavier weight" term that is guaranteed to have certain selectors with built-in semantics. Viewed from the Congress language, the term space is simply a labelled directed graph. Viewed from C++, the nodes of the graph are further classified into an inheritance hierarchy. As explained in § 2.2, the first level of the hierarchy separates nodes into leaf nodes (which are further classified as integers, byte strings, etc.) and internal nodes, which contain pointers to other nodes. Among internal nodes, CAPITL further designates some as *object* nodes, which implement the semantics of CAPITL objects.

A CAPITL object can be viewed as a POL term (*i.e.* a directed labeled graph) and it supports the interface of the POL Term class. Nevertheless, a CAPITL object is best viewed as a set of <*name, value*> pairs, called *attributes*, where the value is a POL term. As C++ class instances, CAPITL objects have methods for manipulating their associated data. The main methods for manipulating CAPITL objects relate to attributes; the POL term interface for objects is created using these methods.

CAPITL distinguishes three kinds of attributes: *simple*, *timestamped*, and *derived*. A simple attribute is a pairing of a name with a term and behaves exactly like a POL term. A timestamped attribute records when its value was last modified and provides a method to retrieve this timestamp. The value of a derived attribute is not represented directly as a term, but as a function application. CAPITL maintains a cache of the most recent value of a derived attribute. The inputs to a derived attribute are timestamped attributes, so that invalid cached values can be detected and only recomputed when necessary.

The value of a derived attribute is represented by a special node called a *function* node. These nodes replace all the read operations of the term interface with code that first validates the cached function result and then performs the requested operation by invoking the corresponding method of that value. Function nodes are read-only; all write operations of the term interface are overridden by operations that return a failure indication.

All objects have simple, integer-valued attributes owner, group, permissions, mtime, atime, and ctime, interpreted as in Unix. Objects also have a *directory* attribute containing a reference to the directory in which the object resides. The primary value of an object is stored in the *contents* attribute whose representation depends on the kind of object.

Objects are further classified as *directories*, *files*, and *symbolic links*. A directory object is similar to a Unix file-system directory. Its contents attribute is a list (constructed of cons nodes) of references to other objects. The directories create a tree-structured name space similar to the Unix file system.

File objects are further classified as *plain*, *delta*, *term*, and *composite*. The contents of a plain file object is a byte-string atom. It has exactly the same semantics as a Unix "plain" file (§ 3.3). Delta files have additional operations to "compress" and "uncompress" their contents. Delta files represent consecutive versions of their contents as delta lists using an algorithm similar to RCS [49].

The contents of a term file is an arbitrary Congress term. A composite file, like a directory, contains a list of references to other objects, but it does not emulate all the behavior of a Unix directory, nor is it constrained to be part of a strict tree structure.

Finally, *symbolic link* objects exist to support Unix compatibility interface (§ 3.3). The contents attribute of a symbolic link is a printable-string atom.

3.2 Versions

CAPITL uses the world mechanism of POL to maintain multiple snapshots of the database. Each operation accessing the CAPITL database is done in the context of a designated *current world*, and any changes made by an operation affect only this world. A world is either *modifiable* or *committed* (read-only). There are mechanisms to choose a current world, commit a world, and spawn a new world as a child of an existing committed world. The last operation behaves as if it were making a complete copy of the parent database state, but is much more efficient. A world can also be unfrozen if it has no children. A modifiable (leaf) world of the database may be thought of as a "workspace." A person who wishes to modify the database generally selects an existing committed world, creates a modifiable world derived from it, and makes the modifications in the new world. When the changes have reached a stable state, the new world may be committed. Policies and mechanisms for mediating shared access to modifiable worlds are still under study.

Each world has a unique *version ID*, which is a non-empty sequence of positive integers. The root world has ID "0". The ID of the first child of a world W is formed by incrementing the final component of W's id. Sibling worlds are formed by appending zeros to W's ID. For example, the children of world 1.3.2 would be labeled 1.3.3, 1.3.2.0, 1.3.2.0.0, etc. This numbering is similar to the scheme used by RCS and SCCS, and seems more natural than "Dewey decimal" numbering in the common case of long sequences of single-child worlds. For example, a sequence of consecutive derivations from 1.3.2 would yield 1.3.3, 1.3.4, 1.3.5, etc. This numbering scheme can, however, become quite confusing when multiple worlds are derived from the same parent. We expect that worlds will normally be selected by symbolic name or other attributes stored in an index structure (itself stored in the database) rather than by version ID. (This part of the database is still under development.)

In general no changes are permitted in a committed world. However, the value of a derived attribute may be safely deleted and replaced by the special atom "not available." Switching the state of a derived attribute between available and not available is considered a "benign" modification of the database and is permitted in committed worlds.

3.3 Accessing a CAPITL database

A CAPITL database can be accessed and manipulated in several ways:

- Directly, through programs written in C++ or Congress.
- Through an interactive X-based browser.
- Through a Unix-compatible interface called EFS.

CAPITL is written in POL, so all of its structures can be accessed as data structures in C++. For example, nodes are all instances of the class `Term`, which exports such methods (member functions) as

```
boolean IsLeaf();
```

which enquires whether the term is a leaf, and

```
Term *Edge(char *selector);
```

which returns the term referenced by a particular selector (if one exists). Class `Integer` is a subclass of `Term` with an `IntVal()` method that returns its integer value, and so on. Documentation for this interface is currently being written [3].

Browser. An interactive browsing interface has been written on top of the X Window System using the InterViews [34] toolkit. The browser supports visiting any object or directory in the object-base and uses type-sensitive displays to depict the `contents` attribute of an object; other attributes are displayed using the Congress expression language (§ 2.4). For example, the `contents` attribute of a source file object is displayed using a text viewer in the *Viewing* box and any other attributes in the *Term View* box (see Figure 1). The current focus can be moved to a neighboring object in the naming hierarchy by double clicking an object named in the *Object Path* or *Object Siblings* box. The focus can also be changed by typing a path name in the *Location Selector* box. "Time travel" is accomplished by typing a version ID in the *Current World* box. Menus exist for creating and destroying objects, invoking the Congress interpreter, and for creating and committing worlds. Multiple simultaneous windows on a database are kept consistent with changes made from any of them.

EFS. The CAPITL object-base can be considered an enhanced version of the Unix file system: More types of objects are supported, the set of attributes of an object is extensible, complex relationships among objects can be represented directly, and versioning of the entire database is efficiently supported. However, the differences between the CAPITL object base and the Unix file system interfere with using existing tools. Consider, for example, the problem of compiling a C source file stored in CAPITL. One approach is to copy the `contents` of the source object into an ordinary Unix file, invoke the compiler, and copy the resulting object module back into CAPITL. A second approach is to store in CAPITL "stub" objects that contain pointers (path names) to Unix files. A third approach is to modify the compiler (perhaps by linking it with alternative versions of the Unix library functions `open`, `read`, `seek`, etc.) so that it can read and modify CAPITL objects. None of these approaches is entirely satisfactory.

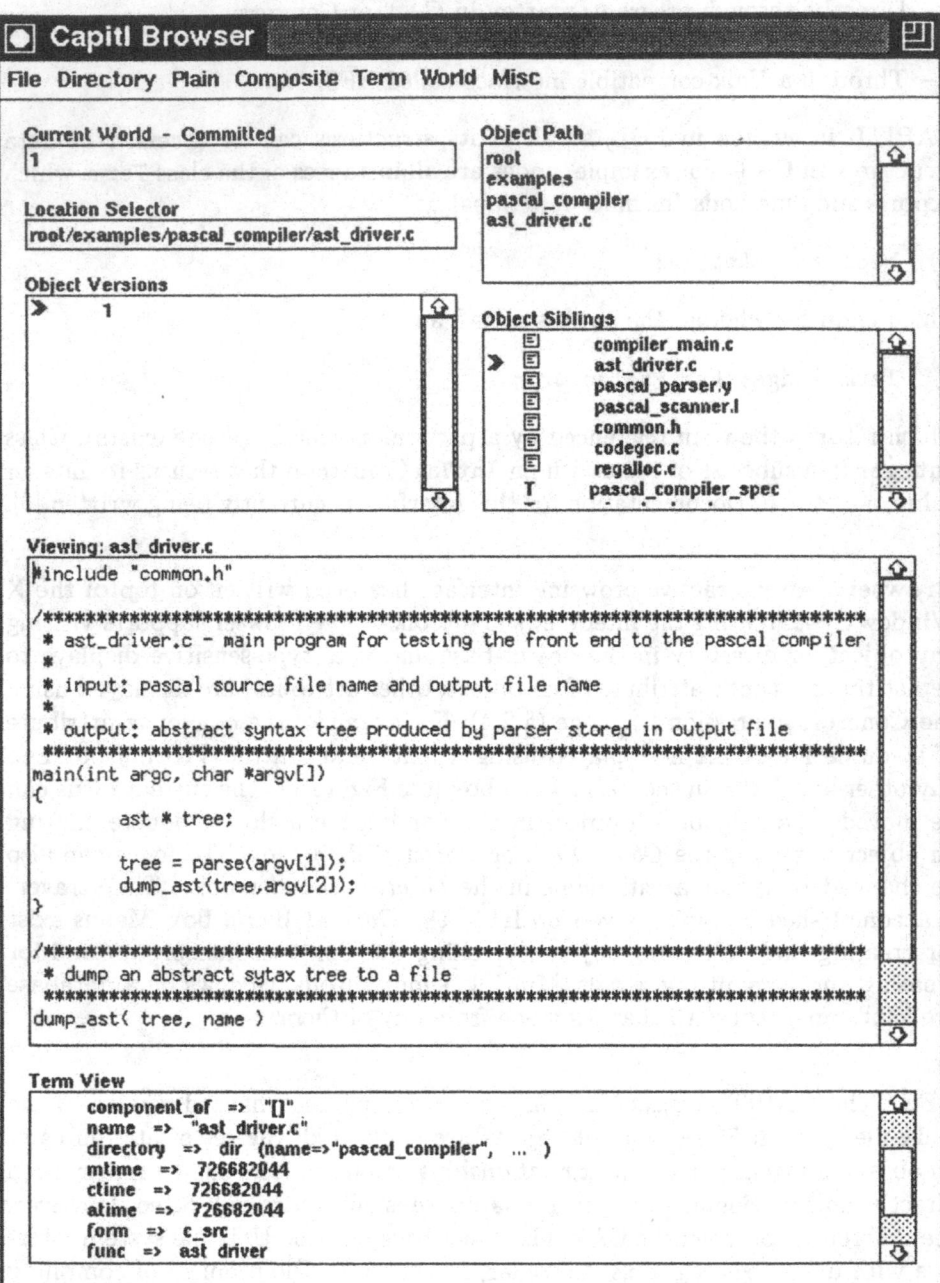

Fig. 1. CAPITL Browser

The *Emulated File System* (EFS) allows programs to access CAPITL objects as if they were Unix files. It is based on the Network File System (NFS) facility [44], which is included in most versions of Unix. NFS was originally designed to support transparent access to remote files. A version of the mount command associates a remote file system with a name, called a *mount point* in the local file system. System calls that request operations on files below this mount point are forwarded to an NFS server. Normally, the server is the Unix kernel on the remote system, which executes the requests on its local disk. The remote file system thus appears to be grafted into the local name space as a subtree of the mount point. It is possible, however, to designate a user-level process as an NFS server (Figure 2).

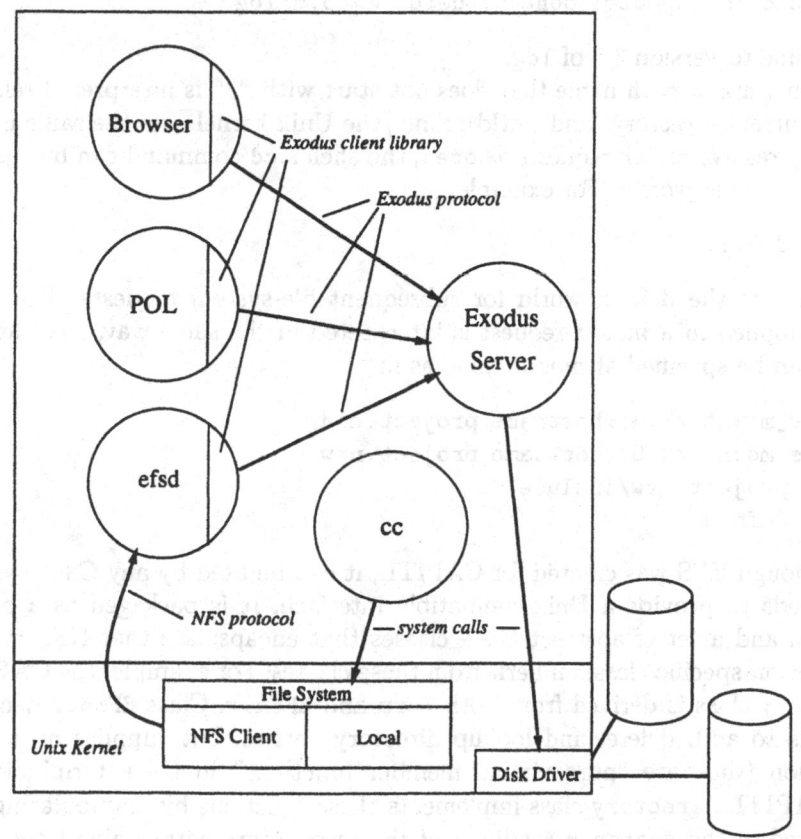

Fig. 2. CAPITL Process Architecture

The EFS daemon *efsd* emulates a Unix file system on a CAPITL database. Once a CAPITL database is mounted, its objects can be manipulated by standard system calls (open, read, write, seek, link, stat, etc.) as if they were actual Unix files, directories, and symbolic links. Neither client programs nor the

Unix kernel need be modified in any way.

Not all features of the CAPITL database are accessible through EFS. For example, a composite or term object appears to be an empty file from EFS (it behaves like /dev/null). However, EFS does allow access to alternative worlds through an extension of Unix path name syntax. A version ID followed by a colon is interpreted as a request to resolve a path name in a designated world of the database. Path names without version ID's are resolved in a *current world* analogous to the current working directory. For example,

```
diff 3.3:prog.c prog.c
```

compares version 3.3 of prog.c with the current version, and

```
(echo -n "updates done "; date) >> 3.5:log
```

adds a line to version 3.5 of log.

As in Unix, a path name that does not start with "/" is interpreted relative to the current directory (and world). Since the Unix kernel uses the same mechanism to resolve chdir requests as open, the shell's cd command can be used to navigate among worlds. For example,

```
cd 3.2.1:
```

sets 3.2.1 as the default world for subsequent file-system requests. The path name supplied in a *mount* request is interpreted in the same way, so a default world can be specified at mount time, as in

```
efs_mount /3.4:@hostname project.old
efs_mount /3.5:@hostname project.new.
cd project.new/include
vi defs.h
```

Although EFS was created for CAPITL, it can be used by any C++ system that needs to provide a Unix-compatible interface. It is packaged as a driver program and a set of abstract C++ classes that encapsulate that NFS model. Application-specific classes inherit from these classes. For example, the CAPITL Directory class is derived from both Term and EFSdir. Class EFSdir declares methods to add, delete, and lookup directory entries, but supplies no implementation (they are "pure virtual member functions" in C++ terminology). The CAPITL Directory class implements these functions by manipulating the list stored in the contents attribute of the term. More details about the EFS package will be contained in a forthcoming report [46].

4   Software Configuration Management in CAPITL

CAPITL provides assistance for constructing and maintaining software products. A product is the output of a series of tools applied to a set of objects. The goal is to produce a "correct" version of a product as efficiently as possible.

Correctness is a fuzzy concept that has possibly different meanings in different situations. Therefore, CAPITL supports a powerful constraint language (POL) allowing system designers to describe attributes and integrity constraints as appropriate to each application. CAPITL guarantees that all derived objects are correctly created by applying tools to inputs in accordance with these specifications. In addition, CAPITL ensures that all products are current (that is, none of the objects used to create the product has changed since the product was constructed). When building (or rebuilding) a product CAPITL speeds up the process by reusing previous work when possible.

CAPITL software objects are classified as *source* or *derived*. A source object is created by a human being or by some other process outside the control of CAPITL. A derived object is created by applying a *tool* object to an input object. Each tool has exactly one input, which can be a set or list of other objects. (Construction of such composite objects is described more fully below.) The tools as well as inputs can be either source or derived. Each derived object can be viewed as the value of a *derivation* – an expression tree whose leaves are source objects and whose interior nodes represent occurrences of a built-in *apply* operator. Objects are all represented in CAPITL as POL terms, and thus can have a variety of attributes. Some of these attributes constrain the set of well-formed derivation expressions (§ 4.1). In particular, each tool object has an in attribute that must match the object to which it is applied, and an out attribute that constrains the attributes of the result. Since the attributes are terms that can contain variables, an object can be partially specified. An incomplete object can be more fully specified by replacing occurrences of variables with other terms[8]. An object with an unspecified contents is called an *abstract object*.

A user requests the derivation of a new object by constructing an abstract *goal* object and invoking the *planner* (§ 4.4) and the *builder* (§ 4.5) which are Congress programs supplied with CAPITL. The planner determines how to create objects and supplies them with code attributes, while the builder creates the contents of planned objects by evaluating expressions in their code attribute. The code attribute of an object is a list of alternative *build expressions*, each of which contains references to a tool object and an input object. When asked to plan an object without a code attribute, the planner searches the database for tools and matching inputs such that the result of applying the tool to the input yields the desired goal. It then recursively plans the tool and the input.

The planner can infer the need to construct new derived objects. If it finds a tool capable of creating a desired goal object but no corresponding input, it tentatively creates an abstract object representing the input and plans it. If the input is a composite object (for example, a list of inputs to the linkage editor), the planner searches for a *template* (§ 4.2) that describes potential collections. The planner can also create new tool objects. A *tool description* (§ 4.3) contains an input/output description of a potential tool. If the planner fails to find a tool that can create a goal object but discovers an appropriate tool description, it

---

[8] A consequence of the definition of unification in § 2.4 is that the absence of an attribute is equivalent to an attribute whose value is a variable.

will instantiate the description as a new tool object and attempt to plan it. For example, the planner may fail to find a cross-compiler capable of building an object module for a particular machine architecture, but a tool description may suggest that such a compiler can be built from existing sources.

The builder completes the process of making an abstract goal concrete by executing one of the build expressions in its `code` attribute. If the build is successful, the result is placed in the `contents`, and a record of the specific tool and input used to create it is placed in the `provenance` attribute of the derived object. If it is unsuccessful (for example, if the tool is a compiler that discovers an error in its input), the build expression is marked as "failed," the planner is invoked to find other alternatives, and another build expression is tried.

4.1 Object Descriptions

The attributes `code`, `contents`, `provenance`, `form`, `functionality`, and `references` are used by CAPITL for the purpose of planning and building. The first three of these have been briefly described above. The attributes `form` and `functionality` jointly describe the "type" of an object. These attributes control the matching of tools to inputs and outputs. The `references` attribute is used to record extra dependencies among objects.

Form. The `form` of an object is its type when used as an argument to a tool. In the simplest case the `form` attribute is a simple atom with an application-defined meaning, such as `c_source` or `object_code`. More detailed information can be specified by more complicated terms. For example, the `form` attribute of an object module might be specified as

```
object_code( opt => no, debug_symbols => yes)
```

Since forms are terms, the partial order induced by unification can be used to express subtype relationships. For example, this term is compatible with (unifies with) `object_code`. The planner interprets two values for the `form` attribute as having special meaning: The value `bag(T)` is interpreted as a homogeneous multi-set of type T, and the value `record(T_1, ... , T_n)` as a heterogeneous collection of types T_1 through T_n. All other values are interpreted as non-structured (atomic) types.

Functionality. The `functionality` attribute of an object is a description of what the object does. For tool objects, the `functionality` attribute is the type signature of the tool and describes its behavior via an in/out pattern. For example, the `functionality` of a C compiler might be specified by the term

```
func(in => obj(form => c_source, functionality => F),
     out => obj(form => object_code, functionality => F)),
```

which states that the input must be C source code, the output will be object code, and the functionality (semantics) of the module is preserved.

Contents, Provenance, and Code. For atomic objects the contents attribute is uninterpreted by CAPITL. For composite objects the contents is the set of sub-objects that comprise the object. The provenance of a derived object specifies the tool and input used to create the contents. Since the provenance names specific objects (by their OID), it is completely synonymous with the contents, in the sense that the same contents could be recreated by rerunning the same tool on the same input. The code attribute is a set of expressions, each of which is type-compatible with the object and is thus a potential recipe for generating the contents; it represents a non-deterministic program for creating the contents. The code, provenance, and contents are in some sense all manifestations of the same value where the code is the least specific and the contents the most specific.

References. The references attribute identifies objects that are referred to inside an atomic object's contents. It can be an assertion from the specification writer or the output of some language-specific tool. For example, suppose a C source file has many "#include" preprocessor directives. If the C compiler and preprocessor are being modelled as one tool, the references attribute would represent the set of include files required to run the compiler/preprocessor tool. These dependencies are needed for maintaining consistency after changes. References are used in checking whether derived objects are up-to-date. They are also useful for browsing source objects.

When describing an object, a specification writer has two ways to refer to other objects. A *generic reference* is a pattern that matches other objects in the object-base. For example, the term

```
obj(functionality =>
        func(in => obj(form => c_source, functionality => F),
             out => obj(form => object_code, functionality => F))
    )
```

represents a generic reference to *any* C compiler. If the environment contained two C compilers, such as "cc" and "gcc," either could match. A *specific reference* defines a unique object. A specific reference can be created from a generic reference by adding enough other attributes to make the reference unique or by using the object's identity. Because it is difficult to guarantee that a set of attributes always identifies exactly one object, the identity of an object is preferred for specific references. For example, the provenance of an object module might contain tool => Gcc where Gcc is a tag for a specific compiler object.

4.2 Templates

A system is a collection of objects that when combined form a meaningful "chunk". Systems are described in CAPITL by specially formed objects called *templates*. (Such descriptions are often referred to as system models.) A template consists of a set of generic references, specifying (at least) the functionality of each sub-object, and a set of constraints. The constraints are used to specialize the generic references prior to *instantiating* the template. Templates are instantiated by making a copy of the template, calling all the predicates listed in the constraints, and then resolving each generic reference via a database lookup. The result is an object that unifies with the template, but has all the generic references in its contents resolved into specific references. Because template instantiations are objects, they can be used as the sub-parts of other template instantiations. Thus, system descriptions in CAPITL can be composed.

4.3 Tool Descriptions

CAPITL uses separate tool descriptions to specify the available set of tools. Tool behavior (as opposed to tool objects) is described via specially formed Congress rules stored in a separate rule-base that can be imported into a Congress program. Tool descriptions serve two purposes. First, the presence of a tool description alerts the planner that it is possible to build a tool with a particular functionality. Hence tool generators can be modelled in CAPITL. Second, tool descriptions allow more complicated descriptions of tool behavior than is possible with simple input/output signature patterns. Section 5.2 contains an example that illustrates this feature.

4.4 Planning

Planning is the process of finding a set of source objects and tool applications needed to satisfy a request. The planner makes use of three kinds of data: existing planned objects, template objects, and tool descriptions. The planner searches the space of all possible "well formed" tool and object combinations for expressions whose results match the goal and that only contain references to atomic objects or fully specified composite objects. These expressions are stored in the code attribute of an object and represent a *potential* recipe for constructing the contents of that object – the planner does not guarantee that an expression will succeed when evaluated. During planning, templates are instantiated and any constraints attached to objects are checked ensuring that all objects used to build a system conform to the constraints specified in the description of the system. Such constraints can easily encode certain kinds of semantic correctness such as "use all debugging versions," by forcing the appropriate sub-types to be used for derived objects (and hence forcing the use of tools that produce debugging information).

The planner avoids repeating work by keeping track of the current state of an object's plan with an additional plan_state attribute. When the planner creates a new object to represent an intermediate result, its state is *attempted*. If a build expression is found, the state changes to *successful*, otherwise it changes to *failed*. Using this attribute the planner can avoid attempting to plan an object that has already failed and avoid derivation loops, which occur if an object is needed in order to derive its own contents.

Planning may be computationally expensive because it exhaustively searches a potentially exponential space. To speed the planning process we are experimenting with lazy generation of expressions and better search strategies. Instead of deriving all equivalent expressions, our prototype stops as soon as a single expression is found. (A "replan" request is available to search for additional expressions.) Currently, the planner uses a blind depth-first search. By ranking choices, perhaps by using approximate tool costs, a branch-and-bound strategy could be used to improve performance.

4.5 Building

Given a reference to a derived object, the job of the builder is to make the contents, provenance, and code attributes consistent. They are consistent if the provenance is one of the expressions in the code and it evaluates to the contents.

The builder traverses the expression graph defined by the code and provenance attributes. Depending on the state of an object there are three cases that arise:

1. The object does not have a provenance or contents attribute. The builder evaluates the first untried expression in the code. If the expression is successful, the builder stores that expression as the provenance of the object. If the expression fails (perhaps due to a syntax error in a source program), the builder annotates that expression as unsuccessful and invokes the planner, which attempts to find a different expression for the object. If the planner is successful, the build continues.

2. The object has a contents (and hence a provenance). In this case the builder must determine if the contents is still valid. In a committed world, the contents must be the value of the expression stored in the provenance, so no reconstruction is necessary. In a mutable world, objects referenced by the provenance may have changed since it was last evaluated. To determine if the contents is still up to date, the builder uses timestamps. The mtime attribute of an object records the time its contents was last modified. Associated with the provenance of a derived object is a provenance_timestamp that records the timestamps of the tool and argument. If the timestamps match, the contents is still valid. Otherwise, the provenance is re-evaluated. A more precise notion of validity that relies on semantic properties of the objects involved could be used, potentially allowing fewer expressions to be evaluated [51].

3. The object has a provenance but no contents, indicating that a user conserved space by deleting the contents. The contents can be regenerated by simply evaluating the provenance.

4.6 Discussion

Separating the planning and building phases has several advantages. The decomposition of a system into sub-systems tends to change slowly, allowing the output of the planner to be used many times. Hence the cost of planning is amortized over many builds. Moreover, the separation simplifies the builder: It is only concerned with equivalence between a functional expression and a "cached" copy of the result of that expression; the planner does all the work of selecting objects and tools.

One can view the planner as a code generator and the builder as a code evaluator. To increase the speed of building a separate optimize phase could be used after planning to perform traditional compiler optimizations such as strength reduction and elimination of intermediate values. These optimized expressions would then be saved in the provenance for future use. For example, the expressions produced by the planner uses an object to hold the result of every tool application. A linear sequence of tool applications in which the intermediate results were not specifically requested could be compressed into a single pipeline invocation.

CAPITL worlds provide a means to group objects with similar semantic properties. This version mechanism assists planning by limiting the search needed to construct a product. Because only one version of an object is visible in a given world, the planner does not need to choose among the (potentially large) set of versions of each source object. Hence the combinatorial explosion associated with combining components represented as version sets is avoided during planning.

5 Examples

To illustrate the concepts of the previous section, we present two examples of simple subsystems. The first example illustrates how an executable program is built from sources in a variety of languages. The second example is drawn from the domain of document processing.

5.1 A Pascal Program Analyzer

The first example is a simple program analyzer that translates Pascal source files into abstract syntax trees (AST's). Such an analyzer might be a component of a compiler or other larger system. We assume that four source objects are available: a Lex [32] specification of tokens, a YACC [22] specification of a grammar, a driver program written in C, and a common file of declarations included by all three sources. These objects are shown in Figure 3. Common is the file of common declarations. It has only two attributes, a format (source for the C preprocessor) and the actual text contents. Main is the main program. Its format is C source, it depends on Common, and its functionality (semantics) is described by the atom "Cast_driver." The Lex and YACC source objects are similar. The references attributes might be supplied manually by the author of the program or it might be deduced by a tool such as the Unix makedepend utility. The functionality attributes would be supplied manually by the designer of the analyzer package.

Pascal_Analyzer describes the functionality of the desired tool: It should translate a Pascal source object into an abstract syntax tree preserving its func-

```
Common:obj(
    form => cpp_include,
    contents => "#include <stdio.h>; ..."
).
Main:obj(
    functionality => ast_driver,
    form => c_source,
    contents => "main(int argc, char *argv[]) ..."
    references => [ Common ]
).
Scanner:obj(
    functionality => pascal_scanner,
    form => lex_source,
    contents => "..."
    references => [ Common ]
).
Grammar:obj(
    functionality => pascal_parser,
    form => yacc_source,
    contents => "..."
    references => [ Common ]
).
Pascal_Analyzer:func(
    in => obj(form => pascal_source, functionality => F),
    out => obj(form => ast, functionality => F))
).
Analyzer_Spec:obj(
    functionality => Pascal_Analyzer,
    form => bag(type => T),
    contents => [
        C1:obj(functionality => ast_driver, form => T)],
        C2:obj(functionality => pascal_scanner, form => T),
        C3:obj(functionality => pascal_parser, form => T),
    constraints => [ debug_level(C1), debug_level(C2), debug_level(C3) ]
).
```

Fig. 3. Source Objects

tionality. Analyzer_Spec is a template that specifies how the component functionalities ast_driver, pascal_parser, and pascal_scanner can be assembled to produce a tool that translates Pascal source into abstract syntax trees. Analyzer_Spec may be thought of as a "tool" that produces a composite object (a package of objects) from components. This specification conveys three pieces of information: First, that the functionality Pascal_Analyzer is the sum of the functionalities ast_driver, pascal_parser, and pascal_scanner; second, that resulting object has form bag(T), where T is the form of each component; and third, that all the components should have a property called debug_level. For example, if it desired that all object files have the debugging property, the debug_level predicate would be defined as

```
debug_level(obj(form => F:object_code)) :-
    !, F = object_code(debug_symbols => yes).
            % object modules must have debugging information
debug_level(obj). % all other objects pass the test vacuously
```

Figure 4 shows a variety of tool specifications. The tool specification **Lex_Spec**

```
Lex_Spec:tool(
    functionality => Lex_Func:
        func(in => obj(form => lex_source, functionality => F),
            out=> obj(form => c_source, functionality => F))
).
Lex:obj(
    form => executable,
    functionality => Lex_Func,
    contents => "..." % the actual executable code
).
Yacc:obj(
    form => executable,
    functionality =>
        func(in => obj(form => yacc_source, functionality => F),
            out=> obj(form => c_source, functionality => F)),
    contents => "..."
).
Cc_debug:obj(
    form => executable,
    functionality =>
        func(in => obj(form => c_source, functionality => F),
            out=> obj(form => object_code(dbg_sym => yes, opt => no),
                functionality => F)),
    contents => "..."
).
Cc_opt:obj(
    form => executable,
    functionality =>
        func(in => obj(form => c_source, functionality => F),
            out=> obj(form => object_code(dbg_sym => no, opt => yes),
                functionality => F)),
    contents => "..."
).
Ld:obj(
    form => executable,
    functionality =>
        func(in => obj(form => bag(type => object_code),
                functionality => F),
            out=> obj(form => executable, functionality => F)),
    contents => "..."
).
```

Fig. 4. Tool Objects

describes the functionality of a Lex processor – it transforms a `lex_source` input into `c_source` preserving semantics. The object **Lex** is an executable program that conforms to this specification. Similarly, each of other tools would have a corresponding tool description. Since each tool description is identical to the input/output signature of the corresponding tool, we omit the remaining descriptions. We have chosen to model the debugging and optimizing versions of the C compiler as two distinct tools.

Calling the planner with the goal

```
obj( form => executable, functionality => Pascal_Analyzer )
```

will create a partial object with the desired functionality and form. If planning is successful, the object will contain a build expression in its code attribute that can be used to create its contents. The planner will also create partial objects for intermediate objects as shown in Figure 5. At this point, the builder may be

```
Goal:obj(
    functionality => Pascal_Analyzer,
    form => executable,
    code => [ build_expr(expr => apply(Ld, Object_Modules, Goal)) ]
).
Object_Modules:obj(
    functionality => Pascal_Analyzer,
    form => bag(type => object_code),
    contents => [ ScannerObj, ParserObj, MainObj]
).
ScannerObj:obj(
    functionality => pascal_scanner,
    form => object_code(debug_symbols => yes, opt => no),
    code => [ build_expr(expr => apply(Cc_debug, ScannerC, ScannerObj)) ]
).
ScannerC:obj(
    functionality => pascal_scanner,
    form => c_source,
    code => [ build_expr(expr => apply(Lex, Scanner, ScannerC)) ]
).
ParserObj:obj(
    functionality => pascal_parser,
    form => object_code(debug_symbols => yes, opt => no),
    code => [ build_expr(expr => apply(Cc_debug, ParserC, ParserObj)) ]
).
ParserC:obj(
    functionality => pascal_parser,
    form => c_source,
    code => [ build_expr(expr => apply(Yacc, Grammar, ParserC)) ]
).
MainObj:obj(
    functionality => ast_driver,
    form => object_code(debug_symbols => yes, opt => no),
    code => [ build_expr(expr => apply(Cc_debug, Main, MainObj)) ]
).
```

Fig. 5. Derived Objects After Planning

invoked on the object Goal. Assuming there were no errors, the builder would fill in the contents and provenance attributes of each object in Figure 5.

Suppose the state of the system is frozen by committing the current world and a new one is created. Consider two different kinds of modifications to the system:

1. The only action in the new world is to modify the contents of Scanner. In this scenario, the same plan can be reused (in fact calling the planner will result in no changes), and the builder will reuse ParserObj and MainObj, rebuilding only ScannerC, ScannerObj, and Goal.

2. No sources are modified, but an optimized version of the analyzer is desired. The definition of the Congress predicate `debug_level` is changed to

```
debug_level(obj(form => F:object_code)) :-
    !, F = object_code(opt => yes).
debug_level(obj).
```

There are two choices for where to store the new version: in a new object distinct from the existing debugging version or in the existing analyzer object (replacing the debugging version in this world). In the latter case, the `code` attribute would need to be cleared before planning (if not, the object would fail the current set of constraints and would fail to be used). In either case the planner would be re-invoked on the appropriate goal object. The existing object `Object_Modules` would not be used because its constraints fail with the current definition of `debug_level`. Instead, the planner would create a new composite object from the `Analyzer_Spec` template that uses the output of `Cc_opt` rather than `Cc_debug`. The derived objects `ParserC` and `ScannerC` from the previous world would be used without modification.

5.2 Document Processing

The Unix *troff* document processing system includes a variety of special-purpose preprocessors. If a document does not use a particular feature, the corresponding preprocessor need not be applied. For example, *eqn* only needs to be run on documents that contain mathematical equations, while *tbl* is only required for documents containing tables. We could model these tools by defining a variety of types as in the previous example, defining *eqn* to be a translator from `troff_with_eqn` to `troff`, etc. However, this approach would require a different type for each subset of the features. A better approach defines one form, `troff`, with subtypes for different sets of required features. For example a document with equations and tables would have form `troff(features => [eqn, tbl])`. The tool description for *eqn* would then be

```
tool(functionality => func(
    in => obj(form => troff(features => L1), functionality => F),
    out=> obj(form => troff(features => L2), functionality => F)))
    :- delete_feature(feature => eqn, in => L1, out => L2) ,
```

where the predicate `delete_feature` searches list L1 for an occurrence of `eqn` and removes it. If a document does not use *eqn* the body of this rule will fail and the planner will not consider it applicable. A more sophisticated version of `delete_feature` can encode the requirement that some processors have to be run before others. As with the `references` attribute, the `features` of a *troff* document could be added manually or by a processor that analyzes a document.

6 Related Work

Many of the ideas in the design of CAPITL are present in other systems. CAPITL's main distinguishing feature is tight integration of a process programming language (Congress) with an underlying versioned, object-oriented database. A software object is not just described by a Congress expression, it *is* a Congress expression. Congress is declarative rather than procedural; it allows system designers to concentrate on the properties of objects and subsystems rather than on procedures to manipulate them.

All of the following systems provide good support for building; they differ primarily in how systems are specified, how version selection is accomplished, and what kinds of consistency are guaranteed.

The related work in this section is organized into three sections: build tools, environments that integrate building, versioning, and other aspects of software development, and work that uses logic as the basis for SCM or building.

6.1 Build Tools

Many successors to Make [20] have been built that keep the basic idea of a Makefile for describing systems. Each of the newer systems addresses deficiencies in Make and adds new features that make it easier to use. There are many variations of these so-called "super makes" and we describe only a sample here. Tools that are comparable to Make are included here as well.

GNU Make. The Make utility from the Free Software Foundation [47] enhances the original Make in several ways. (The authors give credit for these to System V Make, Andrew Hume's mk, and other unnamed sources.) The major improvements include transitive closure of the dependency graph and implicit intermediate files (rule chaining). An *include* facility and conditional execution based on the C preprocessor language eases the maintenance of makefiles since common definitions and machine dependent parts can be stored separately and dynamically chosen. GNU Make extends the syntax for implicit rules to allow simple patterns.

Dmake. Dmake [52] has many of the same extensions as GNU Make such as transitive closure of the derivation graph (rule chaining), an include mechanism, and better rule definition syntax. Dmake further extends Make by supporting parallel construction of a target's prerequisites. The syntax for targets is extended to force sequential construction when desired. The greatest enhancement that Dmake provides is that it saves the state of a Makefile (e.g. macro expansions, tools used, tool flags, etc.) with each target so it can detect out-of-date targets due to changes to a Makefile.

Imake. Imake [10] is a tool for generating Makefiles. It compiles application dependency information along with architecture descriptions to create Makefiles, which are then interpreted by standard Make. The C preprocessor macro language is used to describe systems. Changes to a description require regenerating the Makefiles. Careful use of directories is needed to avoid inconsistent systems (e.g. mixing sparc and mips object files).

Odin. Odin [14] is a system for integrating existing tools into a single environment. Tools are described declaratively and then linked into a *derivation graph* that summarizes all the "type correct" derivations possible using the current set of tools. Given a request for a particular object, the derivation graph is used to infer build steps. As with Make, the programmer must specify all the dependencies of a configuration. Version selection is not integrated into the system, but Odin supports annotations on targets to perform variant (e.g debug versus optimized) selection. Odin uses a separate directory for each tool invocation and creates a derived object cache that associates the provenance with each object so that requests for a different variant are correctly handled.

6.2 Environments

The systems described in this section support more than building software. They include assistance for describing software and they store meta-data about components in addition to their contents. This meta-data is used for configuration management, version selection, and history management. All of the following systems provide good support for building; they differ primarily in how systems are specified, how version selection is accomplished, and what kinds of consistency are guaranteed.

DSEE. DSEE [30, 31] is a commercial environment that manages software in a network of distributed (Apollo) workstations. It supports a notion of "time travel" by compactly storing versions of source files and providing a tool, the History Manager, that associates symbolic attributes with particular versions. A separate tool, the Release Manager, maintains groups of consistent files. DSEE configurations start with a user-supplied dependency relation called the *system model*. Version selection rules are used to bind object references in the system model to specific versions in the file system. DSEE supports many other features needed in a distributed environment such as transparent access to remote files.

ClearCase. ClearCase [7] is a new product from the original DSEE developers that provides many of the same features on a variety of Unix platforms. ClearCase tightly integrates build management and version selection. As with DSEE, source components are versioned and version selection is accomplished with rules. ClearCase extends the versioning model to include directories and modifies the Unix filesystem to create dynamic views based on the current selection criteria (their filesystem is called a Versioned Object Base). ClearCase decouples building from configuration management, allowing any build tool to be used. They provide a Make utility called ClearMake that does "build auditing" to automatically record exact dependencies during a build by tracking file system *open* calls. Derived objects are shared between different developers automatically. ClearCase supports parallel builds using a network of workstations. The repository can be replicated and distributed; changes made to each site are merged on a periodic basis.

Vesta. The Vesta system [33, 13, 21, 9] developed at DEC SRC is a repository and SCM language that uses a functional model. All source components are immutable. Changes are made using a tool that builds a new configuration object from a previous version by replacing new or modified components. The immutability of components (including configuration objects) means that rebuilding a derived object that was erased is easy and is guaranteed to create the same value as before. Derived objects are treated as accelerators for functional expressions and are cached using an algorithm that generates an almost perfect hash of an arbitrary stream of bytes. The functional system models and component immutability are borrowed from Cedar/SML [29].

CaseWare. CaseWare [12] is a commercial SCM system that manages sources, documentation, and derived information. It uses an object-oriented repository that supports extensible attributes. Software systems consist of component hierarchies and CaseWare has graphical tools to create and modify them. An adaptable process model is tightly integrated with the environment and it provides support for life-cycle management, change management, and problem tracking. The environment performs transparent builds and generates Makefiles on demand to support incremental building. Each object is versioned and rules, similar to DSEE, perform version selection of the components in an system.

Shape. Shape [35, 36] integrates Make with a version control system similar to RCS. Shape is backwards compatible with Make and adds version selection rules comparable to those in DSEE. These rules use regular expressions to specify an ordered list of version preferences, such as "use the newest version of all components I am working on", and "use the newest stable version of all other components." The default selection rule is to use the most recent version of all components as in Make. Shape stores source objects in an attributed file system and can distinguish different versions of objects by using "version attributes." Shape's use of Makefiles is convenient, but such files contain a static description of the system, and maintaining that description becomes more and more difficult as the system grows larger. Like DSEE, Shape relies on an external tool for checking that a configuration is consistent.

Jason. Jason is a *generic* software configuration system [53] that constructs a software environment from a given set of parameters. These parameters include class definitions (object schemas), consistency constraints, and build plans (dependency relations). Created environments can later be extended, but because of the "compiled" nature of generated environments, such extensions are limited to additions and refinements. This limitation prevents Jason from supporting certain kinds of evolution (such as re-organizing a two-component system into a three-component system). Jason uses a powerful constraint language (full first-order predicate calculus) and compiles the given constraints into procedures that check the consistency of configurations. A rigorous algebraic model provides Jason with a strong theoretical foundation not present in most other systems.

Adele/Nomade. Adele [17, 18] (and its successor Nomade [19]) is a constraint-based environment for SCM. An attributed filesystem is used to store information about components. Constraints are quantifier-free boolean expressions whose domain is the attribute values. System architects describe systems using constraints and Adele uses them to infer consistent configurations, including the dependency relation between components. Recent work has extended Adele to include process support based on events and triggers [8].

SMILE/Marvel. SMILE and Marvel [23, 24, 25] are two rule based environments that emphasize support for the edit/debug/build cycle. Their goal is to provide a "fileless" environment for programmers by making the environment responsible for invisibly maintaining derived objects. Their rules use Hoare-style pre and post conditions to trigger actions; they can be used for either forward-chaining or backward-chaining inferences. Forward-chaining corresponds to opportunistic computation and backward-chaining corresponds to the method employed by traditional build tools such as Make. Recent work [26] has extended Marvel to include rule-based process support.

6.3 Logic-based Approaches

The similarity between the rules and dependency statements in a makefile and a logic programming language has been noted by others. Logic and logic-programming languages have been used as description languages and as the basis for build tools like Make. All these systems share the desire to use the power of logic languages for consistency checking and make good use of the richer data model provided by terms.

Feature Logic. The NORA [55] system describes components and configurations using feature logic. Feature logic has as its data model terms which are similar to POL terms (both data models are derived from work by Aït-Kaci [4]). The operations of feature logic are selection, complement, intersection, and union of feature terms. Unification in full feature logic is not as easy as in POL since it includes both negation and disjunction. NORA uses feature logic to represent both revisions (changes made to a component that are intended to replace the existing component) and variants (changes in the behavior of a component), providing a uniform representation for these traditionally separate concepts. A subset of feature logic is mapped into the C preprocessor language and used for their prototype editor. Using this editor, programmers interactively pick values for feature terms. The editor supports incremental selection of features and dynamic sensitivity to existing features. In the future they plan to implement a build tool based on feature logic.

Deductive Databases. Asirelli and Inverardi [6] describe how a deductive database could be used to assist configuration management and software construction. Their system (EDBLOG) is a deductive database consisting of three elements: facts, rules and integrity constraints. They implement a Make-like tool by using facts to represent information about components such as their names and last-modified-dates. Rules are used to define implicit and explicit dependencies and to define the "out of date" relationship. Integrity constraints are used to represent transactions, which correspond to invoking the traditional Make command. Concepts like the "history of a component" are defined by rules and enforced by integrity constraints. Their design only covers building; they did not extend their ideas to configuration or version management.

Prolog-based Make. PROM [27] is a Make tool implemented in Prolog. It defines a small language for writing the equivalent of makefiles. Prolog terms are used to represent information, so the data model is an improvement over Make's character string model. In addition logical variables can be used to implement implicit derivation rules. The initial knowledge base is constructed from the "prom-files" and timestamp information of the files constituting an application.

7 Status and Future Plans

A prototype of CAPITL has been implemented that includes all the basic components: the object-base, worlds, EFS, the Congress interpreter, a browser, a planner and a builder. The planner and builder subsume the functionality of Make. We have tested them on small, but complicated examples that have about 10 source objects and 20 tool descriptions. They have been successfully used to construct CAPITL itself, which consists of about 32,000 lines of C++ code and 5,000 lines of Congress code. The planner correctly generates plans, the builder constructs executable binaries (running tools such as the C compiler with the aid of EFS), and the resulting programs can be invoked through the interactive user interface. After changes to only the *contents* attribute of source objects, the planner quickly verifies the existing expressions and the builder is able to rebuild targets taking advantage of unchanged sources and intermediate objects.

Logic-based construction has many advantages. Complex systems are described compactly and precisely easing maintenance costs. Consistency can be guaranteed and programmers freed from having to worry about how to generate a particular variant of a system. Knowledge about tools is shared so not every programmer must be a tool expert. Types and sub-types are easily represented using POL terms. Abstraction using logical variables and constraints is a powerful method of specifying software.

Several areas need more attention before CAPITL can be successfully used in large-scale development.

7.1 Performance

The planner and builder are currently an order of magnitude slower than Make. Although the incremental algorithms reduce this overhead, it is still a significant problem when a version of a system is initially planned. Experiments with the planner showed that for a given project the order in which tools were considered affected performance either upwards or downwards by over fifty percent. Because most projects are use a small set of tools, simple heuristics such as "try the last successfully used tool" should limit the variation due to fixed tool orderings. An estimate of tool costs would enable the planner to use better heuristics for finding an initial plan such as a branch-and-bound strategy.

The performance of the builder is dominated by the cost of applying tools to components. EFS is considerably slower than native or NFS file system access, particularly for updating files, so tool invocations (such as compiling) are severely degraded. The main source of the problem appears to be inappropriate timeouts and buffering strategies in the NFS client code in the Unix kernel. A successor to Exodus, called Shore [15], is being developed by a separate project; one of the goals of Shore is to provide a facility similar to EFS with higher performance.

7.2   User Interface

Several enhancements to the user interface are needed to make CAPITL usable by system architects and developers. From these higher-level interfaces, CAPITL would generate Congress code, effectively using Congress as an "assembly code" of system descriptions.

Syntactic Sugar. Currently, source objects, tool descriptions, templates and goals are all created "by hand" as Congress expressions. Forms-based interfaces would help to streamline this process and eliminate the need for developers to learn about logic programming. The browser understands a few attributes and has special displays for them (for example, the `contents` attribute of a plain file object is displayed in a text window), but most attributes are simply displayed using the Congress expression language. More special-case displays would help.

Idioms. Common terms such as frequently used forms and functionalities (such as the subterm `Lex_Func` in Figure 4 could be collected in libraries and displayed by the graphical interface as icons for pasting into new descriptions. Such terms could be abstractions (*i.e.* contain free variables) from the project domain. For example, the behavior of a generic translator that preserved functionality might have parameters for the source and target languages and could be represented by the term

```
Translator : function(
    in  => object( form => Source, functionality => Func )
    out => object( form => Target, functionality => Func)).
```

They can also serve as the basis for creating new types through subtyping.

Worlds. Currently, a user must set the default world either by navigating the tree of worlds, or by explicitly typing version ID's as sequences of integers. Worlds could be represented explicitly in the object-base as special "world objects" so that mnemonic names and other attributes can be associated with them. Congress could then be used as a query language for the collection of worlds.

Flexibility. The graphical interface of CAPITL uses different views based on the C++ class of the object being visited. The compiled nature of the interface limits the possibilities for customizing the view of an object based on its dynamic type (*form* and *functionality* attributes). A CAPITL object is self-describing. Descriptions of its representation, behavior, and relationships are contained in its associated attributes. This description could be extended to include a graphical view as well. Interfaces based on embedded interpreters such as TCL/TK [38, 39] or a binding of Congress with X windows intrinsics could be used to implement this extension.

7.3 Additional Functionality

The user interface enhancements suggested above are all fairly straightforward. Other usability enhancements require more fundamental research.

Version Management. Versioned worlds are simple to understand, but policies for managing them need to be explored. CAPITL contains no provisions for mediating access to mutable worlds except that provided by Exodus, which only serializes simple updates; more sophisticated kinds of long-term locks are needed. Mechanisms for selecting worlds and maintaining their internal consistency need to be developed. Tools are needed to support an "algebra" of modifications that allow modifications to be added and subtracted. An example of "addition" is reconciling and merging concurrent updates that created sibling worlds. An example of "subtraction" arises when two updates were applied in sequence, and it is desirable to generate the world that would have arisen if the second update were applied but not the first.

Cache Management. A *derived attribute* is one whose value is an immutable function of other attributes. Derived attributes can be elided or recomputed even in a committed world. Currently, a derived value must be deleted by hand. A useful tool would be one that selectively flushes cached values based on their size, time since last use, and cost of reconstruction. More generally, all derived objects may be thought of as a residing in a cache. In some cases there may be more than one equivalent way to build a product. For example, an executable program might be rebuilt from its sources or reconstituted from a compressed version. Thus cache maintenance is intimately tied to the larger issue of planning.

7.4 Other Possibilities

In addition to software development activities related to the construction of software, there are two areas where CAPITL could help. Both of these areas have the potential to reduce the cost of develop software and increase the reliability of the final product.

Reuse. Considerable attention is now being given to reusing software in order to lower the cost of writing new software [1, 2]. Any reuse system must provide a way of storing and locating components. CAPITL would be a good foundation for such environments because of its rich data model, flexible policies, and extendible attributes. In addition Congress is well suited as an ad-hoc query language for locating components for reuse.

Process Support. Most of the effort in CAPITL has been spent on making the job of the software developer and architect easier. In large projects, the majority of time is spent on managing these developers and on communication costs [40, 54]. Support for such activities is called *process programming* or *process modeling*. The requirements for effective process support is an active research area. Nonetheless, there is agreement that in order to support, as well as control, human activities, flexibility is needed. CAPITL has a good data model and language on which to build process support.

7.5 Additional Functionality

8 Acknowledgments

Many people have helped to bring CAPITL to its current state. S. T. S. Prasad was the first to explore the application of Prolog to configuration management. Tony Rich carried this work forward. His thesis is the basis for many of the ideas in Section 4 of this paper, and the current planner and builder owe much of their content to his work. Odysseas Tsatalos, Theoharis Hadjiioannou, and Trip Lazarus have made substantial contributions to the X-based interactive interface. Lazarus also implemented the *worlds* mechanism and integrated EFS into CAPITL. Delta files were implemented by Tsatalos. Tom Ball and Sam Bates offered many helpful comments on earlier drafts of this paper.

References

1. *Proceedings of the 14th International Conference on Software Engineering.* IEEE Computer Society Press, May 1992.
2. *Proceedings of the 15th International Conference on Software Engineering.* IEEE Computer Society Press, May 1993.
3. Paul Adams and Marvin Solomon. POL: Persistent objects with logic. Technical Report 1158, University of Wisconsin—Madison, Computer Sciences Department, August 1993.
4. Hassan Aït-Kaci. *An Algebraic Semantics Approach to the Effective Resolution of Type Equations*, pages 293–351. Number 45 in Theoretical Computer Science. Elsevier Science Publishers B.V., 1986.

5. Hassan Aït-Kaci and Roger Nasr. LOGIN: a logic programming language with built-in inheritance. *Journal of Logic Programming*, pages 181–215, March 1986.
6. P. Asirelli and P. Inverardi. Enhancing configuration facilities in software development: A logic approach. In *Proceedings of ESEC '87 : 1st European Software Engineering Conference*, volume 289 of *Lecture Notes in Computer Science*, pages 55–63. Springer–Verlag, September 1987.
7. Atria Software, Natick,MA. *ClearCase Concepts Manual*, document number 3000-002-a edition, 1992.
8. N. Belkhatir, J. Estublier, and W. L. Melo. Adele 2: A support to large software development process. In M. Downson, editor, *Proceedings of the 1st International Conference on Software Process*, pages 159–170, Redondo Beach, CA, October 1991. IEEE Computer Society Press.
9. Mark R. Brown and John R. Ellis. Bridges: Tools to extend the vesta configuration management system. Technical report, Digital SRC, June 1993.
10. Todd Brunhoff and Jim Fulton. Imake - c preprocessor interface to the make utility. Technical report, Unix Programmer's Manual, X Window System, Version 11, Release 5.
11. Michael Carey, David DeWitt, Goetz Graefe, David Haight, Joel Richardson, Daniel Schuh, Eugene Shekita, and Scott Vandenberg. The EXODUS extensible DBMS project: an overview. In Stan Zdonik and David Maier, editors, *Readings in Object-Oriented Databases*. Morgan-Kaufman, 1990.
12. CaseWare, Inc, Irvine, CA. *Introduction to CaseWare/CM*, part number ic-031-010 edition, 1993.
13. Sheng-Yang Chiu and Roy Levin. The vesta repository: A file system extension for software development. Technical report, Digital SRC, June 1993.
14. Geoffrey Clemm and Leon Osterweil. A mechanism for environment integration. *ACM Transactions on Programming Languages and Systems*, 12(1):1–25, January 1990.
15. David J. DeWitt, Michael J. Franklin, Nancy E. Hall, Mark L. McAuliffe, Jeffrey F. Naughton, Daniel T. Schuh, Marvin H. Solomon, C. K. Tan, Odysseas G. Tsatalos, Seth J. White, and Michael J. Zwilling. Shoring up persistent applications. In *SIGMOD*, Minneapolis, MN, May 1994.
16. James R. Driscol, Neil Sarnak, Daniel D. Sleator, and Robert E. Tarjan. Making data structures persistent. *Journal of Computer and System Sciences*, 38(1):86–124, February 1989.
17. J. Estublier. A configuration manager: the ADELE database of programs. In *Proceedings of the Workshop on Software Engineering Environments for Programming-in-the-Large*, pages 140–147, Harwichport, MA, June 1985. GTE Laboratories.
18. J. Estublier, S. Ghoul, and S. Krakowiak. Preliminary experience with a configuration control system. In *Proceedings of the SIGSOFT/SIGPLAN Software Eng. Symposium on Practical Software Development Environments*, pages 149–156. ACM, April 1984.
19. Jacky Estublier. Configuration management: the notion and the tools. In *Proceedings of the International Workshop on Software Version and Configuration Control*, pages 38–61, Grassau, W. Germany, January 1988. B.G. Teubner, Stuttgart, W. Germany.
20. Stuart I. Feldman. Make—a program for maintaining computer programs. *Software—Practice and Experience*, 9(4):255–265, April 1979.
21. Christine B. Hanna and Roy Levin. The vesta language for configuration management. Technical report, Digital SRC, June 1993.

22. Stephen C. Johnson. YACC—yet another compiler compiler. C. S. Technical Report 32, Bell Laboratories, Murray Hill, NJ, 1975.

23. Gail Kaiser and Peter H. Feiler. Granularity issues in a knowledge-based programming environment. In *2nd Kansas Conference on Knowledge-Based Software Development*, Manhattan, KA, October 1986.

24. Gail Kaiser and Peter H. Feiler. SMILE/MARVEL: Two approaches to knowledge-based programming environments. Tech. Report CU-CS-227-86, Department of Computer Science, Columbia University, New York, NY 10027, October 1986.

25. Gail Kaiser and Peter H. Feiler. An architecture for intelligent assistance in software development. In *Proceedings of the Ninth International Conference on Software Engineering*, pages 80–88, Monterey, CA, March 1987. IEEE Computer Society Press.

26. Gail E. Kaiser. A rule-based process server component for constructing rule-based development environments. In *Proceedings of the 7th International Software Process Workshop*, pages 76–78, October 1991.

27. Thilo Kielmann. Using prolog for software system maintenance. In *Proceedings of the First International Conference on the Practical Application of Prolog*, volume 1, London, UK, October 1992.

28. Kevin Knight. Unification: a multidisciplinary survey. *ACM Computing Surveys*, 21(1):93–124, March 1989.

29. Butler W. Lampson and Eric E. Schmidt. Organizing software in a distributed environment. *ACM SIGPLAN Notices*, 18(6):1–13, June 1983.

30. David B. Leblang and Robert P. Chase, Jr. Computer-aided software engineering in a distributed workstation environment. *ACM SIGPLAN Notices*, 19(5):104–112, April 1984.

31. David B. Leblang and Gordon D. McLean, Jr. Configuration management for large-scale software development efforts. In *Proceedings of the Workshop on Software Engineering Environments for Programming-in-the-Large*, pages 122–127, Harwichport, MA, June 1985. GTE Laboratories.

32. M.E. Lesk. Lex—a lexical analyzer generator. C. S. Technical Report 39, Bell Laboratories, Murray Hill, NJ, October 1975.

33. Roy Levin and Paul R. McJones. The vesta approach to precise configuration of large software systems. Technical report, Digital SRC, June 1993.

34. Mark A. Linton, John M. Vlissides, and Paul R. Calder. Composing user interfaces with interviews. *IEEE Computer*, pages 8–24, February 1989.

35. Axel Mahler and Andreas Lampen. Shape—a software configuration management tool. In *Proceedings of the International Workshop on Software Version and Configuration Control*, Grassau, W. Germany, January 1988. B.G. Teubner, Stuttgart, W. Germany.

36. Axel Mahler and Andreas Lampen. An integrated toolset for engineering software configurations. In *Proceedings of the ACM SIGSOFT/SIGPLAN Software Engineering Symposium on Practical Software Development Environments*, number (24)2 in ACM SIGPLAN *Notices*, pages 191–200, February 1989.

37. John K. Ousterhout. Tcl: an embeddable command language. In *1990 Winter USENIX Conference Proceedings*, 1990.

38. John K. Ousterhout. Tcl: An embeddable command language. *1990 Winter USENIX Conference Proceedings*, 1990.

39. John K. Ousterhout. An x11 toolkit based on the tcl language. *1991 Winter USENIX Conference Proceedings*, 1991.

40. Dewayne E. Perry, Nancy A. Staudenmayer, and Lawrence G. Votta, Jr. Finding out what goes on in a software development organization. Technical report, Personal communication (paper submitted for publication), September 1993.

41. Anthony Rich. *Logic-Based System Modelling*. PhD thesis, University of Wisconsin—Madison, August 1991.

42. Anthony Rich and Marvin Solomon. A logic-based approach to system modelling. In Peter H. Feiler, editor, *Workshop on Software Configuration Management*, pages 84–93, Trondheim, Norway, June 1991.

43. Joel Richardson, Michael Carey, and Daniel Schuh. The design of the E programming language. *ACM Transactions on Programming Languages and Systems*, 15(3), July 1993.

44. Russell Sandberg, David Goldberg, Steve Kleiman, Dan Walsh, and Bob Lyon. Design and implementation of the sun network filesystem. In *Proceedings of the Summer 1985 USENIX Conference*, pages 119–130, Portland, OR, June 1985.

45. R.W. Scheifler and J. Gettys. The X window system. *ACM Transactions on Graphics*, 16(8):57–69, August 1983.

46. Marvin Solomon. EFS: the extensible file system. Unpublished manual, 1993.

47. Richard M. Stallman and Roland McGrath. *GNU Make*. Free Software Foundation, Inc., Cambridge, MA, edition 0.26 beta edition, 1990.

48. Stanley M. Sutton, Jr., Dennis Heimbigner, and Leon J. Osterweil. Managing change in software development through process programming. Technical Report 1, University of Colorado at Boulder, June 1991.

49. Walter F. Tichy. RCS: a system for version control. *Software—Practice and Experience*, 15(7):637–654, July 1985.

50. Walter F. Tichy. Tools for software configuration management. In Jürgen F.H. Winkler, editor, *Proceedings of the First International Workshop on Software Version and Configuration Control*, pages 1–20, Grassau, FRG, January 1988. B.G. Teubner, Stuttgart, W. Germany.

51. Walter F. Tichy and Mark C. Baker. Smart recompilation. In *12th Annual ACM Symposium on Principles of Programming Languages*, pages 236–244, New Orleans, Louisiana, January 1985.

52. Dennis Vadura. Dmake—maintain program groups, or interdependent files. Technical report, University of Waterloo, 1992. Dmake Unix Programmers Manual, Version 3.8.

53. Douglas Wiebe. *Generic Software Configuration Management: Theory and Design*. PhD thesis, University of Washington, Seattle, 1990.

54. Edward Yourdon. *The Decline & Fall of the American Programmer*. Prentice Hall, 1993.

55. Andreas Zeller. Configuration management with feature logics. Technical report, Technishe Universität Braunschweig Report No. 94-01, March 1994.

Untangling Configuration Management

Mechanism and Methodology in SCM Systems

Martin Cagan
Continuus Software Corporation
108 Pacifica, Irvine, CA USA 92718
cagan@continuus.com

Abstract. There is considerable diversity in the SCM methodological needs of today's software teams. The SCM methods a team requires are a function of technical, social and corporate constraints that define how the project team must design, construct, test and deliver software.

Most commercial and academic SCM systems created to date support particular SCM methodologies. Some created specific mechanisms to support their methodology, while others simply support the methods that work given the constraints and limitations of their mechanisms.

If modern SCM systems are to be applicable to the broad spectrum of software development teams, the methodologies must be separated from the mechanisms, the mechanisms must be distilled into a flexible set of widely applicable capabilities, and the definition of methodologies using these mechanisms must be facilitated.

The purpose of this paper is to explore the mechanisms needed to support advanced SCM methodologies, and process-based software configuration management in general.

1 Introduction

Today's software teams span a broad range of languages, team sizes, development and delivery platforms, quality and localization requirements. They often simultaneously support a number of prior releases, as well as new releases under development. Any given team has a unique set of environmental requirements that influence the optimal software development process, and the SCM process in particular.

Those working on team software development support have been investigating processes for facilitating these teams and addressing the problems they face. From these experiments and products have emerged several useful SCM mechanisms and processes [3, 4, 5, 8, 9]. However, these systems have had limited success in four key respects. First, while a particular SCM system might be a good match for one project team, the project teams down the hall often have substantially different requirements and are forced to change the way they operate, look elsewhere for a SCM system, or develop something themselves. The lesson for those who design SCM systems is to provide systems that support a wide range of needs, not just a particular process that is thought to have special value.

Second, most SCM systems provide extremely limited automated process support [5]. They provide mechanisms that are useful when followed up with manual procedures and team discipline, but there is precious little support in the system itself. Perhaps the most extreme example of this occurs when project teams assemble their own SCM system by writing programs and shell scripts on top of standard version control systems. Any process support they put in is a level above the SCM mechanisms, and therefore the mechanisms are not able to provide the automated support for these processes. The lesson here is that the SCM system must consider the automated support of process requirements as a key mechanism.

The third problem has to do with systems which just store the project files but do not manage the process of creating deliverable objects based on the source, or provide automated ways to construct configurations. This "build" process requires a considerably more robust notion of a configuration, and while this may be the most difficult aspect of implementing SCM systems, it is critical.

The fourth problem has been standing the test of time. While the project team may find a match with a SCM system as they begin their project, their needs will no doubt change over time. The SCM system can quickly become an obstacle in accommodating new requirements. This is often the case when the team grows in size, or quality or delivery requirements change. A clear capability of modern SCM systems that emerged through this experience is the ability to evolve the process support over time.[1]

At this point we will enumerate the core SCM mechanisms we believe are required to address these issues.

2 SCM Mechanisms

SCM mechanisms are defined as those capabilities required to support the implementation of SCM processes.

2.1 Objects

In order to characterize what should be placed under control of a SCM system, one must decide which activities will be covered by SCM. A broad variety of activities can sensibly and beneficially participate in the SCM process, including preparation of requirements and design documents, project planning and scheduling, task assignment

---

1. It follows that the SCM system should version control these process descriptions to track their evolution over time as well.

and tracking, program coding and testing, the quality assurance process, defect and change tracking, and finally release generation.

From the above list we can derive an even longer list of artifacts which one may want to control, including requirements documents, design data (drawings), PERT charts, schedules, task descriptions, source files, program build procedures, object files, libraries and executable programs, test plans, test data, test results, quality measurements, user manuals, release descriptions, configurations, and product releases. These types of data include virtually every form of data that one would normally encounter in a modern computing environment including free-form and structured text, structured binary data, multimedia data, databases, executable images, and various structured and unstructured collections of data of the preceding types.

This is not the entire picture either. All of the items have other properties (also referred to as attributes) which need to be stored and referenced, such as who created them, when they were created and last modified, how they are intended to be used, what level of approval they have reached, and what kinds of protections should apply to them. This information is often called "meta-data", and may actually cover the same range of forms as the primary data.

In addition, each item may be related in various ways to other items under control, and these relationships should also be stored.

In order to define a notion of "object" which will be general and flexible enough to encompass all of these different kinds of information, we define the following requirements:

1 An object and its meta-data should be considered to be atomic with respect to overall configuration management. This means that to create, delete, copy, move, or otherwise manipulate an object generally includes the meta-data as well.

2 Objects need not be atomic entities, but rather may be homogeneous or heterogeneous collections of parts. Further, each part may take on any of the forms available to object data.

3 Each object may fit into a classification such that common properties and behavior specified for the class can be used to perform operations on the individual object. The means by which an object acquires behavior from its class is called "inheritance", for consistency with Object-Oriented Programming concepts.

4 In spite of the above, each object instance may have unique character of its own, which overrides the class behavior. Further, new attributes of any type may be added to a given object at any time, unless purposeful access restrictions specifically prohibit this. Unlike popular database concepts used in traditional application development, this means the SCM database should not be ruled by a fixed schema.

5 As is suggested above, a key requirement of objects (or more generally, their classes) is that they describe how to perform most generic or abstract operations upon themselves. Since many users, activities, and processes (pro-

grams) will interact with an object during its lifetime, it is important that the means of performing routine functions (such as creation, deletion, modification, changes of state, or retrieval of primary or meta-data) be transparent to the user or encoded into every application. Thus the notion that behavior be storable and associated with the class is fundamental to our object definition. For the sake of uniformity, stored behavior can also be considered as another type of meta-data, and we refer to this kind of meta-data as "methods".

6 While objects themselves are classified and have behaviors and properties derived from their classes, data members also have a data type and properties leading from that type, such as storage format (integer, string, text, binary) and location (the SCM database, local file-system, remote repository).

7 Objects may participate in various "relationships" with other objects or with structured or unstructured groups (binary and n-ary relationships). Some relationships may be treated as properties (meta-data) of one of the affected objects. For example, the "is a" relationship between an object and its class is a (static) property of the object. Other relationships may not be considered properties of the participants. An example of this is the participation of an object in a configuration. The configuration "contains" the object only by reference, since the same object may be used in a variety of places.

8 Objects must be persistent.

2.2 Versioned Objects

We next turn to defining what is meant by the term "version", and how this relates to objects. We then examine the relationships which inherently exist among versions, in order to create a basis for discussing SCM processes.

In informal discussions, we could talk about objects as being the same as versions of class instances (object = version), or we can consider objects to exist as one or more versions (object = set of related versions). For simplicity, the latter usage will be followed. In fact, we will not make a formal definition of objects, but instead only of versions. The pattern by which versions belong to the same object will be a matter of convention.

It is a clear purpose of SCM systems to store the version history of an object. However, what is not so clear is which of several kinds of relationships between versions should be involved in this history. Thus a SCM system should be able to show users all relationships of which it has knowledge. Which relationships are kept in the SCM database is a function of the SCM process.

Aside from the occasions when an initial version of a new object is created, there exists at least two important implicit properties of a version being created: the other version(s) from which the new one is derived; and the intended use of the new version.

The former is called the "derivation" relationship of the version, and one may say the new version is "derived from" the preceding one (its predecessor). If a merger process is involved in creating the new version, then this version may be considered to be derived from more than one predecessor. It is important to track this relationship for two key reasons: first, it is needed for computing history of changes to the succession of versions leading to a particular one; and second, it allows storage compression mechanisms to operate more efficiently.[1]

The "usage" of a derived version is more interesting from a process perspective. This relationship connects the new version to one or more previous versions which it is either intended or known to replace (in the sense of participation in configurations). In other words, we create a new version to "succeed" a previous one (usually because it contains a correction or enhancement to the predecessor), or to "replace" or "supersede" it (if the new one is considerably different, and not a change to the previous). In the latter case the new version may not actually be considered to belong to the same object, but still constitutes part of the predecessor's history.

2.3 Object Relationships

Managing relationships is a key capability of any SCM system. In Continuus/CM, object instances can be associated with one another through one of three types of relationships:

* Derivation Relationships
* Binding Relationships
* Hyperlink Relationships

Derivation Relationship

When one object version is derived from another to create a new version, a derivation relationship is created. This association records the predecessor/successor relationship. For example, `foo.c-12` has a *derivation* relationship with `foo.c-11`. We discussed this relationship earlier as we described the mechanisms for tracking versioned object histories.

Binding Relationship

A configuration object manages binding relationships. When an object version is a set up as a member of a configuration object (we describe configuration objects formally in the next section), a binding relationship is created between the member object and the configuration object. For example, the C source object `foo.c-12` is a member of the configuration object `proj1-rel2.0` which is recorded with a *binding* relationship between the two object versions.

Hyperlink Relationship

The hyperlink relationship is used to maintain arbitrary relationships between any two object instances. For example, C source object `foo.c-12` may be associated with task object number **491** through a *hyperlink* relationship.

---

1. Knowing which version another is derived from will usually yield the smallest "delta" between the two versions. It is such deltas that are often stored as a means of compression.

Hyperlink relationships are typed (e.g. `is_documented_by` or `is_task_of`).

2.4 Configuration Objects

Another fundamental requirement of a SCM system is to provide the means to construct, manage, and control configurations. Herein the term configuration will be used rather loosely, but there are a few assumptions which we will make about the properties these objects must have.

1 There may be several types of configurations, and all will be first-class objects in the sense of possessing member data, behavior (inherited from the class or defined locally), and version history.

2 In departure from normal object properties, configurations will permit the aggregation of objects (possibly by containment, but certainly by reference), and will permit structural relationships among objects to be stored and navigated.

3 Configurations may form hierarchies such that one configuration "contains", or organizes (again by reference), a set of others just as it can do so for other types of objects.

The reason referential grouping is emphasized is that although containment is an intuitively attractive concept, the referential mode appears to support more capabilities required for SCM purposes. This should become more clear in later sections which examine release management processes, but we will mention one key point here. It is the very nature of the SCM (and software development) process that objects are continually reused and reorganized in ways that were not anticipated initially. Thus objects which have long been non-modifiable (for control reasons) may need to be included in new configurations, and of course in multiple configurations. Thus containment in a single configuration tends to be a less useful concept.

The question now arises as to what kinds of structures configurations may need to represent. Some examples of configuration structures which naturally arise are:

1 Sets (e.g. the set of all program-versions participating in a release)[1]
2 Groupings (e.g. the program versions a user maintains)[2]
3 Trees (e.g. the section/chapter/paragraph structure of a document)
4 Directed graphs (e.g. the "make" dependency structure of a program)
5 A network (e.g. the call graph among a class collection)

Depending on one's habits, processes, or development tools, other structures may need to be represented. Thus a good SCM system should provide a rich set of configuration types and/or a general way of implementing new structures.

Considering the above list, a very general type of structure which may be able to represent most of the cases routinely arising in SCM is the directed graph. We will shortly

---

1. A "set" is thought to have only one version of each member.
2. A "group" may have more than one version of each member.

define a type of configuration which supports directed graph structures but can also be used to represent many other commonly needed object organizations.

At this point we will try to elaborate on why it is so crucial that a SCM system support configurations as first-class objects.

To start with, a primary function of a SCM system is to provide the means to define and control releases of a product (we use this term in the abstract). Consider the case of a software development shop. The goal of such an organization is to deliver software to a set of clients or customers. Over time many versions of this software must typically be delivered. The software shop is expected to deliver versions with known functionality and quality.

This software is usually not a singular entity, but rather some collection of programs, data, documents, and other objects provided on some medium such as disk or tape. So a foremost task of the software shop is to generate the tape with known, correct content. Thus they immediately need to store in their SCM database a representation of this content, and this representation must be constructible in some orderly, reliable and reproducible fashion. Further, since some of the contents of this "tape configuration" consists of constructed objects, each of these constructed objects should also have their component structure stored in the SCM database.

Additionally, the constructed tape image must correspond to these configuration structures, which means that these structures ought to be functional, and not just documentation. To clarify, the configuration should be constructed to represent the required product, and used to drive the product construction process.

As time passes, other uses for this configuration will arise. If the software shop sells additional copies of the product to other customers, and if they also continue to maintain and enhance the software, multiple versions will inevitably be in concurrent use in the field. Thus they will require (at a minimum for support reasons) that they keep a permanent record of each configuration which is delivered, and the SCM database must be able to store and control (i.e. prevent modification) saved configurations.

2.5 Versioned Object Management

Now that we have covered the properties and relationships of object versions, we must examine issues such as how and why versions are created, and what happens to these versions over time. Rules or guidelines concerning creation of versions are certainly a very fundamental aspect of a SCM process, but since the objective is to provide SCM mechanisms that are as process-independent as possible, we must carefully separate process constraints from those SCM principles which are widely applicable. Here the case is made that traditional views on versioning are much too limiting, and that a SCM system should support a much broader range of possible versioning models.

First we will consider the question of when a new version should be (considered to have been) created. The following points are relevant.

1 Anytime the appropriate version of an object is non-modifiable, yet a change must be made to the object, a new version must be created.

2 On the other hand, a user may wish to start with a copy of a modifiable version (even someone elses!) yielding two concurrently modifiable versions. There is nothing inherently wrong with this concept.

3 There are diverse reasons why such creation may occur, not all of which have to do with creating a successor (in the sense of usage) to the version from which the newer one is derived. Thus, the actual time of creation may be less interesting for SCM purposes than the (later) point in time when the new version becomes usable for some purpose.

4 Many revisions (in the sense of edits or other manipulations) to an object may occur between creation and eventual usage, and it may be the case (depending on process) that these intermediate revisions are of no significance to overall SCM matters (release generation). In other words, only revisions which are considered to be "milestones" in some sense are of importance in creating configurations. We call these potentially numerous and small checkpoint revisions the "micro-versions", while those versions which are considered SCM level we call "macro-versions".

5 It is generally useful for versions created as in (1) to be known to other users, though it is especially useful when the new version is intended to succeed an existing one. That is, the intentions of the version creator are more important than the simple existence of the version, since development decisions may not be able to be based on the latter.

6 Versions which initially are considered to be useful for some purpose (e.g. an integration test) may later be promoted to other uses (e.g. an actual release), or be discarded as unusable. This evolution from creation to initial uses, to eventual uses, and/or obsolescence, can be thought of as the "lifecycle" of the object.

From the above points we conclude that in the absence of a more intentionally limiting process, a generalized versioning model should provide the following:

1 All versions of objects must be known to the SCM system without constraining them to a particular use.

2 The intended future use of the object may be known (if and only if the user supplied this information explicitly, or the process provides it implicitly), but is not necessarily implied simply by the existence or derivation of the version.

3 The SCM system must provide some way for the user to convey when a version is suitable and ready for some intended use.

4 The SCM system may or may not provide for tracking of micro-versions, but obviously must provide for full management of macro-versions.[1]

---

1. Micro-versioning may be best handled by the tool which creates and manages the data (e.g. the Program Editor).

5 An important tracking responsibility of a SCM system is to know the state of every version within its lifecycle (although this lifecycle is defined by a users chosen process, and may depend on the class of object).

Note that we do not find that any dependency between versions of different (or even the same) objects exists in the absence of specific processes. Thus we might say that all objects should be thought of as being versioned independently of (or orthogonally to) each other, and any interdependence arises as a result of added operational rules.

Note also that it has not been concluded that any notion of locking is relevant to the general issue of versioning. The idea of locking will arise only when considering strategies for handling concurrency during parallel development, not in the context of simple versioning.

For this reason certain well established beliefs about SCM are rejected. For example, it has long been thought that the "check-in/check-out" (CICO) model is a universal property of SCM systems. The "long transaction" model is essentially equivalent to CICO in this regard, though it suggests an attractive correlation between SCM models of concurrency with those used in general database theories [5]. However, we suggest that more effective processes will be far less trivial than these, and a SCM system must support a more general class of techniques.

The locking aspect of the CICO model is just one example out of myriad examples of potential rules for maintaining some process required conditions on a set of versions of an object. A lock is just a conveyance of a binary property over one (or a set of) version(s). Certainly more information could be conveyed, and with more information perhaps a more efficient overall process can result.

Similarly, the privacy and isolation components of the CICO model are arbitrary (and actually very poor) techniques for achieving insulation between separate concurrent activities. Shortly we will explore the insulation concept more fully to show that more general and effective approaches exist. The CICO model is a two-state lifecycle which is far too trivial for managing most types of data in a quality-focused, team environment.

2.6 Insulation

Another basic problem that SCM systems must solve is that of interference between various elements of a project team. Since many versions of objects are constantly being created during development, each group or individual must use some set of these versions in order to get work done. However, in the interest of working with the "right" set, or in particular an "up-to-date" set, techniques are often employed which frequently cause developers to end up with incompatible, nonfunctional, or otherwise unusable configurations. The prevention of these problems we term "insulation".

Here again it can be stated that traditional SCM processes oversimplify the issue. It must be emphasized that insulation cannot be trivialized to isolating developers until such time as they submit work as completed, after which all such work is immediately shared. Modern SCM systems should not be limited to the "sharing versus isolation" model anymore. Today's software development organizations are usually collections of a number of different teams under some management structure, and each team has different responsibilities and relationships with other teams. For example, a software project may have one team developing core services libraries; another developing application functions; another graphical user interfaces; and another generating releases. Each team can be seen to have different relationships with other teams with regard to communicating results and status or work in progress. Within each team there are still further subtleties in relationships and communication paths. All these factors indicate that results of work must flow among diverse elements in a non-trivial way. This multidimensional and potentially complex aspect of the development process may need to be served by a variety of forms of insulation.

Another way to look at the issue of insulation is to consider it as a matter of controlling the "visibility" of objects. That is, if a particular piece of (complete or incomplete) work is not visible to some individual (or team), then it could be said that the individual is insulated from the source of that work. Further, there is no abstract difference between insulating two developers from each other and insulating new revisions from end-users or customers. This is also just a matter of limiting delivery of changes to customers until such time as the changes are fully tested and approved.

A further refinement of this concept is that visibility should not imply that work which is not ready for some particular use cannot be known ahead of time to that user. What is really necessary is for the existence and purpose of the work to be known, yet unusable due to process restrictions which are supported in the environment. Thus the challenge here is really to accomplish insulation without having to resort to isolation.

2.7 Object Lifecycles

Given that the concept of visibility control as a mechanism for achieving insulation between diverse project elements has been adopted, and that it is understood that the level of control over objects may vary along with the changes in visibility, some way to model the evolution of an object's state is necessary. A general technique for doing this is called "lifecycle modelling". The lifecycle of an object is the set of visibility and control states that it moves through between the time of its creation and its eventual

Fig. 1. Lifecycle of Source Objects

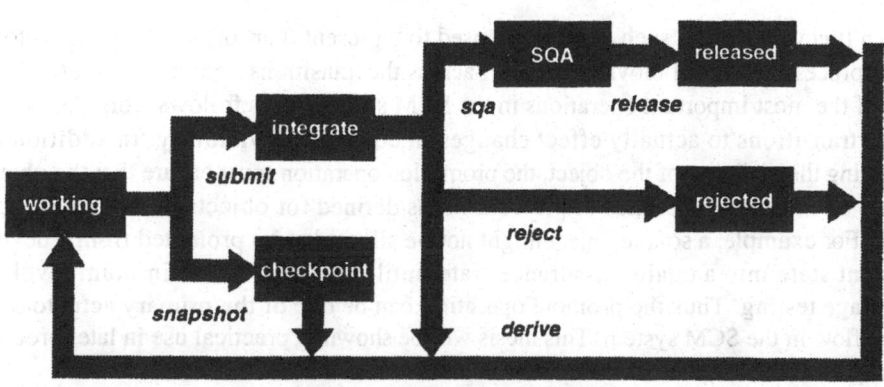

obsolescence, together with the rules governing which state-transitions are permitted and what side effects or pre-conditions occur when making each transition.

No single lifecycle model can be expected to apply to all objects in a system, and life-cycles may be specific to (groups of) classes, or may be particular to certain usages of the objects, rather than to the class of the object. Since these lifecycle models are at the core of a SCM process, a SCM system must be very flexible as to the lifecycles it supports.

Consider the following examples of typical lifecycles. The first is a sample lifecycle for a software object (e.g. a source file) which typically proceeds from a developmental state (*working*), through an integration test stage (*integrate*), and then through a quality control process (*sqa*), and finally to a deliverable (*released*) state (see Figure 1, Life-cycle of Source Objects). Both the initial testing as well as quality assurance procedures can result in the module being passed back to the developer (*integrate -> working*), or being rejected altogether (*sqa -> rejected*). Although it is clearly much more compli-cated than the two-state CICO model, this model is actually fairly simple, once the idea of an object lifecycle is clear.

To illustrate just how different the lifecycles for two object classes may be, consider a lifecycle for a change request object, which rather than unit and integration testing, has a much more complex work-flow-oriented lifecycle (see Figure 2, Lifecycle of Change Request Object).

Fig. 2. Lifecycle of Change Request Object

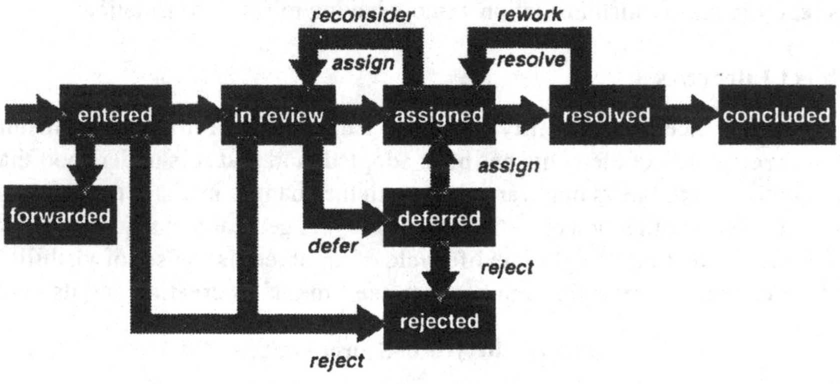

When lifecycle models such as these are used to represent (part of) a software develop-ment process, the act of moving an object across the transitions, termed "promotion", is one of the most important operations in the SCM system. This follows from the use of these transitions to actually effect changes in control and visibility. In addition to changing the visibility of the object, the promotion operation must ensure that the object meets all required properties or pre-conditions defined for objects in the destination state. For example, a source object might not be allowed to be promoted from a devel-opment state into a quality assurance state until it passes some minimum level of coverage testing. Thus the promote operation can be one of the primary actuators of work flow in the SCM system. This thesis will be shown in practical use in later process examples.

2.8 Rule-based Configurations

In addition to the obvious need to be able to explicitly include an object in a configuration, we believe that modern SCM systems require the power and flexibility of rule-based configuration definition.

In rule-based configuration definition, the configuration object contains a method which determines the set of objects and specific object versions that should be included in the configuration.

Common rules include "select the latest versions of the files except those that are private and not owned by me", or "select all the files in Release 2 plus the fixes for Patch 9".

This is a key mechanism for supporting insulation and object lifecycles. This mechanism has proven useful in a wide variety of processes and in dealing with large amounts of data where explicit specification is not feasible [5, 8].

The configuration member selection rules themselves are a key component of the process, in that they provide automated support for the process. Specifically, they support the particular means of insulation desired.

One important aspect of rule-based configuration specification is that since this mechanism is used to update the contents of the configuration, the configuration update process must be under the control of the user due to insulation considerations. Otherwise, a particular user's configuration could change without action on his part, a clear violation of the insulation requirement.[1]

2.9 Security and Access Control

In addition to inducing information flow in the development environment, promotion can also be used to operate the changes in the control state of an object. This is accomplished by defining some set of access types (privileges), and defining the set of privileges that are allowed for each state in the lifecycle. Consider the following example.

A three-state lifecycle could be defined in which the states are *working*, *integrate*, and *released*. The *working* state could allow full privileges to its creator, but only read access to others. (Others could not, for example, change a module in this state, or even use it in their own configurations.) Once the work on the object is initially completed, the object is promoted to *integrate*, which then allows the object to be used in test configurations, and perhaps in working configurations of other team members. At this point it may be non-modifiable (or only modifiable by its owner), though possibly retrievable back to the *working* state by its creator. After sufficient tests have been

---

1. Consider a scenario where a large C application is being built, and that your selection rules say to include the latest checked in versions. Half-way through your build, a new version of a header file is checked in. Part of the application is built with one version, and the rest with another, causing a difficult to locate run-time error.

passed, it might then be promoted to *released* (but only by a QA manager), which would qualify the object for use in deliverable configurations, and would require that the object be permanently non-modifiable, and not dependent on any other modifiable object.

The access rights required for the above scenario can be summarized as *read, write, bind* (use in a configuration), and *promote*. We can also add that perhaps a different set of these applies to the creator or owner of an object than to other team members.

Of course, additional "natural" access rights can easily be thought of, and artificial ones can even be devised to serve purposes of specific processes. (For example, the right to "sign off" a document might be reserved for certain users of certain roles.)

Another behavior which may usefully be tied to lifecycle is that of storage control (or accessibility control). This deals with the fact that an object currently in use must be readily available, while those which are older and possibly obsolete may be archived until the need for them arises. In some processes, both short term archival (for space compression) and long term archival (for historical purposes) are required.

2.10 Workflow Support

The mechanisms of object lifecycle support, rule-based configurations, insulated workareas, and role-based security and access control are key capabilities which enable the higher-level process mechanism of workflow support. At one level of abstraction, an SCM process is all about managing the flow of project data through the development organization.

Workflow support involves facilities for defining, supporting and enforcing the flow of project data from the development team to the test team to release management and out to the end-users. There are any number of potential workflows for the SCM process, each optimized around different objectives (e.g. quality, security, visibility, control, rapid application development, etc.).

A process-based SCM system must incorporate this notion of workflow support in its foundation in order to provide the services needed for to manage higher level SCM processes.

2.11 Representing Process Using Objects

Mechanisms for describing object classes, which include both stored data and stored behavior, and how an object's data and behavior is inherited from its class and its super-class(es) have been discussed. Additionally, it has been explained that data or behavior can be specialized for each instance, and that objects are manipulated through their methods.

In the object-oriented information repository that has been described, all project entities, both physical (e.g. representing configurations, source files, directories, libraries, executables) and logical (e.g. representing groupings, installation instructions) are represented as objects and stored in the database.[1]

Using this object-oriented repository, a software SCM process is represented by creating the appropriate objects, with the desired behavior captured in the object's methods, and the project data encapsulated in the object's data attributes. This collection of classes (methods and data) is referred to as the "SCM Development Model".

The development model supports the desired process. Because the process will evolve, so must the development model. The development model is viewed as a key project object, and should be configuration managed along with the other project information. In fact, the products that are built under the SCM system's control actually have the development model as a dependency.

Because the classes and their methods are completely dynamic and user extensible, this mechanism can be used to support a wide range of behavior.

There is a good deal more to be said about representing SCM process using an object-oriented repository. For a more detailed discussion of this topic, as well as the other SCM mechanisms required in order to support modern SCM systems, see [1].

2.12 Instrumenting the Process

Everything we have discussed under process is a part of the overall software development process. However, there are other forms of process support that can be applied to nearly any process to further specialize the SCM system to support the local process requirements. In this section we will discuss some examples of this.

Pre-conditions, Notifications and Triggers

A very common form of process control is to enforce pre and/or post-conditions on object state transitions or method invocations. For example, certain audit information may be enforced as a pre-condition for promoting an object to a *released* state. Or, Q.A. may be notified each time a new object is ready for testing, or require that a test suite has run before a configuration object can be *released*.

State transitions are not the only situations which are appropriate for pre-conditions and notifications. You may also want to be notified or log in an audit trail when source objects have been compiled, or when design diagrams have been edited. The key lesson learned over the past few years from work in control integration was that it is very difficult to predict in advance the sorts of operations that project teams may need to trigger on and what actions they wish to trigger, and that the best policy is to support customizable pre-conditions and notifications on all operations on all object classes [2].

---

1. Actually, the storage characteristics for a given data type is an attribute of that type, so any data member can physically be stored anywhere. Typically, the meta-data is stored in the database, and the "contents" resides in the file system.

Metrics Collection

It should be clear at this point that definition of the SCM process and supporting its continuous improvement is crucial to the software development process. Moreover, the key to continuous process improvement lies in measuring the process to identify where problems lie [6, 7].

Since modern SCM systems manage the project data, manage access to that data, and manage change to that data, they are an ideal place to collect information on the process.

There is an abundance of useful raw data stored when using the processes described here. For example, the SCM system knows how long it takes from the time a change is requested to the time it is approved for release. It knows who has been doing what operations to what data, and when it was done. It knows how many unassigned change requests are in the system, and how long it takes until they are assigned.

Furthermore, since the SCM mechanisms described here provide for the dynamic addition of user-defined attributes on any object class, it is simple to add an attribute (such as "essential complexity") to the C source class, and instrument the "promote" method to run complexity analysis tools and store the results on the object. Or code stability could be measured just as easily.

The point here is not the value of any particular metric, or set of metrics, but rather to point out both the opportunity for easily collecting project data, and that this data can and should be analyzed in order to identify the process improvements necessary to improve your SCM process.

3 SCM Processes

Thus far we have described a rich set of mechanisms designed to support a wide range of SCM processes. Now we will explore some of the popular SCM processes and consider the applicability of the mechanisms to these processes.

3.1 SCM Usage Models

In [5], Peter Feiler presents a taxonomy of SCM models (processes) and describes four very different models of SCM systems. It is interesting to review each model to see how the SCM mechanisms described here support each of these models.

Checkout/Checkin Model

The Checkout/Checkin model is the simplest of the models, and focuses on the basics of controlling access to files. The usage model is that you retrieve and reserve a version of an object from a repository (checkout), modify the object, and return the updated object version to the repository.

The basic mechanisms described under Versioned Object Management are more than sufficient for modelling any of the popular systems based on this model (e.g. PVCS, RCS, SCCS).

Composition Model

The Composition Model extends the basic component checkout/checkin to address the notion of collections of components, including versioning the collections and rule-based version selection.

This model is at the heart of modern SCM systems, and is well supported by the mechanisms described here, in particular the support for Configuration Objects, Versioned Object Management, Insulation and Rule-based Configurations.

Long Transaction Model

The long-transaction model, exemplified by NSE [3], is oriented around the concept of the flow of objects through a hierarchy of workspaces. This model represents technology and processes to support large-scale parallel development.

From the perspective of the underlying SCM mechanisms, this model is very similar to the Composition Model. To precisely mimic the NSE system, several of the parallel notification mechanisms would not be used, since parallel changes are performed in isolation using NSE. However, this is not so much a feature of NSE as a side-effect limitation of the implementation, so using these mechanisms would be an enhancement to the model.

Change Set Model

The Change Set model approaches changes to software from a logical view rather than a physical one. Rather than the user remembering that six files were changed to fix a single problem, the system remembers this and lets the user operate on the change from this logical "change-set" level.

In order to support this model, the SCM system must support objects other than source objects, and be able to maintain relationships between the logical change object and the actual physical changes. Each of these services is provided by the mechanisms described here.

3.2 Parallel Development Models

Of the many processes a software team performs each day, among the most important is how the team manages (or struggles with) parallel development.

Most modern SCM systems support parallel development. However, the precise form of parallel development can vary widely. We view parallel development as a spectrum, with purely serialized development on a single line of descent at one extreme, and the "optimistic" scheme made popular by Sun's NSE [3] at the other. Most techniques fall somewhere in between. All can be supported using the mechanisms we have described.

It is useful to first define what we mean by parallel development, as this definition varies widely as well.

Parallel development occurs at two levels of granularity. Multiple changes may be made in parallel (either by multiple people or by one person working on multiple tasks) to a single source object (such as a C source file, or a design document), and simultaneous changes may be made to a configuration (for example, one person may add the new file "foo.c", and another add the new file "bar.c").

Parallel development involves access control (to both the source objects and the configuration), notification (keeping people informed of the parallel activity, when desired), comparison (identifying the differences between parallel versions) and merging (combining parallel versions into a new, common version).

One extreme process for dealing with the problems of parallel development is to enforce serialization. This simply says that parallel versions are prevented. The first person derives a new version and begins work. If another person asks to derive from the same ancestor, then that person's derive fails, with a reference to whoever owns the new version. This of course makes the person that currently owns the object a bottleneck (which all too often leads to circumvention of the system), which is why many organizations prefer to support at least one of the forms of parallel development.

The most common form of parallel development involves making an explicit branch in the main line of descent, and later (when and if desired) doing an explicit merge of the parallel version(s). Even with this technique the details vary, especially with respect to how the various owners of the parallel versions are kept informed of each other's activities. All owners of parallel versions may be kept informed of all activity with regard to these objects (such as when they are created, promoted or merged); however, most of the common version control and SCM systems support this scheme without activity notification.

Another approach to parallel development, referred to as the "optimistic" scheme [4], creates parallel versions implicitly (the creator does not know it is a parallel version at the time the version is derived), and only upon promotion is the user informed of a conflict if one exists, at which point the user must enter into a reconciliation process.

The purpose here is not to critique any of these processes, but rather to emphasize the range of styles that can be supported with the general mechanisms described. All forms of parallel development described here are useful in appropriate circumstances.

4 Conclusion

Process is absolutely fundamental to software configuration management. Furthermore, it is the role of SCM systems to support the SCM process, not just simply provide the mechanisms. The SCM process must be able to evolve over time, and the system should in fact facilitate (and track) this evolution (and certainly not hinder it).

The SCM mechanisms described here are able to support all four of the commercial CM models (processes) described in [5].

The SCM mechanisms and processes (development models) described here have been implemented by Continuus Software Corporation and are installed at customer sites world-wide under the product name Continuus/CM.

5 References

1 Cagan M (1995). White Paper, *Continuus Software Corporation*.
2 Cagan M (1990). An Architecture for a New Generation of Software Tools, *Hewlett-Packard Journal*.
3 Courington W (1989). The Network Software Environment, *Technical Report, Sun Microsystems*.
4 Feiler P (1990). Tool Version Management Technology: A Case Study, *SEI Technical Report SEI-90-TR-25*.
5 Feiler P (1991). Configuration Management Models in Commercial Environments, *SEI Technical Report SEI-91-TR-7*.
6 Humphreys W (1989) *Managing the Software Process*, Addison-Wesley.
7 Jones C (1994). *Assessment and Control of Software Risks*, Prentice-Hall.
8 Leblang D (1985). The DOMAIN Software Engineering Environment for Large Scale Software Development Efforts, *Proceedings of the IEEE Conference on Workstations*.
9 Wiebe D (1990). Generic Software Configuration Management: Theory and Design, *University of Washington, Department of Computer Science Technical Report 90-07-03*.

Software Configuration Management:
Why is it needed and what should it do?

David B. Leblang and Paul H. Levine
Atria Software, Inc.
24 Prime Park Way, Natick, MA 01760 USA

Abstract

While "configuration management" has taken on many meanings, the basic requirements for a Software Configuration Management tool are universal. This paper categorizes these core requirements, presents the stress points that motivate the adoption of a professionally supported, industrial-strength tool, and highlights some key benefits offered to the daily users of an SCM system.

1.0 Introduction

"Configuration Management" (CM) is a widely used term, with an equally wide range of meanings. To some, it conjures images of formal, complex policies and procedures, with strict approval and reporting mechanisms. To others, it is merely the name given to an ad hoc layer of scripts over a basic version control facility.

The level of CM required by an organization is driven both by needs and by methodology. No one tool, no single methodology, and certainly no single set of policies will work for everyone. However, there are some basic CM requirements that span all software development environments. This paper presents a practical view of configuration management, describing the requirements of CM tools' harshest critics: the software developers themselves. The paper also describes the pressures that motivate the purchase of a fully supported, product-quality CM tool, and offers a few guidelines for selecting a vendor for a CM tool.

2.0 A Practical View of CM

The need for "configuration management" is not unique to the software industry. In a mechanical design and manufacturing environment, a CM system is used to keep track of how components change over time, and how particular versions of specific components are combined to produce the final assembly. The CM system keeps component-level change logs and produces bills-of-materials, complete with version numbers of the components used and complete assembly instructions. The system records development history in a form that can be used to reproduce the manufactured item.

Just as in hardware and mechanical systems environments, software configuration management (SCM) is the art of keeping track of what has changed and how things are combined. The software engineer edits (changes) some files, and then builds (combines) the software in steps that link the changed elements with the remaining unmodified files. An SCM system must include a history of changes made to each file. It also must reliably record in a software "bill-of-materials" the process by which specific versions of these files are combined to produce a complete software system ("release"). This guarantees reproducibility of running software. The SCM system is responsible for the collection and reliable retention of the "who, what, when, how, and why" of every source code change and every software system build.

Basic SCM requirements encompass the four categories described below.

• *Version control* is the process of keeping track of all changes to every file, supporting parallel development by enabling easy branching and merging; every type of object that evolves in the software development environment must be version-controlled.

• *Environment ("sandbox") management* provides each developer with a consistent, flexible, inexpensive, and reproducible environment to compile, edit, and debug software. Environment management is the process that selects and presents the appropriate version of each file to the developer in a way that enables the development tools to work smoothly.

• *Build management* is the process of building software components and also producing a "bill-of-materials" that documents the contents of each software build. The bill-of-materials must be complete enough and reliable enough to recreate the environment that created the build in the future (for making patches and debugging problems).

• *Process control* is a set of policies and enforcement mechanisms that ensure software is developed according to a defined software development methodology. Process controls include *monitoring* (to track what is being changed and by whom), *notification* (to send messages to interested parties when certain operations are attempted or performed), *access control* (to prevent changes by unauthorized personnel, or at inappropriate times), and reporting (to create permanent records). These controls must be flexible, enabling development organizations to customize their environment to support their chosen policies.

Each organization emphasizes some of these requirements over others. In particular, there is a wide-spectrum of demand for process control and reporting facilities. Some software engineering teams operate under specific and documented procedural guidelines; others prefer a minimalist approach to policy enforcement. A widely acceptable SCM tool must provide building blocks for the implementation of process control without bias toward any specific type of policy.

The SCM process will interact with other processes such as design methodologies, quality assurance policies, and customer support programs. It must be easily integrated with design tools, software quality tools such as test coverage and metrics tools, and with call tracking and problem tracking systems. In general, the SCM system must be "open" and easily integrated into existing environments.

3.0 When Do I Need a CM Tool?

Every software development team already has some SCM tools and methodologies. In the simplest case, developers send email, holler over partitions and tape notes to their monitors. For some teams, such ad hoc mechanisms suffice to create audit trails, record what has changed, coordinate merging, and keep track of which versions were used to build yesterday's baselevel.

Most UNIX shops depend on free UNIX utilities (SCCS or RCS), layered with home-grown scripts, to implement procedures for keeping track of what has changed. Windows shops use similar tools and have similar problems. Many organizations have policies for taking periodic "snapshots" of their source code in an effort to capture the environment in which a particular set of programs was built. Some have elaborate scripts to create developer "sandboxes" that mirror the contents and structure of predetermined baselines.

In most cases, the ad hoc tools are eventually stretched and strained, compromising the productivity of the developers, and the maintainability and quality of the software itself. Parallel development activities are constrained by the sophistication of the version branching and merging facilities (or lack thereof). Often, developers give up -- they revert to making changes to individual files serially, rather than in parallel; and they conduct long-lived experiments outside the normal version-control and SCM environment. Interim releases of software are hard to produce, small incremental changes cannot be verified, and old releases cannot be reproduced. What once everyone could do, now requires the special knowledge and heroic efforts of a superstar -- and soon, even that is not enough.

As the organization hires more people, supports a longer history, and accumulates more code, SCM demands grow continually and inexorably. The complexity of the SCM task scales along several dimensions. The most important of these are the sheer size of the software development effort, the number and diversity of the applications produced by the organization, and the importance of maintaining previous releases.

These factors contribute to the need of an industrial-strength, product-quality, fully supported, and continually enhanced SCM tool.

3.1 Scale

A single programmer can keep track of changes and the build structure for a small application using almost any method. However, most software development organizations consist of tens or hundreds of engineers working in parallel on overlapping tasks, tens of thousands of source files, and millions of lines of code -- all scattered across dozens of machines. In addition, several different delivery platforms are often supported and several releases of a software product may be in use and supported.

For this "programming-in-the-large" environment, CM must encourage parallel development by combining flexibility with absolute safety. It is an SCM failure if an engineer decides not to run an experiment, test a theory, or produce an interim release because the required environment is unknown or too hard to set up.

In very large organizations like today's multi-national corporations, a software system may have some pieces developed at one site while others are developed a geographically separate site (e.g. the GUI is developed in England, the database is built in California, and the real-time subsystem is developed in Japan.) In order to scale to these types of organizations the SCM system should provide support for these types of geographically dispersed development teams.

3.2 Product Complexity

A single programmer combines software modules into only a few running programs. A large-scale software development shop produces dozens of applications, often with versions for execution on multiple computer platforms, and all from different combinations of the same underlying source code. The richness and number of these "configurations" defies simple snapshotting techniques for recording which elements were used to produce a given executable.

In such an environment, there is no single set of versions that defines the baseline for all "current" releases. A developer must be able to select the initial set of file versions that make sense for a particular project, and evolve the software from that point. Powerful merge tools are needed as part of an SCM tool to reconcile parallel changes.

3.3 Importance of History

A professional software development organization must be able to reliably reproduce any software build. Old releases continually need bug fixes and minor enhancements, and an SCM system must be able to compare builds to ensure that there have been no unplanned and unwanted changes. The number of active configurations is especially high for developers who manage "specials" for individual clients, each with its own slight variant of the core software. The guarantee of reproducibility for any software build becomes essential for maintainability. Providing that guarantee falls to the SCM system.

4.0 Picking an SCM Tool – Avoiding Shelfware

The key to successfully selecting an SCM tool is to "know your audience." The daily users of the tool are the software engineers themselves. Although software engineering managers can benefit from use of almost any CM tool, successful SCM adoption depends on enthusiastic acceptance by the user community. These engineering professionals have schedules and deadlines, and they most readily embrace tools that make their jobs easier. While it is sometimes possible to mandate use of a particular tool or methodology, there is no substitute for picking an SCM tool that developers *want* to use. Here are just a few common desires of the mainstream software engineering community:

• *Automate sandboxes* -- Setting up a development environment is a time-consuming and error-prone process. Each developer must create and populate his or her own sandboxes before getting any work done. The SCM system should automatically create and manage these environments reliably and reproducibly.

• *Automate dependency checking and rebuild avoidance* -- When none of the files used in its construction has changed, a binary need not be rebuilt. Making engineers manually maintain the dependency lists for every binary is time-consuming and error-prone. The SCM system should automatically record all dependencies, and whenever possible avoid unnecessary builds by automatically reusing existing binaries.

• *Automate merging* -- The reconciliation of some parallel development will always require human intervention (e.g., I changed x=3 to x=4 and you changed it to x=5), but most changes are mutually independent and can be merged without human intervention. The SCM system should have an easy-to-use, highly automated graphical merge tool, that only asks questions when it has to. It should record merge histories and graphically display merges so that user can easily see the parallel evolution of the source code.

• *Remember what I did* -- Developers change files, build software, test the result and move on. The version control facility must record changes to all file system objects (including changes to the names of the elements). The build management component of the SCM system must automatically record what was built, and using that record be able to reliably recreate the original build environment.

• *Answer questions I can't answer today* -- The SCM system should be able to answer questions that previously went unanswered. For example:
  – How many people are currently modifying 'io.h?'
  – How is this build different from last night's?
  – Were the RLS 3.1 changes merged into 4.0?

• *Preserve current investments* -- Engineers were hired because they have experience in building large, complex software systems, and the expertise to use many development tools. Developers will resist an SCM system that requires them to learn a new way to build or develop software, or that are not culturally compatible with Unix (for Unix programmers) or Windows (for Windows programmers). If the SCM system demands adoption of major new methodologies, and requires months of setup, training, and customization to be useful, the system will never gain widespread use.

5.0 Picking an SCM Tool Vendor

The SCM decision is a long-term one. Once the version history for every software component, development environment management, and software all building and rebuilding depend on a specific tool, it is very difficult to replace that system with an alternative.

For that reason, the vendor behind the SCM system is as important as today's release of the system itself. Will the vendor be in business and be able to support the product in the future? Are the product enhancement plans credible? Can this vendor be trusted to innovate, and to consistently deliver leadership products in conjunction with the SCM system being sold today?

As part of a "vendor audit," four aspects of the SCM supplier should be considered:

• *People* - Do I believe this team can deliver the products I will need over the next 5 years?

• *Focus* - Do these people understand, and are they committed to the SCM needs of development shops like mine?

• *Partnerships* - Will this product operate and be integrated with other products I have or will buy?

- *Stability* - Will this company be around in 5 years, and will they continue to innovate in SCM?

6.0 Bringing it all together

Figure 1 below brings together the concepts of version control, environment management, build management, and process control. It shows Atria's ClearCase™

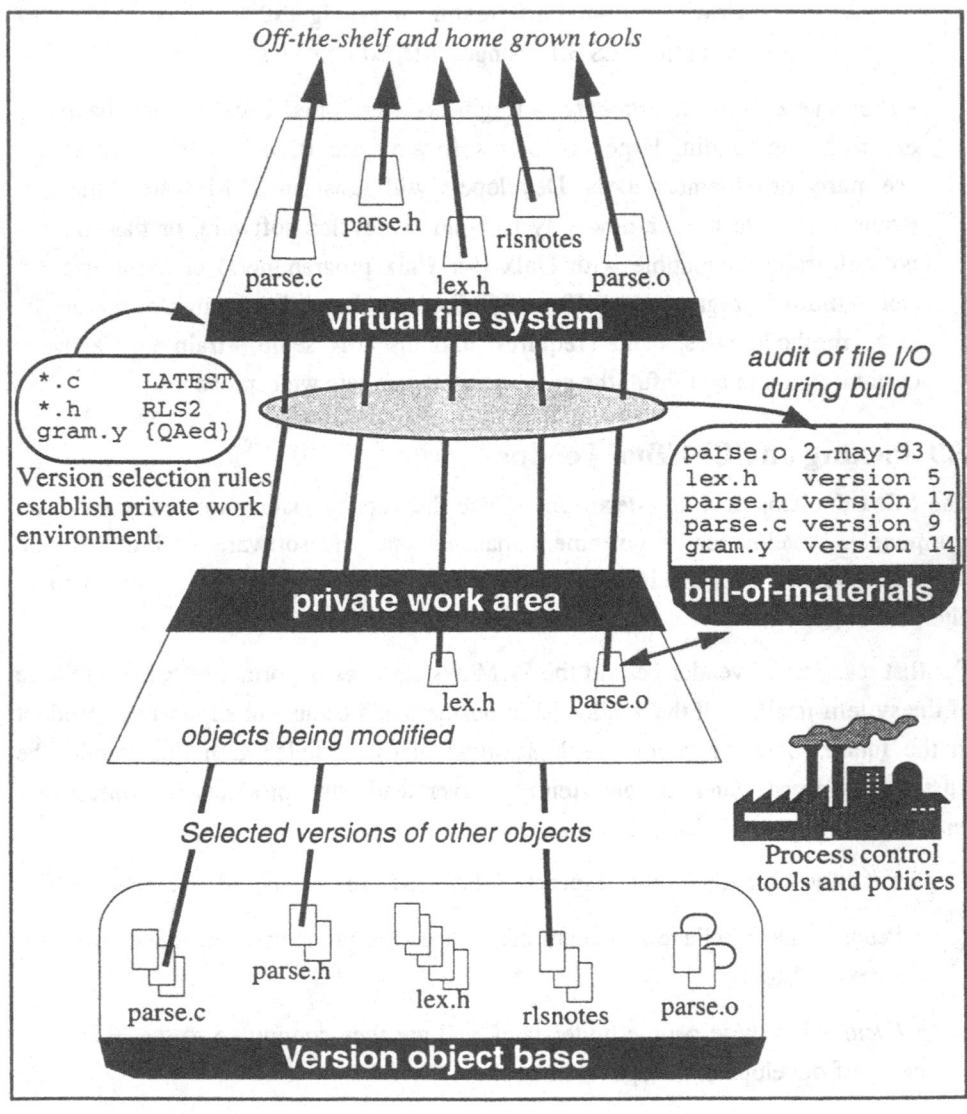

Fig. 1. ClearCase

system which uses a "virtual file system" extension to the base operating system to create private work areas that make user selected configurations available to ordinary applications (such as compilers, debuggers, design, and metrics tools). The system provides highly reliable build management by monitoring all versions read or written during a system build and associating the resulting "bill of materials" with the derived objects produced. Process management, enforcement of development policies, and industrial strength problem tracking are also an important part of this system.

7.0 Conclusions

Picking an SCM system is an important decision so get past the marketing literature and invest the time and resources needed to run the candidate SCM system for a few weeks in your own development environment with real source code and real developers.

VOODOO

A Tool for Orthogonal Version Management

Christoph Reichenberger
UNI SOFTWARE PLUS GmbH
Softwarepark Hagenberg, A-4232 Hagenberg, Austria

<chrei@unisoft.co.at>

Abstract. Version control is one of the fundamental tasks of every software configuration management (SCM) tool. The way how a SCM tool organizes all the emerging versions within a software project influences the overall working method of the whole SCM tool. Most existing version control tools follow the idea of SCCS and RCS. They organize the different versions by managing a revision tree for each single document. This organization – we call it the "intermixed organization" – has some major disadvantages that can be avoided by using an "orthogonal organization" as shown by the author. The main difference between the orthogonal and the intermixed version organization is that the orthogonal organization emphasizes the entire project over its individual components. Consequently, the terms variant and revision span over the whole project and are orthogonal to each other. This paper first summarizes the fundamentals of orthogonal version management and then presents the version control tool *Voodoo*. Voodoo is based on the idea of orthogonal version management and uses a graphical user interface.

1 Overview

Voodoo (Versions Of Outdated Documents Organized Orthogonally) is a version management tool for the simple and clear management of projects in which files are created in numerous versions (variants and revisions). Since Voodoo is capable of managing arbitrary files, the program can be employed for more than just the organization of software projects in a narrow sense (program development). Even the writing of a book, for example, is a project in which multiple elementary building blocks (the individual chapters, illustrations, etc.) evolve in various revisions. Using Voodoo can also pay off here.

For a given project, Voodoo can handle any number of users with *hierarchically ordered access privileges* to the project variants. The problem of simultaneous update of the same component by different users can be handled by a flexible *locking mechanism.*

The versions of files maintained by Voodoo are stored in a space-efficient way by *delta storage*. Contrary to other version management tools, Voodoo stores not only text files in space-saving deltas, but also any other files (in the Macintosh operating system, even those consisting of data and resource forks). We refer the reader to [Reichenberger 91] for details.

One point of criticism of existing version management tools is their poor user interface (usually command-oriented). Thus one major goal in the development of Voodoo was to demonstrate that modern concepts of human/computer interaction can be usefully employed in version control tools as well. Since the operating system of the Macintosh family avails exemplary concepts for human/computer interaction, Voodoo was developed for this operating system. By focusing on the user interface of Voodoo, this paper shows how a graphical user interface can usefully be applied to a version control tool.

2 Thought Model

This section describes Voodoo's underlying orthogonal thought model. After a short description of the disadvantages of the intermixed organization, the fundamental ideas of orthogonal organization are presented. The reader is assumed to be familiar with the most popular terms of SCM as defined in [Tichy 88], [Reichenberger 89] and [Whitgift 91].

2.1 Intermixed Version Management

A major drawback of most existing version control tools (e.g. SCCS [Rochkind 75] and RCS [Tichy 82, 85]) is the jumble of variants and revisions, which we call "intermixed organization" of variants and revisions. The main characteristics of the intermixed organization are that variants and revisions of components are organized together in form of *revision trees*. Variants are generated by branching off new revisions from certain points and developing them in parallel. The component thereby forms the center of attention, and the different versions of the components are organized by maintaining a revision tree for each component of the project. The tree's structure represents the chronological order of branching off variants. As the components' histories of development will in general be different, distinct tree structures will arise within the project, all representing the same variant information. The user of the software version control tool has to consider each of these structures in order to retrieve the specific variants and revisions of the components he wants to work with. Moreover, these trees soon become difficult to survey when the number of variants of the project increases.

2.2 Orthogonal Version Management

The main difference between the orthogonal and the intermixed version organization is that the orthogonal organization emphasizes the entire project over its individual components. As such, variants and revisions of a whole project are managed rather than variants and revisions of individual components. Consequently, the terms *variant and revision span over the whole project* and *are orthogonal to each other*.

With orthogonal version management, the thought model of a software project consists of two main parts – the *object pool* and the *project tree*. The object pool is the collection of all different variants and revisions of all of the project's components. The project tree represents a hierarchical structure between the project's components and defines the association of individual components to specific project variants. A detailed introduction to orthogonal version management can be found in [Reichenberger 89].

2.2.1 The Object Pool

The software project is built up by a set of fundamental *components*. Each of these components may exist in different variants and revisions. We will use the term *object* for one particular instance of a component, i. e., a component in a particular variant and revision. Thus an object might correspond to a particular implementation of a component (e. g., revision 7.3 of module *XY* in variant *A*). We will illustrate an object as a small cube (see Fig. 2.2-1).

Fig. 2.2-1: Object

The collection of all objects of a software project is called *object pool*. As the terms *variant* and *revision* span over the whole project and are orthogonal to each other, we can view the object pool as a three-dimensional space the dimensions of which are *component*, *variant*, and *revision* as shown in Fig. 2.2-2.

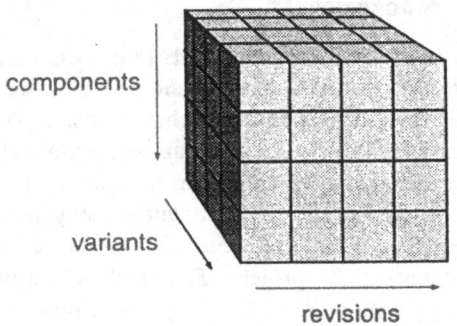

Fig. 2.2-2: Object pool

This tree-dimensional object pool would be too complex to be managed by the user directly. Thus Voodoo uses the project tree to let the user browse through and modify the object pool in a clear and easy way.

2.2.2 The Project Tree

The structure of the software project is modeled in the form of the *project tree*. The project tree represents an extension of the structure tree as introduced in [Reichenberger 89]. It consists of four different kinds of nodes: *structure nodes*, *component nodes*, *version group nodes* and *variant nodes*. It represents the logical associations of the individual components and gives insights into the association of individual components to project variants. Fig. 2.2-3 shows the complete project tree of a small sample project.

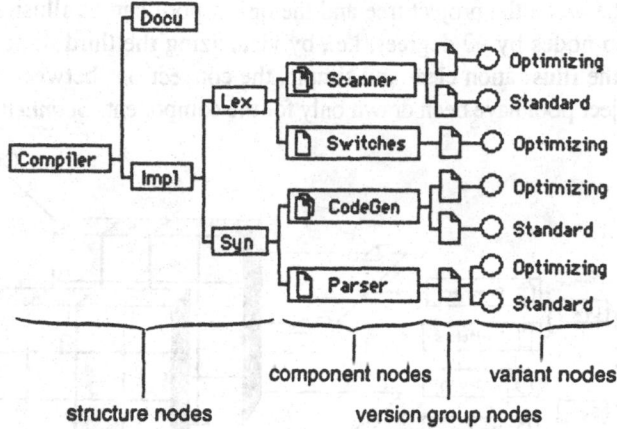

Fig. 2.2-3: Project tree consisting of four kinds of nodes

Let us examine the meaning of the individual kinds of nodes:

Structure node (e.g., Lex)

Structure nodes provide a logical structure of the project. Each structure node can contain structure nodes and component nodes.

Component node (e.g., ☐ Parser)

Component nodes represent the elementa Slding blocks of a project (e.g., a module of a program system, a chapter of the documentation, etc.). A component node does not represent a physical file, however. It represents a project component that can exist in multiple variants and revisions. Each component node is the child of a structure node and can contain any number of version group nodes.

Version group node (☐)

A version group node represents a certain version of a component. Each version group node is the child of a component node and can contain any number of variant nodes.

Variant node (e.g., ○ Optimizing)

A variant node always carries the name of a project variant. Variant nodes identify in which project variants a certain version group is used. If a version group node contains a variant node x, this means that this version group is used in the project variant x. Each variant node is the child of a version group node and cannot have children itself.

As shown in Fig. 2.2-3, the project tree reflects information on both the structure and the variants of the project. The composite project, in our example a compiler, consists of two parts, the implementation and the documentation. The implementation is subdivided into lexical analysis and syntax analysis (including code generation), of which each part again consists of two components. The further structure of the documentation is not yet defined.

The project tree also shows that the project is being developed in two variants, one with and one without optimization. The component *Parser* can be used commonly by both variants (a version group node that contains both variant nodes). The components *Scanner* and *CodeGen* are being developed differently for each of the two project variants (each variant node has its own version group node). The component *Switches* is used only in the variant *Optimizing* (no version group node for the variant *Standard*).

The connection between the project tree and the object pool can be illustrated by turning the version group nodes by 90 degrees, i.e., by visualizing the third dimension (see Fig. 2.2-4). To keep the illustration clear and simple, the connections between the component nodes and the object pool have been drawn only for the components *Scanner* and *Parser*.

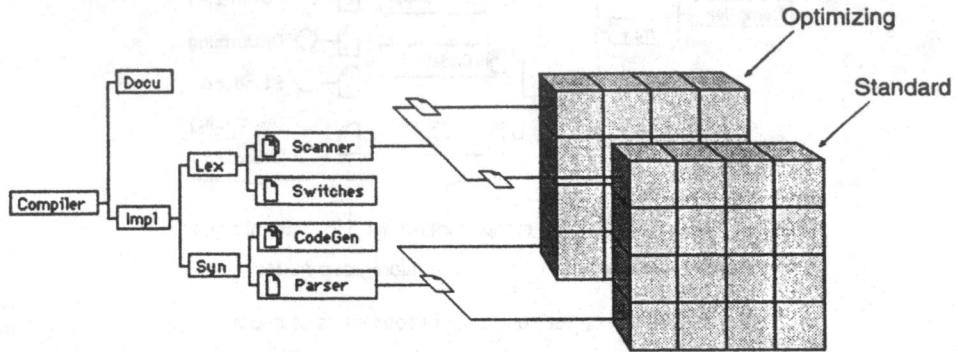

Fig. 2.2-4: Connection between project tree and object pool

It would be beyond the scope of this paper to describe all details of the orthogonal thought model in more detail. The interested reader may refer to [Reichenberger 89].0

3 Orthogonal Version Management using Voodoo

This chapter describes the most essential functions of Voodoo. For a full description of Voodoo's functionality we refer to the user documentation of Voodoo.

Voodoo commands fall into three groups that are represented by menus.

- The **Design** menu contains commands for the definition and maintenance of the project structure and variant information.

- The **Version** menu contains commands for processing the object pool, i.e., for archiving and retrieving objects as well as locking and unlocking version groups. It also contains a command for defining system configurations.

- The **View** menu contains commands for adjusting views of the projects. This includes the selection, activation and deactivation of filter settings as well as showing or hiding the project history window.

Some general-purpose functions are provided in the **File** and **Edit** menus as well as in the **Font**, **Size** and **Style** menus.

In the description of the individual functions of Voodoo, menu commands are noted in the form **Menu:Command**. Thus **File:Quit** represents the command **Quit** in the **File** menu.

3.1 Creating New and Opening Existing Projects

Invoking the command **File:New Project...** allows the user to create a new project. After the user has specified the name of the project, Voodoo creates a folder with that name for the storage of all project-related data in the form of multiple files. Since all these files collectively represent the total information of the project, none of the files may be manually modified or deleted. To assure that the individual files match, Voodoo conducts consistency checks.

The created project is opened and the project tree is displayed in a window. A newly created project always contains a superuser (Administrator); this is the only user with all access privileges within the project (see Section 3.3). With creating a project the user is automatically logged in as administrator. The project tree of a new project consists of a single structure node, the root node of the entire project.

To continue work on an existing project, the project has to be opened with the **File:Open Project...** command. After selection of the project, the user must enter his user name and password in order to log on to the project.

3.2 Defining a Project

Defining a project consists primarily of two subtasks: the specification of the project variants and the specification of the project structure. Since these subtasks are significant events in the life cycle of a software project, the user must enter a special *design mode* with the **Design:Enter Design Mode...** command before changes can be made to the project structure and/or variant information. This command can only be executed by authorized users (see Chapter 3.3).

3.2.1 Defining the Project Variants

Each project variant has a name and can be described further by means of a comment. The command **Design:Define Variants...** displays a dialog box that allows the user to add new variants and to change the names and comments of existing variants.

Fig. 3.2-1 shows the dialog box for modifying the variant information. The project is currently being developed in two variants.

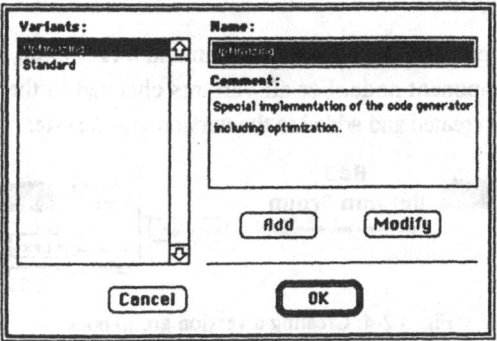

Fig. 3.2-1: Modifying the variant information

Every new project contains by default one variant named *TheOnlyVariant*. The user can change this name at any time; renaming a variant does not affect its identity. If the variant *X* is renamed *Y*, then everything that previously applied for *X* now applies for *Y*.

3.2.2 Defining the Project Structure

Creating a structure node

To create a new structure node, an existing structure node must be selected. The command **Design:Rdd Structure Node...** creates a new structure node and adds it to the project tree as a child of the selected node. The user can freely choose the name of the new structure node.

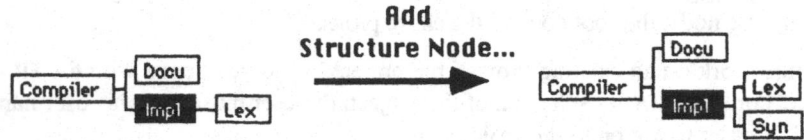

Fig. 3.2-2: Creating a structure node

Creating a component node

A new component node is created with the command **Design:Rdd Component...** as a child of the selected structure node. The name of the node can be freely chosen by the user. It need not match the name of an existing file. As shown in Fig 3.2-3, with the creation of a component node, a version group node with the associated variant nodes can be created. In this case, for all variants at are currently checked in the **View** menu (see Section 3.4.2) a variant node is created.

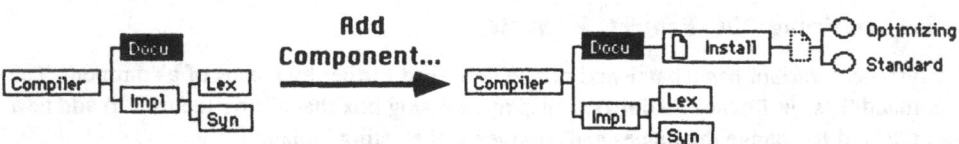

Fig. 3.2-3: Creating a component node with version group and variant nodes

Creating a version group node

A new version group node is created with the command **Design:Rdd Version Group** as the child of a selected component node. For all variants checked in the **View** menu, variant nodes are automatically created and added to the version group node.

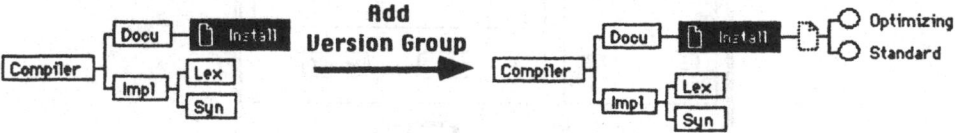

Fig. 3.2-4: Creating a version group node

Creating a variant node

In contrast to the kinds of nodes discussed so far, variant nodes cannot be created in any number and with any name by the user. The variant node always carries the name of the project variant, and within one component node each variant node can occur not more than once. This means that the user can only add a variant node as the child of a version group node if this variant node does not already exist within this component. To prevent the user from unintentionally creating an invalid node structure, there is no menu command to create a variant node. Clicking on a version group node and holding the mouse button raises a pop-up menu from which the user can select the variant for which a variant node is to be added. Variants that are already contained in another version group of this component thus cannot be selected.

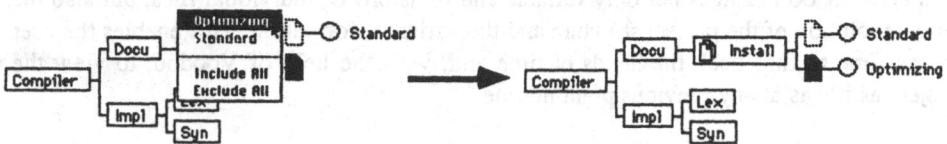

Fig. 3.2-5: Creating a variant node

Moving a node

An existing tree can be modified by simply dragging a node (with its subtree) to its new parent. Voodoo restricts the target nodes to ones that are valid in the node hierarchy. By moving structure and component nodes as shown in Fig. 3.2-6a, the user can modify the structure of the project. Even variant nodes can be moved from one version group node to another (Fig. 3.2-6b). The result is not a change in the project structure, however, but only in the variant association of the respective version groups. For reasons mentioned above, a variant node can only be moved within its component.

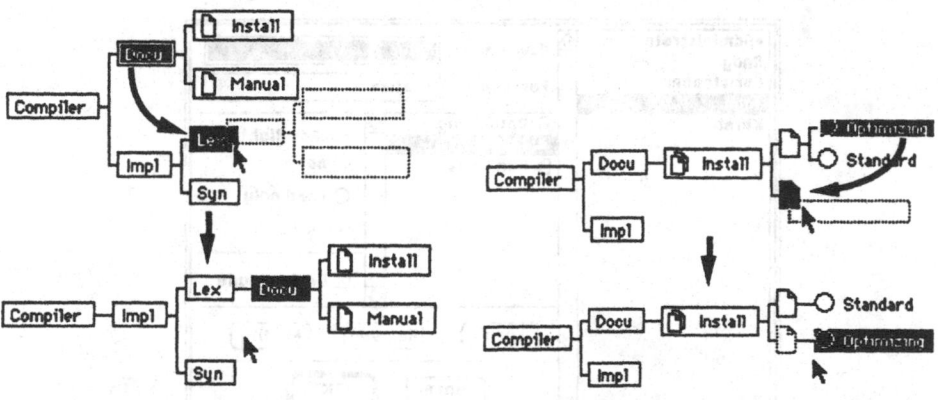

a) Modifying the project structure   b) Modifying the variant information

Fig. 3.2-6: Moving a node

Fig. 3.2-6b shows the typical procedure for splitting off a variant. Up to this point both project variants used the same object for the component Install. After a new (empty) version group node is created, dragging the variant node Optimizing expresses that from now on the two project variants will use different objects for the component Install.

Voodoo offers a couple of other functions for the creation and modification of the project tree that will not be described in more detail here.

3.2.3 Recording the Project's Evolution

After the user has made the desired modifications, the design mode can be left with the **Design:Leave Design Mode...** command. A dialog box appears in which the information about the modifications made can be entered. This information is added to the project history. Voodoo manages not only variants and revisions of individual files, but also the entire evolution of the project structure and the variant information. This enables the user at any time to turn back the hands of time and, with the help of Voodoo, to view the project as it was at any previous point in time.

3.3 Managing Users and Access Privileges

The management of users, passwords and access privileges is reserved for the project administrator. Upon selection of the command **File:Define Users...** a dialog box is presented in which users can be added and deleted and individual user access privileges can be assigned.

Fig. 3.3-1 shows a dialog box for managing access privileges. Besides the *Administrator* the box shows four other users. The user name *John* has been assigned the password *Beatles*. *John* has read and write privileges for the variant *Standard*, but only read privileges for *Bug Fixes* and no privileges for *Optimizing*. *John* also has the right to modify the project tree and the variant information (the option **Design Mode** is checked).

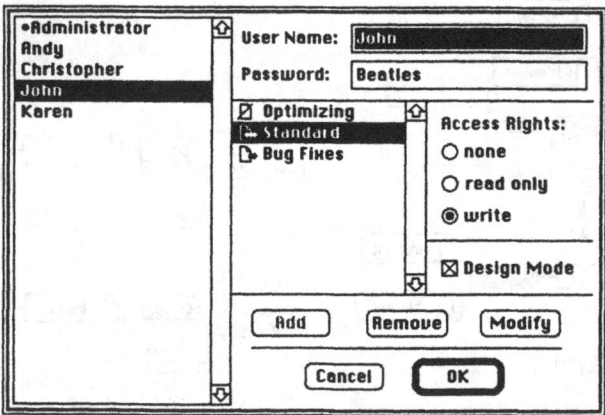

Fig. 3.3-1: Dialog box for managing user access privileges

3.4 The Project Tree Browser as a Navigation Tool for the Whole Project

The project tree serves as the central access route to the software project. All functions that Voodoo provides for the management of the software project are carried out via the project tree.

To provide users with the greatest possible clarity in working on the projects, Voodoo enables different views of the projects by means of various filter settings. The user can restrict a view of the project tree in all three dimensions (components, variants and revisions) as needed. This restricts the display to subprojects that interest the user.

3.4.1 Filtering by Components

In large projects the project tree can be very extensive and unclear. Most personnel do not work on the entire project, but only on certain subprojects. Voodoo makes it possible to collapse parts of the project tree. With the command **Uiew:Collapse** the complete subtree of the currently selected node is collapsed. The node now serves as a placeholder for the collapsed subtree; it is marked as such in the project tree (see Fig. 3.4-1).

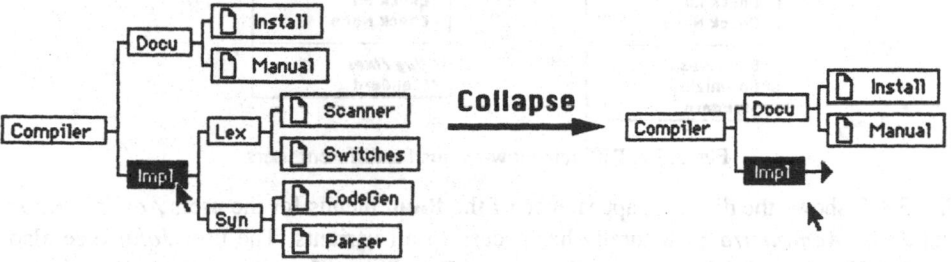

Fig. 3.4-1: Collapsing a subtree

The command **Uiew:Expand** makes a collapsed part of a tree visible again.

Another way to hide parts of the project tree is to hide the variant information, i.e., to cut off version group and variant nodes. Especially for projects that are developed in only one variant, this view of the project tree is convenient.

3.4.2 Filtering by Variants

The clarity of presentation of projects with multiple variants is one of the most significant advantages of Voodoo over other version management tools. The variant information that applies to the project is not mixed with the revisions of the individual components, but is strictly orthogonally managed. Voodoo is thus able to filter the project tree according to variants of the project, i.e., to display only those parts of the project tree that are associated with a certain variant (or a set of variants). The filtering of the project tree is applied in Voodoo in two ways. Parts of the project tree can be hidden based on user access privileges and according to user-defined variant filters.

Filtering a project tree according to access privileges

If a user lacks access privileges to certain variants, then the project tree shows only nodes of variants to which this user has at least read-only privileges. Furthermore, the names of variants to which the user lacks access are not displayed in the **View** menu. The user is thus not even aware that these variants exist.

Filtering a project tree according to user-defined variant filters

Within those variants that are visible to the user based on access privileges, the user can set variant filters that further restrict the view of the project. In the **View** menu the user sees all variants with at least read access privileges. Variants with read-only access are displayed in the menu in italics.

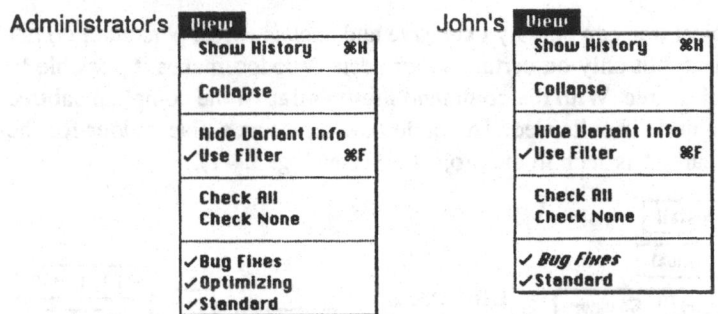

Fig. 3.4-2: Different view menus for different users

Fig. 3.4-2 shows the differing appearance of the **View** menus for the users *Administrator* and *John*. *Administrator* naturally has access to all variants. The user *John* (see also Fig. 3.3-1) has read-only access to the variant *Bug Fixes*. The variant *Optimizing* is not available to him.

By checking the desired variants from the **View** menu and by switching the filter mechanism on/off with the command **View:Use Filter**, the user can select from the available variants those that are to be visible. If the filter mechanism is active (**Use Filter** is checked), then only those parts of the project trees are displayed that are used in the variants checked in the **View** menu.

Fig. 3.4-3 shows a filtered project tree. When you compare the filtered tree with the full project tree of Fig. 2.2-3 you will notice that only those nodes are visible that are associated with the variant *Standard*. Since the component *Switches* is used only in the variant *Optimizing*, this component node is not visible in the filtered display of the project tree.

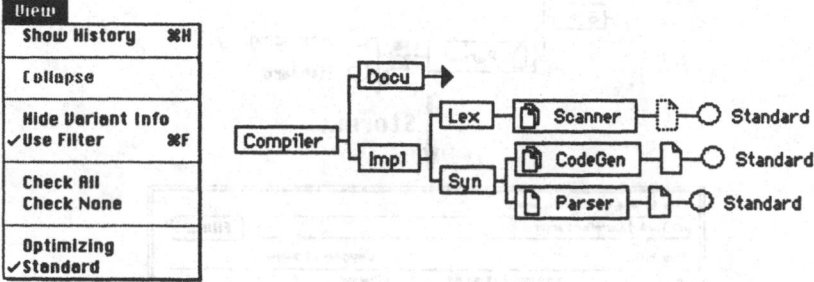

Fig. 3.4-3: Filtered project tree

3.4.3 Filtering by Revisions

Voodoo enables the user to turn back the hands of time at any time and to display the project as it was at any given previous time. This can be interesting, e.g., in determining which objects were associated with a certain project variant at a given time. The desired information can easily be retrieved by appropriate setting of the viewing time. A previous point in time is set via the project history window (see Section 3.7).

3.5 Archiving and Retrieving Objects

In daily work with a version management tool, two operations are central: archiving and retrieving objects. Normally objects are copied from the object pool to a user's private workspace, are modified there, and are later copied back to the object pool.

For this copy/modify/copy procedure, Voodoo offers, similar to other tools, two functions called *Store* (archiving) and *Fetch* (retrieving). Voodoo's user interface, however, distinguishes from other tools. In order to archive or retrieve objects, there is no need to type in commands. Here, too, the project tree provides a simple and clear procedure. The following sections describe how individual objects as well as groups of objects are archived and retrieved.

3.5.1 Archiving Objects (Store)

An object in the object pool represents a specific variant and revision (i. e. a particular implementation) of a component. Archiving an object requires assigning it to a version group node. To archive an individual object, the respective version group node is selected and the command **Version:Store...** is chosen.

This command can only be executed if the user has write privileges to all variants in the version group node and the version group is not locked by another user. Voodoo conducts all necessary tests.

After selection of the command a dialog box appears; the user can specify the file to be archived and add a comment. The user can also specify whether the version group should be unlocked (see Chapter 3.6).

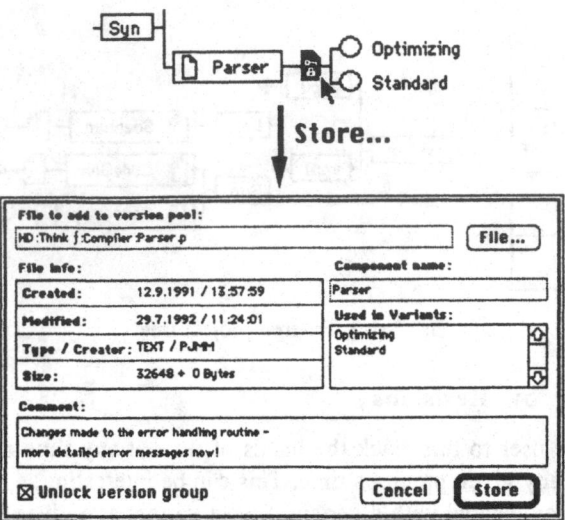

Fig. 3.5-1: Archiving an individual object

Fig. 3.5-1 shows the dialog box for archiving an individual object, here a modified parser. The dialog shows that an object is being stored for the single version group node of the component *Parser*. This object is collectively used in the project variants *Optimizing* and *Standard*. The version group is to be unlocked after archiving.

If multiple objects are to be stored simultaneously, it would be troublesome to carry out the above procedure for each object. Voodoo makes it possible to select a structure node and then to execute the command **Version:Store...**. All components contained in this subtree are presented to the user in a selection list, and the user can enter the respective information for each version group. If a component has multiple version groups, the user must specify the version group in which the objects are to be stored by means of filtering the project tree before selecting the *Store* command. In Fig. 3.5-2 the variant filter was set to the variant *Standard*. The component node *Switches* is thus hidden.

The *Include/Exclude* button allows the user to select components (marked with a check in the list) that are actually to be archived. To permit the actual archiving of the objects without user interaction, possible problems (file not specified, version group locked, inadequate privileges, etc.) are displayed in this dialog and the user can react.

Fig. 3.5-2 shows, e.g., that the file *CodeGen.p* is to be archived for the component *CodeGen*. The question mark in the line for *Scanner* indicates that no file has been specified yet for this component. The option **Newer files only** permits the user to exclude components that have a version in the object pool that is newer than or identical with that in the private workspace. This is the case in Fig. 3.5-2 for the component *Parser*, thus the check mark for this component is a broken line. The option **Unlock version groups** indicates whether a version group should be unlocked after archiving (see Chapter 3.6).

After all settings have been made and the comment (for all objects collectively) has been entered, the **Proceed** button can be pressed to start the archiving of the selected objects.

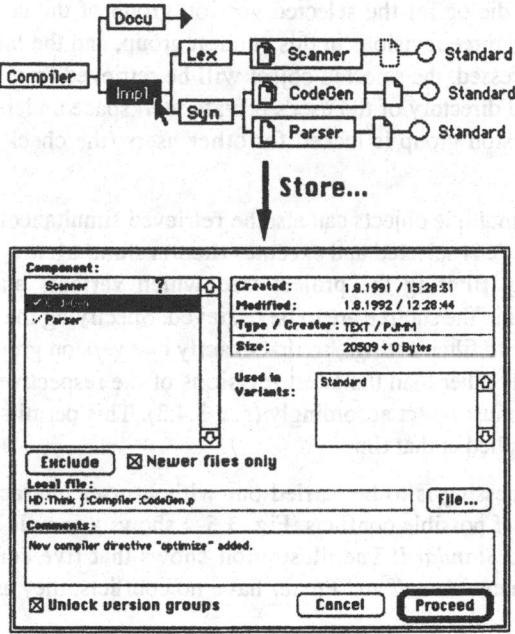

Fig. 3.5-2: Archiving multiple objects

3.5.2 Retrieving Objects (Fetch)

Retrieving objects from the object pool is similar in function to archiving. To retrieve an individual object, the desired component and variant are specified by selecting the respective version group node. If the user selects the **Uersion:Fetch...** command, then a dialog box displays all revisions that exist in the object pool for this combination of component and variant.

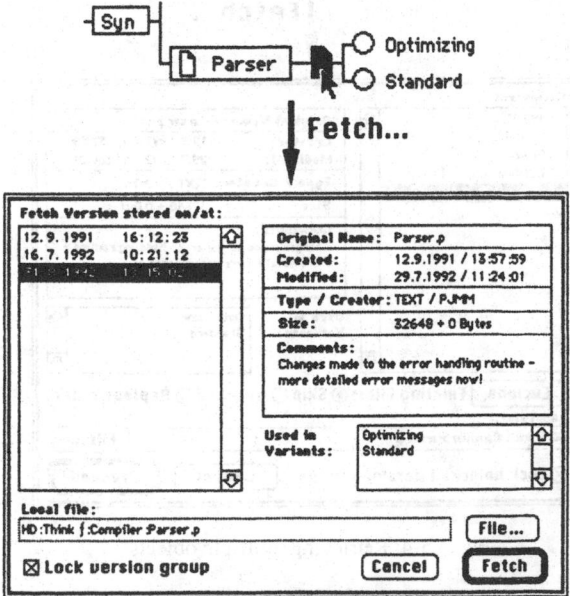

Fig. 3.5-3: Retrieving an object

Fig. 3.5-3 shows the dialog for the selected version group of the component *Parser*. A list is displayed of the three revisions in this version group, and the last one is selected. If the *Fetch* button is pressed, the selected object will be retrieved from the object pool and stored in the specified directory of the user's private workspace under the name *Parser.p*. Furthermore, this version group is locked for other users (the check box **Lock version group** is marked).

Similar to archiving, multiple objects can also be retrieved simultaneously from the object pool. The structure node is selected and executes the **Version:Fetch...** command. First the user must specify by filtering the project tree which variants and revisions of the components contained in the subtree are to be retrieved. Specifying the variant occurs as in archiving by appropriate filter settings, so that exactly one version group node remains for each. If the user wants other than the latest revisions of the respective version group, the project viewing time must be set accordingly (see 3.4.3). This permits the retrieval of the latest revision that applied at that time.

Again the actual processing is to be carried out without user interaction, so the user is informed in advance of possible conflicts. Fig. 3.5-4 shows a sample dialog. The variant filter was again set to *Standard*. The illustration shows that five components are to be retrieved. The components *Install* and *Parser* have no conflicts; they are checked and will

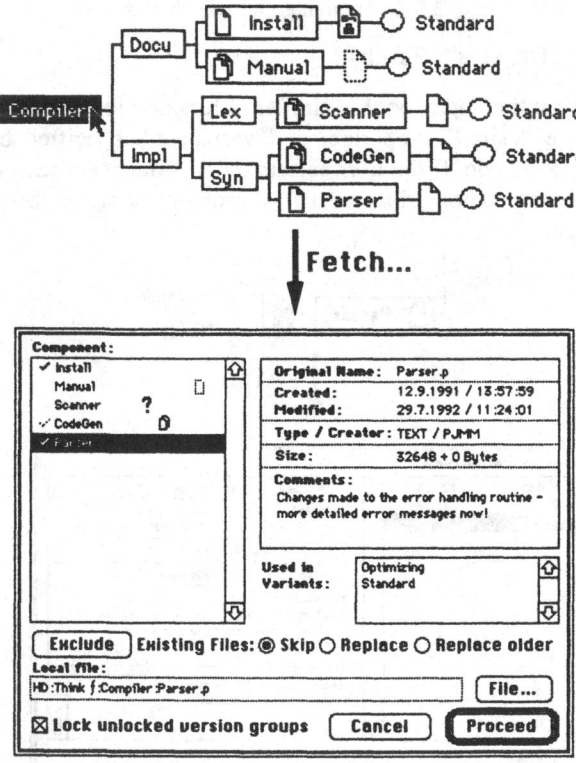

Fig. 3.5-4: Retrieving multiple objects

thus be retrieved. The component *Manual* does not yet have an object in the object pool, and *Scanner* lacks a file name and a directory in the private workspace. A file already exists under the specified directory and file name in the user's private workspace for the component *CodeGen*. The setting **Skip** in the selection **Existing Files** assures that this file is not overwritten. The check box **Lock unlocked version groups** indicates that the unlocked version group nodes are to be locked.

This function again shows the advantage of the orthogonal form of organization. At any time the user can easily view the status of the project at a specific point in time in a certain variant, and the entire configuration can be retrieved from the object pool with a single command.

3.5.3 Connection between Version Groups and Files

When archiving and retrieving objects, there exists a connection between a version group node and a file in the user's private workspace. If the user copies an object from the object pool to a file in a certain directory of the private workspace, this file (although modified) will probably be copied back to the object pool. Thus Voodoo remembers the name and the directory of the file in the local workspace that was last used in connection with the version group node. With the next *Store* or *Fetch* command Voodoo automatically suggests this file and the user only needs to overwrite this suggestion if the directory structure has been changed meanwhile. So the user seldom has to specify the file in the private workspace, which proves particularly beneficial when archiving or retrieving multiple objects.

Since different users are likely to have differing directory structures and naming conventions within their private workspaces, records of the files in the private workspace of each user are kept separately.

3.6 Locking Mechanism

A problem that often arises in software projects with multiple programmers is the uncontrolled simultaneous access of several programmers to a given component [Babich 86]. Version management tools can help to solve this problem by providing a locking mechanism.

Voodoo provides a locking mechanism at the version-group level rather than at the component level. Since various version groups represent different parallel development branches, two version groups of a component can be worked on simultaneously by two team members.

Version groups can be locked and unlocked either explicitly with the commands **Version:Lock** and **Version:Unlock** or as a side effect in retrieving or archiving objects. Of course, a user can only lock version groups to which he has write privileges. The current status of a version group is displayed in the project tree with respective icons (see Fig. 3.6-1).

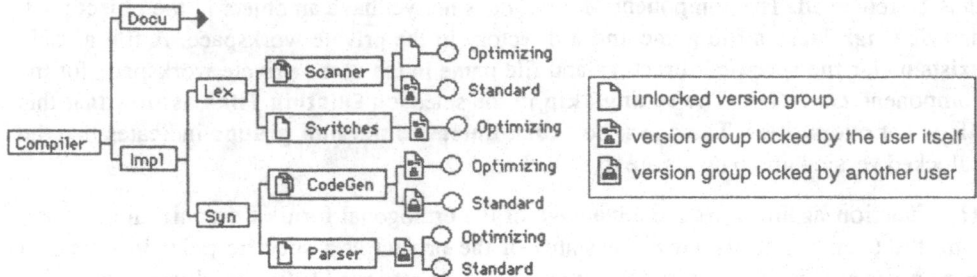

Fig. 3.6-1: Project tree with locked nodes

3.7 Project History

Another important task of a version management tool is the continuous recording of the development history of a software project. Each time a new object is archived or modifications are made to the project structure or variant information, Voodoo generates an entry in the project history. Such an entry consists of the date and time of the modification, the affected components and variants, the name of the user, and a comment.

The user can display the entire project history in a dedicated window. The history window can be displayed/hidden at any time with special commands.

Fig. 3.7-1 shows the history window for the sample *Compiler* project. The illustration shows the two types of entries (modifications to the structure and/or variant information are displayed in bold, all other entries in normal).

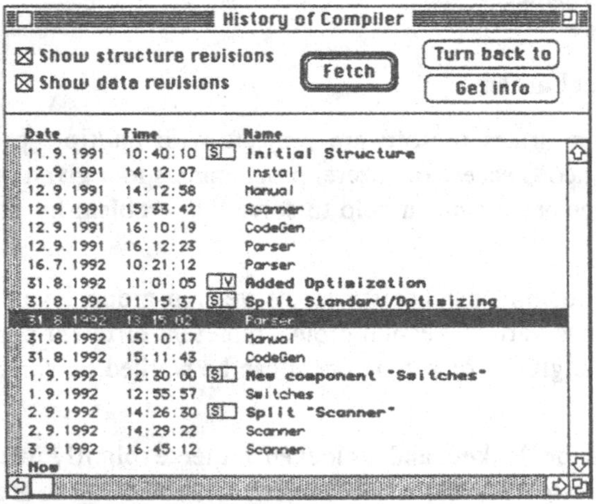

Fig. 3.7-1: History window

To provide the user with the best possible overview of the software project, the entries in the history window can also be filtered according to various criteria. Setting the variant filters affects the history window as it does the project tree: Only the entries for checked variants are displayed.

To restrict the project history to certain nodes, it suffices to select the desired nodes in the project tree. If one or more nodes in the project tree are selected, then only these selected nodes are displayed in the history window. If no node is selected, all entries are displayed.

To set the viewing time of the software project (see Section 3.4.3), the desired line need only be selected and the button **Turn back to** be pressed. The history window and the project tree are then displayed as they appeared at the selected time.

The options **Show structure revisions** and **Show data revisions** toggle the respective kinds of history entries on/off.

3.8 Defining Configurations

When a project tree is modified, Voodoo automatically creates an entry in the project history (the bold lines in the history window). In addition, the user is able to freeze the state of a project at a given time. The command **Version:Define Configuration...** allows the user to assign a name and enter a comment, and to create an entry in the project history with these data.

This enables the user later to reference this point in time by setting the viewing time. Such milestones in a project can then be used to restore a certain past configuration of the project.

3.9 User Preferences

To allow each user to view the project according to private preferences, Voodoo stores various preference settings individually for each user. The user can adjust the alignment of the tree (centered or justified upward) and the horizontal and vertical spacing of nodes. In addition, the default settings for the filter mechanism can be set.

4 Conclusions and Further Prospects

Most existing version management tools use revision trees to organize the evolution of whole multi-variant software projects. Voodoo follows the idea of orthogonal version management, that means it manages the evolution of the whole software project rather than of single components. Voodoo does not mix variants and revisions but considers them to be orthogonal to each other. This allows Voodoo to present the project to the user in a very clear way. Together with a graphical user interface Voodoo is a convenient and efficient version control tool that meets today's requirements.

Version control forms only the basis of SCM and an isolated version control tool like Voodoo might therefore be only of qualified use. However, the orthogonal version organization clarifies the presentation of a software project to such an extent that it would be worth building a configuration management tool based on Voodoo.

Initially Voodoo was implemented just to prove that the idea of orthogonal version management can be used successfully for the management of multivariant projects. However, due to the success of Voodoo it is now available as a product and is used by many satisfied users all over the world. Current development is directed towards client/server architecture, scripting, as well as for porting Voodoo to other platforms.

References

[Babich 86] Babich W. A.:
Software Configuration Management – Coordination for Team Productivity. Addison-Wesley, 1986.

[Leblang 84] Leblang D. B., Chase R. P. Jr.:
Computer-Aided Software Engineering in a Distributed Workstation Environment. Proceedings of the ACM SIGSOFT /SIGPLAN Software Engineering, Symposium on Practical Software Development Environments, Pittsburgh 84. ACM Software Engineering Notes 9 (1984) 3.

[Reichenberger 89] Reichenberger C.:
Orthogonal Version Management. Proceedings of the 2nd International Workshop on Software Configuration Management, ACM SIGSOFT Software Engineering Notes, Vol. 17, No. 7, November 1989.

[Reichenberger 91] Reichenberger C.:
Delta Storage for Arbitrary Non-Text-Files. Proceedings of the 3nd International Workshop on Software Configuration Management (Trondheim, Norway, June 12-14, 1991), ACM Press (Order Number: 594910).

[Rochkind 75] Rochkind M. J.:
The Source Code Control System. IEEE Transactions on Software Engineering, Vol. SE-1, No.4, December 1975.

[Tichy 82] Tichy W. F.:
Design, Implementation, and Evaluation of a Revision Control System. Proceedings of the 6th International Conference on Software Engineering, ACM, IEEE, IPS, NBS, September 1982.

[Tichy 85] Tichy W. F.:
RCS – A System for Version Control. Software – Practice and Experience, Vol. 15(7), July 1985.

[Tichy 88] Tichy, Walter F.:
Tools for Software Configuration Management. Proceedings of the International Workshop on Software Version and Configuration Control (Jan. 27 - 29, 1988 Grassau), Teubner 1988.

[Whitgift 91] Whitgift D.:
Methods and Tools for Software Configuration Management. John Wiley & Sons, 1991.

Versioning Models

Chair: Reidar Conradi, NTH. **Rapporteur**: Eirik Tryggeseth, NTH.

There is not yet a common agreement on basic versioning models. Tichy [Tic88] distinguishes between sequential revisions and parallel variants, both being part of a version group. But the ANSI/IEEE SCM standard uses versions and variants in the reverse meaning [ANS87]. Further, there is no agreement on the following topics: Is the versioning model linked to the data model, the product model (schema), the transaction model (e.g. uni-version subdatabases), or is it independent? At what granularity are "deltas" expressed, computed and merged – on the basis of whole files, text lines, or syntactical entities? And how is versioning combined with e.g. inheritance and parameterization? Does basic versioning only apply to atomic and textual objects, and not to composites or to the entire database? How to version relationships, and thus configurations? How to express intentional version selection, and how to express constraints, defaults and preferences for such selections? Is the selection based on symbolic attribute values, that together constitute a version space. Can the constraints and attribute domains evolve over time? Given a system model with objects and relationships: is the product selection (AND-closure) done before the version selection within each version group (OR-choices), or vice versa, or intertwined?

The session contains 4 papers.

Pearl Brereton, Paul Singleton; Univ. Keele, UK: "SCM: Issues and Pay-offs of a deductive Approach": This discusses rule-based builds.

Bradley R. Schmerl, Chris D. Marlin, Flinders Univ. of South Australia: "CM for dynamically Bound Systems": This discusses versioning constraints for building configurations.

Yi-Jing Lin, Steven P. Reiss; Brown Univ.: "CM in Terms of Modules": This paper discusses a fine-grained versioning of object-oriented modules, using delegation. But how to avoid proliferation of object variants during system configuration?

Jacky Estublier, Rubby Casallas; LGI, Grenoble: "Three dimensional Versioning": This discusses three views of versions – historical revisions, logical (permanent) variants, and cooperative (temporary) variants. A rich basic versioning model is sought, allowing the user to select one of these views. Also, some object attributes may be non-versioned (e.g. status), while others are versioned (e.g. contents).

References

[ANS87] ANSI/IEEE. IEEE guide to Software Configuration Management, STD 1042-1987 (version 1.0). Technical report, ANSI/IEEE, 1987.

[Tic88] Walter F. Tichy. Tools for Software Configuration Management, pages 1–20. In Jürgen F. H. Winkler, editor: *Proc. ACM Workshop on Software Version and Configuration Control, Jan. 1988, Grassau, FRG. Berichte des German Chapter of the ACM, Band 30, 466 p.*, Stuttgart, B. G. Teubner Verlag.

Deductive software building

Dr. Pearl Brereton and Dr. Paul Singleton
Department of Computer Science,
University of Keele,
Keele, Staffs, UK.
email: pearl@cs.keele.ac.uk

ABSTRACT. In this paper we present a deductive approach to modelling complex software systems. As well as highlighting the strengths of the approach in terms of configuration issues we also outline its potential contribution to an exploratory software development process.

1 Introduction

Software configuration management (SCM) is of vital importance to the development and maintenance of quality software products. It can be considered as involving a *product* part, relating to identification, storage and configuration of components or modules; and a *process* part, concerned with the organisation and control of configuration activities. In addition, a sound and simple SCM system should support other software engineering tasks (such as reuse and prototyping).

In this paper we look at the problems associated with the *product* aspects of CM and show how deductive modelling of software items and configurations can alleviate some of these problems. We also look briefly at the way in which deductive modelling of software inter-dependencies can provide added value to the software development process through its support for configuration exploration.

2 Version and Build Management

Many of the problems associated with the product aspect of CM stem from the need to maintain multiple versions, constituting families, of software components, configurations and documents. Versions of components or documents (or other software items) that arise from evolution are usually referred to as *revisions.* The need for such evolution may arise, for example, to correct errors or to enhance an item in some way.

The other important reason for maintaining multiple versions of a software item is when two or more items are in some way equivalent (for example, they may be functionally equivalent) but are different in some (other) way. This *variation* may arise, for example, when code is written in different languages, when different communications protocols are used, when different algorithms are used within a software module (for example, to accommodated different space and storage trade-offs), when variants are for use in different software or hardware environments or to satisfy different standards or legal requirements.

Clearly the problem is complex since revisions can have multiple variants (or vice versa) leading to an explosion in the number of potential combinations of components.

Most SCM systems to date have used the RCS system [Tich85] or its predecessors to manage multiple versions of components held as files in a traditional (UNIX) filestore. Each version of a component is labelled within a tree-structured numbering system which branches when a new variant is created. Each variant evolves as a succession of revisions. The RCS approach has a number of positive features and has been widely used. It provides multi-user control and space management through the use of deltas. However, it has a number of limitations due mainly to its use of sequence numbers to distinguish versions and its underlying dependence on a file-based component repository.

One of the major facilities offered by SCM systems is the ability to create deliverable software systems by (recursively) applying software tools to combinations of selected components. Tool and component selection is based on a system model generated by developers. The system model is usually expressed in some 'programming-in-the-large' language or as a build script and refers to generic components (rather than specific revisions or variations). Creating and maintaining system models is a time-consuming and error-prone manual task.

The best known and most widely used system modelling tools are based on the UNIX make utility [Feld79] and its derivatives. make describes a configuration by a set of rules, where a rule is composed of a target, prerequisites and actions (see Figure 1). The limitations of make are well-known and stem from:

- timestamped destructive update of targets in a public workspace;
- hidden dependencies in prerequisite items;
- opaque imperative actions with side-effects.

Our aim has been to use a computational framework within which these problems do not arise.

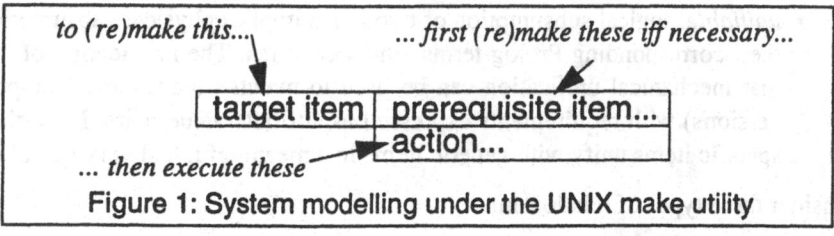

to (re)make this....   *... first (re)make these iff necessary...*

target item	prerequisite item...
	action...

... then execute these

Figure 1: System modelling under the UNIX make utility

3 Deductive Component and Dependency Management

We present here the current state of our data model and build manager. A prototype system, known as DERIVE, has been developed using commercially mature components including: a networked operating system and filestore; a networked relational database kernel and a single-threaded relational application programming language.

A DERIVE software item is defined as an extensible set of attributes, some of whose values may be large (e.g. chunks of source code or text). The attributes constituting a particular item each have one or more associated values. For example, a version of a source code module called "getprice", written in "C" by Fred Jones for use on a Unix system with messages in English is shown in Figure 2.

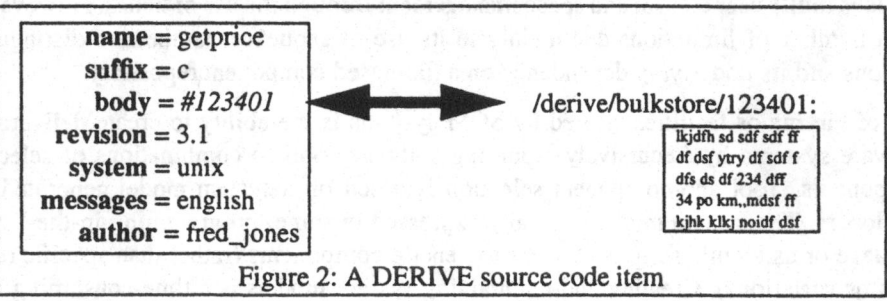

Figure 2: A DERIVE source code item

This item model has several strengths: it treats all attributes in a uniform way; it allows a software item to have several large attribute values and it allows items to be selected by attribute value.

Within DERIVE, items are encoded as incomplete binary trees with each attribute having a fixed position in the tree. This encoding is:

- *extensible*: new attributes can be introduced dynamically without having to re-write existing items;
- *compact*: an item with N attributes in a universe of M recognised attributes (or attribute keys), needs $O(N.\log_2 M)$ nodes where $N \ll M$, and M nodes otherwise;
- *unifiable:* logical subsumption of two items implies physical subsumption of their corresponding Prolog terms, and vice versa. The implication of this is that mechanical unification can be used to match stored items (component versions) with requirements expressed as attribute/value pairs. In particular, specific items unify with generic items in a meaningful and very useful way.

We consider three types of relationship:

- *version/version* - these are relationships **between specific versions** of software items;
- *generic/version*: - refers to the **family membership** relation;
- *generic/generic* - these are the most abstract and useful relationships that exist **between item families**.

84

Version/version relationships have limited but nevertheless useful applications and can be simply handled through the attribute mechanism. For example, the relationship *textually_derived_from* can usefully record the fact that a module body (e.g. a source code version) was created by editing some other module body. This can provide valuable trace information to determine the origin and spread of errors detected in one version of a multi-version module. Such a relationship can be represented as:

textually_derived_from (*#123401, #45631*)

Generic/version relationships are handled through Prolog's unification mechanism (see [Sing92] for more details). Any item which unifies with a generic item is a version of that (abstract) item.

The most abstract (*generic/generic*) relationships, such as build and life cycle dependencies are described by *rules*. In DERIVE, a system model or *generic configuration* is expressed as a set of definite clauses i.e. as inferences predicated on configuration items. Clause heads (the *targets* in make terminology) are generic items and sub-goals are either other abstract items or tool goals. A simple rule, shown in Figure 3, can be interpreted as follows:

"an executable item with name N and body T2 exists (is defined and delivered) if there is a source code item with name N and body T1 and T2 is the compilation of T1"

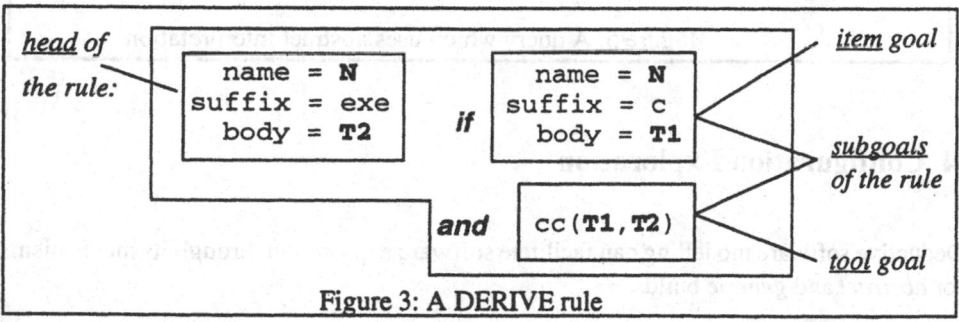

Figure 3: A DERIVE rule

The set of rules describing relationships and the set of facts describing configuration items constitute a deductive database which can be queried to perform a build (see figure 4) or for other purposes.

The capacity to perform arbitrary queries is a major strength of the DERIVE approach. In particular, the rules held in a deductive database are amenable to *abstract evaluation* which means that generic configurations can be evaluated (abstractly) without incurring the costs of instantiated (or concrete) builds. The aspects of evaluation which can usefully be treated abstractly include:

- *version selection*: wherever a choice has to be made between several alternative versions of some component, an abstract interpreter can avoid making this choice;
- *tool invocation*: instead of invoking a compiler, an abstract interpreter can assume that its invocation would succeed. Clearly, the result of the compilation

```
      query:   build(gizmo,6-2-28-1,sun4,ukEnglish,X)?
interpretation:  "Is X a built Gizmo version 6.2.28.1 for Sun 4 kit with
                                                    a UK English GUI?"

      answer:   (eventually) yes

  where X = [[.],        ◄──── complex structured value
            [..,..],           denoting source and binary
            [..,..]]           files, libraries, documentation, etc.
```

Figure 4: Querying the DERIVE database

is unknown, and any dependent compilations must also be performed abstractly.

A query which makes use of abstract interpretation in order to avoid the cost of version selection and tool invocation is shown in figure 5.

```
      query:  absbuild(gizmo, _, _, _)?
interpretation:  "Is there at least one way to build Gizmo for some
                  version number for some environment and for some GUI?"
      answer:  (fairly promptly) yes
```

Figure 5: A query which uses abstract interpretation

4 Configuration Exploration

Deductive software modelling can facilitate software exploration through its mechanisms for *abstract* and *generic* builds.

Abstract builds are, effectively, a "dry run" build of a system. As outlined above, an abstract build may avoid version selection and/or tool invocation. In this way, the feasibility and general structure of the build can be explored without the overheads of a concrete system build. An abstract build can be allowed to proceed even if some components or tools are missing. This facility can be used to answer questions such as: What tools and header files would we need to build *GIZMO 3.1.1* for *VMX 2.2a*? In this way proposed extensions can be explored without the need to develop and integrate all the required additional code.

Generic systems can be built by partial evaluation, with some version selections left unspecified and without invoking all tools. This allows exploration of families of products without the need to consider individual version combinations and again avoiding the overheads of tool invocation.The ability to manipulate generic configurations, to perform partial builds and to automatically generate the build scripts to perform final customisation makes the task of supporting the evolution of such systems more predictable and more efficient.

Explanation is a valuable prerequisite to understanding. Because our build process is deductive the final result, whether concrete, abstract or generic has a derivation proof which serves to justify or explain it. This proof provides a formal basis for explanation tools.

5 Summary and Conclusions

It is not possible, in the space available, to present a full discussion of DERIVE or to contrast it with the many other approaches to software modelling. We conclude, therefore, with a summary of the properties of our approach as exemplified by DERIVE which, in particular, overcome some of the limitations of make:

- dependencies (of targets upon prerequisites) are inferred automatically from the rules;
- generic rules are correctly chained (whether or not intermediate items exist);
- generic rules can have any number of parameters (not just a filename), and can have any number of prerequisites (not just one);
- version selection is performed, ensuring global consistency (no version skew);
- variants of items, rules, and tools are supported by a single mechanism;
- its minimal recompilation is more minimal (being based on file *values*, not timestamps);
- potential tool concurrency can be detected and exploited;
- tools which have several outputs (such as a compiler which produces warning and cross-reference files) are accommodated;
- composite items (e.g. sets of related files) can be treated as single entities.
- redundant items can be identified and destroyed automatically, easing the trade-off between storage space and rebuild costs;
- any build (whether concrete, abstract or partial) can be explained by reference to its proof, which is not merely a history of the build but a *justification* of it;
- generic product distributions can be built, using partial evaluation to special-ise the stored configuration and to mechanically generate makefiles;
- builds may proceed concurrently, without any risk of adverse interaction.

We close with the remark that the strengths of DERIVE come from the underlying declar-ative nature of the approach rather than as the result of individually addressing each 'feature'.

6 References

[Feld79]   S. I. Feldman, "make - a program for maintaining computer programs", *Software - Practice & Experience*, vol. 9, pp. 255-265, 1979.

[Sing92]   P. Singleton, "Applications of Meta-Programming to the Construction of Software Products from Generic Configurations", *Ph.D. Thesis*, Keele University, 1992.

[Sing93]   P. Singleton and O. P. Brereton, "Storage and Retrieval of First-Order Terms using a Relational Database", in *Proceedings of the Eleventh British National Conference on Databases*, Lecture Notes in Computer Science (LNCS), vol. 696, pp. 199-219, Springer-Verlag, 1993.

[Tich85]   W. F. Tichy, "RCS - A System for Version Control", *Software - Practice & Experience*, vol. 15, no. 7, pp. 637-654, 1985.

Designing Configuration Management Facilities for Dynamically Bound Systems

BRADLEY R. SCHMERL & CHRIS D. MARLIN
{bradley,marlin}@cs.flinders.edu.au
Department of Computer Science, Flinders University of South Australia,
GPO Box 2100, Adelaide, South Australia 5001

Abstract

Dynamically bound systems are those software systems which are able to incorporate executable components into themselves during execution. Such systems are clearly very flexible; however, they suffer from problems associated with this flexibility. These problems, which are similar to some of the problems addressed by configuration management, include how to locate and select components, how to manage change to components, how to verify the consistency of configurations of the systems and how to determine the actual system configuration. This paper describes some of the systems which support dynamic binding and discusses some of their associated problems. An approach to the design of configuration management facilities for dynamically bound systems is then outlined. This approach involves the detailed modelling of dynamic binding in a range of systems supporting this notion and the integration of this model with the relevant aspects of a model of configuration management developed by Wiebe. Finally, the paper foreshadows some ways in which the previously mentioned problems with dynamically bound systems can be addressed.

1. Introduction

Dyamically bound systems have the ability to create and recreate themselves during execution; typically, this process of dynamic binding involves the replacement of executable code, but it can also be regarded as covering the rebinding of other aspects of the system (such as on-line documentation). Dynamic binding allows systems to change their behaviour dynamically. Instead of being able to determine all of the components of a system statically (and joining them together into a single binary), the decision about which components to include can be made dynamically, allowing components to remain separate. Dynamically bound systems are flexible because their components can be updated and reincorporated dynamically, rather than having to relink the entire system. Such flexibility is particularly important in systems for which stopping is undesirable, but for which updates are still desirable (e.g. fixing a bug in a component of the life support software on a space station). Frieder and Segal [2] assert that the ability to update a program dynamically may also alleviate the costs associated with stopping such systems in many cases. Dynamic binding also provides a flexible way to support the sharing of components — rather than having copies of binaries in each system, one copy of a component exists and each system binds to it as necessary [16].

An examination of the systems which support dynamic binding to code shows that there are essentially two types of dynamically bound systems: systems which modify themselves and those which are modified externally. In self-modifying systems, dynamic binding facilities can be made available to systems by providing an operating

```
program main (input,output)
var name : string;
    val : integer;
  function read_database:integer; dynamic;
begin
  write('Which database do you want to read?');
  readln(name);
  link 'read_database' to name;
  val := read_database;
end.
```

Figure 1. Dynamic binding in db-Pascal.

system library. Examples of support for this type of dynamic binding are *dld* [3] and the dynamic linker provided by the FIELD [4] integration environment. However, this form of dynamic binding is typically unsafe, because little regard is given to language features related to concepts such as typing and information hiding. The provision of dynamic binding facilities as a language feature has also been investigated; two examples of languages taking this approach are db-Pascal [5, 6] and Napier88 [7]. In these language systems, typing and information hiding are well integrated into the language. Figure 1 illustrates how dynamic binding is supported in db-Pascal. The procedure read_database is declared as a dynamic procedure, causing the compiler to output information about the scope level and declared identifiers at the point of declaration of the procedure; these identifiers may be accessed by implementations of the read_database procedure. At runtime, the user of the code in Figure 1 enters the name of the database from which to read; the name is read via the readln statement and the name is then used to dynamically retrieve, and bind to, the matching implementation of the read_database procedure (using the link statement). This implementation is then used in the penultimate line of Figure 1 to retrieve a value. When an implementation of the read_database procedure is compiled, it accesses the information output from the compilation of the program in Figure 1, and so identifier access and type checking can be performed statically.

Programs need not drive the dynamic binding, but may be changed by the environment in which they run. Conic [8] is a distributed system which supports dynamic reconfiguration. Program elements in Conic have a well defined interface, and do not explicitly access modules external to the component. The *configurer* of Conic allows one to connect ports defined in the interface of one module to ports in another module; in this way, a system is constructed. Conic allows port connections to be broken and connections remade to other modules dynamically. PODUS [9] is a system which provides updating which is transparent to the user. Whole programs are able to be updated incrementally, without the language having to support dynamic binding explicitly. Some approaches to software architectures are also addressing the question of how to allow components of a system to be updated dynamically, and this is an area of ongoing research [10,11].

All of these systems suffer from one or more of the following problems:

- **Location and Selection of Components:** Self-modifying systems typically cannot rely on the existence of a component, and cannot be assured that the component being retrieved will behave in the intended way; this is because these systems generally only select components on the basis of a filename[1].

- **Coping with Change:** Most self-modifying systems rely on a file system to store their components. This typically means that the program has no control over changes to the components. For example, a filename may not change, but the component contained within the file may. Even in Napier88, where files are not used, components can be changed without breaking even static links, because they can be L-value bindings. Although this makes the systems very flexible, it increases the difficulty of knowing what comprises the "program" at some given point during its execution.

- **Consistency:** The conditions under which a component can be replaced differ between dynamically bound systems. In db-Pascal, procedures cannot be relinked if there is an instance of that procedure already in existence. In dld, procedures can only be relinked by first unlinking them. In Napier88, procedures can be replaced at any time. These issues can be thought of as being related to some notion of consistency. For some systems, consistency means having only one implementation of a component in existence at any given time; for other systems, this consistency constraint is relaxed, but there may be other conditions which would mean that the incorporation of some component would make the executing system inconsistent.

- **System Configuration:** Because the system essentially composes itself when it binds dynamically, and the components to which it binds may have changed since the system last bound to them, discerning the configuration of the system statically is impossible without sacrificing the flexibility of dynamic binding. If the components which comprise a system are known statically, then static binding would suffice. Knowing the system's actual configuration is, however, important if an error occurs.

Dynamic binding is used to facilitate the evolution of executing programs, and configuration management also addresses the evolution of software systems. Problems such as those above can be thought of as problems of identification, control and validation, problems which are typical of those addressed by configuration management systems (as discussed, for example, in [12]). It is therefore clear that dynamically bound systems would benefit from configuration management, and that the integration of configuration management and dynamic binding is worthy of investigation.

In considering how to provide configuration management support for dynamically bound systems, it is important to do so within a framework or model which focuses on the relevant design issues and allows one to reason about matters such as an appropriate

---

1. An exception is Napier88, which uses the name and type of an object in its persistent store.

definition of consistency. Thus, one of the goals of this work has been the development of a model of configuration management in dynamically bound systems; this model will be used to design suitable configuration management facilities in the manner of the approach to design described in [13], an approach which involves the use of models in the comparison of design alternatives.

This paper is organised as follows: in Section 2, we briefly introduce a model for configuration management which is fully described by Wiebe in [1]. This model is to be used as inspiration for modelling the configuration management aspects of our design space. In Section 3, we outline some preliminary work on modelling dynamically bound systems. Finally, Section 4 discusses some issues which arise in providing configuration management for dynamically bound systems.

2. A Model for Generic Configuration Management

Wiebe's work [1, 14] was concerned with providing a generic software configuration management system called Jason. This system is generic in the sense that it makes no assumptions about the types of components which it is managing (including their attributes), or any constraints which must be met for a configuration to be consistent; these are defined by the user of Jason. Thus, Jason is more flexible than existing configuration management systems, and can actually emulate a range of configuration management systems. Wiebe's model is comprised of two levels of abstraction: the *configuration language* for Jason is an object-oriented formalism used for modelling

```
Component : class
(
    name : String,
    modified : TimeStamp,
    modified-by : String
)

Config : subclass of Component
(
    modules : set of Component,
    components : set of Config
)

Source : subclass of Component
(
    code : Text
)
Binary : subclass of Component
(
    code : Byte-String,
    sources : set of Source
)
```

$S_{Binary} = \{\text{String, Source, TimeStamp, Byte-String}\}$

$\Gamma_{Binary} = \{\text{Component}\}$

$\Omega_{Binary} = \{\text{code, sources, name, modified, modified-by}\}$

$\tau_{Binary} = \{\text{code} : \lambda \rightarrow \text{Byte-String,}$
$\text{sources : Source} \rightarrow \text{boolean,}$
$\text{name} : \lambda \rightarrow \text{String,}$
$\text{modified} : \lambda \rightarrow \text{TimeStamp,}$
$\text{modified-by} : \lambda \rightarrow \text{String}\}$

$\Pi_{Binary} = \{\Pi_{constants} = \{\text{code, name, modified, modified-by}\},$
$\Pi_{sets} = \{\text{source}\},$
$\Pi_{subsets} = \varnothing,$
$\Pi_{set-elements} = \varnothing,$
$\Pi_{relations} = \varnothing,$
$\Pi_{functions} = \varnothing\}$

$\delta_{Binary} = \{\text{name} \rightarrow (\lambda, \lambda),$
$\text{sources} \rightarrow (\lambda, \lambda), ...\}$

(a)   *(b)*

Figure 2. Objects in Jason and their algebraic description.

```
Newer : constraint on (bin : Binary)
(for-all source in bin.source)
(bin.modified > source.modified)
```

Figure 3. Definition of a constraint.

various aspects of configuration management, and there is also an underlying rigourous *algebraic formalism* on which Jason is based.

Software components which are managed by Jason are stored in an object-oriented database; part of a specification in Jason is the definition of the types of components which will be managed. An example can be seen in Figure 2(a), which contains the definitions of the classes Component, Config, Source and Binary. A Component is a composite object which consists of three attributes: name, modified and modified-by. Classes at the Jason level are modelled as *signatures* in the algebraic formalism; the name of the composite class Component is a *composite sort*. The equivalent definition of Binary in the algebraic model is given in Figure 2(b)[2]. A signature is a tuple $(S_\Sigma, \Gamma_\Sigma, \Omega_\Sigma, \tau_\Sigma, \Pi_\Sigma, \delta_\Sigma)$, where Σ is the *signature name*, S is the *sort set*, consisting of a set of symbols referred to as *sorts*, Γ is a set of symbols called the *supersort set* (representing the inheritance hierarchy of the signature), Ω is the *operator set*, symbols in which are called *operators*, τ is the *type function*, Π represents a partitioning of the operators in Ω, where:

$$\Pi = \{\Pi_{constants}, \Pi_{sets}, \Pi_{subsets}, \Pi_{set-elements}, \Pi_{relations}, \Pi_{functions}\}$$

and δ is a domain restriction function. Signatures merely define the class definitions of the objectbase; for instances of the class, *many-sorted algebras* are used. Given this formal model, properties such as the inheritance relationship between classes (modelled as the *subsignature* relation between *signatures)* are well defined, and characteristics such as the reflexive and transitive nature of the subsignature relation can be established. Furthermore, they form the basis for formally describing more complex notions such as consistency, refinement and version selection.

For the purposes of verifying a configuration, *constraints* are defined which verify whether a snapshot of the objectbase is valid. Constraints in Jason are comprised of a set of first-order logic formulas. For example, the constraint Newer in Figure 3 says that the modification time of a Binary object must be later than the modification time of all its sources. The parameter is passed to the constraint by the user[3].

Version families are collections of software components which encapsulate the evolution of a component. Jason represents version families as partial objects (modelled as partial algebras in the algebraic formalism), examples of which are given in Figure 4(a). The definition of the family main-src specifies that all objects of the Source

---

2. In Figure 2(b), the symbol λ denotes the null string.
3. How a user invokes constraints, and the actions to be taken on the failure of a constraint, are discussed only briefly in [1], but were essentially beyond the scope of the work.

```
main-src : family of Source          system template (
   (name = "main")                      database1:subfamily of database
main-bin : family of Binary           (
   (name = "main")                         modules = {rdatabase-src,
rdatabase-src : family of Source                     rdatabase-bin,
   (name = "read database")                          ...}
rdatabase-bin : family of Binary       )
   (name = "read database")
                                       main1 : subfamily of main
database : family of Config            (
   (name = "database system")            modules = {main-src,
main : family of Config                            main-bin},
   (name = "main system")                components = {database1}
                                       )
                                      )

            (a)                                   (b)
```

Figure 4. Defining version families and system templates in Jason.

class which have their name component bound to the value "main" are members of this family. The example in Figure 4(a) defines the families which would represent the components of the example in Figure 1. This configuration consists of four components: the sources and binaries of both the main procedure and the read-database procedure. In addition to this, there are two configuration components: database would represent the subsystem of the database and main corresponds to the main system. Families are an important concept in Jason, as they represent the primary mechanism for defining and referring to collections of related components.

The *system template* of Jason represents a generic configuration. It lists all the source and derived objects, as well as their organisation into subsystems, in the form of a hierarchy. Figure 4(b) shows the definition of a possible system template for the example in Figure 1. As can be seen, the system template has families as its members. The hierarchy is composed using the container objects. In the figure, database1 is a subfamily of the container object database, which is a family of Config. Therefore, database1 is comprised of all Config objects whose names are "database system" *and* whose modules set contains rdatabase-src and rdatabase-bin. A system template is modelled algebraically as a *partial algebraic closure*. Building is the process of refining this partial algebraic closure to a *total algebraic closure*, i.e. replacing families in the system template with individual members of the family. Constructing the total algebra is a process which utilises *selection rules* to select components, and *build rules* to construct derived components. A selection rule is declarative and is also expressed in first order logic notation. For example, Figure 5 shows a selection rule, Latest, which will select the component which has the most recent modified time. It is also possible to specify tool signatures, and various other properties concerned with building systems; descriptions of these facilities are beyond the scope of this paper.

The key point of Wiebe's model is that every construct in the high-level language of Jason has a corresponding construct in the algebraic model. It is then possible to ac-

94

```
Latest: select comp from f:family of Component
  (for-all mem in f)
    (comp.modified >= mem.modified)
```

Figure 5. Expressing selection in Jason.

curately define and prove relationships between the various constructs in a Jason specification, and to be able to have confidence in predicting and understanding the
behaviour of the specification.

3. Investigating Configuration Management for Dynamically Bound Systems.

The model of configuration management described by Wiebe covers the various essential aspects of configuration management for software systems and provides a suitable
base on which to construct a model of configuration management for dynamically
bound systems. Our work has thus far been to examine a number of existing systems
which support dynamic binding, and to construct a model of dynamic binding, in which
each system can be described; these descriptions in terms of the model highlight how
these systems differ, and what their notion of configuration is. This model is to be used
as a basis for a model of configuration management for dynamically bound systems
which addresses the deficiencies raised by the model of dynamic binding, and which
borrows from the relevant aspects of Jason.

In this context, it is possible to state some requirements for the model of dynamic
binding:

- Because the main point of the investigation is the interaction of dynamic binding
  facilities and configuration management, the model must be able to be easily
  extended to model configuration management in the manner of Wiebe's model.

- Often, dynamic binding involves very low-level actions relating to a particular
  operating system; the model must abstract over such low-level details.

- It is desirable that the model be amenable to the generation of suitable prototype
  implementations of the dynamically bound systems being described.

- Descriptions in terms of the model must facilitate the comparison and design
  process by focusing on the essential issues in dynamic binding.

- The structure of the system, and how this changes during execution, needs to be
  discernable.

Most implementations of dynamically bound systems seem to have been performed
in an *ad hoc* fashion; if comparisons have been made with other systems, they have been
informal. Certainly, no existing model meets all the above requirements.

In our model of dynamic binding, a description of a dynamically bound system consists of several class definitions. Each class represents the structure of objects which will be manipulated by the dynamic linker, such as files and symbols, as well as constructs such as modules. One of the objects will represent the interface between the dynamic binding facilities and the programs which use them; such an object will be required whether the interface is direct, as in the case of self-modifying dynamically bound systems, or is used indirectly as part of an external linker. Each object in the model has four parts, all of which are optional:

- **Public Attributes:** These attributes may be viewed and modified by any other objects.

- **Internal Attributes:** These attributes contain the internal state of objects, and as such cannot be modified by other objects (except via constraints). However, other objects may read the values of these attributes.

- **Constraints:** A constraint is a condition which must be satisfied if the object is to be in a consistent state. Constraints may read public attributes of objects, but not modify them; they may, however, modify the internal attributes of objects. An object is *consistent* if all of its constraints are satisfied. Constraints take the form of predicates in first order logic. Constraint evaluation may either check whether a certain constraint is true, or ensure that it will be true. In the model, the keyword **check** denotes the former case, whilst **assert** causes the latter behaviour. For example, consider the constraint:

  check ($\forall o \in$ objects)
      ((o.name$\notin$def) $\to$ (o.code = default))

  The evaluator checks to see that all objects whose names are not in the set def have their code attribute set to default. If this is not the case, an exception will be raised. However, changing the keyword **check** to **assert** means that in order to satisfy the constraint, the evaluator is permitted to change the code attribute of an object to default if its name is not in def. The evaluator contains rules that indicate which object attributes involved in an assert constraint it is able to change. Thus, constraints in this model are different from constraints in Wiebe's model, in which constraints are simply evaluated to validate the consistency of a configuration which has already been constructed. In our model, constraint evaluation may also involve an attempt at constraint satisfaction.

- **Operations:** An operation is an imperative set of statements supplied by an object. Unlike constraints, whose order of evaluation is determined by which objects' attributes are involved in the constraints, the statements are evaluated in sequence. Operations may change public attributes of themselves and other objects, but only the internal attributes of its own object.

Figure 6 illustrates part of the model for dynamic binding in db-Pascal. The model of db-Pascal is represented as a collection of objects which can be of the type Configuration, Component or Implementation. A Configuration is simply a set of Component objects. The class Component represents names which require implementations, represented by the class Implementation. Hierarchy within the con-

```
    Configuration : class (
      components : set of Component)

    Component : class (
      in : Configuration,
      name : String,
      multiple_implementations : Exception
    internal
      impl : Implementation,
      activations : Integer = 0
    constraints
 ①   assert (∀c∈ in.components)
         (∀c₂∈ impl.uses)((c₂.name=c.name)→(c₂.impl=c.impl))
 ②   check (name = impl.environment)
    operations
      link(i : Implementation)
      (
        if activations>0 then
          raise multiple_implementations
        else
          impl ← i
      )
    )

    Implementation : class (
      name : String,
      environment : String,
      code : Binary,
      uses : set of Component,
      subconfig : set of Configuration
    )
```

Figure 6. A fragment of the description of db-Pascal.

figuration is expressed in the Implementation objects. For example, the main program of Figure 1 would be an Implementation object attached to the Component for main. The subconfig attribute of main would contain the component corresponding to read_database, which has no implementation when main begins execution. With this arrangement in mind, let us look more closely at the class Component.

The class Component has three public attributes. The attribute in specifies the configuration to which a component belongs. The attribute name is the name of the component (in terms of Figure 1, its name would be "read_database"). Because db-Pascal does not allow a procedure to be dynamically linked if an activation of the procedure is already in existence, the third public attribute, multiple_implementations, is an exception to be raised to deal with this constraint. The internal attribute, activations, records the number of activations for this component (initially 0). The implementation currently bound to the component is stored in the attribute impl (which is initially undefined).

The constraints section of Component has two members, providing an example of each of the assert and check forms. Constraint ① ensures that a component used by an implementation has the same implementation as a component with the same name in the configuration of the component responsible for firing the constraint, if such a component exists. If this is not the case, the evaluator will ensure its truth (if it can't, an exception will be raised). Constraint ② says that the environment of the implementation must be the same as the name of the component that it is implementing. Consider the example in Figure 1; the Component object referring to read_database would have "read_database" as its name attribute. In db-Pascal, any procedure which implements read_database must quote read_database as its environment[4]. Therefore, only implementations which are compiled in the environment of read_database may be linked to read_database. Constraint ② checks this. If the check fails, an exception will be raised.

The link operation of the Component class defines the steps involved in linking. The first step is to ensure that there are no activations of the component already in existence; if there are, the exception multiple_implementations will be raised. The linker will then set the impl attribute of the component to be the parameter passed in to link. This assignment will cause the evaluation of any constraints which depend on the impl attribute (in this case, both constraints ① and ②).

Future work with this model will be concerned with merging it with the concepts of the model of configuration management as defined in Jason. Although this is in its initial stages, there are a number of observations which can be made at this time:

- In the above model, the Component could be treated as a version family; assigning an implementation can be seen as refining that version family to a particular member. The way that refinement would be performed would be via selection rules similar to those from Jason.

- In general, it is possible for an executing program to have more than one implementation for a component, but still be in a consistent state[5]. Currently, Jason does not allow this.

- Jason does not perform constraint satisfaction, which is currently needed in the model for dynamic binding.

4. Configuration Management Issues for Dynamic Binding

Some of the problems associated with dynamically bound systems were outlined in Section 1 and a formalism for describing dynamic binding has been outlined in Section 3. This formalism will form the basis of a model of configuration management for dynamically bound systems, which will be used in the process of comparing and understanding

---

4. This is so that identifier usage can be checked statically.
5. Although this is not true of the model for db-Pascal, other dynamic systems may allow this; the merits or otherwise of this behaviour is a matter which is beyond the scope of this paper.

various alternative approaches to providing configuration management in the context of dynamic binding. This section briefly presents several issues involved in providing configuration management for dynamically bound systems; in later work, these issues will be more carefully elucidated, and solutions formulated, using the model of configuration management for dynamically bound systems.

One of the issues which arises in the context of configuration management for dynamically bound systems is that of how to locate and select appropriate components to be incorporated dynamically. The problem associated with this, as described in Section 1, arises from the fact that traditional dynamically bound systems rely on the file system, and so simple names are used. This means that the expressive power associated with selection and location is limited; it is not easily possible to support selection based on, say, the type of the component needed. One way to alleviate this problem is to allow the executable program to interact with a software repository in a similar manner to configuration management systems. Software repositories can be arbitrarily attributed, as occurs with Shape [15] for example, so that the characteristics of components can be further expanded. In Napier88, once a link (L-value) is established, it is guaranteed to always contain an object of the appropriate type, thus improving the safety of programs written in Napier88, but still allowing the object to change dynamically [16]. This referential integrity could be extended by ensuring that links, once they have been established, can only be updated to reference components which have compatible attributes.

In configuration management systems, a version independent generic configuration [17], or system model, is typically used to denote the structure of a software system as a hierarchy of subsystems and components. If a system model were to be imposed on the executing program, then the system model could aid in the location of components by providing the program with knowledge about its own structure. Initially, the system model for dynamically bound systems will be concerned with describing the system structure. This is a subset of the functionality of system models from traditional configuration management, which also describe how a build tool derives a configuration. In this sense, the system model may be more related to descriptions of software architectures [18, 19]. One problem with using a system model is the fact that even the structure of the program may not be known statically. Consider again the example in Figure 1. When main starts, the configuration is known to contain main and a component called read_database (although it has no implementation). Once an implementation of read_database is bound, it is possible that it has other dynamic (or static) components that were unknown at the time that main commenced execution. This is expressed in the model in Figure 6 by the fact that subconfigurations are dependent on particular implementations. Any formalism for describing system models for dynamically bound systems must provide for this dependency.

Another interesting possibility is for dynamically bound systems not to bind to particular components, but to bind to selection rules which are used to select specific components. This approach is used in some existing database systems, but typically to bind to data, not code (see, for example, [20]).

Selection rules, such as those in Wiebe's model, exploit attributes of components in the repository. It would therefore be possible for a system to refer to components as *latest version, debugging version, Unix-compatible version,* etc. The selection rules would be evaluated as part of the binding process. Such selection rules would also help in controlling the evolution of the system, by ensuring that only those components with suitable attributes are incorporated.

Dynamically bound systems deal with derived objects rather than source objects. In traditional configuration management systems, derived objects are treated as second class because they can be readily recomposed, while source objects are treated as "sacred"[17]. If configuration management is to be integrated with dynamically bound systems, derived objects may need to be treated with more reverence if the existence of components needs to be assured to the same extent as source in traditional configuration management systems.

In traditional configuration management systems, requesting *"version X of the object code for component Y"* may involve building the object from the source. It may be possible for the interaction between dynamically bound systems and configuration management systems to also take advantage of such build capabilities. Questions such as when should derived components be deleted, and under what circumstances can they be rebuilt during execution, need to be explored further. Therefore, the status of object code in dynamically bound systems and its ramifications for configuration management warrants further investigation.

Acknowledgements

The on-going work described in this paper represents part of a long-term collaborative software engineering research programme involving the Department of Computer Science at Flinders University and the CSIRO-Macquarie University Joint Research Centre for Advanced Systems Engineering; funding from the CSIRO Institute of Information Science and Engineering is gratefully acknowledged. Earlier support from the Defence Science and Technology Organisation is also gratefully acknowledged, as are the helpful comments of Keith Ransom on an earlier version of this paper.

References

[1]   D. Wiebe. *Generic Software Configuration Management: Theory and Design.* PhD thesis, Technical report 90-07-03. Department of Computer Science, University of Washington, Seattle, Washington, 1990.

[2]   O. Frieder and M. E. Segal. On dynamically updating a computer program: From concept to prototype. *Journal of Systems Software*, 14:111–28, 1991.

[3]   W. W. Ho and R. A. Olsson. An approach to genuine dynamic linking. *Software - Practice and Experience*, 21(4):375–90, 1991.

[4]   S. P. Reiss. FIELD: A friendly integrated environment for learning and development. 1994.

[5]   R. E. Gantenbein. *Dynamic Binding of Separately Compiled Objects Under Pro-*

gram Control. PhD thesis, Technical report 86-08. Department of Computer Science, The University of Iowa, Iowa City, Iowa, 1986.

[6]   R. E. Gantenbein and D. W. Jones. The design and implementation of a dynamic binding feature for a high-level language. *The Journal of Systems and Software,* 8:259273, 1988.

[7]   R. Morrison, A. L. Brown, R. C. H. Connor, Q. I. Cutts, A. Dearle, G. N. C. Kirby, and D. S. Munro. The Napier88 Reference Manual (Release 2.0). Technical report, University of St. Andrews, St. Andrews, Scotland, 1993.

[8]   J. Kramer and J. Magee. Dynamic configuration for distributed systems. *IEEE Transactions on Software Engineering,* SE-11(4):424–35, 1985.

[9]   M. E. Segal and O. Frieder. On-the-fly program modification: Systems for dynamic updating. *IEEE Software,* 10(2):53–65, 1993.

[10]   R. N. Taylor, N. Medvidovic, K. M. Anderson, E. J. Whitehead Jr, and J. E. Robbins. A component- and message-based architectural style for GUI software. In *17th International Conference on Software Engineering,* pages 295–304, 1995.

[11]   Chiron-2 - a component- and message-based architectural style for GUI software, 1995. Arcadia Pamphlet.

[12]   E. H. Bersoff. Elements of software configuration management. *IEEE Transactions on Software Engineering.,* SE-10(1):79–87, 1984.

[13]   C. Marlin. Modelling, comparison and design. In *Proceedings of the 1994 Western Australian Computer Science Symposium,* Claremont, Western Australia, 1994.

[14]   D. Wiebe. Object oriented configuration management. Presented at *the 4th International Workshop on Software Configuration Management,* 1993.

[15]   A. Mahler and A. Lampen. Integrating configuration management into a generic environment. In *SIGSOFT '90 Proceedings on the Fourth ACM SIGSOFT Symposium on Software Development Environments,* 1990.

[16]   R. Morrison, R. C. H. Connor, Q. I. Cutts, V. S. Dunstan, and G. N. C. Kirby. Exploiting persistent linkage in software engineering environments. *The Computer Journal,* 38(1):1–16, 1995.

[17]   W. F. Tichy. Tools for software configuration management. In *Proceedings of the International Workshop on Software Configuration and Version Control,* pages 1–20, 1988.

[18]   D. E. Perry and A. L. Wolf. Foundations for the study of software architecture. *Software Engineering Notes,* 17(4):40–52, 1992.

[19]   A. van der Hoek, D. Heimbigner, and A. L. Wolf. Does configuration management have a future? In *Proceedings of the 5th Workshop on Software Configuration Management,* pages 173–6, 1995.

[20]   P. Lambrix. Aspects of version management of composite objects. Thesis No. 328, Department of Computer and Information Science, Linköping University, Linköping, Sweden, 1992.

Configuration Management in Terms of Modules

Yi-Jing Lin and Steven P. Reiss
Department of Computer Science
Box 1910, Brown University
Providence, RI 02912
yjl@cs.brown.edu spr@cs.brown.edu

Abstract. Modern programming languages support constructs like functions and classes that let programmers decompose source programs into modules. However, existing programming environments do not allow programmers to handle configuration management directly with them. Instead, system building and version control are usually handled with different decomposition structures. The modules used in configuration management do not always match the modules in the source code. This is both inconvenient and error-prone, since there is a gap between handling the source code and managing the configurations.

In this research we propose a framework for programming environments that handles configuration management directly in terms of the modules in the source code. We define the operations required for this purpose, study their semantics, and find a general strategy to support them. We show that with the ability to handle a large module as a single unit, software reuse and cooperative programming becomes easier. We also design and implement a prototype environment to verify our ideas.

1 Introduction

Modulization is one of the most important techniques used to harness the complexity of software. It is a common practice to decompose source programs into units such as functions, procedures, and classes that represent modules. However, existing programming environments do not handle configuration management directly in terms of these logical modules. In more traditional environments, versions are managed in terms of files and directories, which only roughly correspond to the modules in the source code. Some advanced environments replace the underlying file system with object-oriented databases, but usually the organization of objects in these environments do not match the structure of the source code either. Most existing environments also describe the process of system building with separate descriptions (e.g. makefiles). These descriptions decompose a software system in a separate structure that does not necessarily match the decomposition structure of the source code.

Managing configurations and source code with different structures is not only cumbersome but also error-prone. Maintaining a mapping between the logical structure of source code and the physical structure of software artifacts is an unnecessary burden on programmers. Whenever the source code is modified, programmers have to check if some corresponding modification is required at the configuration management level.

When software systems become larger, this mapping between source code and configuration management may become very complicated.

Another problem with most current environments is that the configuration management tasks are not well decomposed into modules with simple interfaces. At the source code level, since a function or a class hides the details about the functions and classes it uses, using a high-level function or class is as easy as using a low-level one. However, this is usually not true in configuration management. If we want to use a large module, we have to handle the derived objects generated by its submodules. If a module contains many submodules and uses many files, then managing the modules's versions becomes difficult.

In this research, we present a new framework for programming environments that handles configuration management directly in terms of the functions and classes in the source code. Under this framework, users can create and use versions of a large module with simple operations, no matter how many submodules the module contains. Users can also describe the system building process by establishing the module-submodule relationships. We show that with the ability to handle a large module as a single unit, cooperative programming becomes easier, since programmers will be dealing with modules, instead of files, that are generated by other programmers.

Our framework has a strong object-oriented flavor, but it is not limited to supporting object-oriented programming. Any programming language that supports separate compilation can fit into our framework. Currently, we are focusing on supporting C and C++, though our framework can also handle languages like Modula-2, Modula-3, Ada, and Pascal without major modification.

There are limitations to our approach, though. Since our framework is based on the modulization of programs, it cannot properly handle documents generated before the modulization. Our environment is designed to support configuration management in software design, implementation, and maintenance, but not for activities like requirement specifications and feasibility studies.

1.1 The Model

In current environments, configuration management is handled with tools that run *on top* of data repositories. For example, traditional UNIX programming environments manage configuration with tools like MAKE [8] and RCS [25] that operate on files and directories. STONEMAN [4] envisioned configuration management in an Ada Programming Support Environment (APSE) as tools running on top of a database. In the ECMA [6] "Toaster Model," low-level configuration management is supported by a database, but higher level activities are still carried out by separate tools.

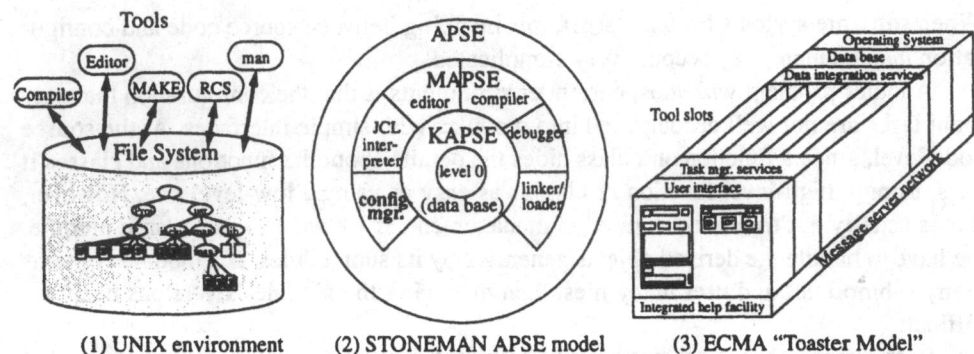

(1) UNIX environment (2) STONEMAN APSE model (3) ECMA "Toaster Model"

Figure 1: Models of current environments.

As illustrated in Figure 2, our framework represents functions and classes of a program as objects called *software units*, and represent the relations between them as links. A software unit encapsulates all the source code, derived objects, documentations, and building script of the corresponding function or class, and supplies a set of operations to programmers. In this environment, programmers manage software by invoking the operations of software units, instead of using tools that are separated from the data repository.

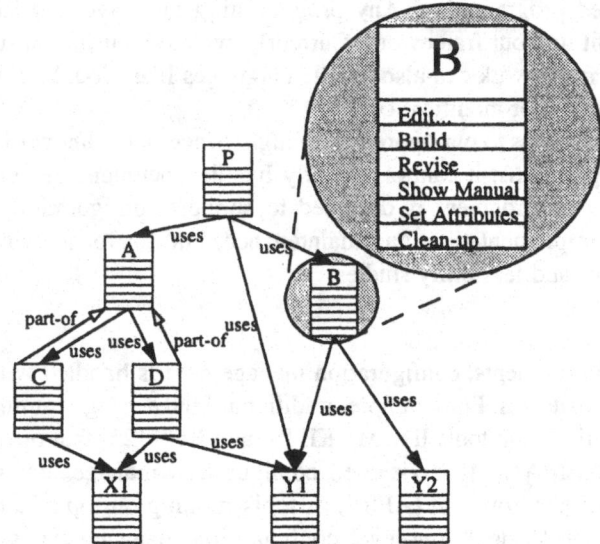

Figure 2: An object-centered programming environment.

We organize software artifacts at the *configuration management* level in parallel with the modulization at the *source code* level. A software unit plays two roles at the same time. It represents a function or a class in source code, and it corresponds to a configuration in configuration management. Since we use the same decomposition structure, the gap between handling source code and managing configurations is narrowed. Additionally, since we represent the relations between modules explicitly as links, programmers can examine and traverse them directly without looking into the source code.

This helps programmers to understand the general structure of a program.

Our approach applies the principles of modulization and encapsulation in configuration management. It is well known that modulization and encapsulation is very useful in managing source programs. Similarly, they can help us greatly in handling configuration management. As pointed out by Osterweil [19], software processes can be considered as special programs that are enacted by both human and computers. The data used by these special programs are software artifacts like source code, derived objects, system models, documentation, version history files, etc. By applying the principles of modulization and encapsulation on these software artifacts, we can simplify configuration management greatly. Modulization helps us to decompose the configuration management tasks into manageable units. Encapsulation helps us to hide the different configuration management requirements of individual modules.

1.2 Software Unit, Module, and Work Area

From a user's point of view, our environment consists of a set of software units that are interconnected by links. Software units represent modules, and links represent the module-submodule relations. More specifically, if we are programming in C or C++, a software unit corresponds to a function or a class. A link corresponds to the relation traditionally represented by a "#include" directive. It may be the calling of a function, the usage of a class, or the inheritance between two classes.

As illustrated in Figure 3, a software unit contains a set of *data attributes*, a set of *operations*, and a set of *links*. Data attributes are encapsulated and not directly accessible to programmers. Operations can be invoked by other software units or directly by programmers. Links are considered as parts of the software units they originate from, but can be modified directly by programmers.

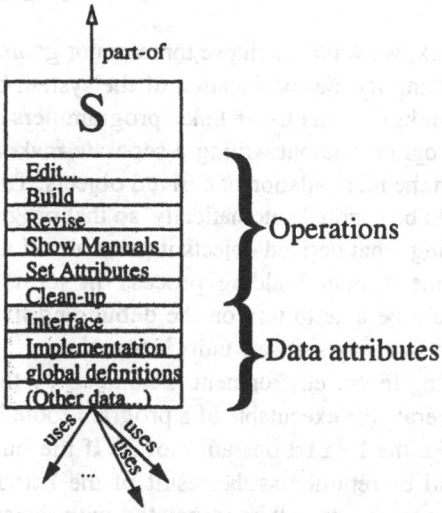

Figure 3: A software unit.

Among the data attributes of a software unit, *interface*, *implementation*, and *global definitions* are source code that is filled in by programmers. The interface part specifies the facilities provided by a module. The implementation part realizes what is specified in the corresponding interface. The global definitions contain the definitions to be time. Usually, a programmer will edit mutable software units in one work area, and at the same time access immutable software units in other work areas. Immutable software units in remote work areas can be accessed directly without check-in or check-out operations.

Different kinds of software units need different data attributes and different implementation of their operations. For example, some software units used in a C program may contain YACC code instead of plain C code, and some software units may be library functions that do not have implementation parts. We use the *delegation model* [15][26][22][18] instead of the more conventional *class/inheritance model* to describe the sharing of behavior between software units. Delegation can simulate the class/inheritance mechanism while supporting the sharing of attributes between individual objects.

With the delegation mechanism, we define a set of *prototypes* for commonly used software units, like those for C, C++, and YACC. These prototypes work like *classes* in a conventional object-oriented system. All software units are created from these prototypes, and a software unit inherits the operations and default attribute values from its prototype. But with delegation, we can also add new attributes and redefine operations on individual software units to meet special requirements.

Our framework requires no modification to the syntax of C and C++. But since the uses links and part-of links already describe the exchanging of definitions between software units, the "#include" directives should not be used when the corresponding links exist. Using links and "#include" directives simultaneously is redundant and may cause integrity problems.

2 System Building

With our framework, we want to achieve three major goals in handling system building. First, we want to simplify the specification of the system building process. After establishing the uses links and part-of links, programmers should be able to generate the executable of a program without writing a separate makefile. Second, we want to free programmers from the manipulation of derived objects. The identification of object files and libraries should be handled automatically, so that programmers can use a large module without knowing what derived objects it generates. Lastly, we want to let programmers customize the system building process in terms of modules. For example, programmers should be able to turn on the debugging flag of a module with a simple action, no matter how many software units it contains.

System building in our environment is handled by the build operations of software units. To generate the executable of a program rooted at software unit X, programmers should invoke the build operation of X. If the building is successful, then the executable file will be returned as the result of the build operation. If the building fails, then the error messages will be associated with the software units that contain the erroneous code. Programmers can also build the derived objects of individual modules by invoking the build operations of their root software units.

Internally, this system building process is carried out collaboratively by the build operations of all software units in a module. Each software unit compiles its source code shared by submodules. If we are programming in C or C++, then the implementation part corresponds to a ".c file" under a traditional programming environment. The interface part corresponds to a public header file that declares the facilities defined in the ".c file." And the global definition parts correspond to a private header file that declares the common definitions to be shared by all ".c files" of a module.

There are two kinds of links in our framework - *uses* links and *part-of* links. Each software unit has a set of uses links pointing to the software units representing its submodules, and an optional part-of link pointing to the software unit representing its parent module. These links define the set of definitions to be imported from other modules. A uses link imports the interface from a submodule, and a part-of link imports the global definition from the parent module.

Part-of links are the inverse links of uses links, but they are required only when software units need the global definitions of their parents. Use of part-of links should be avoided whenever possible, because they increase the interdependence between modules. As we will see later, software units without part-of links have nice properties for software reuse and cooperative programming.

In our framework, a *module M(X)* is defined as a *root software unit X* and all the software units that are reachable from *X* by uses links. A module can be handled as a single unit by invoking the operations of its root software unit. For example, invoking the build operation of a software unit *X* will generate the derived objects of the whole module *M(X)*, not just those of the root software unit *X*.

During the design and implementation stages, software units work like templates. Programmers create new software units and then fill in their interface, implementation and global definitions by invoking the edit operation. The edit operation brings up editors for this purpose. Uses links and part-of links can be specified either before or after the contents of software units are filled in. Therefore, programmers may layout the general structures of their programs before doing any coding.

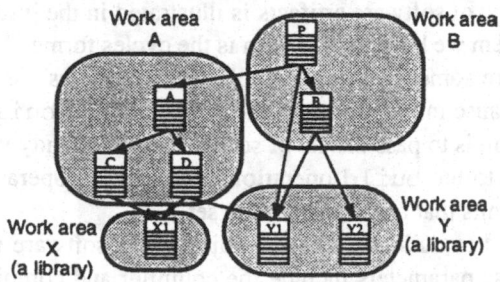

Figure 4: Software units are grouped into work areas.

As illustrated in Figure 4, software units are grouped into mutually exclusive *work areas*. Work areas serve two purposes in our framework. First, they divide the name space of software units into manageable units. Second, they define the boundaries between programming tasks. Each work area contains some mutable software units that are under development, and some immutable ones that represent old versions. The immutable software units are accessible to all programmers, but the mutable ones are visible only to the *owner* of a work area.

To reduce interference, only one programmer can be the owner of a work area at a if its derived objects are outdated, propagates the build message along the uses links, and then collect derived objects from its submodules. As illustrated in Figure 5, the propagation of build messages is essentially a depth-first traversal of the graph formed by software units and their uses links.

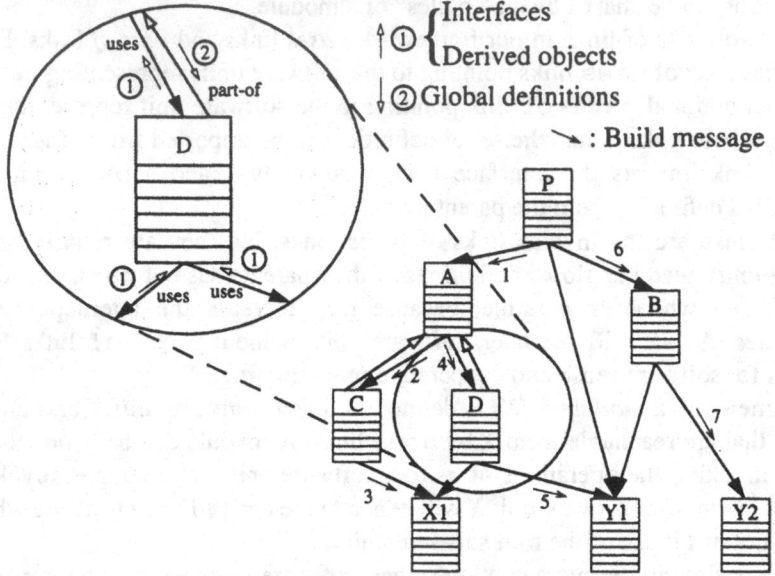

Figure 5: Propagation of the build operation.

During the system building process, software artifacts are passed along the uses links and part-of links. When compiling, a software unit gets the interfaces of its submodules along its uses links, and gets the global definitions of its parent module along its part-of link. In the meantime, derived objects are passed upstream along the uses links. This flow of software artifacts is illustrated in the inset of Figure 5.

An important problem we have to deal with is the cycles formed by the uses links. Cycles of uses links are sometimes unavoidable when modules are mutually dependent. These cycles may cause infinite loops in the propagation of build messages. One way to avoid this problem is to pass the set of software units already visited in the propagation as an argument to the build operation. The build operation is propagated only to those software units that are not yet in the set.

The parameters used to build the derived objects of a software unit are stored on each software unit. These parameters include the compiler and compilation flags being used. Programmers can change these parameters by invoking the set_attributes operations of a software unit. For example, programmers can request a software unit to put debugging information in its object code by turning on its debugging flag. By default, the set_attributes operations are also propagated along the uses links, so that the same setting will take effect on the whole module. This propagation can be prohibited when programmers want to confine the effects of the new setting to the root software unit.

3 Version Control

Our version control system also has three major goals. First, we want to provide facilities that allow programmers to create, select, and use versions in terms of modules. Second, we want to simplify the access to old versions while reducing the space they occupy. Finally, we want to handle the sharing of derived objects automatically.

In terms of version control, we classify software units into *fixed versions* and *active versions*. A fixed version represents an immutable snapshot of a module. An active version represents a working copy of a module. An active version provides a *freeze* operation that turns itself into a fixed version. A fixed version provides a *revise* operation that creates a new active version as its successor. In the beginning, every new software unit is created as an active version. Then by repeatedly applying `freeze` and `revise` operations, we can create a version history tree for each software unit.

Since a fixed software unit represents an immutable snapshot of a module, it should always produce the same derived objects during the system building process. To insure this property, a fixed software unit should freeze all the software units it uses. If a fixed software unit has a `part-of` link, then the parent software unit should also be frozen.

Similarly, since an active software unit represents a developing module, it should use active software units in the local work area. Invoking the `revise` operation of a fixed software unit will create a module that contains active software units in the local work area and fixed software units in remote work areas. The `revise` operation does not create active versions in remote work areas because active software units cannot be accessed across the work area boundaries, and because it is seldom what programmers want.

Figure 6 shows the effect of `revise` and `freeze` operations on a module. Notice that since we do not modify C and X in Figure 6(c), they are *reverted* to their previous versions in Figure 6(d). However, although D is not directly modified either, a new version of D is created because it uses a modified version of Y.

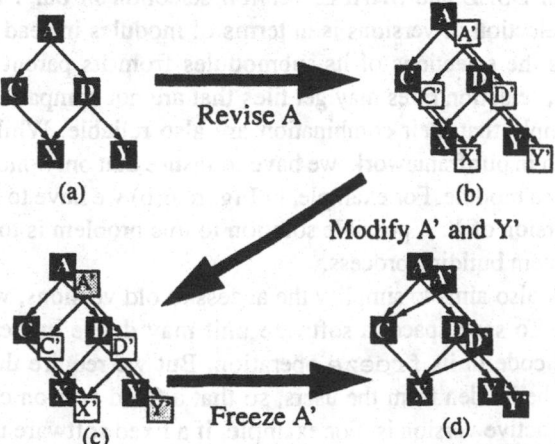

Figure 6: Version control of a module.

Like the system building process, the revising and freezing of a module is carried out by the collaboration of individual software units. When revising a module, the `revise` message is propagated along the `uses` link until it hits the boundaries of a work area. Each software unit then uses its own `revise` operation to process its data attributes. The freezing of a module is carried out similarly by propagating the `freeze` message. Basically, a `freeze` operation should reduce the space occupied by a software unit. A `revise` operation should make modifiable copies of its data attributes.

Our model to handle composite objects is similar to that of PCTE [9][3]. But there are two major differences. First, while all the attributes of a *stable* object in PCTE are immutable, a fixed software unit in our framework may modify its attributes internally. For example, it may delete its derived objects and compress its source objects to save space. The only requirement is that each fixed software unit should keep enough information so that the same derived objects can be regenerated. Second, instead of using the same predefined operations for all objects, we allow different software units to have different implementation of their `revise` and `freeze` operations. This is necessary because different kinds of software units may have different data attributes.

Our framework allow users to choose versions directly in terms of modules. If programmers want to use a certain version of module $M(X)$, they can simply point a `uses` link to the corresponding version of the root software unit X. Programmers do not have to know which software units $M(X)$ uses, or whether different versions of $M(X)$ use a different set of software units.

Like DSEE [13], SHAPE [16], and Adele [7], we use *version selection rules* to make the selection of versions more flexible. But since versions are selected by the `uses` links in our framework, we associate these rules with `uses` links instead of putting them in a separate description. A version selection rule contains a predicate made in terms of the attributes of software units. The effective destination of a `uses` link with a version selection is the latest version of a software unit that satisfies this predicate. However, since the `uses` links with version selection predicates do not have fixed destinations, they cannot be used by fixed software units. A `freeze` operation should freeze them into normal `uses` links.

Compared with DSEE and SHAPE, version selection in our framework is more hierarchical. The selection of versions is in terms of modules instead of files, and each software unit hides the selections of its submodules from its parent software unit. In DSEE and SHAPE, selection rules may get files that are not compatible, since two reliable files do not imply that their combination are also reliable. While this problem is less likely to happen in our framework, we have to insure that only one version of a software unit is used by a module. For example, in Figure 6(b) we have to insure that C' and D' use the same version of X. A possible solution to this problem is to detect these conflicts during the system building process.

Our framework also aims to simplify the access to old versions, while reducing the space they occupy. To save space, a software unit may delete its derived objects and check-in its source code in its `freeze` operation. But we require that all these space conserving actions be hidden from the users, so that a fixed version can be accessed in the same way as an active version is. For example, if a fixed software unit checked in all of its source code into some version repository, then when its `edit` operation is invoked, it should check out its source code internally before bringing up an editor. We also require that the `freeze` operation not change the semantics of a module. In other words, a fixed module should keep enough information so that it can regenerate the same derived objects.

Since a fixed software unit may check out its source objects and regenerate its derived objects internally, we need an operation to remove these objects when the fixed software unit is no longer used. We define a `clean-up` operation for this purpose. A `clean-up` operation should reduce the space occupied by a module without affecting its behavior. Again, we propagate the `clean-up` messages along the `uses` links, and let individual software units decide what to do with their data attributes. The `clean-up` operation may be invoked either explicitly by programmers, or internally by the system. When a work area is short of disk space, it may invoked the `clean-up` operations of its least-recently-used software units.

We also use the delegation mechanism to save space in version control. The basic idea of delegation is that if an attribute is not defined on an object, the underlying system will try to find that attribute on the *prototype* of the current object, and use that value as if it is locally defined. In our environment, a new version internally uses its predecessor version as its prototype, and stores only the attributes that are modified on the new version.

Delegation, in this respect, is similar to version control systems like RCS [25] and SCCS [20], where only the deltas between versions are stored. But using delegation has an additional benefit - versions can be accessed directly without check-in and check-out operations. Internally, attributes are shared between versions. But to users, it looks as if every version keeps its own copy of all the attributes.

4 Software Reuse

The ability to handle a large module as a single unit simplifies the process of incorporating reusable modules into new projects. It makes the reuse of library modules easier. It also helps in reusing modules that are not made into libraries.

In existing environments, reusable software is usually represented as libraries. To reuse a library module, programmers have to locate its archive file and its header file, and then modify the description of the system building process (e.g. a makefile). At the same time, programmers have to locate the corresponding manual pages in some remote directory. This is both tedious and error-prone. If there are multiple versions of the same library, then programmers may accidentally get the header file from one version and the archive file from another version. The manual pages read by programmers may not match the software either.

In our framework, we represent library modules as software units. These software units have different internal structures but bear the same interface as other software units. To reuse one such software unit, programmers can simply establish a `uses` link to it. With this single action, its header file, archive file, and manual pages are all incorporated into the new project. It also guarantees that all these components will come from the same version.

Another problem with existing environments is that modules can be reused easily only when they are made into libraries. Since making large modules into libraries is not trivial, programmers seldom do this with their code. As a result, many chances for software reuse are missed.

In our framework, modules can be reused directly without being made into libraries. Because we designate each modules by a single root software unit regardless of its internal complexity, a large module can be used in the same way as a library module is used. As illustrated in Figure 7(a), if a module does not have a `part-of` link, we can reuse it by pointing a `uses` link to it. With this single operation, the reuser gets not only the derived objects of the reused module, but also its source code, manual pages, version history, and the operations to handle it. In contrast, if we want to reuse a module that are not made into libraries in a traditional environment, we have to know the location of all the object files it generates, and all the libraries it uses. Besides, modifying makefiles to incorporate a large module is usually difficult.

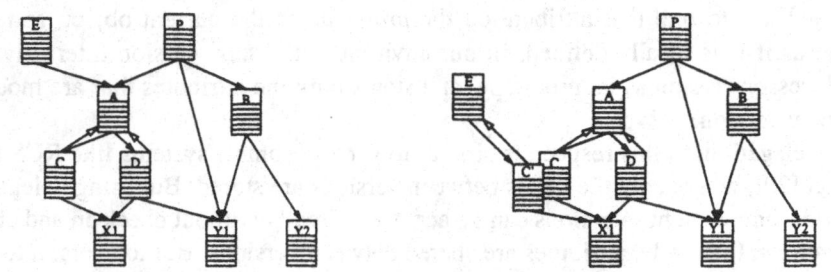

(a) Reusing a module without a `part-of` link.   (b) Reusing a module with a `part-of` link.

Figure 7: Reusing modules.

Modules with `part-of` links represent modules that need information from their parent. To reuse one of them, we should create an active version of the reused software unit and make its `part-of` link point to the new parent software unit. The reuser software unit is responsible for providing appropriate global definitions to the reused one. This is illustrated in Figure 7(b). Although different derived objects will be generated internally when this kind of module is reused, no other action is required. Since new derived objects will be kept as attributes of the new active version instead of overwritten to the existing version, the reuse will not interfere the original project. In contrast, to reuse this types of modules in a traditional environment, we have to copy all the source files of the module, or create a separate directory for the new derived objects and modify the makefile in a non-trivial way.

Our framework does not differentiate between a reused module and a locally created one. All software units in a project are treated the same. We can follow the `uses` links to a reused module just like browsing any other modules. If users want to modify the source code of a reused module, they can invoke the `revise` operation of the reused module to get a modifiable version. The ability to tailor a reused module is important when we are reusing large modules.

5 Cooperative Programming

The major goal of our support for cooperative programming is to let programmers deal directly with modules, instead of files or individual objects, that are generated by other programmers. Our framework also enables us to reduce the interference between programmers, and increase the sharing of software artifacts more naturally.

Our scenario for cooperative programming follows the general strategy of DSEE [13] and SHAPE [16]. Programmers should use the older but more stable versions of code from their colleagues, and work on the newer but experimental versions of their own code. But instead of dealing with *files*, our framework allows a programmer to choose and use *modules* generated by other programmers.

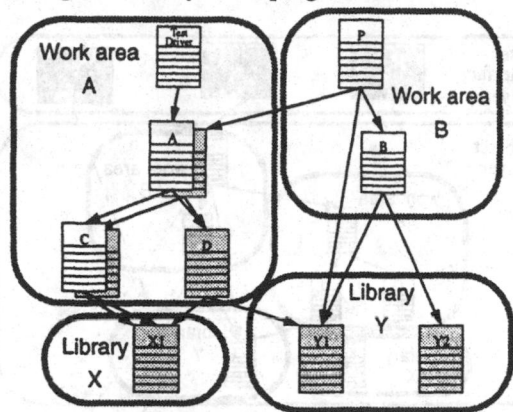

Figure 8: Cooperative programming.

Figure 8 shows a simple example of cooperative programming. Suppose that a program *P* is cooperatively developed by two programmers *A* and *B*. Programmer *A* works on module *M(A)*. Programmer *B* works on the main program *P* and module *M(B)*. In order to use *M(A)*, programmer *B* points a uses link from software unit *P* to software unit *A*. With this single uses link, the whole module *M(A)* is incorporated into the program. Programmer *B* does not have to know which software units *M(A)* contains, or what derived object it will generate. All the internal complexity of *M(A)* is hidden from programmer *B*. This is especially helpful when *M(A)* is very large, or when *M(A)* itself uses modules from other programmers.

Work areas are used to reduce the interference between programmers. Since active software units in a work area are visible only to the work area owner, the on-going work will not interfere or be interfered by other programmers. On the other hand, fixed software units of a work area can be accessed by all programmers. No check-out operation is required and they can be treated just like fixed software units in local work areas. Programmers can browse them, send build messages to them, and create their version successors in local work areas.

Our framework also handles the sharing of software artifacts between programmers naturally. If two programmers use the same version of a module, then they will automatically shared all the source objects and derived objects of that module. For example, in Figure 8 since the same version of module *M(D)* is used by both programmer *A* and programmer B, all its data attributes will be shared. Moreover, because of the delegation mechanism described in section 3, programmers A and B will also share the attributes of software unit A and C that are not modified in the new version. In DSEE and SHAPE, the sharing of derived objects are handled by more complicated mechanisms.

6 POEM - A Prototype Environment

To verify the ideas of our approach, we are developing a prototype environment called POEM (Programmable Object-centered EnvironMent). As illustrated in Figure 9, the architecture of POEM is composed of a *user interface layer* and an *object layer* on top of the file system.

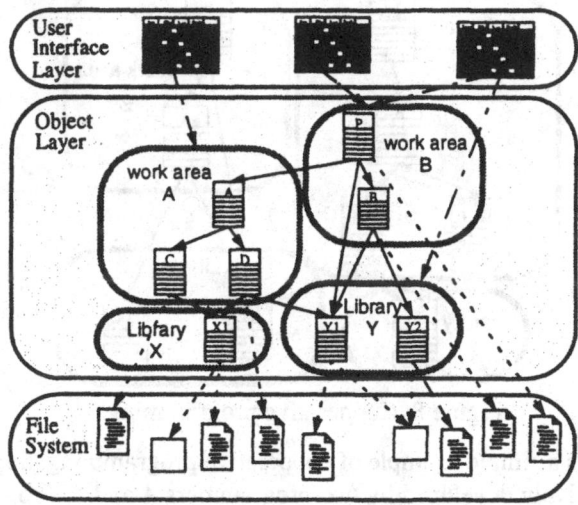

Figure 9: The architecture of POEM.

The object layer is where the software units are stored. It is basically an object-oriented database. Currently we are using an object-oriented database system called ObjectStore [12] to implement this layer. ObjectStore is basically an extension of the C++ language that supports persistent objects. It allows multiple clients to work on the same database simultaneously in a distributed environment, and it supports transaction facilities to serialize the operations on objects.

To increase the flexibility of this environment, we supply an interpretive language that allows users to define new classes of software units, or change the definition of individual software units. Therefore, users can tailor the environment to their needs. The compatibility between user-defined software units is enforced by requiring that all new classes of software units inherit existing classes.

In POEM, users do not directly access files and directories of the underlying file system. But instead of storing everything in the object layer, POEM still stores large software artifacts like source code, object code, and documents as files in the underlying file system. Doing so makes POEM more open to the outside world. Existing tools like editors, compilers, and debuggers can be invoked by the operations of software units to process these files. We can also utilize existing code and documentation by creating software units that reference existing files.

The purpose of the user interface layer is to let programmers access software units in the object layer. This layer is fairly simple because most functions of POEM are already supported by software units in the object layer. Its major responsibilities are to display the contents of software units, to let users invoke operations of software units, and to show the relationship between software units. A graphical user interface can easily be built, since software units and their links map naturally to icons and edges. Operations of a software unit can also be represented as items in a pop-up menu.

7 Related Work

MAKE [8] is the most commonly used system building tool, but it has rather weak support for the modulization of makefiles. There is no formal channel of communication between makefiles. If we want to use multiple makefiles in a large project, then the passing of arguments has to rely on implicit protocols. The lack of formal arguments also makes the reuse of makefiles more difficult. The VESTA configuration management system [14] aims to solve these problems by the modulization and parameterization of system models. It uses a functional language to describe system models, and emphasizes the modulization and parameterization of system models. However, since the nature of system building requires lots of parameters for each system building functions, and since it is impractical to supply all these parameters on each call to these functions, VESTA has to introduce a complex binding mechanism to manage the parameters of system building functions. Our framework shares the same goals with VESTA in system building, but uses an object-oriented approach instead of a functional approach. The parameters for system building are stored on software units instead of passed as arguments to functions.

Early version control systems like SCCS [20] and RCS [25] handle the versions of files only. CVS [2] enhances RCS by letting programmers handle versions of directories. DSEE [13] allows version selection in terms of *threads* that refers to files or other threads. Version control in terms of objects is studied in the area of software development environments as well as in the area of computer aided design (CAD). Zdonik describes an object-oriented database system that includes a built-in version control mechanism [27]. PCTE+ [3] supports operations to manage versions of composite objects. Katz surveyed version modeling in engineering databases, and proposed a unified framework [11].

Several other systems also aim to free programmers from the management of derived objects. Cedar [23] and DSEE [13] use *source oriented system models*. Derived objects are not directly managed by programmers, but programmers still have to address them indirectly by some functions. VESTA hides the management of derived objects by passing them as the results of building functions.

Most existing configuration management systems use separate document to describe the system building process. CaseWare [5] stores the information about how to build a particular type of object on the object type definition itself, and places the build context information on objects. But the compositions of configurations are still described by separate collections called *assemblies*.

In Ada [1], since packages and subprograms are units of source code as well as units for compilation, the gap between handling system building and managing source code is smaller than in other languages. Besides, an Ada environment is responsible to decide which units need to be re-compiled based on the logical relations between them. However, Ada organizes compiled packages in libraries, which have flat structures and thus cannot directly capture the relationship between packages and subprograms. Ada also needs additional mechanisms to handle a mapping between versions of libraries and their elements. CMVC [17] presented one of such mechanisms.

Gandalf [10] uses a module concept where a set of versions implement a single interface. Adele [7] extends this model so that interfaces themselves may have versions. It also describes the relation between interfaces and implementations as an AND/OR graph. Compared with our framework, Adele is more flexible to handle variants of versions, but it is also more complicated.

Rumbaugh [21] proposed a framework to control the propagation of operations between objects. The propagation policy is based on attributes associated with relations. Our framework also relies on the propagation of operations to handle composite objects. But instead of using the full power of that rather complicated model, we found that treating all operations equally and using work areas to control the propagation is suffice to meet our requirements.

8 Conclusion

The major goal of this research is to find a framework that makes configuration management simple yet powerful. We have shown that it is possible to provide a programming environment that handles system building and version control according to the logical structure of source code. This makes programming easier because programmers no longer have to maintain the mapping between the structure of source code and that of the physical software artifacts. Our framework also handles derived objects automatically, and allow programmers to handle large modules as a single unit.

While the basics of this framework is established, there are still many problems to be solved. Our framework does not have enough support for managing variants of modules at this moment. We plan to enhance this part by exploiting the delegation mechanism, so that module variants with many overlapping parts can be created without actually duplicating the data.

Acknowledgments

We want to thank Clarence Clark at IBM for giving us numerous ideas and suggestions. Thanks also to Anthony Cassandra and Hsueh-I Lu for giving us suggestions on writing this paper.

References

1. J. G. P. Barnes, "An Overview of Ada," in *Software Practice and Experience*, vol. 10, pp. 851-887, 1980.

2. Brian Berliner, "CVS II: Parallelizing Software Development," Prisma, Inc., 5465 Mark Dabling Blvd, Colorado Springs, CO 80918.

3. Gerard Boudier, Ferdinando Gallo, Regis Minot, and Ian Thomas, "An Overview of PCTE and PCTE+," in *Proceedings of the ACM SIGSOFT/SIGPLAN Software Engineering Symposium on Practical Software Development Environments*, (Peter Henderson, ed.), pp. 248-257, November 1988. Published as ACM SIGSOFT Software Engineering Notes, Vol 13, No 5, November 1988, and ACM SIGPLAN Notices, Vol 24, No 2, February 1989.

4. John N. Buxton and larry E. Druffel, "Requirements for An Ada Programming Support Environment: Rationale for STONEMAN," in *Proceedings of COMPSAC 80*, pp. 66-72, 1980.

5. Martin R. Cagan, "Software Configuration Management Redefined," CaseWare, Inc., 108 Pacifica, Irvine, CA 92718, March 1992.

6. ECMA, "A Reference Model for Frameworks of Software Engineering Environments (Version 2). *ECMA Report Number TR/55 (Version 2), NIST Report Number SP 500-201*, December 1991.

7. Jacky Estublier, "A Configuration Manager: The Adele data base of programs," in *Workshop on software engineering environments for programming-in-the-large*, June 1985

8. Stuart I. Feldman, "Make - a Program for Maintaining Computer Programs," in *Software - Practice & Experience*, 9(4), pp. 255-265, April 1979.

9. Ferdinando Gallo, Regis Minot, and Ian Thomas, "The Object Management System of PCTE as a Software Engineering Database Management System," in *Proceedings of the ACM SIGSOFT/SIGPLAN Software Engineering Symposium on Practical Software Development Environments*, (Peter Henderson, ed.), pp. 12-15, December 1986.

10. A. Nico Habermann and David Notkin, "Gandalf: Software Development Environments," in *IEEE Transactions on Software Engineering*, Vol 12, No 12, pp.1117-1127, December 1986.

11. Randay H. Katz, "Toward a Unified Framework for Version Modeling in Engineering Databases," *ACM Computing Surveys*, Vol 22, No 4, pp. 375-408, December 1990.

12. Charles Lamb, Gordon Landis, Jack Orenstein, and Dan Weinred, "The ObjectStore Database System," in *Communications of the ACM*, Vol. 34, No. 10, pp. 50-63, October 1991.

13. David B. Leblang and Robert P. Chase, Jr., "Computer-Aided Software Engineering in a Distributed Workstation Environment," in *SIGPLAN Notices*, vol. 19, No. 5, pp. 104-113, April 1984.

14. Roy Levin and Paul R. McJones, "The Vesta Approach to Precise Configuration of Large Software Systems," DEC System Research Center Research Report No. 105, June 1993.

15. Henry Lieberman, "Using Prototypical Objects to Implement Shared Behavior in Object Oriented Languages," in *ACM OOPSLA '86*, pp. 214-223, September, 1986.

16. Axel Mahler and Andreas Lampen, "An Integrated Toolset for Engineering Software Configurations," in *Proceedings of the ACM SIGSOFT/SIGPLAN Software Engineering Symposium on Practical Software Development Environments*, (Peter Henderson, ed.), pp. 191-200, November 1988. Published as ACM SIGSOFT Software Engineering Notes, Vol 13, No 5, November 1988, and ACM SIGPLAN Notices, Vol 24, No 2, February 1989.

17. Thomas M. Morgan, "Configuration Management and Version Control in the Rational Programming Environment," in *Ada in Industry - Proceedings of the Ada-Europe International Conference*, pp. 17-28, June, 1988.

18. Lynn Andrea Stein, Henry Lieberman, and David Ungar, "A Shared View of Sharing: The Treaty of Orlando," In *Concepts, Applications and Databases*, pp. 31-48, Addison Wesley, Reading, Massachusetts, 1989.

19. Leon Osterweil, "Software Process are Software Too," in *Proceedings of the 9th International Conference on Software Engineering*, pp. 2-13, Monterey CA, March-April 1987.

20. Marc J. Rochkind, "The Source Code Control System," in *IEEE Transactions on Software Engineering*, pp. 364-370, Vol 1 No 4, December 1975.

21. James Rumbaugh, "Controlling Propagation of Operations using Attributes on Relations," *ACM OOPSLA '88 Proceedings*, pp. 285-296, September 1988.

22. Lynn Andrea Stein, "Delegation is Inheritance," in *ACM OOPSLA '87*, pp. 138-146, October 1987.

23. Warren Teitelman, "A tour through Cedar," in *IEEE Software*, pp. 44-73, Apr. 1984.

24. Ian Simmonds, "Configuration Management in the PACT Software Engineering Environment," in *Proceedings of the 2nd International Workshop on Software Configuration Management*, (Peter H. Feiler, ed.), pp. 118-121, October, 1989.

25. Walter F. Tichy, "RCS - A System for Version Control," in *Software - Practice & Experience,* Vol. 15, No. 7, pp. 637-654, July 1985.

26. David Ungar and Randall B. Smith, "Self: The Power of Simplicity," in *ACM OOPSLA '87*, October 1987.

27. Stanley B. Zdonik, "Version Management in an Object-Oriented database," in *Advanced Programming Environments*, (R. Conradi, T. M. Didriksen, and D. H. Wanvik, ed.), pp. 405-422, 1986.

Three dimensional versioning

Jacky ESTUBLIER and Rubby CASALLAS

ABSTRACT

Versioning, in Software Engineering, has become synonym to the revision/variant graph, as proposed 20 years ago by SCCS. It is claimed here that this version graph is only a mechanism, and that it does not provide a clear description of the versioning concept. Consequently, the same mechanism is now used for very different purposes which lead (1) to a great confusion in the concepts involved, and (2) the services provided are low level and inadequate in most situations.

The other claim is that the irruption of software process support in SE introduced new needs which can also be solved by another kind of versioning.

In this paper we try to clarify the situation, introducing three orthogonal versioning dimensions: historical, logical and cooperative. We show that the associated concepts services and needs are clearly different, and how this model was (partially) implemented in the Adele project.

Key Words: Temporal database, Version model

1 Introduction

Software Engineering Environments (SEE) must support agents in their efforts to reach a common goal: the development and maintenance of a software product. The entities these agents operate upon are the resources involved, e.g., software objects, documents, tools, etc. The agents not only create but, most often, *make evolve* these entities. Product evolution support is thus a fundamental requirement for SEE.

SEE must be able not only to support but also to preserve (part of) this evolution. This is, not only, because a single value for an object is not sufficient (various versions may be needed simultaneously) but also because old versions must be kept (for later rebuilding, bug tracking, etc.).

More recently, it was understood that product quality control can only be achieved if the process by which software is produced is itself controlled. But for measuring, evaluating, controlling, improving the software process, extended traceability services are needed. This traceability needs the recording of intermediate product (and process) states all along the software production process (i.e. during a very long time).

Finally there is an increasing pressure to reduce the market lead time, thus to allow and to control parallel work, even when sharing (copies of) the same objects.

Versioning is the natural answer to all these problems, but in the current situation there are several difficulties:

- Versioning is considered as a *mechanism*, not as a *concept*; and thus is used for many unrelated purposes: cooperative works, copies, transient or work version, variants, histories, traceability etc. There is a big confusion in the concept involved.
- Almost all SEE are file-oriented with a confusion between the physical level and the conceptual level of versioning [Sci91].
- In all cases, only a sub set of the aspects which need versioning are supported by the system.

The result of the *concept* of version not being supported by the system, is that applications must define themselves their version concept, they must define the semantics for creating and retrieving versions, and must also assume the same understanding from other applications sharing the same objects. This is a heavy job, and an error prone situation.

In this paper we propose a clear separation between three version concepts: historical, logical and cooperative versioning. We show that these versioning dimensions are orthogonal and we describe for each one, the concept involved and the services provided by our platform (Adele) to support the concept.

This paper is organized as follows. In the second section is presented a basic data model and one example to illustrate the various concepts used in this paper. In section three, our versioning model. The last section contain the conclusion and the perspectives of our work.

2 Concepts

2.1 The version concept

Versioning was worked out by different communities; essentially Software Engineering Environments (SEE), Computed Aided Systems (CAD) and Temporal database communities.

The basic and most famous versioning systems, from SEE community, are the SCCS/RCS systems. These systems [Roc75], [Tic82] propose a solution for the management of a single file regardless of its content. A file is a sequence of revisions, one for each change to the object; considering that evolution is not a single sequence of revisions (a single branch) but forms a graph where each branch (or variant) follows its own evolution as a succession of revisions.

This is a valuable intend to clearly distinguishing the version concept: revisions as successive versions (evolution according to the time dimension) and variants representing logical variations or development in parallel. In fact the distinction between variant and revision is unclear and still subject to much confusion. The main reason of this confusion is the fact all versioning needs such as versioning graph, parallel work, alternative versions, object evolution and historical information are solved using the same simple mechanism.

Almost all commercial SCM tools like NSE [Cou89], DSEE [LC88], ClearCase [Leb94], CaseWare[CW93], Aide-De-Camp[adc90] or Adele[EC94], to mention a few, retain the solutions proposed by SCCS and RCS. Cooperative work support is provided using Work Space control, implemented still with the same version mechanism to solve the concurrence control problem.

CAD systems use more complex data models because they are based on database technology [Kat90]. Orion [KGW91], a "federated database systems", provides the concept of shared database and private database also for cooperative work support; the solution to control concurrence problem between the different databases, in turn, is implemented using the version mechanism.

2.2 Basic data model

The data model we use extends the object-oriented formalism with relationships. Objects and relationships being treated in almost a homogeneous way.

Objects can represent files, activities, documents, etc. Relationships are independent entities (external to objects) because they model associations with different semantics such as derivation, dependency and composition.

A Type describes the common structure and the behavior of the instances of that type. The structure corresponds to a set of *attributes* modelling properties of the instance.

Attributes model the properties of the instances. An attribute is defined by a name and its domain type.

Types are organized in a type hierarchy corresponding to specialization. A type can have one or more super types (i.e multiple inheritance).The subtype relationship is a relation of inclusion between corresponding extensions.

External names must be assigned to objects at creation time, and are directly manipulated by the user to retrieve information.

Querying the database takes place using *path expressions*. Objects and relationships can be seen as graphs: objects are the nodes and relationships are the arcs. The query language uses this graph to reach the instances navigating through the graph.

2.3 Example

The goal of this example is to illustrate the different concepts of versioning in a typical Software Engineering context. The example is the maintenance of the graphical interface of an existing system. The interface must be developed both for X11 and Open_win libraries.

Suppose in our system, software components (called here modules) are defined in the following way. By convention basic types are capitalized, user defined types have first letter capitalized, attribute are not.

```
TYPE Object;
 name: STRING;
 creationdate : DATE;
END;
TYPE Module IS Object;
 specification : Document;
 documentation: set_of Document;
 interface : Interface;
END;

TYPE Interfaceinterface IS Object;
 system      : {unix, hp, vms};
 graphics    : {X11, Open_win};
 responsible: User;
 belongs-to : Conf ;
 bug-reports: Document;
 header      : FILE;
 body        : Realization;
END;

TYPE Realization IS Object;
 source      : FILE;
 moddate     : DATE;
END;
```

Object type *Object*, root of the type hierarchy, has two attribute definitions: *name* and creation date; object type *Module* contains the specification, documentation and the interface of the corresponding module. In the example, object GraphInt is a Module instance and represents the module to develop.

The object type *Interface* has the attributes *system* and *graphics* representing the development platform and window systems. *belongs-to* attribute records the configuration including this interface and *bug-reports* contains a description of problems found on the interface. The *header* attribute contains the exported definitions; it is the module interface, the value of this attribute is a source file (the *.h* file); the *body* attribute contains the realization of the functionalities defined in the *header* attribute.

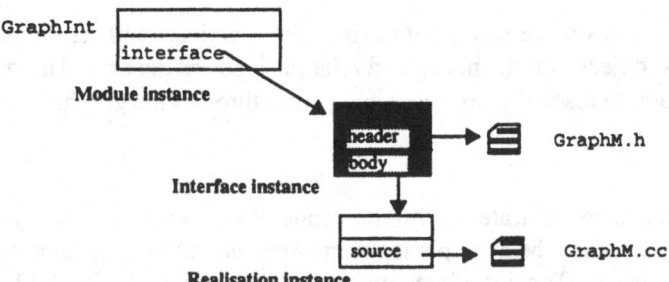

Figure 1 GraphInt is an instance of Module type. It contains a reference to an Interface object and its *body* attribute contains a reference to a Realization object.

2.4 Three dimensions

We identified three classes of versioning:

- **Historical**. It contains the evolution of the object according to the time dimension. It will be used for record intermediate object values and for extended *traceability*.
- **Logical**. Objects may exist in multiple *variants* for logical reasons. In our example a variant is needed for each window system. It is the "real" versioning.
- **Cooperative**. Multiple and concurrent *activities* are taking place in an SEE. At a given point in time, concurrent activities may have a cooperative version of the same object.

These three dimensions are completely orthogonal. The first is the time dimension, designed for history and traceability reasons; The second arises from the need to support logical versioning, i.e., *real* versioning. The third dimension is related only to the support of processes and so called long transactions, i.e., dynamic and transparent versioning.

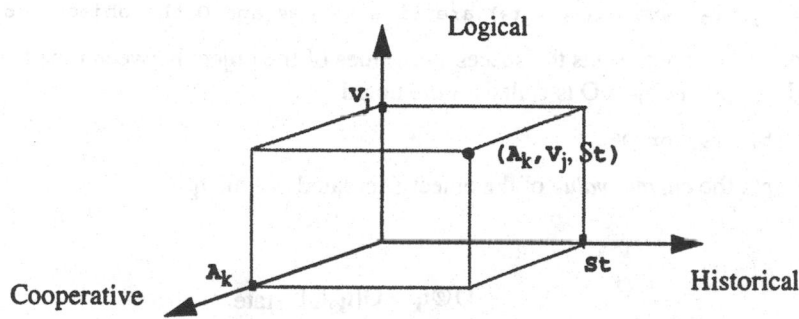

Figure 2 . Orthogonal versioning. $O(A_k,V_j,St)$ represents the version V_j of the object O in the activity A_k at state St.

This space is managed by two basic operations: creating and retrieving specific occurrence(s). It is advocated here that these operations are conceptually different for each dimension. For example, creating a new historic version differs widely from creating a new logical version (identification, naming, characterization and so on are different); similarly, retrieving the "good" variant involves different techniques than retrieving the good historical version (queries over semantic characteristic are expressed differently than temporal queries).

This work is motivated by the fact powerful versioning services can only be provided if the corresponding concepts are clearly defined. In the following sections, each one of these versioning dimension, are successively presented with their concepts and services.

3 Historic Versioning

When the value of an object is modified, normally, the previous value is overwritten, thus lost. This is not always acceptable in a Software Engineering Environment. Traditionally, the file value of an object is considered as *immutable,* i.e., the value can not be overwritten.

The natural solution to this problem is to create an historic version (a revision) each time an immutable value needs to be changed. This kind of versioning is usually implicit and produces a linear sequence of values, ordered by time. The corresponding relationship *revision_of* is a complete order relationship.

3.1 Definition

In our model, objects are temporal entities, i.e., their value is a function of time. Then, an object is defined as a pair: $<oid, value(t)>$ where *oid* is the object identification and *t* a time identification.

The values of an object O, for a time interval is called an *historic object* noted as:

```
O[t₁, t₂] where (t₁ < t₂) are time values and O the object oid.
```

This historic object represents the successive values of the object between time t_1 and t_2. A single value of object O is called a *state* noted

```
O[tₖ, tₖ] or O@tₖ
```

and represents the *current value* of the object *O* created at time t_k .

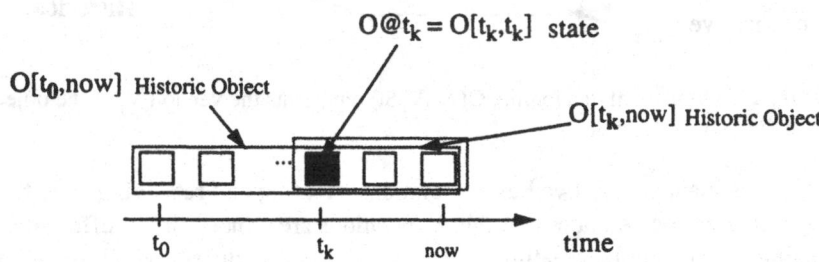

$O@t_k = O[t_k, t_k]$ state

$O[t_0, now]$ Historic Object

$O[t_k, now]$ Historic Object

t_0 t_k now   time

Figure 3 An historic object corresponds to a life-span of the object defined by a time interval.

Between two successive states, the object is assumed to have been unchanged, thus

```
O@t = O@ti, ti <= t < ti+1
```

Values contained in recorded state attributes should not be modified, since they correspond to a past reality, and past can not be changed!. They are the *immutable* attributes. In our example, *header* is immutable, once recorded the header cannot be modified. This property is fundamental in software configuration management; it ensures that

124

under a given identification (*O.header@ti*), the corresponding value is constant, and thus it avoids identification confusion.

Not all attributes are immutable. For instance the *bug-reports* attribute, which indicates the bugs found in the corresponding header, must remain *modifiable* at any point in time. Modifiable attributes are often characteristics of the immutable attributes.

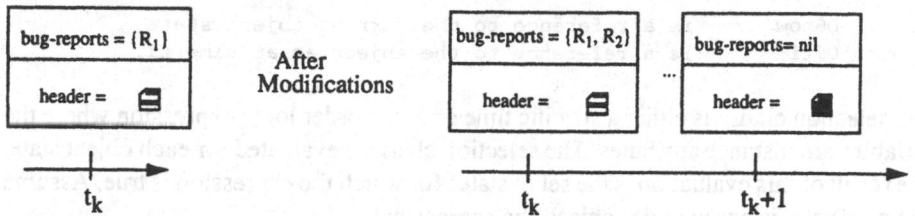

Figure 4 *bug-reports* is a *modifiable* attribute; its value can be modified at any time. *header* is an *immutable* attribute its value cannot be changed on a given state.

Some attributes are not characteristics of any specific state but of the historical object as a whole. For instance if the *responsible* attribute indicates the responsible of the historical object, it can be defined in each state, and updated in each existing state when the value is changed. This is expensive and inconvenient, because it is left to the application. Instead our model provides the concept of *common* attributes for that. The example can now be rewritten in our model as follows.

```
TYPE Interface IS Object;
COMMON
      system    : {unix, hp, vms};
      graphics  : {X11, Open_win};
      responsible: User;
MODIFIABLE
      belongs-to : Conf ;
      bug-reports: Document;
IMMUTABLE
      header     : FILE;
      body       : Realization;
END;
```

In this model, updating an *immutable* attribute creates automatically a new state of the object. The simultaneous update of more than one immutable attribute needs to be done in the same transaction. It is worth noting that the classic Check-in/Check-out paradigm was designed exactly for that reason: changing an immutable attribute, if not an atomic operation (like editing a source file) needs to be done out of the control of the system, otherwise a state would be created for each basic editing operation.

3.2 Retrieving Historic Objects

If O is an historical object, it refers all its states from creation to current time:

$$O = O@[t_{creation}, t_{now}]$$

A reference to a specific state is build by the concatenation of the object name with the "@" character and a selection clause.

```
O@now       is a reference to the current object state
O@ti        is a reference to the abject as at time ti.
```

The selection clause is either a specific time or a first order logic expression where the variables are instance attributes. The selection clause is evaluated for each object state. The result of this evaluation is the set of states for which the expression is true. Assume that GraphInt is an (historic) object, the expression:

```
GraphInt.interface@(belongs-to = ConfUnix AND creationdate < 93-
02 )
```

returns all the GraphInt interface states belonging to ConfUnix and created before February 93 (creationdate is an inherited attribut for any object).

The language has been extended with functions. Basic aggregate functions (first, last, min and max) are provided in standard, users can define their own functions. The expression

```
GraphInt.interface@(last | belong-to = ConfUnix AND creationdate
< 93-02)
```

returns the most recent GraphInt interface state contained in ConfUnix before february 93

3.3 Annotations

Recently, process support in SEE introduced more emphasis on historic services. Monitoring, assessing, evaluating processes need extended historic services. This is because the information to keep is not necessarily related with immutable attribute changes. Suppose we are interested in recording the access to a module, the number of activities having a copy of an object and so on. We need to record information concerning the use and behavior of an object, not only its changes. This is not new, the history mechanism of SCCS includes such an annotation mechanism, containing the comments, date and authors information and recorded on the occurrence of event check-in. This is far to be sufficient.

Annotations can be represented by attributes in the state definition as for instance the Check-in comment. However, this approach leads to confuse the object definition if different kinds of information are to be recorded, and creates performance problems (stored historic information may be huge).

An annotation is a piece of information associated with an object or a state. This information is independent of the object properties. It is associated to activity execution on which the objet participated.

Annotations are represented in the model as objects, and an annotation instance looks like a state. However, annotations are special characteristics: (1) they have only immutable attributes (the recorded facts); (2) there is not *revision_of* relationship between successive records and (3) "current state" is a meaningless concept. Annotations are typed, an annotation types looks like object types, but are all subtype of the root type "*annotation*". An annotation has an identifier built from the name of the associated object, followed by "#" symbol and the annotation type.

```
1 TYPE Consult IS Annotation ;
2    date := !date ;
3    author := !author ;
4    Comment COMP = STRING := READ () ;
5    ON read (x) DO RECORD (x) ;
END Consult ;
```

This is the definition[1] (1) of the *Consult* annotation type. Lines (2,3,4) define the information to record (*!date* and *!author* are built-in attributes meaning current date and current user). Line (5) is a trigger which expresses that a new *Consult* record must be associated to an object x (*RECORD (x)*), each time x is read i.e. each time event *read (x)* is true[2]. Each *Consult* record will contain the *date* the *author* and a *comment* dynamically requested to the author.

For all command, annotations will be considered as an historic object, in particular historic queries can be used in an homogeneous way:

```
GraphInt.interface#Consult@[t₁, t₂] (NUM | author = John) ;
```

This expression provides the number of time user john have read the *interface* of *GraphInt* between time t_1 and t_2.

States appear as a special case of annotation; they are simply the object implicit annotation. States are recorded implicitly each time an immutable attribute is modified: the state annotate the immutable attributes evolution.

Annotations subsume and generalize both the history and the revision concepts as found in usual SEE tools.

Our database looks like a set of parallel databases, one containing the objects and their state (the state annotation), and one for each annotation type. If fact GraphInt.interface@ti is a shortcut for GraphInt.interface#Interface@ti. If annotations are omitted, any query works as if no annotation (other than state) were existing, and with no computing overhead.

---

1. The syntax we use here is a relaxed syntax of the Adele system.
2. Triggers are out of the scope of this paper.

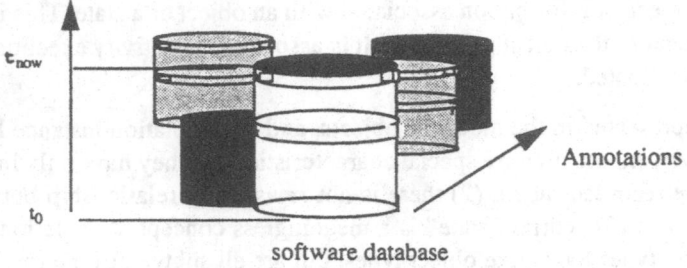

t_{now}

Annotations

t_0

software database

Figure 5 . The software object database and its associated annotation databases. It can be seen as specific annotations linked to an activity, a product, a user, etc.

3.4 Comparison and evaluation

Historical databases maintain *all* past and present data; entities are *temporal entities*, for example the salary-employee history, the student-record history, etc. Almost all works in this domain are limited to Relational Data Model, usually each relation is extended with attributes to represent time intervals [MP93], [GN93].

The main requirement in temporal databases is to query information concerning entities on the past. Most of these models distinguish between *valid time* and *transaction time*. The former represents the time a fact was observed in reality, while the latter indicates when the fact was recorded in the database. The temporal query language TQuel [Sno93] typically supports these two dimensions.

The control of the temporal dimension in SEE is underestimated; it is currently limited to revisions of files; files being the unique implicit immutable entities. Only some prototype databases provide extended versioning facilities. Our system allows to define, at model level, which are the attribute classes in relation with time and evolution, and thus how the system knows how to record and query.

In previous systems our 3 attribute classes were defined in different types. This was proved very powerful, but different types containing attributes were confusing for users. We expect this new definition will overcome this problem.

Annotation is our answer to: (1) how to generalize, record and store efficiently historic information, and (2) how to provide the traceability required in the PERFECT Esprit project (project No. 9090) for process improvement. Annotation have been recently implemented but we have no experience of its real use so far.

4 Logic Versioning

Historic versioning deals with the linear evolution of an entity; since RCS it is accepted that evolution makes evolve the same object simultaneously in different directions. For instance, the graphical interface evolves simultaneously to support X and Open_wind libraries.

If all these evolutions cannot fit in a single object instance, various *variants* of the same object will exist in parallel, each one corresponding to a logic variation.

The set of variants of an object is called a *versioned object*. Each element in the set is a variant and represents the same entity. Between two variants there are a *variant_of* equivalence relationship. *Variants* can only be distinguished when selecting a given point of view, called a *logic dimension*. In our example the logic dimension is the *graphic* point of view, represented by the *graphic* attribute; *system* is another dimension.

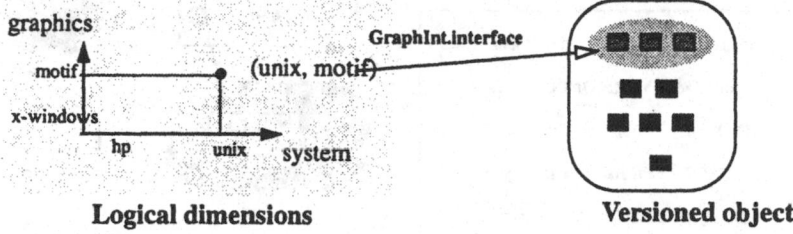

| Logical dimensions | Versioned object |

Figure 6 To access a set of instances into the generic object the domain function is an multidimensional space where each dimension defines a logical version of the object.

A *versioned object* is a *generic object* which can be seen as a function which *generates* objects given a parameter [Fav94]. The parameter is a *selection expression* which allows to find out specific instance(s). From this perspective, the function domain is a multi-dimensional space where each coordinate represents a choice, and the function co-domain is the set of objects.

4.1 Definition

In our model, a versioned object is a component of another object and an object may have several versioned components. Key-word VERSIONED is used to indicate that the value of an attribute is a versioned object. Basic attributes (integer, string, date,...) cannot be versioned.

Our example can be rewritten as follows.

```
TYPE Module IS Object;
  specification: Document;
  documentation: set_of Document;
  interface: VERSIONED Interface;
END;

TYPE Interface IS Object;
```

```
COMMON
    system: {unix, hp, vms};
    graphics : {X11, Open_win};
    responsible : User;
MODIFIABLE
    belong-to : Conf ;
    bug-report : Document;
IMMUABLE
    header   : FILE;
    body : VERSIONED Realization;
END;
```

This definition makes clear that different *interface* for a module may exist, and that different *bodies* may exist for a given *interface*. Both modules and interfaces are versioned objects. Version nesting may be arbitrary.

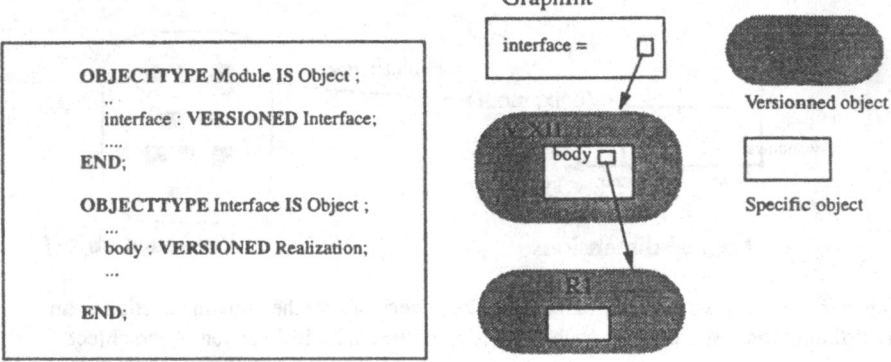

Figure 7 GraphInt.interface attribute is a reference to a generic object. Its value is a reference to a set of variants.

4.2 Retrieving variants

The database is queried using *path expressions* i.e. a *navigation* expression and a *selection* clause. Navigation allows instances to be reached starting from a set of instances and following a path through the graph, while the *selection* clause filters this set of instances for each navigation step.

Path expression are used, also, to reach versioned objects, for instance (figure 6) the expression GraphInt.interface is a reference to a versioned object, and GraphInt.interface.body references all bodies for the GraphInt object whatever the interface version.

The *selection* clause can be used to filter specific variants

```
GraphInt.interface (graphics = X11)
GraphInt.interface (graphics = X11).body (algo = min_memory)
```

A reference to a variant is a reference to an historic object[1], thus we can combine with historical queries. For example:

```
GraphInt.interface(system=unix and
                   graphics=motif)@(last | moddate < 10-10-94)
```

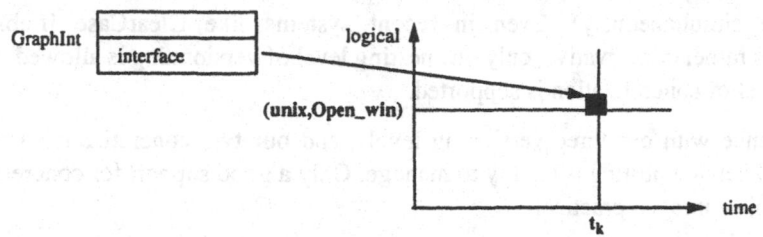

Figure 8 GraphInt.interface (systems= unix, graphics = Open_win)@t_K state.

An object is said to be composite-versioned, if it contains a versioned attribute; conversely an object is said composite-specified, if it does not contain any versioned attribute, or if each versioned attribute is reduced to a single element. The process which generates an specific object from a composite-versioned object is called *concretization*.

Building configurations is a process which concretizes all composite-versioned objects found when computing the transitive closure of set of relationships. A configuration thus concretizes one level of versionning, another configuration step may be needed to concretize embedded composite-versioned objects, until all levels of versionning are concretized: we have a fully concretized configuration.

4.3 Evaluation and comparison

In [Sci91] and in [Wie93] are presented two different object-oriented versioned data models. In both models, cooperative versionning is not taken into account and there is not distinction between historic and logic versionning. The [Sci91] model allows multi-dimensional versioning and arbitrary version nesting. The versioning model allows applications to provide semantics to versions by means of parameterized selection predicates. The same concept of version is used to model immutable properties and variants. Thus, for a given object, only one component can be versioned.

The [Wie93] model proposes extensions for the modelling of version families. This model involves the use of partial objects, i.e., objects where some attributes are bound to a value. A class may define different partial objects; all instances of that class whose attributes match the bound value pertain to that partial object family. The same family concept is used to model revisions and variants.

In SEE, versionning is most often SCCS-like. No commercial system propose (yet) multidimensional versioning and arbitrary nested versioning. In the COV system

---

1. If its type contains immutable attributes.

[MLG⁺93] all the versionning is logical, any change produces the creation of a new binary dimension (an option). The lack of historic versionning along with the large number of dimensions make the (prototype) system complex.

It is not surprising in that context that configuration selection is not very well advanced. The Adele system proposes a static three nesting levels of versionning (similar to our example), but only two level configuration steps (the two first concretization steps being done simultaneously). Even in recent systems like ClearCase [Leb94], versioning is rather conservative, only one nesting level of versionning is allowed, and only one level of concretization is supported.

The experience with our three versioning levels, and our two concretization levels proved deep version nesting is uneasy to manage. Only a good support for concretization make this approach practical.

5 Cooperative Versioning

A SEE supports the production/maintenance of the software product. There is an increasing pressure to severely reduce the "time to market". It is no longer possible to work sequentially; parallel work must be possible.

Several trends of work tried to solve that problem, e.gr., Databases and SEE. Database community tried to relax the serialization constraints as found using classic ACID transactions. Advanced and exotic transaction models have been proposed [DBAV94]. For SEE, none of these propositions fit our requirements; this is because our transactions are very long (weeks, months) and because consistency, in collaborative work, has a very high level meaning, far above the read/write knowledge of the DBMS [MLG⁺93], [BSK94].

In SEE, the solution proposed by almost all systems is the Work Space (WS) concept[1]. A WS looks like a transaction, in that it supports an activity managing isolated objects. Protocols are (should be) provided to coordinate the changes done in concurrent otherwise isolated WSs (breaking thus the Atomicity and Isolation properties). These protocols are out the scope of this paper [BSK94], [God93], we concentrate only on the fact isolation between concurrent WSs and transparency must be provided [5].

5.1 Definition

Cooperative versioning is a versionning designed to solve the isolation and transparency requirements for concurrent work control.

Isolation means that changes performed in a workspace are "visible" only from the workspace; and conversely changes done in another workspace are not visible.

---

1. Some data base work, and notably the Orion system, proposed a concept of sub Database which looks like a Work Space, except it does not provide a File System representation.

Transparency means each activity must believe it works on the (only) real object.

If concurrent work is possible, the only solution is to provide each workspace transparently with a different version of the (changed) objects. Suppose activity A_1, created at time t_i, and A_2, created at time t_j, share an (historic) object O. A_1 and A_2 updated O adding new states, and A_1 created a relationship between X and O.

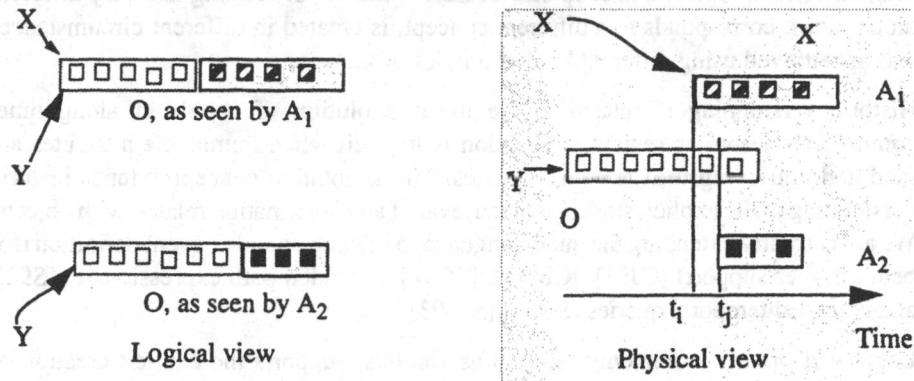

Figure 9 Each activity works on the O object independently. The cooperative versions are created dynamically and create for each activity the illusion of managing the unique real object O

The SEE knows if the current activity is executing in a workspace; if so, cooperative versioning is automatically applied to all objects managed by that activity. Cooperative versioning creates transparently a "cactus" branch as soon the activity changes the object. To a cactus branch is associated a "filtering" information allowing all utilizations of the virtual object to behave in exactly the same way as with the unique real object; in particular deleted relationships (from or toward the object), changing the modifiable state attributes, and so on.

5.2 Evaluation

Cooperative work became an important topic in SEE, and particularly in Process Centered SEE (PCE). Current implementations are highly ineffective, or very partial, because no cooperative versioning is available at kernel level. Instead of working at the level of read/write transactions, we provide transparent versions, along with the integration of merging mechanisms.

The Adele Work Space manager is an example where cooperative versioning was simulated using the usual branch mechanism and an intensive use of triggers to compute dynamically the logical view, to create transparently the cooperative versions and so on. Unfortunately, we do not have currently cooperative versioning capabilities and many aspects of cooperative versioning cannot be simulated; the Work Space manager cannot implement fully isolation and transparency. It is the building our WS manager which clarified the needs for cooperative versionning. It is our belief that cooperative versioning, provided by the kernel, is mandatory to support cooperative work properly.

6 Conclusion

Our long experience in SCM, as well as our research work in DB and process support showed that versioning is not an atomic concept. We identified three classes of versionning: historical, logical and cooperative. Each class of versionning has very different motivations, corresponds to a different concept, is created in different circumstances and, is retrieved using different kind of queries or services.

Historic versionning is related to the linear evolution of an object along time, commonly referred as revisions. Creation is implicit when immutable attributes are modified, retrieving uses temporal queries. The annotation concept extends historic versionning to the explicit storage and retrieval of any information related with objects. We are currently extending the query language to include complex event definition (for better trigger support) [GJ91], [CM91], [SG94], extended path expression [KKS92], and extended temporal queries [SG93],[Sno93].

Logic versionning, commonly referred as variants, supports the explicit creation of competing versions. We have extended the usual mechanism to multi-dimensional and multiple nested versionning. Creation is explicit, and queries are closely related to the concretization operation which lead to the creation of configurations, at different levels of binding (concretization). Extensions toward the support for any kind of "built object" is under way.

Finally cooperative versioning deals with cooperative work support. It provides the isolation and transparency properties to activities sharing object, while avoiding the duplication of information. Creation is transparent, retrieving is transparently related to the current activity, and provides the illusion of working alone on the object.

We do think these three versioning dimensions are all needed for a good support of SEE activities. It is clear that each one of these dimensions is currently ill supported, and that they are all subject to further research.

7 References

[adc90] "Aide-De-Camp, Product Overview,SMDS, P.O. Box 555 ". Technical report, 1990.

[BSK94] I.Z. Ben-Shaul and G. E. Kaiser. A paradigm for decentralized process modeling and its realization in the oz environment. In *Proc. of the 16th Int'l Conf. on Software Engineering*, Sorrento, Italy, May 1994.

[CM91] S. Chakravarthy and Deepak Mishra. Snoop: An expressive event specification language for active databases. Technical Report UF-CIS-TR-91-007, University of Florida, 1991.

[Cou89] W. Courington. *The Network Software Environment*. Sun Microsystems, Inc, 1989.

134

[CW93] M. Cagan and A. Wright. Untangling configuration management: Mechanism and methodoloy in cm systems. In *Proc, 4th International workshop on Software Configuration Management*, Baltimore, May 1993.

[DBAV94] D.Agrawal, J.L. Bruno, El Abbadi, and V.Krishnaswamy. Relative serializability: An approach for relaxing the atomicity of transaction. In *Proceedings of the ACM SIGACT/SIGMOD Symposium on Preinciples of DatabaseSystem*, pages 139–149, May 1994.

[EC94] J. Estublier and R. Casallas. *The Adele Software Configuration Manager*, chapter 4, pages 99–139. Trends in Software. J. Wiley and Sons, Baffins Lane, Chichester West Sussex, PO19 1UD, England, 1994.

[Est94] J. Estublier. The adele work space manager. Adele Technical Report, available bt ftp.imag.fr, July 1994.

[Fav94] J.M. Favre. Vers un support pour la maintenance et re-ingenierie globale des logiciels, 1994.

[GJ91] N. H. Gehani and H. V. Jagadish. Ode as an active database: Constraints and triggers. In *Proceedings of the 17th Conference on Very Large Databases, Morgan Kaufman pubs. (Los Altos CA), Barcelona*, September 1991.

[GN93] S. Gadia and S. Nair. *Temporal Databases: A Prelude to Parametric Data*, chapter 2, pages 28–66. Benjamin/Cummings, 1993.

[God93] C. Godart. Coo: A transaction model to support cooperation software developers COOrdinaton. In I. Sommerville and M. Paul, editors, *4th European Soft. Eng. Conference*, volume 717 of *LNCS*. Spring-Verlag, September 1993.

[Kat90] R. H. Katz. Toward a unified framework for version modeling in engineering databases. *ACM Computing Surveys*, 22(4):375–408, [12] 1990.

[KGW91] W. Kim, N. Ballou J.F. Garza, and D. Woelk. A distributed object-oriented database system supporting shared and private databases. *ACM Transactions on Information Systems*, 9(1):31–51, January 1991.

[KKS92] M. Kifer, W. Kim, and Y. Sagiv. Querying object-oriented databases. In M. Stonebraker, editor, *sigmod*, volume 21, pages 393–402, San Diego, California, June 1992. acm, Acm Press.

[LC88] D. Leblang and R. P. Chase. Parallel building: experience with a case for workstations networks. In *International Workshop on Software Version and Configuration Control*, Grassau, FRG, January 27–29 1988.

[Leb94] D. Leblang. *The CM Challenge: Configuration Management thats work*, chapter 1, pages 1–37. Trends in Software. J. Wiley and Sons, Baffins Lane, Chichester West Sussex, PO19 1UD, England, 1994.

[MLG+93] B.P. Munch, J.O. Larsen, B. Gulla, R. Conradi, and E.A. Karlsson. "Uniform Versioning: The Change-Oriented Model". In *in Proc. of the 4th International Workshop on Software Configuration Management*, Baltimore, Maryland USA, May 1993.

[MP93] A. Montanari and B. Pernici. *Temporal Reasoning*, chapter 21, pages 534–562. Benjamin/Cummings, 1993.

[Roc75] M. Rockhind. The source code control system. *IEEE Trans on Soft. Eng.*, SE-1(4):364–370, Dec 1975.

[Sci91] E. Sciore. Multidimensional versioning for object-oriented databases. *Proc. Second International Conf. on Deductive and Object-Oriented Databases*, December 1991.

[SG94] K. Dittrich S. Gatziu, A. Geppert. The samos active dbms prototype. Technical Report TR-94-16, Zurich University, 1994.

[Sno93] R. T. Snodgrass. *An Overview of TQuel*, chapter 6, pages 141–182. Benjamin/Cummings, 1993.

[Tic82] W.F. Tichy. Design, implementation, and evaluation of a revision control system. In *Proc. of the 6th Int'l Conf. on Software Engineering*, Tokyo, Japan, September 1982. IEEE Computer Society.

[Wie93] D. Wiebe. Object-oriented software configuration management. In *Proc. of 4th Int'l Workshop on Software Configuration Management*, Baltimore, Maryland, USA, May 1993.

Process Session

Jacky Estublier

SCM is often defined as "the discipline of controlling and supporting product, teams and activities...", or "the control of the evolution of families of systems". In both (and most other) definitions, the software process aspect is explicitly mentioned. For a number of aspects, including change control, status accounting, work space control and collaboration control, an SCM tool IS a software process tool.

Two series of questions arise when contemplating the relationships between SCM and process support. (1) What kind of process support is needed for SCM and (2) What is the relationship between SCM and general purpose Process support tool.

1 What kind of process support is needed.

The SCM5 attendance was primarily interested in this question. There is a large consensus, including SCM designers and vendors, that SCM must include, in one way or another, some process support. This is a major change in relationship with previous workshops, where most industrials consided this topic as academic.

It seems to be agreed, by most of the attendance that, ideally, all the SCM processes should be explicit, defined in a high level language easy to understand and to customize.

The current state of practice is pretty far away from this ideal. Current tools have either nothing, or barely a product state life cycle, most processes, like change control, being predefined and inflexible.

There was no consensus on how process support should be provided, or which paradigm is better suited for SCM (Rule, imperative, active base,...). State of practice considers almost only a state transition diagram approach (i.e. the product state life cycle). This is interesting, but far from being sufficient. There is a clear need for deeper knowledge and understanding of software process technology. This topic should be much more elaborated in future workshops.

2 What relationship with general process support

Since SCM (should) includes process support, and since modern environments will rely on general purpose process support, how will both process supports cooperate. Different scenarios have been proposed, and attendants tried to indicate what is their solution.

The SCM tool ignores other process support tools.

Almost all vendors are in this category.

The SCM tool relies on an existing and independent process support tool.

This solution looks promising, but since there is almost no satisfactory process support tool available on the market today, this solution is not (yet) practical. It could, in the future, be a good solution.

The SCM tool IS the process support tool of the environment.

More exactly, if the process support provided by the SCM tool is general enough, it could be used as a general purpose process tool. The difficulty is that general process support involves many difficulties usually not found in SCM applications; the SCM tool may become too big and complex. The Adele system is in this category.

The SCM tool provides a layer on top of which process support tools can be built.

Different prototype SCM systems are investigating this possibility, Epos (Conradi, see his paper in this session), COO (Godart, see his paper in next session), as well as the Adele product (Estublier). The authors are all advocating that the SCM system should provide a layer with services for work space management, including advanced transaction management features (for cooperation control). The "low" level aspects, related with product and work space are managed by the SCM tool, all other services by another process tool. In this approach, many SCM processes are supported by the general process tool.

In this session, many discussions focused around the Work Flow and CSCW (Computer Supported Cooperative Work) tools. Discussion centred on the meaning of these words, the functionalities of these tools and around the interest (or not) to include such aspects in an SCM system. This topic is open.

3 Conclusion

Most think the major challenge for future SCM tools will be the process support dimension. In the future, it is expected an SCM tool will be selected based on its ability to support processes. The current state of practice is pretty far away from ideals.

The conclusion of this session was certainly that industrials think they need much more understanding of the process dimension. The "best" paradigm to use, the kind of support to provide, how far to go in process support is a hot topic for vendors.

The second topic attracted the interest of academic people. The openness to other process tools, how process support tools can interoperate, the architecture of a CASE environment, the place of SCM in a process centred environment are topics of interest, with many open issues.

This workshop was the first one with an explicit process support session. No doubt it will not be the last.

A Rationale for
Automated Configuration Status Accounting

Juha Viskari, KONE Elevators
P.O.Box 677, 05801 Hyvinkää, Finland / Juha.Viskari@hat-fi.kone.com

Abstract. Configuration status accounting has been traditionally considered to perform the recording and reporting tasks within CM. We discuss the motivations for extending it with support for project control activities, and lay down requirements for integrating it with a software engineering environment that provides mechanisms for process integration.

1 Introduction

The discipline of controlling a product and its components over the whole life-cycle of the product is called *configuration management*, CM [1], [2]. CM is responsible for

- the unique identification of the components within the product structure,
- auditing and reviewing the product completeness and conformance to contract requirements and organization standards,
- controlling changes to the product both during development and maintenance,
- *configuration status accounting*, CSA, traditionally seen as consisting of recording and reporting the information which results from applying other configuration management functions and which is needed for managing the product, formed of *configuration items*, CIs, effectively [1], [10], [2].

Over the last years, research and tool development in the field of CM have mainly focused on the management of component versions and builds, derivations of component versions resulting from various types of processing by tools [4]. New CM concepts are needed for e.g. industrial-scale production of custom-tailored embedded systems. It differs from the traditionally supported development time CM in that the number of variants of the complete product can be magnitudes greater. This is mainly due to the fact that every delivery can be unique. The new concepts pose new questions to be answered by CSA, thus increasing its importance. Such tools that assist in software life-cycle activities, including CM, as an integrated whole, have been available a relatively short time. The current trend among these tools is towards the support of all stages of software creation and evolution, and the possibility to integrate own methods and tools. *Software engineering environments*, SEEs, are tools that provide an integrated set of runtime facilities and tools to support the whole software life-cycle, providing an access to a repository database, a common user interface, and means for integrating new interoperable tools [11].

This paper aims at laying a rationale for rising the integration level of a SEE by enhancing the process model with CSA. As a part of this, we want to motivate the use of CSA also as a means for automating product control. We do not try to provide an all-encompassing SEE solution including a database and sophisticated tool integration mechanisms, but rather to provide such a process integration approach which allows easy and effective use of existing tools within controlled processes.

2 CSA as a Mediator between CIs and CM Processes

2.1 Need for change management

The changes implied by the need for maintenance can be performed in a controlled manner only if we know exactly what we are going to change and when. From CM point of view, this establishes a fundamental need for *product control*. An absolute prerequisite for it is that we have means for *monitoring and measuring product state*.

We want to suggest that it is CSA which could be exploited for both of these purposes more effectively than what traditionally has been done. In our view, CSA places itself between different CM processes taking a dualistic role in managing CIs. Firstly, it monitors CI status changes that result from various activities within processes, thus providing valuable information as input for human decision processes. Secondly, supposing that we have a rigidly refined rule set for specifying how and when some activity may change the status of a CI, we could apply CSA as an automated process that uses its own measurement information to implement product control processes.

2.2 The recording and reporting aspect

The recording and reporting activities of CSA focus on monitoring the status values and status changes of CIs, being able to provide useful information both for the whole project and for individual project members. After the planning phase, a project should move to a state where controlled and argumented adjustments of the schedule and resourcing are possible. For achieving this, project management needs reliable information about progress in the project. That is, it must have means for collecting the status of each work activity, as well as summing up the information and comparing it with existing plans. When a project has lots of members, it may not always be straightforward to grasp the current state of work with respect to progress in the near future. CSA reports could point out possible bottlenecks in resourcing. If or when resourcing problems occur, the project management must be able to argue why more resources are needed. Of course, a pure statistical report about the state of a project cannot tell *why* the project is late, but it can point out *where* the problems are. A project member needs to be aware of the current status of all CIs to be produced, as well as capable of preparing the right material for reviews and audits. Usually several people's activities are intertwined in such a way that they must be able to follow how the others are proceeding.

In practice, the reporting activities of CSA are rarely performed because of the labor intensity of the process. Also the diversity of the groups causes that the reports produced would have to be available in various forms and tailored to the different users' needs.

2.3 The change request process

Change requests (CRs) are commonly used for tracing the histories of proposed and implemented changes. We regard a CR as an object that has two-way connections to product CIs. Also the status evolution of related CRs and CIs is dependent. Falkenberg [3] even considers CRs as the only objects that are subject to CSA.

A *CR process* is needed for receiving incoming CRs, making decisions about the actions that they cause, and maintaining pending, active, and completed CRs. It is important not to lose the connections between CRs and the corresponding CIs, because they are the link that connects the two major CM processes. A formalized CR process is given in [6].

Related to the change request process, among others following questions might arise for CSA to be answered:

- What is the status of proposed and approved changes dealing with a certain piece of software?
- What design decisions and modifications in them have lead to a certain implementation solution or change in it?
- What is the list of all updates that must be made?
- Which CIs were affected when a given fault was corrected? Which CRs were generated because of it?

The organ that is responsible for managing the CR process inside a project is called *configuration control board* (CCB) [1]. It has the required knowledge for making decisions about pending CRs, changes to be made, but it requires information about such things like

- given a CR, are there any related CRs, or has the proposed change been already implemented,
- when a certain change can be implemented,
- in which components a CR has caused changes, or
- what earlier changes there have already been in a certain component.

E.g. [8] identifies the need for automating change management.

2.4 The product control aspect

We may as well consider the version control process from the point of view of automated product control. The motivation for this is enlightened by considering concurrence taking place in software processes [9]. The separate activities performed by individual project members are tied together by means of various forms of concurrence control. Most modern version control tools provide facilities for preventing unintended simultaneous updates to the same version of a CI [4]. In addition to those services, an integrated SEE should provide support for controlling process-related project standards, like preventing writing an implementation before accepted design documentation. CSA comes into picture in that it is capable of retrieving the status values of CIs to be used as pre- and postconditions for processes and activities. CSA extended with product control capabilities could prevent both premature modifications of such CIs that first require the acceptance of modifications to earlier CIs, and unintended simultaneous changes to a CI outside the control of a CM tool. Status reporting that is based on progress in software processes contains what is the current status of work as well as what events have occurred so far, when and in which processes or project phases. It also makes it possible to examine the product status with respect to work activities and resourcing.

3 Augmenting SEE integration with automated CSA

Our SEE philosophy [7] is based on automating the software processes following the idea of SEE integration through process integration [9]. Our work so far has consisted of creating a general model for defining software development projects. This models is based on the idea that every project consists of consecutive and concurrent process phases. Their hierarchy and contents can be specified generally for the whole project and specifically for each project member. Every phase exists to produce some intermediate result of the whole product. In addition to phase and product structure, various tools are needed for achieving the required output. The SEE framework consists of the project modelling concepts and a tool that can be used for generating customized SEEs to be used by project members. By a customized SEE we mean a specific instance of the SEE tool providing a personal environment for use. Customization itself means careful planning of project policies and goals and their formal modelling in a tool-understandable form, which is easily modifiable when the project proceeds.

In general, there are several ways and levels for enabling SEE customization [5]. One of them, integration by common tool access, provides a common user interface and standardized means for accessing the tools, but no higher data or message integration. In our work we have consciously wanted to stay on this integration level. This is because we have wanted to achieve the ease of integration of tools and processes without having to make any modifications to the tools themselves [7]. This is especially important when we are speaking of small projects that cannot afford either replacing their tool set completely or spending effort on developing new interfaces for their tools.

The process support facilities of a mechanism that provides only the basic means for tool usage are rather limited in the sense of integrating tools to form a consistent and interoperable environment. The approach we want to take is to combine CSA and process control in order to raise the common tool access integration on a higher level without committing ourselves to some external tool architectures - or forcing the users to adopt their tools to solutions that should be internal to our SEE only.

Our approach, therefore, makes a clear distinction between the roles of the SEE and the tools integrated to each customized environment. The tools are needed for taking the responsibility of the actual work to be performed. The SEE exists for assisting in coordinating the work within the project and acting as a platform for individual project members for organizing and performing the work conveniently.

In order to derive the real benefit from CSA, we need concepts for integrating it as a seamless part of our process-based SEE framework. It raises following questions to be formally answered, work which will be our interest in the future:

- What are the objects that can carry status? How are the product structure and process phases reflected?
- How do we define status values for these objects, what are the internal structures of the status values, and how do they change?
- How can we use status values for helping in the enactment of processes?
- How could we integrate CSA as a part of some measurement system, i.e. how could we collect and what kind of information that originates from status changes and the behavior of processes?

As a summary of the requirements and possibilities for utilizing CSA, we would like to highlight some of the activities that could be automated. They include:

- Making summaries from the current progress of the project (like "x% complete") without a need to have a special CM database with related query capabilities.
- Support for automatic product construction especially in initialization phases, e.g. through template usage support
- Making a snapshot of the current project state: freezing all currently dynamically and statically bound object references in an environment configuration that can later be used for one-to-one restoring of the project state.
- Process control in the form of access and concurrence control on a higher abstraction level than what the operating system can provide, as well as in the form of using status changes as postconditions that trigger specified activities. This kind of support approaches tool integration paradigms based on message passing.
- Integrating the CR process as a part of other software engineering activities, providing traceability between product components and related CRs, and supporting the activities of the CCB.

Our intention is to study more thoroughly these kinds of possibilities of automated CSA on the way to realizing it in practice.

4 References

[1] Buckley, F.J., Implementing Configuration Management. IEEE PRESS / IEEE Computer Society Press. New York, NY 1993. 249 p.

[2] Dart, S.A., The Past, Present, and Future of CM. Technical report CMU/SEI-92-TR-8. Software Engineering Institute. Pittsburgh, PA 1992. 28 p.

[3] Falkenberg, B., Configuration Management for a Large (SW) Development. Proceedings of the 2nd International Workshop on Software Configuration Management. Princeton, NJ 24.10.1989. Software Engineering Notes 17(1989)7, p. 34-37.

[4] Feiler, P.H., Configuration Management Models in Commercial Environments. Technical report CMU/SEI-91-TR-7. Software Engineering Institute. Pittsburgh, PA 1991. 54 p.

[5]   Forte, G., In Search of the Integrated Environment. CASE Outlook 3(1989)2, p. 5-12.

[6]   Lacroix, M. and Lavency, P., The Change Request Process. Proceedings of the 2nd International Workshop on Software Configuration Management. Princeton, NJ 24.10.1989. Software Engineering Notes 17(1989)7, p. 114-117.

[7]   Laine A. and Viskari J., UISER - a Customizable Software Engineering Environment for Development-in-the-Large. Proceedings of Euromicro 92. Paris 14.-17.9.1992. Microprocessing and Microprogramming 35(1992)1-5, p. 505-512.

[8]   Lehman, M.M., Software Engineering, the Software Process and Their Support. Software Engineering Journal 6(1991)5, p. 243-258.

[9]   Mi, P. and Scacchi, W., Process Integration in CASE Environments. IEEE Software 9(1992)2, p. 45-53.

[10]   Sprague, K., The Role of Software Configuration Management in a Measurement-Based Software Engineering Program. ACM SIGSOFT Engineering Notes 16(1991)2, p. 62-66.

[11]   Terry, B. and Logee, D., Terminology for Software Engineering Environment (SEE) and Computer-Aided Software Engineering (CASE). ACM SIGSOFT Software Engineering Notes 15(1990)2, p. 83-94.

Transaction Planning to Support Coordination

Patricia Lago[1], Reidar Conradi[2]

1 Introduction

Traditional transactions fulfill ACID[3] properties, and use strict access management policies to preserve data consistency. Software engineering transactions relax such properties to support cooperation and work independence: following strict serialization of accesses (e.g., using strict locking), work would be delayed and hindered. On the other hand, with relaxed accesses (e.g., using temporary parallel version histories of shared components, and delegating conflict resolution to late merge), the amount of conflicts would explode in untraceable independent version histories, rendering later merge almost impossible. Furthermore, traditional database applications are simple (read and write operations), pre-programmed and short, while software engineering applications are interactive, long-lasting, and depend on many factors, like human creativity, data- and team- complexity, and parallel work of development teams, which often follow loosely coupled work procedures.

Careful planning is therefore needed to find out a balanced approach that allows flexible development, and still keeps consistency. In this work, data access and cooperative work problems are viewed from an organizational viewpoint. Project activities are mapped on a hierarchy of transactions, which forms the basis where to perform planning.

The paper focuses on the partitioning step of the planning process: Initial partition represents the formal base for planning, and helps in avoiding potential conflicts. Impact analysis helps in detecting and solving un-expected conflicts, and accordingly reorganizing work. The language to specify transaction intentions is also described, and impact analysis application is sketched out.

---

1. Dipartimento di Automatica e Informatica, Politecnico di Torino, I-10129 Torino, Italy, Phone: +39 11 564.7008, Fax: +39-11-564.7099, Email: patricia@athena.polito.it.
2. Department of Computer Systems and Telematics, Norwegian Institute of Technology, N-7034 Trondheim, Norway, Phone: +47 73 594485, Fax: +47 73594466, Email: conradi@idt.unit.no.
3. (A)tomicity, (C)onsistency, (I)solation, (D)urability.

2 The planning process

The planning process is a management activity usually performed by project managers, that states costs and time constraints on an up-starting or already running project, (re)organizes work breakdown and resource allocation, and enables cooperation among teams of developers that possibly work concurrently (see [4]).

The planning process can be refined into three main steps: partition, schedule, and cooperation protocol definition (see [1]). *Partition*, after an initial breakdown of a project into sub-activities, performs impact analysis based on data ownership and access. Impact analysis calculates the set of data objects transactions overlap by, and minimizes the possibility of conflicting accesses. Depending on results, activity breakdown is re-organized. *Schedule* states when activities are to be executed. Transactions may be: Serial (e.g., $t1;t2$, where $t2$ relies on $t1$'s work); Parallel and overlapping (e.g., $t1 \mid t2$ where temporary work on replicated versions is allowed, and later merge is needed); Parallel and independent (e.g., $t1|t2$, where work is completely disjointed and no conflict may arise, i.e., no merge is required); Cooperating (e.g., $t1 \Leftrightarrow t2$, where work is run in parallel and proper communication ensures that no conflicts arise). The best suited schedule depends on both time and work context, as we will see in the example of section 5. *Cooperation protocol definition* chooses the way activities cooperate. Cooperation is defined by a set of high-level communication patterns (suitable for a more high-level, project management view), refined into low-level cooperation protocols (using low-level transaction mechanisms to implement patterns).

The planning process has a twofold advantage: First, it helps in coordinating team activities, by means of proper data access and activity partition. Second, is represents a means to tackle conflict avoidance, detection, and resolution.

The purpose of the presented work is to give formal support to project partition. We use transaction technology to support project enaction: i.e., project activities are mapped onto transaction hierarchy, and data structure is partitioned to it. We have developed a language to model intentions of planned future transactions. This language is called TiDL (Transaction-intention Description Language). TiDL specifications are textual, and specify each transaction that is part of a certain software process. TiDL specifications are stored in EPOSDB: Schema entities and relationships represent information needed to perform automatic impact analysis. I.e., build impact sets and possible solutions. The complete planning process has been deeply described in [1].

3 Partition and TiDL

The information needed to map project activities onto a hierarchy of transactions, is:

Structure: determining for each project activity the properties and number of transactions enacting it, transaction schedule and hierarchy;

Data access: the part of the data model (i.e., which data objects) each transaction intends to work on, and the access rights the transaction grants to perform that work;

Cooperation policy: the role that each transaction will have w.r.t. the whole transaction hierarchy, i.e., the interconnection with other transactions, the most suitable execution mechanism.

These information must be specified into the transaction model (or plan), in order to perform impact analysis and partitioning.

3.1 TiDL

TiDL is a language for defining properties of and pre-declaring work intentions for a (sub-)transaction, i.e., a project (sub-)activity. TiDL specifications are declarative, and their purpose is to define in advance which objects will or may be accessed, and at the same time to supply project managers with a high level view they are used to. In fact, TiDL represents the bridge between high level project description and low level computerized support for project execution.

```
TRANSACTION t1                    /* (mandatory) Unique within parents sub-tree */
PROPERTIES
        OWNER programmer          /* (mandatory) user name or role */
        DURATION 2                /* {1=eternal|2=user|3=session} */
        NR_SESSIONS 1
        TIME_STAMP 011195         /* starting time */
        STATE 1                   /* (mandatory) {1=planned|2=activated} */
STRUCTURE
        ft_parent:  develop       /* parent trans. name */
CONTEXT
    AMBITION                      /* --------- versioning space ----- */
        SET ... : value           /* options and boolean value */
      CHOICE
        SET ... : value           /* options and boolean value */
    PROD_ROOT /eposdb/p1          /* ---------- product space ------- */
    READ_SET                      /* for-each lock type, specify data objects */
        * : ... ;
    WRITE_SET                     /* for-each lock type, specify data objects */
        a.c, a.h, d.h : ... ;
END_TRANSACTION t1
```

Figure 1   TiDL specification of future transaction t1

The language covers part of the above listed mapping information, i.e., structure and data access (cooperation policy is currently under development). An example of TiDL specification is given in Figure 1.

First, transaction name and properties are defined: the owner is either the responsible person, or the role (if nobody is assigned yet); state is either planned (when the transaction is stored in EPOSDB), or activated (when it is running). In the last case, when stored in the database, the future transaction will be connected to the running transaction instance. Other properties are related to time schedule. Then, the position in the transaction hierarchy is given: in the example, transaction t1 is a child of transaction develop. The rest of transaction specification regards required data (i.e., the transaction work context): EPOSDB implements Change-oriented Versioning (CoV) (see [3]) for software configuration management: ambition (for write) and choice (for read) define the *version space*, and are described by a set of boolean *options*. Option values may be set to true, false, or unset. Version choice is a complete option binding (i.e., options are either true or false), and univocally states visible database version; version ambition may have unset options (defining a multi-version space), and states which database versions will be impacted by future modifications. The *product space* is defined by prod_root, along with read_set and write_set. For each product component, the access mode is given. In the example, t1 works on product subsystem p1 (version space specification is not detailed, for sake of simplicity): all components are included in the read-set, while three of them are included in the write-set. TiDL specifications available to users are *modular*: they are organized in textual files, each representing the information related to one transaction, and referring to the parent and to other entities by using relations. Since the language specifies work intentions, it is assumed that TiDL specifications can be modified until transactions activation. Specifications are stored in EPOSDB as entities and relationships. It is possible to reproduce TiDL specifications out of the database schema: comparing initial plans to those obtained by impact analysis, it is possible to acquire experience about changes involved during execution.

4 Impact analysis

In cooperative transactions, overlapping ambitions indicate that a potential conflict may happen. Two ambitions do not overlap if at least one common option is set to opposite values. Further, a conflict takes place if product spaces overlap too: i.e., if either the transactions modify the same object, or modify two different objects that have dependencies one to the other. In these cases, non-strict and commonly used solution is merge. Using CoV, textual (traditional) merge comes for free, while semantic merge is facilitated thanks to cooperative transactions pre-commit facility. Nevertheless, in complex data configurations, textual merge becomes very hard, while semantic merge does not ensure complete automatic consistency. Impact analysis reduces potential conflicts to minimum. When a planned future transaction has to be started, impact analysis is performed. The needed information can be obtained by the following calculations:

$$WS_i \text{ and } RS_i, \quad WS_i \subset RS_i$$

are respectively the read- and write- set of *Transaction$_i$*.

$$TC_i = \{ o_j \in RS_j \mid \exists\, o_i \in WS_i, \exists\, Rel(o_j, o_i),\ j \neq i \}$$

calculates the transitive closure TC_i of WS_i, by traversing the relevant relations in the reverse direction. TC_i contains all the objects impacted by the changes in WS_i.

$Rel(o_j, o_i)$ is the relationship connecting the two objects, and oriented from o_j to o_i.

$$IM_{ij} = TC_i \cap RS_j, \text{ where } i \neq j$$

is the impact set IM_{ij} of $Transaction_i$ on $Transaction_j$, and indicates which part of the read-set RS_j of $Transaction_j$ is impacted by the changes in the write-set WS_i of $Transaction_i$.

$$(IM_{ij} \cap WS_i) \rightarrow move \rightarrow WS_j$$

determines which components impacted by $Transaction_i$, and part of WS_i, should be moved to WS_j.

5 An example

This section presents an example of transaction planning: impact analysis is explained, and some rational about cooperation is given. Two different sub-projects (and corresponding transactions t1 and t2) under the same parent project, work on sub-configurations p1 and p2. We suppose that transaction t2 starts during transaction t1. Initial transaction product-space definitions are viewed in the TiDL specification fragments shown in Figure 2 .

```
(for t1)                              (for t2)
. . . . .                             . . . . .
PROD_ROOT /eposdb/p1                  PROD_ROOT /eposdb/p2
  READ_SET                              READ_SET
    * : ... ;                             * : ... ;
  END_READ_SET.                         END_READ_SET.
  WRITE_SET                             WRITE_SET
    a.c, a.h, d.h : ... ;                 s.c, s.h, b.c : ... ;
  END_WRITE_SET.                        END_WRITE_SET.
```

Figure 2 Example:TiDL specification fragments

The planning process (shown in Figure 3) takes place through the following steps (step numbers correspond to labels put on dotted arrows of Figure 3):

Step 0: TiDL specification of t1 and t2 are stored in the database as future_transaction entities.

Step 1: The work context for t1 is created according to specification. As the transaction is currently the only running one, no overlaps with other transactions work context exist.

Step 2: The user connected to the running transaction starts working.

Step 3: During t1 execution, as scheduled in plans, transaction t2 has to be started (i.e., t1 | t2). Impact analysis is performed to find out if overlaps with other running transactions (in the example with t1) exist. The results of impact calculations (refer to section 4) are:

$$RS_1 \cap RS_2 = \{p1.c, a.h, a.c, s.h, s.c, d.h, b.h\} \cap \{p2.c, s.h, s.c, b.c, b.h, d.h\} =$$

$$=\{s.h, s.c, d.h\}.$$

We do not have problems as long as no common data component is updated.

$$RS_1 \cap WS_2 = \{s.h, s.c\} \text{ and } RS_2 \cap WS_1 = \{d.h\}.$$

Certain operation sequences (e.g., t1:read, t2:write, t1:read) may lead to inconsistencies.

$$WS_1 \cap WS_2 = \varnothing.$$

We do not encounter any problem, as no write-write conflict is possible.

Thus, the only possible conflict can occur for non-serialized read-write operations. To find out the best work context partition we calculate the impact that the two transactions have each other (impact sets are included in the dotted groups in Figure 3):

$$IM_{12} = TC_1 \cap RS_2 = \{p2.c, d.h, b.h, b.c\}. \; IM_{21} = TC_2 \cap RS_1 = \{p1.c, s.h, s.c, a.c\}.$$

We notice that impact sets are large compared to product size. Further, they overlap with write-sets:

$$IM_{12} \cap WS_2 = \{b.c\} \neq \varnothing \quad \text{and} \quad IM_{12} \cap WS_1 = \{d.h\}$$

mean that t1's changes on d.h could impact t2 on b.c.

$$IM_{21} \cap WS_1 = \{a.c\} \neq \varnothing \quad \text{and} \quad IM_{21} \cap WS_2 = \{s.h, s.c\}$$

mean that t2's changes on s.h could impact t1 on a.c. Following the last rule in section 4, a possible choice to reduce the interconnection between transactions is to move d.h from WS_1 to WS_2, and $\{s.c, s.h\}$ from WS_2 to WS_1 (see objects drawn in black in Figure 3). Transactions' read-set remains stable, while write-sets are modified to:

$$WS_1 = \{a.c, a.h, s.c, s.h\} \quad \text{and} \quad WS_2 = \{b.c, d.h\}.$$

The result is that impact sets are limited to read-read conflicts, as $IM_{12} = \{p2.c, s.h, s.c\}$, $IM_{12} = \{p1.c, d.h, b.h\}$, and $IM_{12} \cap WS_2 = IM_{21} \cap WS_1 = \varnothing$.

Step 4: The best suited cooperation protocol is based on real-time communication, i.e., changes performed by each of the two transactions are immediately propagated to the other, and notification is sent to make the reading transaction aware of it.

Step 5: Transaction t2 can start working.

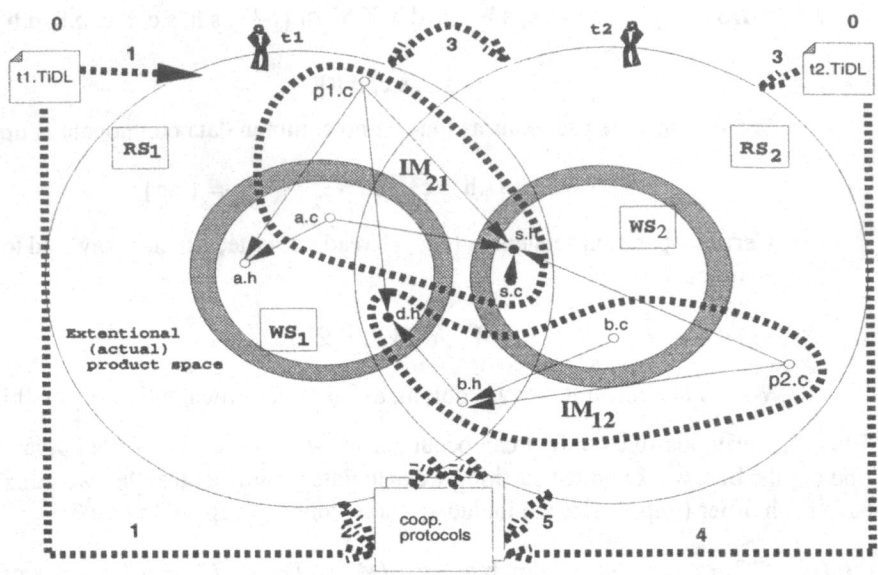

Figure 3 Example: Planning process

The achieved result is that read-write conflicts have been solved by organizing the work context in a better way, and by adopting the most suited communication pattern between overlapping transactions. Further, transaction schedule has been modified from $t1 \mid t2$ to $t1 \Leftrightarrow t2$. In the case where write-write conflicts cannot be removed by planning, i.e., $IM_{ij} \cap WS_i \neq \emptyset$, *for some* $i \neq j$, transactions must either run isolated and be followed by merge actions, or be scheduled to $t1 ; t2$. The presented approach exploits dependencies (relationships) between configuration components to perform impact analysis (e.g., to calculate transitive closure and impact set formulas, or to choose partition). Further work is to better exploit semantics of component dependencies (to refine impact analysis and visibility), and to investigate problems related to protocols integration. TiDL has to be enhanced with protocol definition, too.

References

1 R. Conradi, C. Liu, and M. Hagaseth. Planning Support for Cooperating Transactions in EPOS. *Information Systems*, page 22, 1995.

2 S. I. Feldman, editor. *Proceedings of the Fourth International Workshop on Software Configuration Management*, Baltimore, Maryland, May 21–22, 1993.

3 B. P. Munch, J. Larsen, B. Gulla, R. Conradi, and E. Karlsson. Uniform Versioning: The Change-Oriented Model. In [2].

4 D.D. Roman. *Managing Projects: A Systems Approach*. Elsevier Science Publishing Co., Inc., 1986.

Cooperation Session

Jacky Estublier

Cooperation implicitly means that the same object can be changed simultaneously by the cooperating activities. Until recently, SCM consided cooperation essentially by the technical side of the problem: "how to reconcile 2 simultaneous evolution of the same file". This is the problem of file merging. All SCM systems are now including a file merger, but merging is still a research topic. J. Buffenbarger in his paper "syntactic Software Merging", makes a very good overview of the current approaches and state of the art in merging techniques.

However, with the introduction of the software process dimension in SCM, cooperation must (also) be consided from a methodological point of view. What happens and what can be done to foster and control cooperation. But what is really cooperation.

C. Godart defined that "there is cooperation when people accept to provide intermediate results". Following this definition, cooperation refers to the definition and control of data interchange during long transaction. In SCM, long transactions are often highly related with Work Space control. For most authors cooperation is synonymous to inter Work Space data exchange.

This approach, considering cooperation as the definition and control of inter Work Space exchanges, is also represented in the paper from R. Conradi, in the previous session. In this session, C. Godart & all. tried to define more formal constancy properties between cooperative transactions. The authors insisting on the fact cooperation support has deep influence on the underlying environment architecture. This is probably why current SCM systems are pretty weak in this dimension.

This session was split up in two, fist we discussed the traditional merging topic, where no real progresses were made in the last years, and where practitioners seems to conform with the usual line merger.

The second half was dedicated to analyse the relationships between cooperation, as presented above, with concepts and mechanisms found in other domains as CSCW (Computer Supported Cooperative Work), DataBases, and Work Flow.

It was discussed in particular what is really CSCW and if it should be included in SCM systems. It was may be a conclusion of this session that these domains are addressing pretty much the same problem, with different point of view, and that we can envision an SCM system supporting CSCW and Work Flow services.

The other conclusion is that more work is needed to clarify concept and techniques for cooperation support. We still lack the ability to formally model collaboration, and the needed underlying mechanisms are still to define.

Syntactic Software Merging

Jim Buffenbarger

buff@cs.idbsu.edu

Boise State University

Abstract. Software merging is the process of combining multiple existing versions of a source file, to produce a new version. Typically, the goal is for the new version to implement some kind of union of the features implemented by the existing versions. A variety of merge tools are available, but software merging is still a tedious process, and mistakes are easy to make. This paper describes the fundamentals of merging, surveys the known methods of software merging, including a method based on programming-language syntax, and discusses a set of tools that perform syntactic merging.

1 Introduction

Software is often developed as a set of items, where each item records the development history of a single file. For example, an item might record the important versions of a particular source file. Multiple versions of a file must be maintained to record changes and support variants.

When a file has variants, they are developed concurrently, perhaps for different hardware configurations or mutually exclusive features. A change made to one variant of a file must often be made to other variants of the same file. Such changes can be accomplished by editing one of the variants and merging it with each of the other variants.

A programmer can merge variants manually or with the help of a merge tool. This paper is concerned with traditional and experimental methods of merging variants of a source file.

1.1 Terminology

A software component's *source code* is the form of the component that a person would prefer to change first, when modifying the component. A *source file* is a file containing source code.

Software is developed and maintained as a set of named items. Conceptually, an *item* is a directed acyclic graph associated with a file. Each of an item's nodes is a *version* (aka, a revision) of the file. Each of an item's arcs denotes succession from one version to another. An item's name is typically derived from that of its associated file.

A version is immutable. When a version requires a change, a successor is created. When a version requires multiple concurrent changes, a successor can be created for each change, thereby creating *branches*. Versions of an item on different branches are *variants*.

When a variant requires a change that has already been made to another variant, a successor can be created by *merging* variants. A programmer can use a text editor to copy changes from one variant to another. A file-comparison tool can help, by locating differences. Alternately, a merge tool can locate and sometimes select differences, based on the nearest common ancestor of the contributor variants. When a difference cannot be selected automatically, a conflict is reported. A conflict may produce a message or require programmer interaction.

As with medical-test results, a merge-conflict indication may be correct, false positive (i.e., a semantic conflict is reported but none exists), or false negative (i.e., a semantic conflict exists but none is reported). A false-positive result is preferred to a false-negative result, since the former is easily resolved at merge time, while the latter may not be discovered until the program is translated or tested.

Figure 1 illustrates a simple three-way merge of two variants of a C program. Version p is a common ancestor of variants a and b. Version p reads ten numbers into an array. Version a modifies p to compute and write the mean of the numbers. Version b modifies p to compute and write the maximum of the numbers. Version q is the result of the merge: it computes and writes both the mean and the maximum of the numbers.

In subsequent sections, versions from Figure 1 are also used to illustrate various methods of merging.

1.2 Software Merging is Difficult

Although merge tools are helpful, merging remains a tedious and error-prone task.

> A merge tool is a very useful component of a software engineering environment, but it should not be trusted blindly. Even if the tool registers no conflicts, the result of the merge operation should be carefully reviewed. [75]

> Existing merge tools are either very crude, or very sophisticated but of limited applicability. [36]

> Integrating programs via textual comparison and merging operations is accompanied by numerous hazards. [25]

1.3 Merge Methods

Merge methods can be organized into a taxonomy, as follows. The methods are listed in order sophistication (i.e., difficulty of implementation).

Cut-and-Paste Merging A programmer can merge changes manually, using a text editor.

```
#include <stdio.h>
#define SIZE 10

void Read(int a[], int size)
{
  int i;
  for (i=0; i<size; i++)
    (void)scanf("%d",&a[i]);
}

main()
{
  int a[SIZE];
  Read(a,SIZE);
  return 0;
}
```

```
#include <stdio.h>
#define SIZE 10

void Read(int a[], int size)
{
  int i;
  for (i=0; i<size; i++)
    (void)scanf("%d",&a[i]);
}

void WriteMean(int a[], int size)
{
  int i;
  float sum=0;
  for (i=0; i<size; i++)
    sum+=a[i];
  (void)printf("%f\n",sum/size);
}

main()
{
  int a[SIZE];
  Read(a,SIZE);
  WriteMean(a,SIZE);
  return 0;
}
```

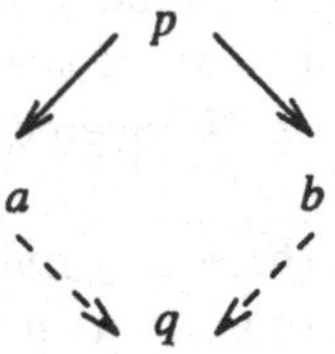

```
#include <stdio.h>
#define SIZE 10

void Read(int a[], int size)
{
  int i;
  for (i=0; i<size; i++)
    (void)scanf("%d",&a[i]);
}

void WriteMax(int a[], int size)
{
  int i;
  int max=0;
  for (i=0; i<size; i++)
    max=(a[i]>a[max]) ? i : max);
  (void)printf("%d\n",a[max]);
}

main()
{
  int a[SIZE];
  Read(a,SIZE);
  WriteMax(a,SIZE);
  return 0;
}
```

```
#include <stdio.h>
#define SIZE 10

void Read(int a[], int size)
{
  int i;
  for (i=0; i<size; i++)
    (void)scanf("%d",&a[i]);
}

void WriteMean(int a[], int size)
{
  int i;
  float sum=0;
  for (i=0; i<size; i++)
    sum+=a[i];
  (void)printf("%f\n",sum/size);
}

void WriteMax(int a[], int size)
{
  int i;
  int max=0;
  for (i=0; i<size; i++)
    max=(a[i]>a[max]) ? i : max);
  (void)printf("%d\n",a[max]);
}

main()
{
  int a[SIZE];
  Read(a,SIZE);
  WriteMean(a,SIZE);
  WriteMax(a,SIZE);
  return 0;
}
```

Fig. 1. An example merge.

Text-Oriented Merging A tool can try to use the result of character-string comparisons on the contributor versions, to determine and merge changes.

Operation-Oriented Merging A tool can try to use information recorded during the development of the contributor versions (e.g., editor commands), to create a merged version.

Syntax-Oriented Merging A tool can try to use the result of parse-tree comparisons on the contributor versions, to determine and merge changes.

Semantics-Oriented Merging A tool can try to understand the behavior of the contributor versions, to create a merged version.

Each method is discussed in a section below. The focus of this paper is syntax-oriented merging, so it is discussed last. Syntax-oriented merging is proposed as a reasonable compromise between desirability, practicality, and tractability.

2 Cut-and-Paste Merging

In its simplest form, cut-and-paste merging is what a programmer does when a merge tool is unavailable, inappropriate, or inconvenient.

Referring to the version names in Figure 1, a programmer decides which of version a and b is the best initial version q. This decision is based on the programmer's prediction of whether most conflicts will be resolved in favor of a or b. If q is to be more like a than b, the programmer should start with a copy of a rather than a copy of b (and vice versa). Assuming the initial q is a copy of a, the programmer then begins editing b and q concurrently, repeatedly performing the following steps.

1. A region of b is copied to some buffer.
2. A (possibly empty) region of q is deleted.
3. The buffer's content is inserted in q, at the deletion point.

Referring to versions in Figure 1, q can be created from a copy of a by copying the definition (and call) of `WriteMax()` from b into q after the definition (call) of `WriteMean()`.

Cut-and-paste merging seems very primitive. However, conditional-inclusion mechanisms, which are provided by many compilers and assemblers, lead to this kind of merging [47]. The most well-known conditional-inclusion mechanism is probably the `#ifdef` directive of C and C++. For example, consider the following fragment.

```
#if   PLATFORM == SYSV
      /* code for SYSV    */
#elif PLATFORM == BSD
      /* code for BSD     */
#elif PLATFORM == MSDOS
      /* code for MSDOS   */
#elif PLATFORM == MAC
      /* code for MAC     */
```

```
#else
      /* code for generic */
#endif
```

The first four comments represent platform-specific variants of source code, while the last comment represents a platform-independent variant. However, the SYSV and BSD platforms are both UNIX, so a change to the SYSV-specific code often suggests a change to the BSD-specific code. A programmer would typically accomplish a multiple-platform change by "typing it in" for one platform and copying it to other platforms. This is essentially cut-and-paste merging. Surprisingly, programmers typically believe that conditional-inclusion mechanisms avoid merging, since all variants are already in one file. Not surprisingly, some organizations have banned conditional inclusion [22].

3 Text-Oriented Merging

Text-oriented merging assumes that each variant comprises a sequence of lines or characters.

Typically, each variant is assumed to comprise a sequence a lines. Lines are considered to be atomic: a line is either exactly the same as, or completely different from, another line (whitespace or character-case differences may be ignorable); only whole lines are replaced; and different lines are never combined into a single line. Line-oriented merging is implemented by the vast majority of merge tools, including those provided by: SCCS [56], RCS [69] [67], EMACS [60], DSEE [32] [33] [34] [37], and CLEARCASE [2] [3].

Less frequently, each variant is assumed to comprise a sequence a characters. This method is sometimes implemented by change-file or context-diff tools, and is discussed below as context-oriented merging.

3.1 Line-Oriented Merging

A typical line-oriented merge requires a common ancestor p and two variants a and b, as in Figure 1. When a difference is detected among the variants, the ancestor's content sometimes allows the correct variant's content to be chosen automatically.

First, a three-way text comparator partitions each version into a sequence of n regions. Each version has the same number of regions. The comparator determines n and the content of each region. A version's regions are not necessarily of the same length, corresponding regions of each version are not necessarily of the same length, and a region may have zero length. An example of a three-way text comparator is the UNIX program diff3. An algorithm is presented in [44].

After the versions are partitioned into regions, they can be merged according to Figure 2 and the algorithm shown below.

```
for i:=1 to n
    if p[i]=a[i] and p[i]=b[i] then q[i]:=p[i]
    if p[i]=a[i] and p[i]#b[i] then q[i]:=b[i]
    if p[i]#a[i] and p[i]=b[i] then q[i]:=a[i]
    if p[i]#a[i] and p[i]#b[i] then q[i]:=conflict(a[i],b[i])
```

Figure 3 shows a partition and merge of the versions in Figure 1. In this example, $n = 5$, regions 2 and 4 in version p are empty, and version q contains conflicts at regions 2 and 4.

The UNIX program **merge** constructs a q similar to that of Figure 3. However, **merge** also highlights the conflicting regions by bracketing them with conspicuous lines. Because of the conflicts, **merge** returns an indication of failure.

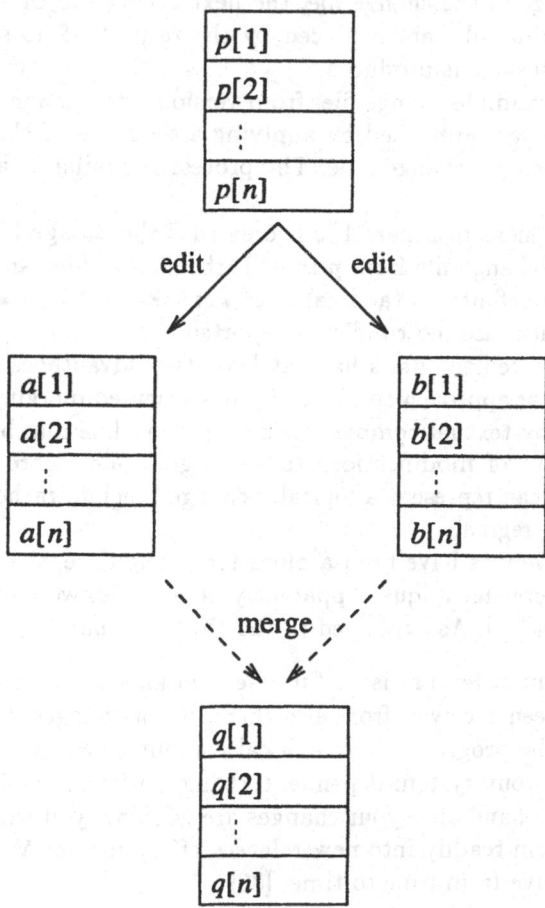

Fig. 2. A textual merge.

3.2 Context-Oriented Merging

Context-oriented merging is implemented by change-file or context-diff tools. Change files are primarily used for version control, but the technique also supports merging.

A *change file* records changes made to an *original file*. Each change is stored as a replacement pair comprising text to delete and text to insert, called the *from* part and *to* part (respectively).

There are two kinds of change file tool. One kind applies a change file to an original file producing a *changed file*, and perhaps a conflict message. The other kind creates a change file from an original file and a changed file.

When a change file is applied to an original file, its changes are applied in sequence. The first change is applied starting at the beginning of the original file, the second change is applied starting after the replacement performed by the first change, and so on. Only one pass is made through the original and change file. For each change in the change file, the next occurrence of the *from* part is located in the original file, and replaced by the *to* part. If no such occurrence exists, a conflict message is produced.

Figure 4 is an example change file, from version p to version a of Figure 1.

A merge can be accomplished by applying a sequence of change files to an original file, producing a changed file. The process is similar to a UNIX pipeline of filters.

Referring to versions in Figure 1, q is created if the change file from p to b is applied before the change file from p to a. If the change files are applied in the opposite order the definitions (and calls) of WriteMean() and WriteMax() are transposed. In either case, no conflict is reported.

Change-file replacement pairs have at least two advantages over the three-way text-comparator approach employed by line-oriented merging. A change-file change is located by textual comparison, rather than line number, so a change file is often tolerant of modifications to its original file. More importantly, a change-file change can represent a logically changed region, rather than just the physically changed region.

Although change files have been around for a long time, they can hardly be called a popular merge technique. Apparently, change files were first used as part of the WEB system [31]. As explained in the WEB manual:

> This dual-input feature is useful when working with a master WEB file that has been received from elsewhere, when changes are desirable to customize the program for your local computer system. You will be able to debug your system-dependent changes without clobbering the master WEB file; and once your changes are working, you will be able to incorporate them readily into new releases of the master WEB file that you might receive from time to time. [30]

Change files are part of at least two other large projects. Hewlett-Packard's printer laboratories use them for interproject firmware merging. Austin Kyoto Common Lisp (AKCL) uses them to avoid modification of its Kyoto Common

```
#include <stdio.h>
#define SIZE 10

void Read(int a[], int size)
1 {
   int i;
   for (i=0; i<size; i++)
     (void)scanf("%d",&a[i]);
  }

main()
3 {
   int a[SIZE];
   Read(a,SIZE);
   return 0;
5 }
```

```
#include <stdio.h>
#define SIZE 10

void Read(int a[], int size)
1 {
   int i;
   for (i=0; i<size; i++)
     (void)scanf("%d",&a[i]);
  }

void WriteMean(int a[], int size)
2 {
   int i;
   float sum=0;
   for (i=0; i<size; i++)
     sum+=a[i];
   (void)printf("%f\n",sum/size);
  }

main()
3 {
   int a[SIZE];
   Read(a,SIZE);
4  WriteMean(a,SIZE);
   return 0;
5 }
```

```
#include <stdio.h>
#define SIZE 10

void Read(int a[], int size)
1 {
   int i;
   for (i=0; i<size; i++)
     (void)scanf("%d",&a[i]);
  }

void WriteMax(int a[], int size)
2 {
   int i;
   int max=0;
   for (i=0; i<size; i++)
     max=(a[i]>a[max]) ? i : max;
   (void)printf("%d\n",a[max]);
  }

main()
3 {
   int a[SIZE];
   Read(a,SIZE);
4  WriteMax(a,SIZE);
   return 0;
5 }
```

$$p$$
$$a \qquad b$$
$$q$$

```
#include <stdio.h>
#define SIZE 10

void Read(int a[], int size)
1 {
   int i;
   for (i=0; i<size; i++)
     (void)scanf("%d",&a[i]);
  }

void WriteMean(int a[], int size)
  {
   int i;
   float sum=0;
2a for (i=0; i<size; i++)
     sum+=a[i];
   (void)printf("%f\n",sum/size);
  }

void WriteMax(int a[], int size)
  {
   int i;
   int max=0;
2b for (i=0; i<size; i++)
     max=(a[i]>a[max]) ? i : max;
   (void)printf("%d\n",a[max]);
  }

main()
3 {
   int a[SIZE];
   Read(a,SIZE);
4a WriteMean(a,SIZE);
4b WriteMax(a,SIZE);
   return 0;
5 }
```

Fig. 3. A textual-merge partition.

```
Usage \n@s[Original text\n@s|Replacement Text\n@s]
Anything not between '\n@s[' and '\n@s]' is a comment.

****Change:(orig (10 10 a))
@s[     (void)scanf('%d',&a[i]);
}


@s|     (void)scanf('%d',&a[i]);
}

void WriteMean(int a[], int size)
{
  int i;
  float sum=0;
  for (i=0; i<size; i++)
    sum+=a[i];
  (void)printf('%f\n',sum/size);
}


@s]

****Change:(orig (14 14 a))
@s[  int a[SIZE];
  Read(a,SIZE);

@s|  int a[SIZE];
  Read(a,SIZE);
  WriteMean(a,SIZE);

@s]
```

Fig. 4. An example change file.

Lisp (KCL) code base, which is philosophically similar to how they are used in WEB.

The change-file technique is equivalent to the combination of UNIX's **diff** and Larry Wall's **patch** commands.

Change files are similar in concept to the "change sets" supported by AIDE DE CAMP [42]. In AIDE DE CAMP, a version is a sequence of change sets, which is applied to a base file to produce a changed file.

Change files also seem to be similar in concept to "change-oriented" versioning [35], where operations on a relational database of text fragments can construct or reconstitute a desired variant.

4 Operation-Oriented Merging

Operation-oriented merging is still in the research stage. The technique requires each item to be annotated with the sequence of editor operations or transformations comprising its actual development history. Two variants of an item are merged by applying their two operation sequences, in an interleaved fashion, to the initial version. A conflict occurs when a pair of interleaved operations are not commutative. Operation-oriented merging is described in [36].

Referring to the versions in Figure 1, and assuming that the each operation inserted an entire function definition or call, conflicts would be detected in two places. The first conflict occurs where both new function definitions would be inserted; the second at the location for both new function calls.

This approach is limited to specialized development environments. Since typical text editors do not store editing operations with the files they edit, operation-oriented merging is impractical for many large projects, where developers inherit an existing code base and development occurs in a heterogeneous environment [22].

5   Semantics-Oriented Merging

Semantics-oriented merging is also still in the research stage. The technique attempts to detect and compare the semantic differences between contributing variants and their common ancestor. Two versions are semantically different if, starting from the same initial state, they compute final states that differ in the value of at least one variable. Two semantic differences interfere if they involve the same variable. If two variants are produced by two changes to the common ancestor, and the two associated semantic differences do not interfere, the variants can be merged.

A project that attempts to implement semantics-oriented merging is described in [25], [55], [54], and [76]. Semantics-oriented merging is (in general) undecidable, so a "safe approximation" based upon program-dependence graphs and program slices is used to "integrate" programs. In the following two quotations, variable names have been changed for consistency.

> This paper concerns an algorithm for this operation; it provides the foundation for building a language-based program-integration tool. The integration algorithm takes as inputs three programs A, B, and P, where A and B are two variants of P; whenever the changes made to P to create A and B do not "interfere" in a certain sense, the algorithm produces a program that integrates A and B. [55]

> As for interference criterion, we assume that any change to version A or B that could lead to a behavior different than that of P is significant and must be preserved in the integrated program. [55]

Referring to the versions in Figure 1, p and a are semantically different because a produces output and p does not. Likewise for p and b. Clearly, "input" and "output" must be considered as part of the initial and final states. The two semantic differences involved interfere, since they both involve the "output" variable. Consequently, the variants cannot be merged.

Semantics-oriented merging relies on inputs being partitioned into named components [25]. An editor or programmer must establish and maintain these names. Furthermore, the current methods for semantics-oriented merging apply only to a significantly restricted programming language.

While this algorithm provides a strong foundation for solving the program-integration problem, it is not yet applicable to real programming languages. We are currently extending the algorithm to handle languages with arrays, pointers, and procedures. [55]

6 Syntax-Oriented Merging

Syntax-oriented merging is a compromise between the simplicity of line-oriented merging and the complexity of semantics-oriented merging. During a syntax-oriented merge, each variant is parsed, and a variant's syntactic structure determines its partition of regions (regions are discussed in Section 3.1). Regions are then selected from the variants to form a merge result.

Syntax-oriented merging can be accomplished at several levels of granularity. For example, in C, a merge can occur at the level of tokens, statements, blocks of statements, or external declarations. External declarations are the "unit of merge" in the merge tool described below, for several reasons:

- External declarations are the unit of abstraction in C, so a programmer is typically interested in potential conflicts at this level. For example, if two statements conflict, a programmer usually needs to consider the whole function definition containing them. Other approaches to variant management recognize this [47] [22].
- External declarations are already named, so region deletion and rearrangement is easily recognizable. Furthermore, a conflict report is very concise, listing source-code identifiers rather than conflicting text. A programmer reading the conflict report immediately understands the logical location of each conflict. Other approaches to "smart" merging require a special editor that assigns "tags" to regions [74] [25]. Such tags have no meaning to a programmer.
- Concurrent changes tend to affect different declarations [13].

One approach to syntax-oriented merging is described in [74] and [73], where abstract syntax trees are merged, and the approach is called structure-oriented merging. The technique is language independent, as long as the language has syntax for alternatives, lists, and structures. This approach uses tags to identify tree nodes. The tags must be maintained by a special editor.

> The price we pay is that all edit operations have to be performed within our environment. [74]

In addition, cut-and-paste operations (i.e., region rearrangements) are not currently supported, because tags are serial numbers rather than source-code identifiers.

6.1 A Syntax-Oriented Merge Tool

As part of this research, a syntax-oriented merge tool is being implemented for
C. It performs the following:

1. scans and parses each of its inputs into a set of named declarations (e.g.,
   variable declarations and function definitions)
2. compares the name sets
3. compares declarations with the same name, textually
4. (if necessary) compares declarations with the same name, as token sequences

Assuming the contributor files in Figure 1 are named p.c, a.c, and b.c, a
syntactic merge is accomplished with the following UNIX command.

```
$ cmerge -fileBase p.c -file1 a.c -file2 b.c -fileResult q.c
```

For Figure 1, the command above produces the following conflict report.

```
main: differs in p.c, a.c, and b.c
```

The output file is constructed to contain Read(), WriteMean(), WriteMax(),
and main(). The output main() is the result of executing a text-oriented merge
tool on the three input versions of main().

6.2 Some Implementation Details

Although C declarations are named, the language has more than one name space.
This small problem is solved by prefixing a declaration's name with the name of
its name space. For example, in the fragment

```
struct x;
struct x1 { int a; int b; };
struct x2 { int a; int b; } sx2;
struct x3 { int a; int b; } sx31,sx32;
struct x4 sx4;
struct x5 sx51,sx52;
main() { return; }
```

the nine declarations are named struct:x, struct:x1, sx2, sx31, sx32, sx4,
sx51, sx52, and main. Other kinds of C declaration are processed analogously.

Before the actual merge, each input is partitioned into a table of named
external declarations. The structure of this table is described, bottom-up, in the
paragraphs below. The notation is borrowed from VDM [27].

A Decl is a record representing an external declaration (a postfix asterisk
denotes a list and curly braces denote an enumeration).

```
Decl =
    name:    DeclName
    kind:    DeclKind
    tokens:  TokenValue*      # e.g., "int", "x", ",", "y", ";"
    file:    File
    lineBeg: Natural
    lineEnd: Natural
    colBeg:  Natural
    colEnd:  Natural

DeclName =   String           # e.g., "x,y"

DeclKind =   {
    "declaration",
    "function definition"
}

TokenValue = String           # e.g., "total"

File =       String           # e.g., "foo.c"
```

A declaration's **File** is recorded to facilitate management of preprocessor file inclusion. A declaration's beginning and ending location in a file (i.e., its region) is recorded to allow a text-oriented comparison and (if necessary) a text-oriented merge to be performed. Note that each **TokenValue** comes from a file created by preprocessing a source file, but its region in the actual source file must be maintained for text-oriented operations. The region of a **TokenValue** includes any preceding whitespace, comments, and preprocessor directives.

Each of an input's declarations are stored in a table, keyed on a name constructed for the declaration.

```
ExtDeclTab =  ExtDeclName => Decl

ExtDeclName = String                  # e.g., "x"
```

Once an external declaration table is constructed for each input, their key sets are compared to detect added or removed declarations. A declaration added to, or removed from, only one variant is included in the output. Declarations corresponding to names in the intersection of two key sets are compared for textual equality and, if necessary, token equality. Textual equality is just character-string equality. Token equality is tested by performing pairwise character-string comparisons of the two declarations' **tokens** fields.

If corresponding declarations from the two variants are text and token equal, either variant's declaration can be output. If they are only token equal, one variant's declaration must be chosen (e.g., for whitespace, comments, and preprocessor directives); the tool arbitrarily outputs the declaration from the variant corresponding to the -file1 option. If they are text and token unequal, they, and the corresponding declaration from the common ancestor, are merged with UNIX's merge. An interesting alternative would be to merge the token sequences, but the practical value of token merging has not yet been investigated.

7 Conclusion

Software merging is a difficult task that deserves sophisticated tool support. This paper has presented five methods for software merging: cut-and-paste, text-oriented, operation-oriented, syntax-oriented, and semantics-oriented merging. This section argues that syntax-oriented merging is the best compromise between capability and complexity.

7.1 Comparison to Cut-and-Paste Merging

Cut-and-paste merging is immediately discounted as a method without tool support.

7.2 Comparison to Text-Oriented Merging

Text-oriented merging comes in two flavors. Here, they are called line-oriented and context-oriented merging. The inadequacy of both flavors of text-oriented merging can be demonstrated by the production of an uncompilable merge result from compilable merge inputs, without the detection of a conflict. This merge-conflict indication is a false-negative, which is the worst kind of incorrectness (false-negatives are discussed in Section 1.1).

Consider the merge in Figure 5. Version a adds a call to f2(), while version b removes all trace of f2(). Version q is constructed according to the algorithm of Section 3.1, and is uncompilable. UNIX's merge (i.e., a line-oriented merge) produces this output regardless of interchanging a and b. AKCL's merge (i.e., a context-oriented merge) produces this output if the change file for a is applied first. If the change file for b is applied first, function f2() is deleted, but a conflict is detected in function main(). Essentially, algorithms for text-oriented merging are biased toward insertions rather than deletions.

A syntax-oriented merge of the input versions in Figure 5 produces a result containing the definitions of functions f1(), f2(), and f3(); but a conflict is reported for the definition of function main(). To most programmers, this behavior is correct. They want a merge tool to operate according to the following rules.

- Do not remove an external declaration unless a and b both remove it.
- If a and b both change an external declaration, report a conflict. At worst, this merge-conflict indication is a false-positive, which is the preferred kind of incorrectness (false-positives are discussed in Section 1.1).

```
#include <stdio.h>

int f1()
{
  int x=1;
  return x;
}

int f2()
{
  int x=2;
  return x;
}

int f3()
{
  int x=3;
  return x;
}

main()
{
  printf("%d\n",f2());
  printf("%d\n",f3());
}
```

```
#include <stdio.h>

int f1()
{
  int x=1;
  return x;
}

int f2()
{
  int x=2;
  return x;
}

int f3()
{
  int x=3;
  return x;
}

main()
{
  printf("%d\n",f2());
  printf("%d\n",f3());
  printf("%d\n",f2());
}
```

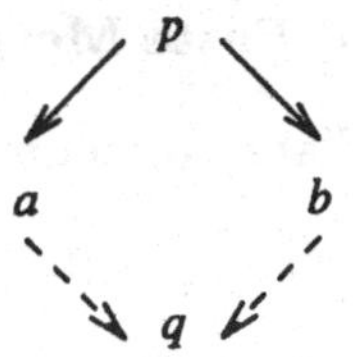

```
#include <stdio.h>

int f1()
{
  int x=1;
  return x;
}

int f3()
{
  int x=3;
  return x;
}

main()
{
  printf("%d\n",f3());
}
```

p

a b

q

```
#include <stdio.h>

int f1()
{
  int x=1;
  return x;
}

int f3()
{
  int x=3;
  return x;
}

main()
{
  printf("%d\n",f3());
  printf("%d\n",f2());
}
```

Fig. 5. A text-oriented merge problem.

One can argue that context-oriented merging could recognize the conflict, regardless of the order of application of change files. The trick would be to manually construct a single change whose *from* part includes both the definition and call of function f2(). However, this trick requires programmers to edit change files rather than source files. Such an approach has been used in practice, but it is not recommended.

To summarize, syntax-oriented merging has several advantages over text-oriented merging:

- A merge is not disrupted by differences caused by whitespace and comments.
- Differences caused by declaration deletion or rearrangement are recognized as such.
- Conflicts are identified by declaration name, rather than by listing the conflicting text. Thus, conflict reports are more concise and comprehensible.
- Conflicts are identified at an appropriate level of abstraction.

7.3 Comparison to Operation-Oriented Merging

Operation-oriented merging requires a specialized development environment, where editing operations are recorded and stored with source files. This requirement is much too restrictive for real software-development projects. For example, a programmer should not be forced to use a particular text editor. Syntax-oriented merging places no special demands on the development environment.

7.4 Comparison to Semantics-Oriented Merging

Semantics-oriented merging is very intriguing. Potentially, it is the most accurate method of merging. However, programs that try to understand other programs tend to stay in research laboratories. Semantics-oriented merging is not ready for industrial use, and it may never be. In contrast, syntax-oriented merging is much easier to implement than semantics-oriented merging. It allows real programs, written in real programming languages, to be merged.

References

1. E. Adams, W. Gramlich, S. Muchnick, and S. Tirfing. SunPro: Engineering a practical program development environment. In *Lecture Notes in Computer Science 244*. Springer-Verlag, 1986.
2. Atria, Inc. *ClearCase Concepts Manual*, 1992.
3. Atria, Inc. *ClearCase Reference Manual*, 1992.
4. W. Babich. *Software Configuration Management*. Addison-Wesley, 1986.
5. N. Belkhathir and J. Estublier. Protection and cooperation in a software engineering environment. In *Lecture Notes in Computer Science 244*, pages 221–229. Springer-Verlag, 1986.

6. N. Belkhathir and J. Estublier. Experience with a database of programs. In *Proceedings of the Software Engineering Symposium on Practical Software Development Environments*, pages 84–91. ACM, 1987.

7. E. Bershoff, V. Henderson, and S. Siegel. *Software Configuration Management*. Prentice-Hall, 1980.

8. V. Berzins. On merging software extensions. *Acta Informatica*, 23:607–619, 1986.

9. G. Boudier, F. Gallo, R. Minot, and I. Thomas. An overview of PCTE and PCTE+. In *Proceedings of the Software Engineering Symposium on Practical Software Development Environments*, pages 248–257. ACM, 1988.

10. G. Clemm. The Odin specification language. In *Lecture Notes in Computer Science 244*. Springer-Verlag, 1986.

11. G. Clemm. *The Odin System*. PhD thesis, University of Colorado, Boulder, 1986.

12. G. Clemm. The Workshop system: A practical knowledge-based software environment. In *Proceedings of the Software Engineering Symposium on Practical Software Development Environments*, pages 55–64. ACM, 1988.

13. G. Clemm. Replacing version-control with job-control. In *Proceedings of the Second International Workshop on Software Configuration Management*, pages 162–169. ACM, 1989.

14. E. Cohen, D. Soni, R. Gluecker, W. Hasling, R. Schwanke, and M. Wagner. Version management in Gypsy. In *Proceedings of the Software Engineering Symposium on Practical Software Development Environments*, pages 201–215. ACM, 1988.

15. S. Dart. Spectrum of functionality in configuration management systems. Technical Report CMU/SEI-90-TR-11, Software Engineering Institute, 1990.

16. S. Dart, R. Ellison, P. Feiler, and A. Habermann. Software development environments. *IEEE Computer*, 20(11):18–28, 1987.

17. V. Donzeau-Gouge, G. Huet, G. Kahn, and B. Lang. Programming environments based on structured editors: The MENTOR experience. In *Interactive Programming Environments*, pages 128–140. McGraw-Hill, 1984.

18. J. Estublier. Configuration management: The notion and the tools. In *Proceedings of the International Workshop on Software Version and Configuration Control*. IEEE, 1988.

19. J. Estublier. A configuration manager: The Adele database of programs. In *Workshop on Software Engineering Environments for Programming-in-the-Large*, pages 140–147, 1988.

20. P. Feiler and R. Medina-Mora. An incremental programming environment. *IEEE Transactions on Software Engineering*, pages 472–482, September 1981.

21. C. Fraser and E. Myers. An editor for revision control. *ACM Transactions on Programming Languages and Systems*, pages 277–295, April 1987.

22. W. Gentleman, S. MacKay, D. Stewart, and M. Wein. Commercial realtime software needs different configuration management. In *Proceedings of the Second International Workshop on Software Configuration Management*, pages 152–161. ACM, 1989.

23. A. Habermann and D. Notkin. Gandalf: Software development environments. *IEEE Transactions on Software Engineering*, 12(12):1117–1127, 1986.

24. P. Heckel. A technique for isolating difference between files. *Communications of the ACM*, pages 264–268, April 1978.

25. S. Horwitz, J. Prins, and T. Reps. Integrating noninterfering versions of programs. *ACM Transactions on Programming Languages and Systems*, pages 345–387, July 1989.

170

26. J. Hunt and T. Szymanski. A fast algorithm for computing longest common subsequences. *Communications of the ACM*, pages 350–353, May 1977.
27. C. Jones. *Systematic Software Development Using VDM*. Prentice-Hall, second edition, 1990.
28. G. Kaiser, P. Feiler, and S. Popovich. Intelligent assistance for software development and maintenance. *IEEE Software*, pages 40–49, May 1988.
29. B. Kernighan and D. Ritchie. *The C Programming Language*. Prentice-Hall, 1988.
30. D. Knuth. *The WEB System of Structured Documentation*.
31. D. Knuth. Literate programming. *Computer Journal*, pages 97–111, 1984.
32. D. Leblang and R. Chase. Computer-aided software engineering in a distributed workstation environment. *ACM SIGPLAN Notices*, pages 104–112, May 1984.
33. D. Leblang and R. Chase. The Domain software engineering environment for large-scale software development efforts. In *Proceedings of the First International Conference on Computer Workstations*. IEEE, 1985.
34. D. Leblang and R. Chase. Parallel software configuration management in a network environment. *IEEE Software*, pages 28–35, November 1987.
35. A. Lie, R. Conradi, T. Didriksen, E. Karlsson, S. Hallsteinsen, and P. Holager. Change oriented versioning in a software engineering database. In *Proceedings of the Second International Workshop on Software Configuration Management*, pages 56–65. ACM, 1989.
36. E. Lippe. Operation-based merging. In *Proceedings of the Fifth Symposium on Software Development Environments*, pages 78–87. ACM, 1992.
37. D. Lubkin. Heterogeneous configuration management with DSEE. In *Proceedings of the Third International Workshop on Software Configuration Management*. ACM, 1991.
38. B. Mack-Crane and A. Pal. Conflict management in a source version management system. In *Proceedings of the Second International Workshop on Software Configuration Management*, pages 149–151. ACM, 1989.
39. A. Mahler and A. Lampen. An integrated toolset for engineering software configurations. In *Proceedings of the Software Engineering Symposium on Practical Software Development Environments*, pages 191–200. ACM, 1988.
40. A. Mahler and A. Lampen. Shape: A software configuration management tool. In *Proceedings of the International Workshop on Software Version and Configuration Control*, pages 228–243. IEEE, 1988.
41. A. Mahler and A. Lampen. Integrating configuration management into a generic environment. In *Proceedings of the Software Engineering Symposium on Practical Software Development Environments*, pages 229–237. ACM, 1990.
42. Software Maintenance and Development Systems. Aide de Camp. Product Overview, 1992.
43. K. Marzullo and D. Wiebe. Jasmine: A software system modeling facility. In *Proceedings of the Software Engineering Symposium on Practical Software Development Environments*, pages 121–130. ACM, 1986.
44. E. Meyers. An $O(ND)$ difference algorithm and its variations. *Algorithmica*, 1(2):251–266, 1986.
45. T. Miller. A schema for configuration management. In *Proceedings of the Second International Workshop on Software Configuration Management*, pages 26–29. ACM, 1989.
46. W. Miller and E. Meyers. A file comparison program. *Software: Practice and Experience*, 15(11):1025–1040, November 1985.

47. K. Narayanaswamy. A text-based representation for program variants. In *Proceedings of the Second International Workshop on Software Configuration Management*, pages 30–37. ACM, 1989.

48. D. Notkin. The Gandalf project. *Journal of Systems and Software*, pages 91–105, May 1985.

49. W. Obst. Delta technique and string-to-string correction. In *Lecture Notes in Computer Science 289*, pages 64–68. Springer-Verlag, 1987.

50. D. Parnas. Designing software for ease of extension and contraction. *IEEE Transactions on Software Engineering*, 5(2):128–137, March 1979.

51. D. Perry. Version control in the Inscape environment. In *Proceedings of the Ninth International Conference on Software Engineering*, pages 142–149. IEEE, 1987.

52. J. Plaice and W. Wadge. A new approach to version control. *IEEE Transactions on Software Engineering*, 19(3):268–276, March 1993.

53. S. Reiss. Pecan: Program development systems that support multiple views. *IEEE Transactions on Software Engineering*, 11(3):276–285, March 1985.

54. T. Reps and T. Bricker. Illustrating interference in interfering versions of programs. In *Proceedings of the Second International Workshop on Software Configuration Management*, pages 46–55. ACM, 1989.

55. T. Reps, S. Horwitz, and J. Prins. Support for integrating program variants in an environment for programming in the large. In *Proceedings of the International Workshop on Software Version and Configuration Control*, pages 197–216. IEEE, 1988.

56. M. Rochkind. The source code control system. *IEEE Transactions on Software Engineering*, pages 364–370, December 1975.

57. G. Ross. Integral C: A practical environment for C programming. In *Proceedings of the Software Engineering Symposium on Practical Software Development Environments*, pages 42–48. ACM, 1986.

58. R. Schwanke and G. Kaiser. Living with inconsistency in large systems. In *Proceedings of the International Workshop on Software Version and Configuration Control*. IEEE, 1988.

59. I. Simmonds. Configuration management in the PACT software engineering environment. In *Proceedings of the Second International Workshop on Software Configuration Management*, pages 118–121. ACM, 1989.

60. R. Stallman. *GNU Emacs Manual*. Free Software Foundation, 6.18 edition, 1987.

61. D. Swinehart, P. Zollweger, R. Beach, and R. Hagman. A structural view of the Cedar programming environment. *ACM Transactions on Programming Languages and Systems*, October 1986.

62. R. Taylor, F. Belz, L. Clarke, L. Osterweil, R. Selby, J. Wileden, A. Wolff, and M. Young. Foundations for the Arcadia environment architecture. In *Proceedings of the Software Engineering Symposium on Practical Software Development Environments*, pages 1–13. ACM, 1988.

63. T. Teitelbaum and T. Reps. The Cornell program synthesizer: A syntax directed programming environment. *Communications of the ACM*, pages 563–573, September 1981.

64. W. Teitelman. A tour through Cedar. *IEEE Transactions on Software Engineering*, 11(3):285–302, March 1985.

65. W. Teitelman and L. Masinter. The Interlisp programming environment. *IEEE Computer*, 14(4):25–33, April 1981.

66. W. Tichy. Software development control based on module interconnection. In *Proceedings of the Fourth International Conference on Software Engineering*, pages 29–41. IEEE, 1979.

67. W. Tichy. Design, implementation, and evaluation of a revision control system. In *Proceedings of the Sixth International Conference on Software Engineering*, pages 58–67. IEEE, 1982.

68. W. Tichy. The string-to-string correction problem with block moves. *ACM Transactions on Computer Systems*, pages 309–321, November 1984.

69. W. Tichy. RCS: A system for version control. *Software: Practice and Experience*, 15(7):637–654, July 1985.

70. W. Tichy. Tools for software configuration management. In *Proceedings of the International Workshop on Software Version and Configuration Control*, pages 1–20. IEEE, 1988.

71. H. van Vliet. *Software Engineering: Principles and Practice*. Wiley, 1993.

72. W. Waite, V. Heuring, and U. Kastens. Configuration control in compiler construction. In *Proceedings of the International Workshop on Software Version and Configuration Control*, pages 228–243. IEEE, 1988.

73. B. Westfechtel. Revision control in an integrated software development environment. In *Proceedings of the Second International Workshop on Software Configuration Management*, pages 96–105. ACM, 1989.

74. B. Westfechtel. Structure-oriented merging of revisions of software documents. In *Proceedings of the Third International Workshop on Software Configuration Management*, pages 68–79. ACM, 1991.

75. D. Whitgift. *Methods and Tools for Software Configuration Management*. Wiley, 1991.

76. W. Yang. *A New Algorithm for Semantics-Based Program Integration*. PhD thesis, University of Wisconsin, 1990.

About some relationships
between configuration management, software
process
and cooperative work: the *COO* Environment

C. Godart*, G. Canals**, F. Charoy** and P. Molli

CRIN-CNRS
BP239,Vandoeuvre Cedex, France
*ESSTIN-Nancy I **IUT-A Nancy II
godart@loria.fr

Introduction

Based on our experience in the Coo project, this paper discusses some issues on the relationships between Software Process (SP) and configuration Management (CM). We particularly discuss about the support to cooperation between processes and we show how introducing cooperation affects the way configurations and configuration items are transferred between work contexts.

Coo[1][4, 5, 2] is a research project whose goal is to provide for an active framework for software process support. It is particularly focused on consistent support to cooperation between processes and recognizes configuration management as a core problem. It is mainly based on a workspace hierarchy which allows to cooperatively work on software configurations while protecting their consistency. In this project, we particularly point out the close relationships between CM and SP, especially through workspaces specification and data transfer between workspaces.

An overview of Coo

The main idea in *Coo* is to base software process execution on a safe transaction[2] mechanism. However, classical database transaction protocols are inefficient in the context of long termed and cooperative processes. This mainly due to the property of *isolation* they impose to parallel executions.

In *Coo* a process recursively breaks down into sub-processes and a process executes as a nested transaction. Thus, a process hierarchy maps to transaction tree. To support cooperation between processes, our nested transactions are open: a transaction (i.e. a process) can make visible a (may be partial) result before it completes. This breaks the isolation property of classical transactions. In other

---

[1] COO stands for cooperation and coordination in the software process
[2] Using the word transaction indicates that we are concerned with correctness of execution and with data integrity maintenance.

words, processes can interact when executing: this is our view of *cooperation*. In this context, a workspace is associated to each transaction, resulting in a workspace hierarchy similar to the transaction tree and processes cooperate by transferring objects from/to its workspace to/from other workspaces.

Workspaces

Workspaces provide services to constrain processes visibility on the object base, to manage and identify objects versions and to transfer objects between workspaces.

Due to the workspace hierarchy, all accesses to objects done by a process are done from the perspective of its workspace: a process is only able to modify objects that belong to its workspace, and can only identify objects that belong to its workspace or one of its ancestors.

Two basic operations are provided for the transfer of objects between workspaces:

check_out: transfers a (group of) object from a parent to a child workspace by creating a copy of the transferred objects in the child,

check_in: transfers a (group of) object from a child to its father workspace by creating a new version of the transferred object in the father.

Thus, when a process wants to modify a configuration, it must: (1) check_out the configuration in its workspace, (2) do the modification locally, and (3) check_in the configuration in its father's workspace. This modification always results in the creation of a new version.

Software Process and Configuration Management

Configurations are built and updated by running software processes. Processes are described by process models which define rules about the way configurations are manipulated and evolve. Fisrt, a process model defines the *structure* of the configuration (and its items) it modifies by means of an E/R diagram. Second, a process model defines a *goal* which describes a state the configuration must reach before the process ends. This goal is specified by a 1st order wf formula. Finally, a process model imposes constraints on the configuration it updates. In Coo, we use two kinds of constraints, both specified using temporal logic formulas and implemented by means of pre- and post-conditions. *Static constraints* define safety properties that must be protected over a time interval. Static constraints allow the specification of integrity and compatibility properties between the items of a configuration and between configurations. *Dynamic constraints* define vivacity properties, i.e. states that must be reached over a time interval. Dynamic constraints allow the specification of transition rules that apply on the evolution of the configuration and on the way it can be rebuilt when one (or several) of its component items is updated.

Cooperating to update configurations

In the framework described above, a configuration is updated by a particular software process (say P1, see figure 1) which in fact delegates its modifications to enclosed sub-processes (e.g. P2 and P3) that operate on sub-parts of the whole configuration (e.g. C2 and C3 respectively). Each sub-process checks_out the sub-configuration on which it operates and modifies it. Then, they have to check_in their results. In this context, an important question is: what to transfer?, and when? Note that in the case of processes that do not cooperate, i.e. that execute in isolation (as classical nested transactions), the question is null: both processes P2 and P3 transfer the whole configuration they update only when they complete.

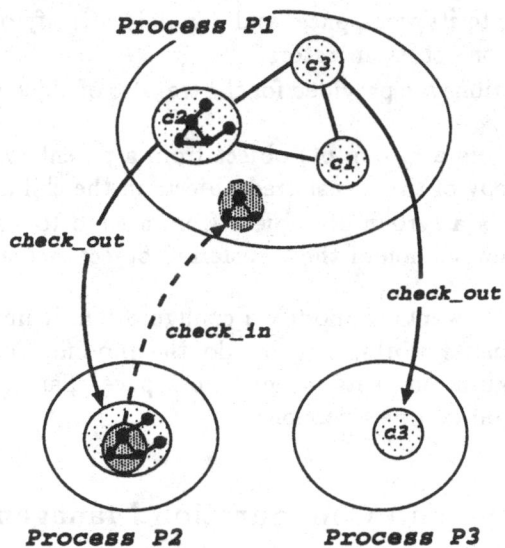

Fig. 1. configurations transfer between workspaces

In the case of cooperating processes, and as previously defined, processes must be able to transfer partial results before they complete. Thus, the question is: how to choose the sub-configuration to transfer? and what is the consequences on consistency?

Our first approach was to base transfer policy on the current software process rules. In other words, the process P2 can transfer a limited part of its configuration only if this part is consistent with regards to its constraints and goal. This transfer will results in the creation of a new version of the sub-configuration at the level of P1. P1's constraints will then enforce this process to rebuild, in collaboration with human agents, the whole configuration to make it consistent with the new released version.

However, the problem with this approach is that a (sub-)configuration is consistent with the SP-rules only if it is consistent with all objects it recursively depends on : in the general case, this can be checked only when the process completes. In other words, **P2** cannot transfer a consistent (sub)-configuration before it completes. And in general, with this first approach, configurations can only be transferred when processes completes: the organization of configuration transfers is completely, and statically, predefined by the software process decomposition. Note that this is not surprising since transfer policy as many to do with testing (general) upward consistency between two arbitrary objects, that is known to be undecidable. It is only possible with a limited semantic check which makes possible the test. And in our case, it is the software breaking-down which limits the semantics to check.

The COO approach to cooperation support

Our approach in COO is based on the one described above, but provides for cooperation in a more pragmatic way. The Coo transfer policy is based on a clear distinction between *final results* and partial, *intermediate results* (see figure 2).

Final results are those transferred when processes completes, and thus are consistent with regards to software process rules. At the upper level, a final result of a sub-process is always considered as a new stable version of a configuration component, from which the whole configuration can be rebuilt.

Intermediate results are those transferred before the process completes and thus can be, in opposition with the final ones, partial and inconsistent. These transfers also result in new version at the upper level, but at this level, consistency rules are not checked on these (may be inconsistent) version. However, since intermediate results are considered as new versions, they can be accessed by other processes when they need it.

Consistency is now maintained by providing new mechanisms. The first one allow to make a logical distinction between final stable results on one hand, and intermediate, partial and may be inconsistent results on the other hand. This is done by adding new operators for intermediate results transfer, the main one being **upward_commit** (see figure 2), which allows to transfer from a child to a father by creating a new version. The second mechanism allow processes to always access the latest version of a configuration, even if it corresponds to an intermediate version. However, in this case, a third mechanism apply : a process which accessed an intermediate results can only apply on it compensatable operations, and it is constrained to resynchronize itself (using the **refresh** transfer operator) with the corresponding final result before to complete. This mechanism assures that final results, and thus the whole configurations, are always produced from other final results and not from intermediate, inconsistent ones.

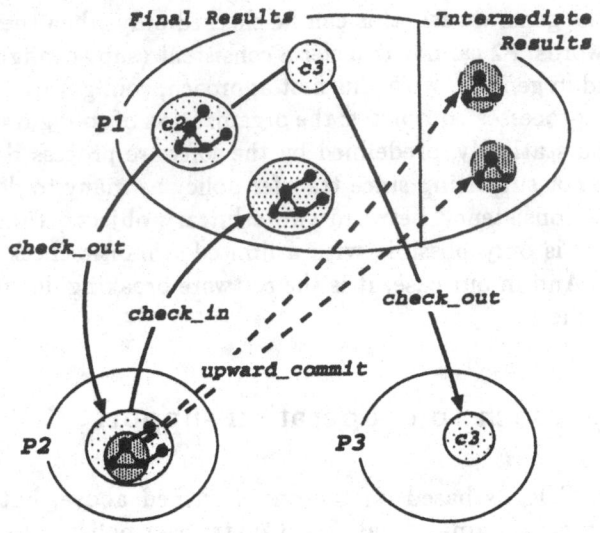

Fig. 2. configurations transfer between workspaces

Conclusion

To conclude, we think that:

– CM and SP are more and more close each to the other since they share, in some sense, the same objective. They are both concerned with building, rebuilding and protecting consistency among sets of constrained objects. A first difference may be that CM is (was) rather concerned with a limited set of object types, those who are well provided with tools when the scope of PM is more large, want to cover all the software life cycle and includes object type whose existence is more dependent on human creativity. However, at this time new types of objects are considered in configuration management (including documents of all phases of the software life cycle and some aspects of resource management) and the application field of configuration management becomes more and more large. As a consequence, technics for configuration management become more and more complex: workspaces, transactions, general constraints,... [3, 1, 6], close to the technics used to develop Process Centered environments. In some way, PM seems to be a natural descendant of CM.

– A second important point is about cooperation. Our experience in the *Coo* project clearly indicates that supporting cooperation in a consistent way has a great influence on the underlying environment architecture. Particularly, we think new mechanisms dedicated to cooperation support are necessary, in addition to the classical ones found in traditional database systems and software engineering environment and probably that traditional CM technics are of the highest interest to support this aspect.

References

1. N. Belkhatir, J. Estublier, and W. Melo. Adèle 2: A Support to Large Software Development Process. In *Proceedings of the First International Conference on the Software Process*, 1991.
2. G. Canals, F. Charoy, C. Godart, and P. Molli. P-Root & Coo : Building a Cooperative Software Development Environment. In *Proceedings of the 7th Conference on Software Engineering Environments (SEE'95)*. IEEE Computer Society Press, 1995.
3. R. Conradi and C. Malm. Cooperating transactions against the EPOS database. In *Software Configuration Management Workshop 3*, Trondheim, 1991.
4. C. Godart. COO: a Transaction Model to support COOperating software developers COOrdination. In *4th European Software Engineering Conference, Garmisch, LNCS 717*, 1993.
5. C. Godart, G. Canals, F. Charoy, and P. Molli. An Introduction to Cooperative Software Development in COO. In *3nd International Conference on Systems Integration, IEEE Press*, 1994.
6. M. Lacroix, D. Roelants, and J.E. Waroquier. Flexible Support for Cooperation in Software Development. In *3rd International Workshop on Software Configuration Management*, pages 102–108, 1991.

Distribution Session

Jacky Estublier

The increasing availability of both local and wide area networks (LAN and WAN), with its corollary on the evolution of working practices is a permanent challenge for SCM systems.

Gradually, the LAN problem is better understood. Distributed rebuilding systems, for example, was proposed more than a decade ago. Nevertheless, some difficulties remain.

The paper from S. A. MacKay is a good overview of the different aspects of the distribution problems. He presented how the DaSC system solves the problem.

This session focused essentially on more recent WAN support. The problem is not recent, geographically distributed development has always existed. Attempts to fully support geographically distributed development is, conversely, a recent domains for SCM. The same problem have been tackled in other domain, and notably by the database community.

The general problem is how to control and/or reconcile the changes made by teams working freely on their own copy of the same software, if there is no direct communication (or too slow communication).

Some SCM system developed solutions for this general problem, as for example the Adele system in 1989; however this experience, and other similar experience showed that a general solution is almost intractable, and result in very complex and fragile solutions. The schema evolution problem alone is currently unsolved.

The ClearCase team took the opposite approach. They defined a "good way" to work when geographically distributed. In their approach, some rules and conventions are applied, the main one is that, on a site, only the local branch can be modified. Reconciling consists simply in copying a distant branch, and then eventually in merging developments.

The excellent paper from the ClearCase team, provides at evidence that looking for a simplified problem, can reach both simple and realistic solutions. Authors claim that, at least until now, the proposed solution fits practical user needs.

The State of the Art in Concurrent, Distributed Configuration Management

Stephen A. MacKay

Institute for Information Technology—Software Engineering
National Research Council of Canada
Ottawa, Ontario K1A 0R6 Canada

Phone: 613-993-6553, Fax: 613-952-7151
E-Mail: MacKay@iit.nrc.ca
WWWeb: http://wwwsel.iit.nrc.ca/

Introduction

The most widely used definition of software configuration management (SCM) comes from the standards community [IEEE87, IEEE90a, IEEE90b, Buck93]. *Configuration management* (CM) is a discipline that oversees the entire life-cycle of a software product (or family of related products). Specifically, CM requires *identification* of the components to be controlled (configuration items) and the structure of the product, *control over changes* to the items (including documentation), accurate and complete *record keeping*, and a mechanism to *audit* or verify any actions. This definition is not complete. Dart [Dart92] suggests that the definition should be broadened to include *manufacturing issues* (optimally managing the construction of the product), *process management* (ensuring adherence to the defined processes) and *team work* (supporting and controlling the efforts of multiple developers). Tichy [Tich88] provides a definition that is popular in the academic and research communities: software configuration management is a discipline whose goal is to control changes to large software system families, through the functions of: *component identification, change tracking, version selection and baselining, software manufacture*, and *managing simultaneous updates* (team work).

We prefer these definitions because the emphasis is on evolution of and access to software components by teams of developers, rather than control or prevention of access in the standards definition. *Concurrent (or parallel), distributed configuration management* is simply a recognition of the true state of software development in the 1990's—managing the evolution of software produced by geographically distributed teams, working semi-autonomously, but sharing a common software base.

We recently conducted a survey of both commercial and freely available SCM systems for an industrial collaborator and were struck by the lack of support, in most systems, for true concurrent, distributed software development. The purpose of this paper is to examine why distributed and concurrent activities in software development are important, to describe some of the currently popular mechanisms for handling concurrency, and to describe how we handle distributed, concurrent software development in our own research vehicle, the Database and Selectors Cel approach to configuration management (DaSC). This paper ties some of the survey results together with thoughts based on over ten years of research into software configuration management. The survey examined the features and limitations of 33 commercial and free CM systems [MacK94] through data provided by the suppliers of each CM system

NRC Number 38359

(marketing literature, manuals, and conversations with staff). The following categories of data were collected:

- name,
- supplier,
- CM model,
- repository abstraction,
- repository mechanism,
- system/subsystem modelling ability,
- distributed development support,
- concurrent modification support,
- branching support,
- merge support,
- user interface,
- revision numbering,
- handling of non-ASCII files,
- multiple development architectures support,
- handling of historical releases,
- logging facilities,
- directory tracking,
- ability to generate deltas,
- price, and
- other comments.

In a broad survey such as this, there is a tremendous amount of overloading of terminology. In this paper we will use terms that we have been using throughout our research project, but to ensure there is no confusion, we provide the following definitions:

Variants of configuration items are different implementations that remain valid at a given instant in time, created to handle environmental differences (for example, different execution platforms). *Revisions* are the steps a configuration item goes through over time, whether to handle new features, fix bugs or to support permanent changes to the environment (e.g., operating systems upgrades, if the old one is no longer supported). Variants and revisions provide a two-dimensional view into the repository, with variants incrementing along one axis as required and revisions incrementing through time on the other.

Versions of configuration items are understood by the SCM community to be synonymous with either revisions or variants [Tich88]. Therefore a version of a single configuration item denotes an entry in the two-dimensional view of the repository reached from an origin through some path of revisions and variants. In this paper we will use the term, *version-set[†]*, to denote a collection (module, product, package, program, system) of configuration item variants taken from specified revision levels.

A *release* is a version-set that has passed some defined quality assurance measures (which, in some cases, are regrettably defined as "none") and is ready for a "customer" (which may be another group within the development organization).

[†] In the DaSC project, we have been using the tighter *version-set* definition of the term *version* since about 1986. We do not refer to versions of individual configuration items because it tends to diminish the concept of variants, which were so long ignored [Mahl94]. To reduce confusion for the reader, we will refer to DaSC versions as version-sets.

Distributed Development

There was a time, not long ago, when distributed development in a software project meant that some programmers could connect their VT100 terminals to the central mainframe through telephone or other slow communication lines. While the computer viewed them as equal participants in the project, using the same tool set as the other developers, the remote developers themselves often saw it differently. Low bandwidth or expensive communication lines (sometimes both), coupled with revision control tools that simply locked them out of particular pieces of source without explanation or indication of when it would be available, made this type of environment virtually unworkable. An alternate strategy was to break the project into completely self-contained pieces that could be worked on in isolation without sharing or on-going communication among the teams. The problem was that development proceeded in isolation without sharing or on-going communication among the teams.

Today, the bulk of software development has moved to the desktop. Workstations and personal computers dominate the workplace and networking is a necessity. Software development has changed greatly, but some things remain the same. The software repository generally resides on one node (or is split across a small number of nodes), so from the point of view of the computers, everyone is still equal, accessing the repository using the same protocols through a standard shared file system (like NFS). Bandwidth is higher and costs have decreased so that even developers continents away have almost immediate access to the source. Most of the current commercial configuration management tools are designed to work in this type of environment.

Intermittently Connected Developer

While today's modern high-speed networks allow remote developers to share code at speeds almost as high as on the local networks, temporary access by the *intermittently connected developer*—someone who, for a variety of reasons, may unpredictably come and go from the network—presents a problem. For example, a software field installer with a notebook computer may need to make minor field customizations or bug fixes with customer 'A' this week, 'B' next week, etc. From the point of view of the field developer, assuming that he is a full-fledged member of the team, it is the software repository that is intermittently connected.

Additionally, large multi-company software projects, typified by military contracts or realtime, embedded system projects, cannot make use of shared software repositories. Joint projects come and go and today's partner may be tomorrow's competitor. Prime contractors depend on subcontractors (likely physically remote) to deliver specific components of the final systems. For reasons of security or physical incompatibility, companies cannot grant each other full network access, leaving the software development effort stuck in the isolation model of the past. This is a recognized area for further SCM research [vand95].

Software Customer

Distributed configuration management not only affects the development organization—the needs of the customers must be considered as well. It is not infrequent that, over time, a customer will obtain a sequence of releases of a piece of software from a developer. Upon receiving each release the customer will need to apply his own changes. It is rare however, for the customer and developer to have the software under common configuration management (particularly when the customer is only one of many for some commercial software product). Another view of the same problem is when a subcontractor delivers a product, which the customer incorporates and changes, and then the customer goes back to the subcontractor for revision and further development. Questions arise such as, "What should the prime contractor provide to the subcontractor as a base for CM on the revisions?", "What kind of CM hooks should developers supply for the customers?", or "Given that the developer ships with no CM support for the customer, how can the customers do an appropriate merge?"

Commercial Support

Virtually all of SCM systems available today support some amount of distributed development. At the very least, all systems support a single repository available on some kind of network (usually a LAN) that is accessible to a distributed group of users. Remote CVS extends the LAN to a WAN to allow worldwide connectivity. Microsoft Delta, and SPARCworks/TeamWare from SunPro, like our DaSC methodology, allow users to take a copy of all or part of the repository and synchronize any modifications at convenient times so that intermittently connected developers may benefit from full configuration management. Only the CCC family of products from Softool advertise an ability to include vendors' products under configuration control, which is surprising, given the number of organizations that experience the upgrade problem.

Concurrent Modifications

To fully support environments composed of intermittently connected developers or cooperating independent contractors, complete concurrent access to individual software configuration items (read *and* write) is a requirement. However, any notion of developers making concurrent modifications to the same configuration item has traditionally been seen as contrary to the concept of configuration management—if an item could be modified in parallel, then it could not be controlled! Fortunately, concurrent development is increasingly being recognized as an important tool in good software engineering. If developers are allowed to take their time, develop changes carefully, and test extensively, before returning code to the repository (with a high degree of confidence of correctness), then it is inevitable that more than one developer is going to touch the same configuration item. In 1993, support for true concurrent development was found in few commercial CM systems, mainly in very high-end tools, such as CaseWare/CM from CaseWare (now Continuus/CM from Continuus Software), and Expertware's CMVision/CMFacility and in Aide-de-Camp from Software Maintenance and Development Systems. In 1994 various forms of distributed concurrency are appearing in product upgrades or in new, more comprehensive products (not all of which are available for review at the time of this writing)—SPARCworks/TeamWare has CodeManager to coordinate simultaneous development across multiple sites on multiple development platforms, Atria has released ClearCase MultiSite to support parallel development across geographically distributed teams and Adele, from Verilog, has recently added rich workspace support to its branch and merge features [Estu94, Estu95]. New offerings or upgrades are also available from Softool (CCC/Harvest), Continuus (Continuus/CM), IBM (CMVC) and Legent (Endevor/WSX, formerly TeamTools from TeamOne Systems).

The two most common mechanisms for handling concurrent modification of software configuration items are branching (usually found in tools implementing the check-out/check-in model of development) and optimistic methods such as copy-modify-merge, workspaces and transactions. We will examine these techniques in more detail as well as looking at how concurrency is handled with tools implementing change sets.

Branching

Branching is a low-level revision control technique, usually found in tools supporting the check-out/check-in model of development. Branching allows a configuration
item to follow simultaneously several paths of development and may be employed to
accomplish a number of goals. Branching is generally represented as directed acyclic
graph, often called a version tree or version graph.

Branches may be created when a variant of a configuration item is needed for a new
version of the product (e.g., new software development platform). Such branches are
likely to be long lived and merging will rarely take place (Figure 1). A similar situation exists when bugs need to be fixed in released software, perhaps several genera-
tions old, usually in large legacy systems (e.g., telephone switches). Merging rarely
takes place because the baselines will have changed substantially or the type change
required may be quite different, if it is needed at all. These branches usually do not
survive as long as in the variant example (Figure 2). When a configuration item is
required to fix a bug in the midst of new development, branches usually exist only
while the configuration item is locked on the main development path for new enhancements or until a release point when many bug fixes may be incorporated into the
main branch for testing. A structure where branching is used solely for bug fixes on
the current development path is shown in Figure 3.

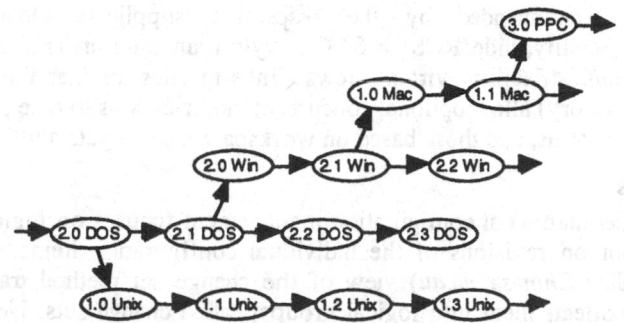

Figure 1. Branching to support new variants. Ovals represent the changing configuration
item—horizontal arrows represent revisions, diagonal arrows, variant creation. Terminal
ovals indicate that a particular variant is no longer maintained (e.g., hardware no longer
available or market sector no longer considered worthy of support).

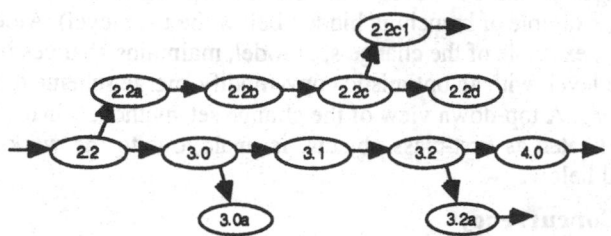

Figure 2. *Branching to support historical revisions.* Ovals represent the changing configuration item—horizontal arrows represent primary revisions, diagonal arrows, creation
of another revision that is part of an earlier release. Terminal ovals indicate that a particular
version is no longer maintained (e.g., all customers have finally upgraded to a newer
release).

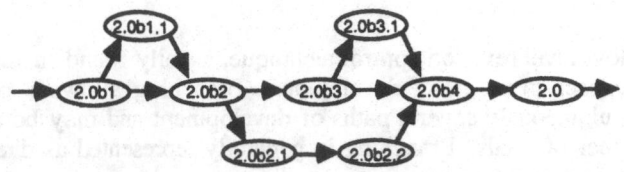

Figure 3. *Branching to support simultaneous bug and feature revisions.* Ovals represent the changing configuration item. A horizontal arrow represents a main development revision and a diagonal arrow leaving an oval represents a bug fix revision. Multiple arrows entering an oval represent a merge.

More commonly, branching is used in all three forms simultaneously, complicating the situation significantly, such that drawing a complete picture, even for an individual configuration item, is difficult to attempt. Branching for full concurrent development is not an effective tool—the model becomes difficult to understand and maintain. Commercial CM systems that support branching, usually discourage its use for full concurrency, even though it is the only mechanism they provide for development to proceed simultaneously on a single configuration item. Some products, including many of those derived from RCS, provide emergency commands to override check-out locks or permit the locks to be turned off, but these features are treated as back-doors and are not recommended by the respective suppliers. Others, such as CMVision/CMFacility, hide RCS or SCCS style branching under a richer interface. With CMVision/CMFacility, virtual views (links to files so that they only appear once in the repository) allow optional concurrent modifications to take place. The line between these systems, and those based on workspaces, often gets a little fuzzy.

Change Sets

The change set method of configuration management focuses on logical changes to the product, not on revisions of the individual configuration items. A bottom-up (sometimes called *Chinese menu*) view of the change set method tracks individual revisions, but collects them into logical groups, called change sets. New versions of the product are then created by applying relevant change sets to a previously baselined version. Different change sets define alternate versions. The change set model would appear to be a natural way of dealing with parallel modifications, however concurrency control is outside this view of the change set abstraction and is handled separately. For example, Peter Miller's aegis, a free program that implements the change set model, maintains changes at the file level, but sits on top some other revision controls system (another example of branching hidden below the user level). Aide-de-Camp, the only commercial example of the change set model, maintains changes in a database, at the line-of-code level, with an optimistic copy-modify-merge scheme to handle concurrent modifications. A top-down view of the change set method, where the change sets themselves are treated as first-class objects, is analogous to the workspace model of SCM, discussed below.

Optimistic Concurrency

Optimistic concurrency is not a single method but a different way of thinking about doing software development. It is a recognition that the software development organization encourages multiple development threads to happen simultaneously, widely distributed or at a single site, but that at some well-defined points in the development cycle some coordination and synchronization of the different streams will have to happen. For optimistic methods to be effective, there is an underlying assumption that management practices will insure that having multiple developers working on a single configuration item is not the norm, but when it is required, there will be no penalty.

One of the most effective ways of managing concurrency and minimizing overlap is to ensure that the granularity of the configuration items is as small as appropriate. This is not to say that developers must continually work with fine-grained fragments that do not present enough context, but the CM tools must take care of the mapping between what the developer needs to see and what is stored in the repository.

The most commonly implemented mechanism for optimistic concurrency among the current generation of CM tools can be categorized as copy-modify-merge. Upon request, a developer is provided with a copy of the requested software configuration item—a direct copy from a file-based repository, or generated from delta-based repository or from a database repository. The developer then has an unlocked copy of the item and the time to modify it properly, but no one else is blocked from working with the same item. When the modification is complete and fully tested, the item is returned to the repository. Because other modifications may have been made while the local copy existed, the procedure for returning the configuration item must check for potential clashes. Depending on the implementation, a merge may be done on each write to the repository, or more intelligently, the parallel changes are managed separately until a human authorizes and supervises the merge.

Workspaces and Transactions

Dart presented a set of 14 categories that describe the functionality of CM systems [Dart90, Dart92]. Of these, three are particularly suited to model concurrent software development: workspaces, transparent views and transactions. The workspace model is a more general form of copy-modify-merge. A *workspace* is an area where a user can take configuration items from the repository and modify them independently, without disturbing or being disturbed by other developers. Any changes committed to the repository by other users after the files are placed in the workspace are not automatically visible, however developers can choose to see what has changed in the repository at convenient milestones. Dart refers to this as insulated, not isolated [Dart94]. When a certain level of satisfaction is reached (such as completion of a major feature or approval by the CM administrator), the items in the workspace are returned to the central repository. There is an implication that the workspace itself is under revision control (possibly private), rather than simply a working directory (i.e., a local history is maintained). A workspace can be used to implement a top-down view of a first-class change set. The *transparent view* extends the workspace model by providing a view into the central repository, but only the variants and revisions of interest are visible. Configuration items may exist in either the workspace or the repository. All those requiring a particular view may share the workspace. Continuus/CM, CMVision/CMFacility, and DRTS from ILSI implement various flavours of workspaces. *Transactions* further enhance the workspace and transparency categories with a set of commands or protocols that coordinate and synchronize the workspaces with each other and with the repository. Feiler, in his attempt to classify CM systems [Feil91], provides more detail on transactions. Often referred to as "long transactions" to differentiate them from simple database transactions, the configuration items can remain out of the repository for weeks or even months. In the extreme case, the workspaces and transactions last indefinitely and become the repository. The focus is on revisions of the configuration and concurrency control. Endevor/WSX from

Legent (formerly TeamTools from TeamOne Systems) is a good example of transaction-based CM.

DaSC Approach

The Database and Selectors Cel (DaSC) approach to software configuration management, developed in our laboratories at the National Research Council of Canada, includes top-down change set, workspace, transparency and transaction features. The concepts of DaSC have evolved over 10 years of practical software development experience, but from the beginning support for concurrent, distributed development was fundamental. The first published description of DaSC and early results from our research into software configuration management appear in [Gent89], a discussion of DaSC and the importance of a good visual metaphor for configuration management can be found in [Wein92], and the evolution of our DaSC model and of the supporting tools will be discussed in a forthcoming paper [Wein95].

Assumptions

The initial target for DaSC was the realtime and embedded systems community, however we have found it applicable to a wide range of applications. As yet, the only environments where DaSC gave us little advantage were those where the configuration items were extremely large-grained and, due to project requirements, we were not able to sub-divide them into smaller entities. The chief assumptions behind DaSC are:

- *Small companies or small teams*—groups of cooperating individuals, numbering in the tens.
- *Distributed development* (within *and* across teams *and* companies)—the intermittently connected developer model is assumed.
- *Software components*—the basic building blocks are fined-grained entities.
- *Cost-sensitive*—no expensive, highly specialized development tools or environments are assumed.
- *Not device independent*—the software structure must be such that alternate implementations are easily integrated.
- *Not just a temporal evolution*—a family of programs sharing common components and evolving together (not necessarily in lock-step) over a long period of time (typically decades).
- *Two-box world*—separate host development environment and specialized target hardware is the norm (also assumed that development may occur simultaneously on a variety of hosts, using a variety of file systems and cross-compilation tools).

Source Code Database

DaSC is based on the principles of managing multi-version software through a software database, and handling concurrent, distributed evolution through a multi-layered approach (analogous to the cel used by film animators). DaSC represents a methodology for configuration management and may be implemented in a number of valid ways. Our examples frequently will refer to source code, but the DaSC model can be applied to any other configuration items, such as documentation and other binary files, as long as there is some form of fine-grained database representation and an appropriate method of selection.

Figure 4 shows a simple example of a DaSC database. Five configuration items are represented by rectangles and two sets of database selectors are represented by ovals.

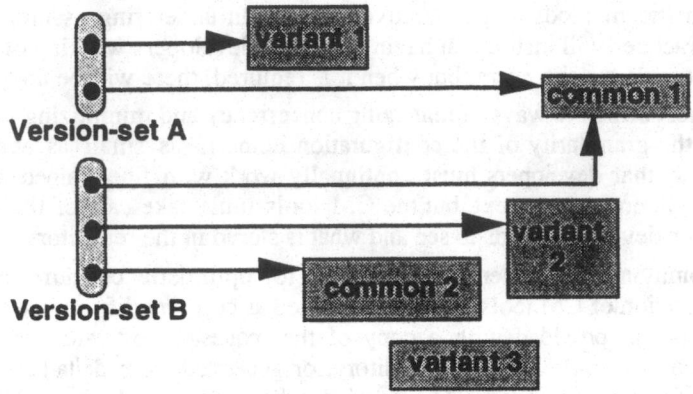

Figure 4. *Database and selectors.*

Individual configuration items may be characterized as *common* or *variant*. Common items, common 1 and common 2 in Figure 4, are those that are (or are expected to be) referenced by a number of selector sets. Variants variant 1, variant 2, and variant 3 provide the same functionality and are selected based on the context. For example, they may represent code appropriate for Unix, Macintosh, or DOS file systems, or for three different compilers, GNU, Borland, or MPW. A DaSC version-set (or selector set) is simply a collection of selectors into the database of common and variant configuration items. In Figure 4, Version-set A selects common 1 and variant 1, and Version-set B selects common 1, common 2, and variant 2.

In order to achieve our goals of portability of host environments and to provide small companies with a low cost entry point, our initial implementation of the DaSC software repository used the file system tree as the database and an inclusion file technique (e.g., files that consist solely of a number of C language #include statements) for database selectors. In addition to providing an effective selection tool, inclusion files also isolate all local file system dependent names in a single substructure.

In DaSC, revisions are represented by new cels or layers. Figure 5 shows an example of a revision layer that might be placed on top of the baseline in Figure 4. Additions are simply shown by new rectangles or ovals, depending on whether a version-set or a database item is being added (e.g., Version-set C, common 3, and variant 4). Changes to an item are represented by a newer copy appearing at the same location on the new layer (e.g., Version-set A and variant 2). A special marker that "paints over" the original item below it is used to denote deletions—the item is not physically removed (e.g., the cross-hatches over the position of variant 1).

Revisions therefore extend the concept of version-sets. A version-set can select common code or a variant from any valid revision layer. In Figure 5, note that the selectors on the revision layer always point to the appropriate spot on the baseline. We provide a tool in DaSC, called derive, which given a version-set and a list of revision layers to be considered, will generate a version-set description that points to the correct configuration items. Figure 6 shows what the database would look like if we looked through the revision layer of Figure 5 onto the baseline of Figure 4.

In the initial implementation of DaSC, cels were realized as parallel file system trees. A set of scripts and tools free the user from concerns about the mapping between the file system and the layered model.

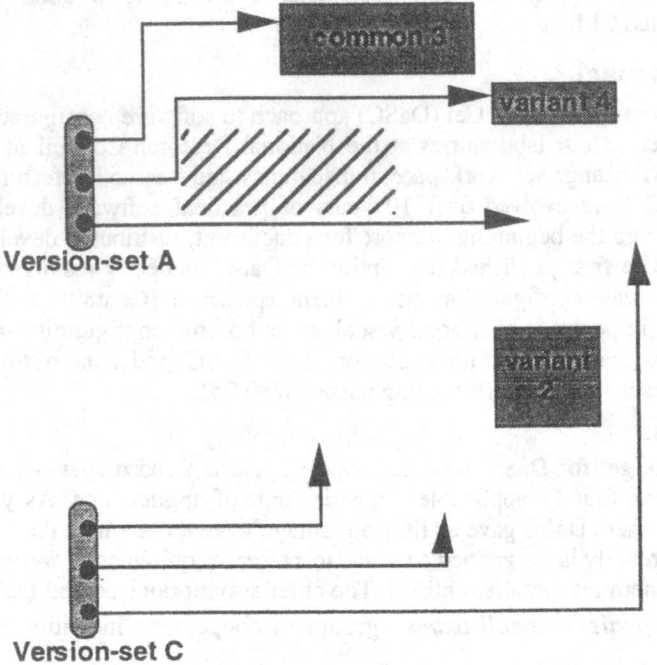

Figure 5. *A revision layer.*

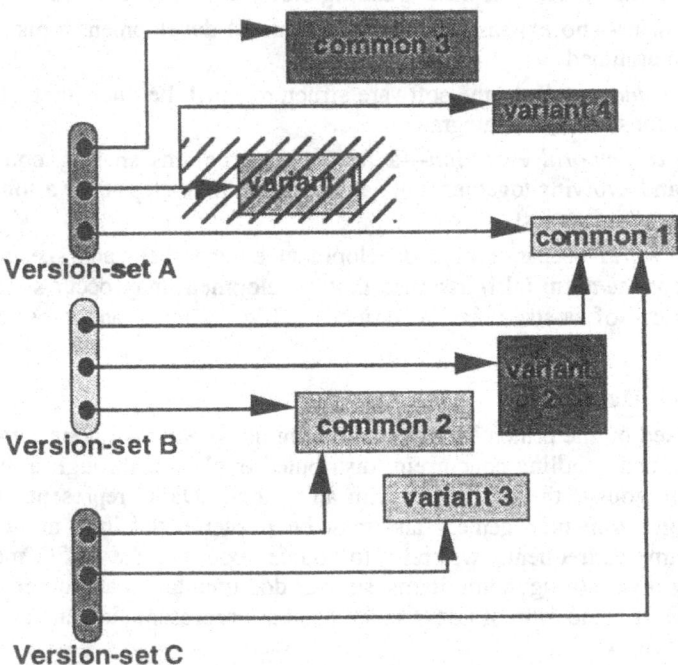

Figure 6. *Figure 5 overlaid on Figure 4.*

DaSC for Concurrent, Distributed Development

The layered approach to software evolution is ideally suited to software development by a group of developers working in parallel in a distributed environment. Cels provide a representation of change without violating the integrity of the original source—first-class change sets. Evolution in time (revision) is supported by adding subsequent layers to a master repository. Layers may be exchanged among developers to synchronize their activities.

Layers exist for as long as is necessary. Layers can exist for short periods of time, to allow a developer to experiment temporarily with a creative idea (later expanded to a full feature or thrown away), for quick bug fixes (later combined with other layers), or even as a sketch for a feature that may eventually be implemented, but is not part of the current product. As in the transaction model of configuration management, individual layers can last "forever" and become the repository of software history. Usually a new layer is created to facilitate a single logical change to the software. It is a logically complete entity—applying the new layer to the layer (or layers) below it will result in stable and complete rendition of the software with the change applied to it. Thus long developer assignments are encouraged. Unlike the check-out/check-in model of development where individuals are urged to return the configuration item to the repository as soon as possible so that others can have access to it, DaSC allows for fully distributed development in the workspace model. The developer is given the time necessary to implement and test changes because the layer is invisible to other developers. They continue to access and modify items in their own layers, taken from the same baselined, master repository. Note that because there are never any check-out locks, intermittently connected developers can take a local copy of all or part of the repository as required.

As development proceeds, many layers are created and they are either considered stacked or adjacent, depending on their relationship with the other layers. Conceptually, a new layer may be *stacked* on top of previous layers if it has been developed with prior knowledge of the layers below it (e.g., an individual developer making a series of modifications). Any configuration item appearing on an upper layer will always appear to overwrite the identically specified item on any lower layer (as shown in Figure 6). Layers are *adjacent* to each other if each layer was developed independently of the other—most commonly by separate developers working in parallel. At convenient times, the layers from individual developers can be combined for integration testing and release, in a process we call *consolidation*.

We have built a tool, consolidate, that manages the process. Figure 7 shows a typical layer diagram and the steps toward consolidation. In step (a), the consolidate tool collapses stacked layers B, C, and D downwards to create a new temporary layer, T^1. Likewise, layers E and F are simultaneously collapsed onto T^2, layers H, I, J, and K onto T^3, and M, N, and O onto T^4. In step (b), adjacent layers T^3, L, and T^4 are reconciled for clashes by comparing each layer with the others to find identically specified configuration items. If any clashes are detected among the three layers, some minor manual intervention will be needed before consolidating sideways to create layer T^5 (if no clashes are found the layers are simply merged to create T^5). In step (c), T^5 is collapsed with G to create T^6. Layers T^1, T^2, and T^6 are then reconciled in step (d) and the resulting temporary layer, T^7, is collapsed, in step (e), with A to create layer Z, the result of the consolidation. While any consolidation of this size, results in some clashes being detected, it is extremely rare that the same line of code was touched, so correction is

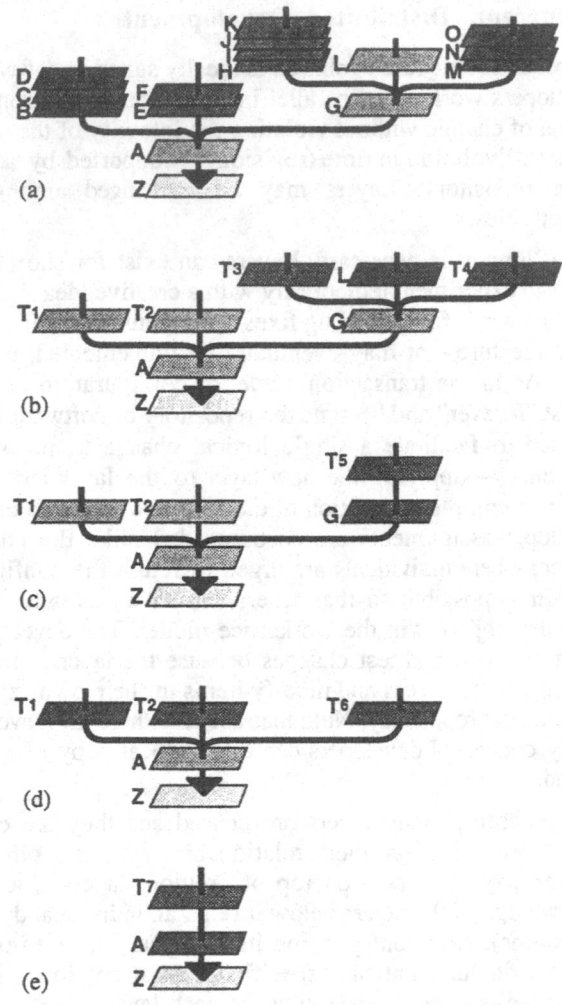

Figure 7. *Typical consolidation in 5 steps.*

usually trivial. Planned improvements to the consolidate tool will allow it process situations, like the one shown in Figure 7, with even less manual intervention [Nodd94].

The layer resulting from a consolidation can then be re-tested and considered part of the master repository. The new layer can be sent to customers as an upgrade or it can be distributed to other developers who may not have been involved in the consolidation (for example, if they are working on more long term development paths). They can then consolidate their code with the new layer at a time that is convenient, such as when they reach a milestone—they are not forced to co-exist with possibly incompatible code until they reach a point when it is reasonable to consider all the ramifications of the new layer and make the appropriate changes, if any are required, to their own code.

Conclusions and Further Research

Modern software development is a team effort, and in today's global marketplace, we cannot assume that the teams are in the same geographic location. We also cannot assume that it is possible to provide continuous shared access to the same software repository. As a result, concurrent development is becoming the norm and vendors of commercial CM systems are reacting with improved features for full optimistic concurrency. The SCM research community needs to investigate a unified representation for concurrent development [vand95]—the branching model is no longer adequate and workspace/change set concepts are too general. The DaSC layer model (or similar models, such as Tandem's Fully Populated Paths [Schw95]) could serve as the basis for such a representation.

In surveying the currently available CM tools, we were struck by the lack of support for dealing with configuration items that were not represented in ASCII text, including word processor produced documentation, databases (e.g., test cases), the project files for advance graphical user interface generators (e.g., XVT), and "source code" for non-textual languages (e.g., Prograph CPX). Most tools will allow the entire "binary" entity to be placed under configuration control, but they do not have the ability to answer such basic questions as, "What has changed in this non-textual configuration item?", "What are the differences between these version-sets?", "How can we revise item B in a manner similar to the revision already applied to A?" We believe that DaSC is ideally suited to work in this environment and plan to extend the implementation fill the void.

Acknowledgments

Thanks are due to the entire DaSC team for their efforts in this research project: Morven Gentleman, Charles Gauthier, Darlene Stewart, Marceli Wein and Anatol Kark. I would also like to thank the many readers of the early drafts of this paper and of the CM survey for their helpful suggestions and references to additional CM systems.

References and Bibliography

[Berl92]   H. Ronald Berlack. *Software configuration management.* John Wiley and Sons, New York, NY, USA. 1992. 330 pages.

[Buck93]   Fletcher J. Buckley. *Implementing configuration management: hardware, software, and firmware.* IEEE Press, New York, NY, USA. 1993. 249 pages.

[Dart90]   Susan Dart. Spectrum of functionality in configuration management systems. Carnegie Mellon University, Software Engineering Institute Technical Report: *CMU/SEI-90-TR-11,* December 1990. 38 pages.

[Dart92]   Susan Dart. The past, present, and future of configuration management. Carnegie Mellon University, Software Engineering Institute Technical Report: *CMU/SEI-92-TR-8,* July 1992. 28 pages.

[Dart94]   Susan Dart. Configuration Management: the KEY to Process Improvement. Talk to the Groupe d'amélioration des processus de génie logiciel, Centre de Recherche Informatique de Montréal, April 20, 1994.

[Estu94]   Jacky Estublier and Rubby Casallas. The Adele Configuration Manager. *Configuration Management* (Walter F. Tichy, ed.). John Wiley and Sons, Chichester, England. 1994. pp. 99–133.

[Estu95]   Jacky Estublier. Work Space Management in Software Engineering Environments. Private communication.

[Feil91]   Peter Feiler. Configuration management models in commercial environments. Carnegie Mellon University, Software Engineering Institute Technical Report: *CMU/SEI-91-TR-7*, March 1991. 54 pages.

[Gent89]   W.M. Gentleman, S.A. MacKay, D.A. Stewart, and M. Wein. Commercial realtime software needs different configuration management. *Proceedings of 2nd International Workshop on Software Configuration Management (SCM)*, Princeton, NJ. October 24-27, 1989. Published as *Software Eng. Notes*, 17(7): 152-161; 1989. NRC 30695.

[IEEE87]   IEEE/ANSI. IEEE Guide to software configuration management. *ANSI/IEEE Std 1042-1987*. IEEE Press, New York, NY, USA. 1987. 92 pages.

[IEEE90a]   IEEE/ANSI. IEEE Standard glossary of software engineering terminology. *IEEE Std 610.12-1990* (revision and redesignation of *IEEE Std 729-1983*). IEEE Press, New York, NY, USA. 1990. 83 pages.

[IEEE90b]   IEEE/ANSI. IEEE Standard for software configuration management plans. *IEEE Std 828-1990*. IEEE Press, New York, NY, USA. 1990. 16 pages.

[MacK94]   Stephen A. MacKay. An Evaluation of Configuration Management Systems and Tools. In preparation.

[Mahl94]   Axel Mahler. Variants: Keeping Things Together and Telling Them Apart. *Configuration Management* (Walter F. Tichy, ed.). John Wiley and Sons, Chichester, England. 1994. pp. 73–97.

[Nodd94]   K.E. Noddin. Derive and Consolidate in the DaSC Configuration Management Model. National Research Council of Canada, Institute for Information Technology Technical Report. In preparation.

[Schw95]   Bill Schweitzer. Fully Populated Paths: A Conservative, Simple Model for Parallel Development. *Proceedings of 5th International Workshop on Software Configuration Management (SCM-5)*, Seattle, WA. April 24-25, 1995. (These Proceedings).

[Tich88]   Walter F. Tichy. Tools for Software Configuration Management. *Proceedings of the International Workshop on Software Version and Configuration Control*, Grassau, FRG. January 27–29, 1988. pp. 1–20.

[vand95]   André van der Hoek, Dennis Heimbigner, and Alexander Wolf. Does Configuration Management Research Have a Future? *Proceedings of 5th International Workshop on Software Configuration Management (SCM-5)*, Seattle, WA. April 24-25, 1995. (These Proceedings).

[vend94]   Various papers, manuals, advertising brochures, electronic mail messages, etc. supplied by the CM vendors.

[Wein92]   M. Wein, Wm. Cowan, and W.M. Gentleman. Visual Support for Version Management. *Proceedings of the 1992 ACM/SIGAPP Symposium on Applied Computing (SAC)*, Kansas City. March 1–3, 1992. pp. 1712–1723. NRC 33170.

[Wein95]   M. Wein, S.A. MacKay, W.M. Gentleman, D.A. Stewart and C.-A. Gauthier. Evolution is Essential for Software Tool Development. *Proceedings of the Eighth International Workshop on Computer-Aided Software Engineering (CASE '95)*, Toronto. July 9-14, 1995.

ClearCase MultiSite:
Supporting Geographically-Distributed
Software Development

Larry Allen, Gary Fernandez, Kenneth Kane,
David Leblang, Debra Minard, John Posner

Atria Software, Inc.
24 Prime Park Way
Natick, Massachusetts
U.S.A.

Abstract

For a software configuration management system to support large-scale
development efforts, it must address the difficult problem of geographically-
distributed development. This paper describes the rationale and design of Atria
Software Inc.'s *ClearCase MultiSite™* software, which extends the ClearCase®
configuration management system to support geographically-distributed
development through *replication* of the development repositories. This paper
considers alternatives to replication and discusses the algorithms used by ClearCase
MultiSite to ensure replica consistency.

1 Introduction: Parallel Development and ClearCase

The size and complexity of software projects has increased greatly over the years. It is
common to find a single software system with many million lines of code under
development by several hundred software engineers. Large projects need to have several
independent "lines of development" active at the same time. The process of creating and
maintaining multiple variants of a software system is termed *parallel development*. A
particular variant might be a major project (porting an application to a new platform), or
a minor detour (fixing a bug; creating a "special release" for an important customer).
Good support for parallel development is a key requirement for any version control and
configuration management system targeted at large development environments.

Atria Software's *ClearCase* product provides configuration management and software
process control for parallel development in a local area network. *ClearCase MultiSite*
extends the single-site parallel development model of ClearCase to provide
geographically-distributed parallel development. Accordingly, we first describe the
fundamental concepts of ClearCase, and then describe the MultiSite approach.

1.1 ClearCase Basics

ClearCase is a comprehensive software configuration management system. It manages
multiple variants of evolving software systems, tracks which versions were used in
software builds, performs builds of individual programs or entire releases according to
user-defined version specifications, and enforces site-specific development policies and
processes.

A ClearCase *versioned object base* (VOB) is a permanent, secure data respository. It contains data that is shared by all developers: this includes current and historical versions of source objects (*elements*), along with *derived objects* built from the sources by compilers, linkers, and so on. In addition, the repository stores detailed "accounting" data on the development process itself: who created a particular version (and when, and why), what versions of sources went into a particular build, and other relevant information. In addition to source, derived, and historical data, a VOB stores user-defined *meta-data*, such as mnemonic version labels, inter-object relationships, and object attributes.

VOBs are globally accessible resources, which can be distributed throughout a network. They act as a federated database: they are independent but cooperative, and can be linked into one or more logical trees. A project may have some private VOBs, and also use shared VOBs that hold common interfaces or reusable components. The VOB is the unit of data that is replicated with MultiSite.

There are many versions of each file in a VOB, and there may be many names and directory structures for the files (reflecting reorganizations of the source tree over time). Rather than copying versions into a physical workspace, ClearCase uses virtual file system technology to create a virtual workspace called a *view*. A view makes a VOB look like an ordinary file system source tree to users and their off-the-shelf tools (Figure 1). A set of user-specified rules determines which version of each file and directory is visible through a view.

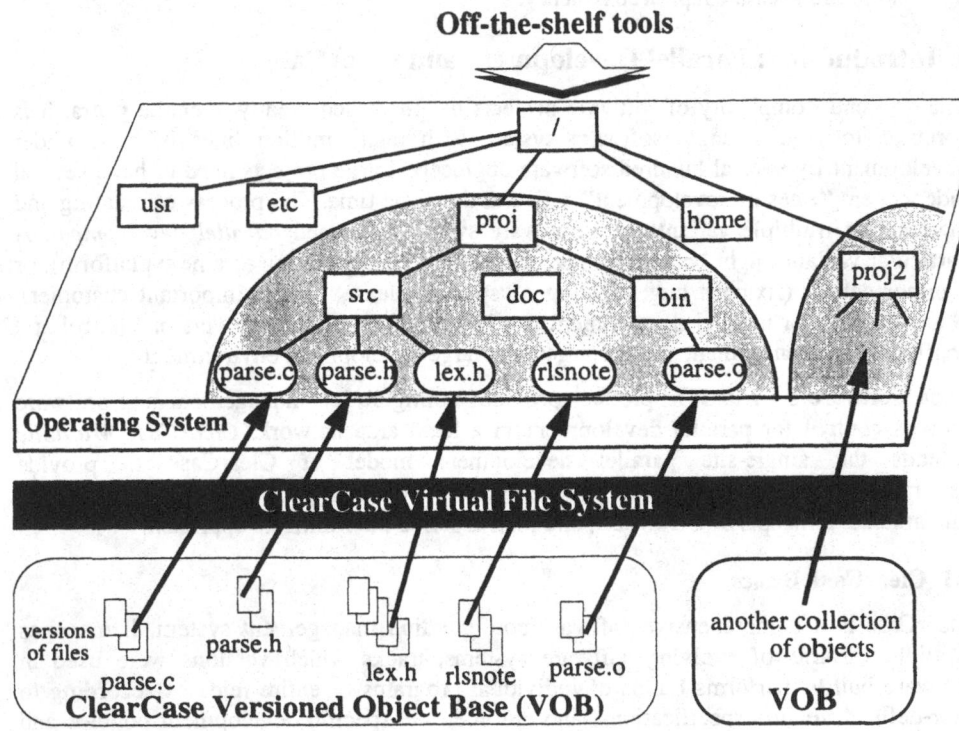

Fig. 1. ClearCase Virtual File System

1.2 Parallel Development with Branches

ClearCase allows multiple developers to modify a single source file simultaneously, without contention or loss of changes. This parallel development capability is accomplished through *branching* — the maintenance of multiple independent lines of descent in the version tree, each of which evolve independently (Figure 2).

For example, a product may require ongoing bug fixes to Release 1.0, while development of Release 2.0 continues in parallel. ClearCase supports this scenario by maintaining separate branches for new development ("main" branch) and for bug fixes (subbranch). This ensures that bug fixes do not accidentally pick up new development work, which has not yet been fully tested. Each branch can be independently checked out and checked in.

ClearCase also has the notion of *branch types* to provide central administration of branches. A branch in an element is really an instance of a particular branch type — that is, it points back to the branch type for common information such as the branch name, access control rights, and comments describing the purpose of the branch.

Eventually, changes made on multiple branches should be reconciled or *merged*. ClearCase provides powerful tools for finding branches that need to be merged, for performing the merges (automatically where possible, and obtaining human input if required), and for tracking merges that have been performed, both for reporting purposes and to optimize subsequent merge operations.

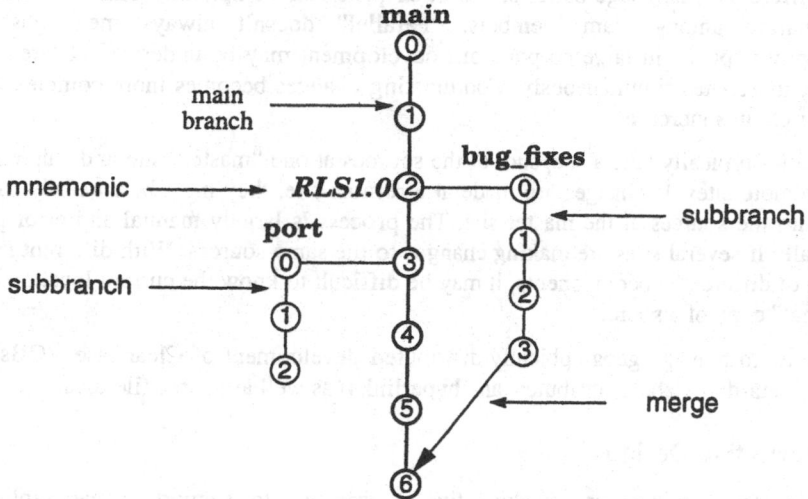

Fig. 2. ClearCase Branching Model for Parallel Development

1.3 ClearCase Meta-Data

In addition to source files and change histories, a VOB holds several of other types of important information, called *meta-data:*

- *Version labels* are mnemonic names for particular versions. For example, *foo.c* version 21 might be tagged with the label "RLS2" in order to indicate that the version was used in the build of the second release.

- *Attributes* are name/value pairs, which can be attached to individual versions, to entire branches, or to entire elements. Attributes are often used to represent state information about a version, for purposes of integrating process-control mechanisms with the version control system. For example, an attribute may be attached to a source file version in order to indicate the bug(s) fixed by that version.

- *Hyperlinks* enable users to define structured or ad hoc relationships between pairs of objects. For example, *foo.c* can point to *foo.doc* via a "design_for" hyperlink. Hyperlinks are useful for requirements tracing and, with a graphic display of the relationship network, navigating between related objects.

2 The Challenge of Geographically-Distributed Development

In a large development organization, software developers typically are located at several physical sites; each site develops one or more subcomponents of a large software system. Sites may be physically near each other and connected by a high-speed network, or they may be on different continents with poor network connectivity. Sites may have private sources but they also may need to share sources, libraries, and header files with other sites. (This is particularly true of header files and libraries, which act as component interfaces.)

Parallel development is more difficult in a geographically-distributed environment; time-zone differences, language barriers, and other problems complicate communication and coordination among team members. "Parallel" doesn't always mean just two development paths; in large corporations development may be underway at three, four, five, or more sites simultaneously. Coordinating changes becomes more complex as the number of sites increase.

Companies typically take a snapshot of the sources at one "master" site and ship them to other remote sites. If changes are made at a remote site, they must be carefully merged back into the sources at the master site. The process is largely manual and error prone, especially if several sites are making changes to the same sources. With different sites in charge of different subcomponents, it may be difficult to know the current location of the "original" copy of a source.

A scheme to manage geographically-distributed development of ClearCase VOBs must handle meta-data (labels, attributes, and hyperlinks) as well as source file data.

3 Alternative Designs

We considered a number of alternative approaches to supporting geographically-distributed software development. This section describes several of these alternatives.

3.1 Global Access to a Centralized Repository

The simplest approach is to extend the tools used for local software development, providing all users at all sites with access to a centralized shared repository across a wide-area network. In fact, several ClearCase customers used this approach to permit, for example, developers working in California to access and update a repository located in Massachusetts. This approach has significant usability problems, however:

- The need to access the central repository frequently makes the system vulnerable to network problems such as partitions.

- Frequent accesses to the central repository have an unacceptable effect on ClearCase performance when they occur over a relatively low bandwidth wide-area network.

- Remote access to a central repository presents problems with scaling the system to very large numbers of users, since the load on the central server increases with the number of users in the entire network.

3.2 Locally-Caching File Systems

The problems of using a global repository might be alleviated by caching information locally at each development site, perhaps by making use of a caching remote file system such as AFS [5]. Unfortunately, such a solution does not go far enough in addressing the problems of sophisticated configuration management system. A ClearCase VOB includes both version data (stored in standard files) and *meta-data* (stored in a database). At best, a caching file system would allow a development site's version data to be cached locally; it does not (and cannot) help with the meta-data.

In fact, databases such as those embedded in ClearCase VOBs represent a worst case for this kind of caching file system: they are frequently written from multiple machines, and their pages are accessed randomly, thereby defeating both the caching and the pipelining of the file system. So, the introduction of a caching file system does not solve the problems of robustness, performance, and scalability caused by use of a central repository; at best, it can only reduce the file I/O load imposed by remote access to version data on the central server.

3.3 Repository Replication

These considerations led us to conclude that an adequate solution to the problem of distributed software development would have to be based upon replication of the entire repository, including both the database and the version data storage, to each local site. Replication carries with it the possibility that the sites may change their replicas independently, with the potential for conflicting changes and subsequent inconsistency of replicas.

The problem of replicating a version-data repository has much in common with the general problems of file and database replication [1,2]. In particular, the key problem to be solved is how to allow multiple replicas to be updated independently without losing changes or allowing inconsistent changes (that is, changes that violate data structure invariants).

3.4 Serially-Consistent Replicas

There are algorithms for updating replicated data at multiple sites, keeping all the replicas continuously synchronized and avoiding the possibility of lost or conflicting changes [3,4]. Replicas synchronized by such an algorithm are termed *serially consistent*. The serial consistency constraint, however, imposes a significant penalty on the availability of data in each replica: either reading or writing of data at any replica requires that at least a majority of all replicas be accessible. It is possible to trade off the number of sites that must be contacted when reading data against the number of sites that must be contacted when writing data, but a majority of all the extant replicas must be available for either reading or writing operations to occur.[1]

This majority-consensus requirement also means that the serially-consistent replication approach has even worse scaling characteristics than the approach using a central repository. With the central repository, both the load on the central server and the aggregate network traffic are proportional to the number of users. With serially-consistent replicas, the load on *each* replica is proportional to the number of users (since each user must contact at least half of the replicas for each read or write operation), while the aggregate network load increases as the square of the number of users.

3.5 Weakly-Consistent Replicas

Relaxing the requirement of serial consistency allows the contents of individual replicas to temporarily diverge, with no guarantee that a change made at one replica is immediately visible at the other replicas. The presumption is that eventually (perhaps on a periodic basis) the replicas will be resynchronized. A number of approaches have been taken to the problem of resolving inconsistencies that may be detected during the resynchronization, but none seemed directly applicable to the problem of distributed software development.

The Locus system, for example, demanded manual intervention upon detecting that conflicting changes had been made to a particular file.[2] This approach may be adequate in a system in which individual files are infrequently modified at multiple sites, and in which only a small number of replicas exist (so that the person who originated the changes is readily available to resolve such conflicts). But it is not suitable for the complex database of a software repository, which is modified continuously at all active development sites. With a large number of replicas and a complex pattern of replica updates, it is easy to imagine that a conflict may be detected at a "third-party" replica, far from those at which the conflicting changes were originally made, and not readily able to resolve the conflict. So, a system that depends on manual intervention at replica synchronization time to resolve conflicting changes to the repository is not acceptable.

An alternative approach to weakly-consistent replication of a database is that taken by Grapevine. In Grapevine, each modification made to a particular data item in the database is assigned a modification time, and modification times are totally ordered (if necessary, by including the replica identifier as part of the modification time to break ties). When two potentially conflicting changes to the same data item are detected, the most recent change (the change with the later modification time) wins. This rule ensures that all replicas will eventually reach the same state, but allows some changes to be lost without notification – adequate for a mailing-list registration database such as Grapevine, but not for a software configuration management system.

---

1. Gifford's weighted-voting approach actually allows the implementor to trade off network load against availability, by weighting some sites more heavily than others. A majority of *votes* is still required for either reading or writing, however.

2. The description of Locus' support for replication in this paper is necessarily incomplete. Locus supported serial consistency of replicas within a single network *partition*; only when two previously-disconnected partitions reconnected was manual intervention as described here required.

4 The MultiSite Solution

To make the weakly-consistent-replicas approach usable for distributed SCM, it is necessary to partition the objects being replicated into disjoint sets, each of which can only be modified at a single replica. The branch and merge development model employed by ClearCase provides a natural way to partition the development activities occurring at multiple replicas in way that is practical and does not unduly restrict the utility of the system, allowing development work to proceed in parallel at each replica while still avoiding conflicting changes.

With MultiSite, geographically distributed development is structured in the same way as parallel development at a single ClearCase site: different development projects proceed concurrently and independently, each project using a different branch of an element's version tree. The only difference between local and multiple-site parallel development is that MultiSite *enforces* the rule that different sites work on different branches, by assigning mastership to individual branches. This ensures *automatic resynchronization*, eliminating the need for manual intervention to resolve conflicts. Only one site can extend a particular branch; thus, all those changes can be trivially grafted onto the corresponding branch at other sites. When a remote effort is complete, or at a convenient integration point, it can be merged into an integration branch; integration of parallel work, testing, and release, can happen at any site.

For example, a multinational company has groups developing compilers in different parts of the world (Figure 3). All the compilers use a common code generator, and all the groups want to share and modify the same code generator sources.

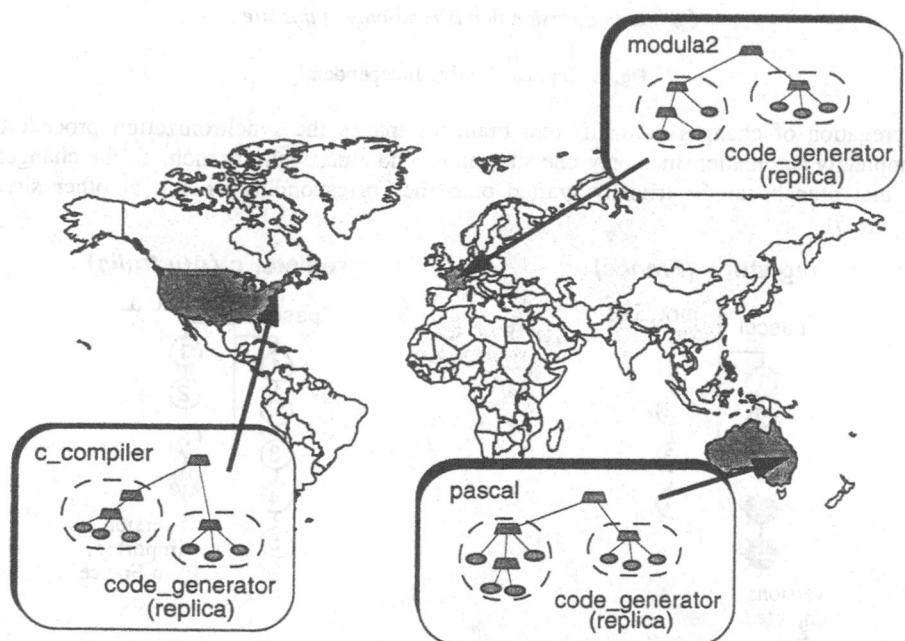

Fig. 3. Multinational Project Sharing Sources

Each site has a copy (*replica*) of the VOB that contains the code generator source files. The Pascal group in Australia makes changes to the source files on a "pascal" branch in its local copy; similarly, the Modula2 group in France makes its changes to the same source files on a "modula2" branch in its local copy (Figure 4).

To support this strategy for geographically distributed development, MultiSite provides these services:

- Maintenance of a local *replica* of a VOB at each site. Each site can "see" the entire VOB through its local replica (i.e. all versions of all files are present).

- Enforcement of the rule that different sites work on different branches of an element.

- Synchronization of the multiple VOB replicas, communicating the changes among the sites via network connections or magnetic tape.

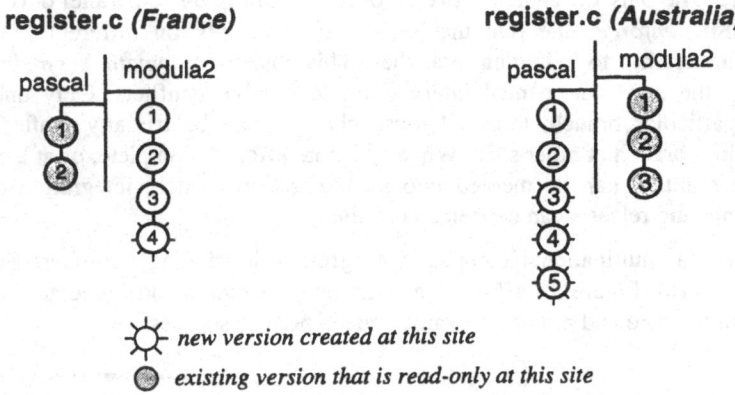

Fig. 4. Replicas Evolve Independently

Segregation of changes onto different branches makes the synchronization procedure completely automatic; since only one site can extend a particular branch, all the changes on that branch can be trivially grafted onto the corresponding branch at other sites (Figure 5).

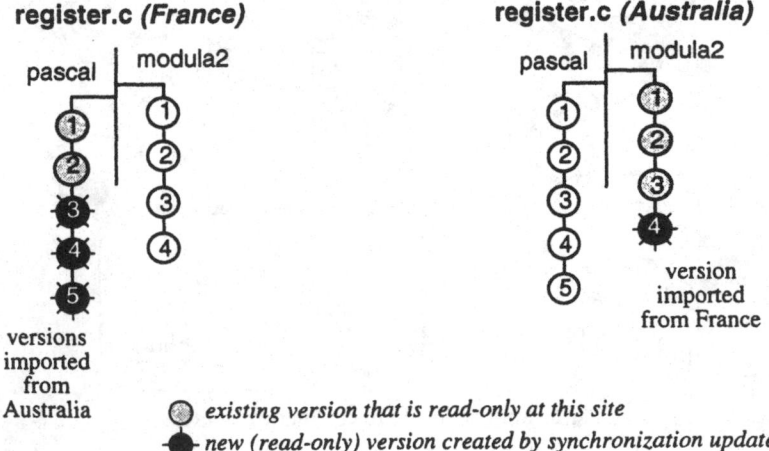

Fig. 5. After the next Periodic Update

After synchronization, independent changes to the same source file can be merged together, using the standard ClearCase merge tools. (Typically, merges are deferred to meet relatively infrequent "integration" milestones, even if synchronization takes place frequently.)

4.1 VOB Replicas

For each ClearCase VOB, MultiSite can maintain any number of *VOB replicas*, distributed at different sites. The original VOB and its replicas form a *VOB family*. All of the replicas are peers — any one can be modified, any one can spawn a new replica, any one can be deleted when no longer needed, and any one can send updates to any other.

The replicas in a VOB family are loosely consistent. Local updates to replicas (new versions checked in, files renamed, labels and attributes added, etc.) make their contents diverge; synchronization makes their contents converge again.

The VOB is the MultiSite "unit of replication" — users cannot restrict replication to a particular element or directory tree.

4.2 Branch Mastership

Enforcement of MultiSite's branch-development strategy is accomplished by assigning *mastership* to individual branches — new versions can be created on a branch only in the replica that masters that branch.

Branch mastership provides the right level of granularity for parallel development. Coarser-grained mastership, such as at the element (file) level, precludes parallel development because people at two sites can't work on the same file at the same time. Without any mastership, if any site can change anything, automatic resynchronization is not possible.

The concept of mastership extends to other objects, such as symbolic version labels. In order to prevent conflicting operations from being performed at different replicas, MultiSite assigns each object a mastering replica that is the only replica permitted to modify the object. For example, each element in a VOB is assigned a mastering replica, only that replica is permitted to delete the element or change its type. Mastership can be transferred between replicas if needed.

4.3 Synchronization

Synchronization updates circulate changes among the replicas in a VOB family. The replica update topology can be a star, a multi-hop chain, or any graph that enables updates to eventually flow from one replica to all others.

Sites that are not connected by TCP/IP can use a file-transport mechanism (e.g. one based on electronic mail) or magnetic tape. All updates are idempotent, so import of an update can be restarted or repeated without difficulty.

5 Implementation of MultiSite

Synchronization of VOB replicas in MultiSite is implemented using a mechanism similar to the multiple-part timestamp schemes found in other replication systems [6,7,8]. As changes are made to a replica, a record of each change is stored as an entry in an *operations log* in the VOB database. A replica exports its changes to other replicas by generating a *synchronization packet*. This packet (file) contains all of the operations log entries made in the replica since the last generated synchronization packet. This includes changes that originated at the replica, as well as changes received from other replicas. The data is stored in XDR[1] format so it can be processed by any target architecture. At the destination replica or replicas, the mechanism *imports* the changes contained in the packet by replaying them in order. Any such changes previously seen (imported) by the replica are ignored.

MultiSite ensures that operations are imported and performed in a consistent order. The dependencies between operations originating at the same and/or at different replicas form a partial order that reflects the potential flow of information between the operations [9]. Any operation performed on a VOB replica may depend on any preceding operation performed on that replica, including both operations that originated at the replica as well as operations imported from other replicas. The MultiSite synchronization mechanism is designed to ensure that no operation is imported into a replica before any of the operations on which it potentially depends (i.e. the mechanism guarantees that the state of each replica reflects a consistent cut in the dependency graph of operations).

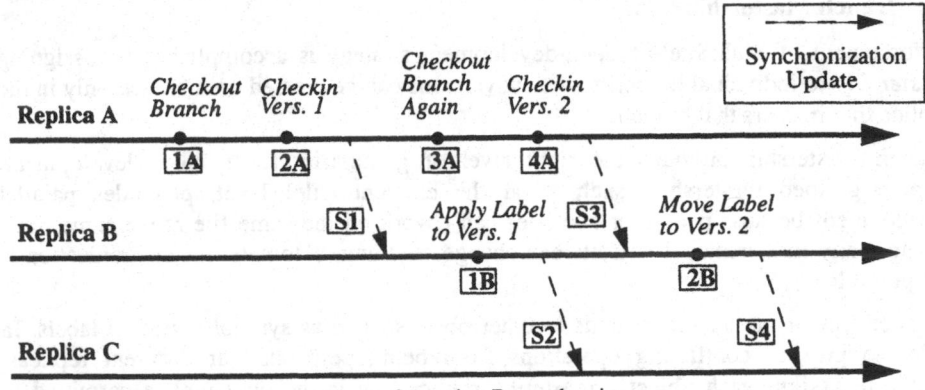

Fig. 6. Operation Dependencies

In Figure 6, creating a symbolic label (e.g. "Beta-Release") on version 1 of the file at replica B clearly requires that version 1 has already migrated to replica B. In other words, the label creation operation (1B) depends on the first checkout/checkin operation pair (1A/2A) made by replica A. These operations were later imported by replica B, creating version 1 (synchronization S1).

The label moving operation (2B) at replica B moves the symbolic label from version 1 of the file to version 2. It depends upon the earlier label application (1B) at that replica, as well as on the second checkout/checkin pair of operations (3A/4A) made at replica A. MultiSite guarantees that all replicas will import these operations in an order consistent with their dependencies. A replica might import both checkout/checkin pairs before either labelling operation, or each labelling operation might immediately be imported after the corresponding checkout/checkin pair. Either order of operations is consistent with the operations' dependencies. However, no replica will import either of the labelling operations without previously having imported the corresponding checkout/

---

1. eXternal Data Representation (used by NFS and other tools)

checkin pair. And, no replica will import the label movement without previously having imported the original label application.

5.1 Logging and Virtual Timestamps

Each VOB replica records in its operation log every operation performed on that replica, including both operations that originated at the replica as well as operations imported from other replicas. The operation log for a replica is maintained as part of the VOB database itself, and operations are logged immediately as part of the transaction of the operation. As a result, the log always reflects exactly the set of operations performed on the replica, and the order in which the operations were performed.

In order to track the potential dependencies between operations, each operation logged by MultiSite is tagged with both the identity of the VOB replica at which the operation originated, and a virtual timestamp reflecting the order of the operation with respect to others that originated at the same replica. The virtual timestamp is implemented as a counter of the number of operations that originated at the replica, and is termed an "epoch number".[1]

Each replica also attempts to track the state of each other replica, using a table of virtual timestamps maintained in the VOB replica's database. The table contains one row and one column for each replica in the VOB family. The virtual timestamp in row A of column B of the table reflects the last known operation originating from replica B that was imported by replica A. Each row of the table therefore represents a multiple-part timestamp (i.e. a cut on the operations dependency graph) reflecting the last known state of the corresponding replica. This is not necessarily the actual current state of that replica, but a conservative estimate of it.

Figure 7, based on Figure 6, shows the state of replica B's table immediately after the first update generated to replica C (S2). Note that replica B is not aware of the second pair of checkout/checkin operations (3A/4A) being performed concurrently at replica A. It is only aware of the operations sent to it by replica A in the earlier update (1A/2A), as well as its own operations.

	FROM		
	A	B	C
A	2	0	0
TO B	2	1	0
C	2	1	0

Fig. 7. Table of Virtual Timestamps at Replica B

Note that a replica's table also contains a row for the replica itself. This row represents the highest numbered operations performed or imported at the replica, and is always kept

---

1. In the original MultiSite design, groups of operations sent to other replicas in a single update were assigned the same virtual timestamp and were considered to constitute an "epoch" of changes. Their order within the operations log determined the potential dependencies between them. The implementation of the product was later simplified by assigning each operation a unique virtual timestamp. However, the term "epoch" has remained with the product.

up-to-date with the actual state of the replica (i.e. it always reflects the VOB replica's actual state).

5.2 Generating Updates

In order to generate an update from one replica to another, MultiSite scans the log of the sending replica looking for operations that are not known to have already been imported by the destination replica. It does this by scanning for entries with timestamps (epoch numbers) higher than those reflected in the table row for the destination replica. A record of each such operation found is XDR encoded and recorded in the update packet, along with the identity of the replica at which the operation originated and the operation's virtual timestamp. Operations are recorded in the packet in the same order in which they occur in the log. Note that because the destination replica's row in the table reflects a conservative estimate of its actual state, the update packet may contain operations already performed or imported by the destination replica. These are discarded later by the destination replica when importing the packet.

In the earlier example, the second update generated from replica B to replica C would contain the second checkout/checkin pair of operations followed by the label movement operation. These are the only operations in the log of replica B with virtual timestamps larger than the corresponding entries in its table row for replica C.

MultiSite takes an optimistic approach to maintaining virtual timestamp tables. Immediately after generating an update packet, the sending replica increments the entries in the table row for the destination replica in order to reflect the operations sent in the packet. No acknowledgment of receipt is required from the destination replica. The next update generated from the replica will pick up where the last update left off, without duplicating any of the operations contained in the previous update. Although this is optimal during normal operation, it requires special actions to detect and handle lost updates when they occur. This issue is discussed in more detail below.

Each update packet contains the virtual timestamp table row (for the destination replica) that was used to determine which operations to include in the packet. This row represents the starting state of the packet (i.e. the set of operations already expected to be possessed by the destination replica before it imports the operations contained in the update packet). This row is also useful for determining the order in which the destination replica should process update packets. This issue is discussed further in the following section.

Each update packet also contains the sending replica's virtual timestamp table row from its own table. This allows the destination to track the actual state of the sending replica without substantial overhead.

5.3 Importing Updates

Before allowing a replica to import the operations contained in an update packet, MultiSite first checks to determine if doing so would create an inconsistency in the importing replica. MultiSite compares the "starting state" virtual timestamp row contained in the packet to the importing replica's own table row for itself. If any entry in the packet row is larger than the corresponding entry in the replica's table row, then the importing replica is missing operations that the sending replica expected the receiver to have already imported. These may be operations contained in other packets that have not yet been imported, or they may be operations contained in a packet that was lost before being imported. In either case, importing the packet could create an inconsistency, and its processing is deferred until the missing operations are imported.

Note that because successive packets from the sending replica will use successively larger "starting state" virtual timestamp rows (i.e. the rows will contain larger entries on a component-by-component basis), the destination replica can determine the order in which the packets were created by the sending replica and the order in which they should be processed.

In the earlier example, if the first update from replica B to replica C were lost, then this situation would be detected by replica C when it attempted to import the second update from replica B. The "starting state" timestamp row in the second packet would be the last row from the table on page 10, and would indicate that replica C was expected to have already imported the first two operations originated from replica A, and the first operation originated from replica B.

If the importing replica has already performed or imported all of the operations identified by the "starting state" row in the packet, then the operations contained in the packet are also imported into it. All operations are imported in the order in which they appear in the packet, and the importing replica's own table row is updated to reflect each operation as it is imported. If the packet contains an operation previously imported into the replica from some other packet (i.e. an operation with a virtual timestamp smaller than the appropriate component of the importing replica's table row), then the operation is ignored. Note that this implies that the importation of update packets is idempotent. If the receiving host fails part way through the importation of a packet, then it is safe to restart the importation from the beginning once the host has recovered.

In proof that this mechanism preserves consistency of VOB replicas, observe that if one replica imports an operation from another replica, then the importing replica must previously have performed or imported every operation preceding the imported operation in the sending replica's log. This follows because each such operation must either have originated at the importing replica (and is therefore already possessed by that replica), or be contained in the importing packet at some location preceding the operation being imported, or be tagged with a virtual timestamp that is no larger than the corresponding component of the importing packet's "starting state" timestamp row. In the last case, the fact that the packet is being imported implies that all such operations must previously have been imported from some other update packet. By induction, if the sending replica's log reflects a consistent ordering of operations, then the importing replica's log (and VOB state) will also be consistent.

It follows as a corollary that if a replica imports an operation that originated at some replica, then the importing replica must previously have imported *all* other operations with lower virtual timestamps that also originated at the same replica. This follows because each such operation with a lower virtual timestamp is a potential dependent of the operation with a higher virtual timestamp.

5.4 Purging Operations Logs

In order to prevent operation logs from growing without bound, entries must eventually be purged from the logs. MultiSite uses an age-based mechanism to decide when an entry should be removed from a log. By default, an entry is deleted after it has been in a log for 180 days (this value can be configured by the site administrator to reflect their

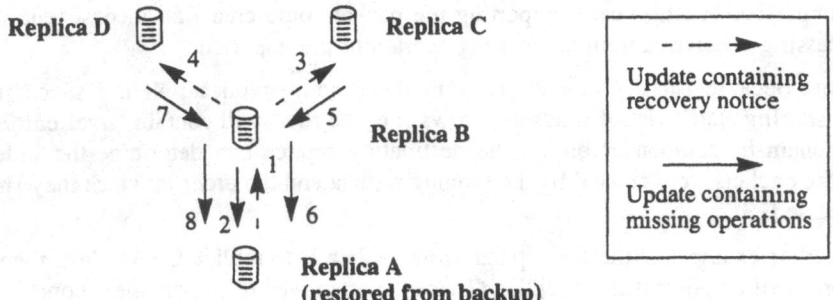

Fig. 8. Recovery from Backup

5.6 Recovery Details

When a replica is restored from backup tape, it is immediately locked to prevent users from making any new changes that would generate operations log entries. A special entry is added to the operations log to indicate that the replica was restored from backup tape, and the restored replica's virtual timestamp table row is added to that entry to indicate its restored state. The entry is assigned a special virtual timestamp (the highest possible timestamp) and treated specially by the synchronization mechanism. Note that the special entry cannot be assigned a normal virtual timestamp because any such timestamp may conflict with one previously used by the restored replica before the failure. The normal process of updating and importing packets then resumes (although the importing of most packets will be deferred by the restored replica due to the "starting state" check).

When other replicas import the special operations log entry, they reset their virtual timestamp table row for the restored replica to the value indicated by the entry. The importing replica also adds the special entry to its operations log so that it can be propagated to other replicas that may not be being directly updated by the restored replica. The importing replica also adds a special acknowledgment entry to its operations log to indicate that it has seen the entry from the restored replica.

When the restored replica imports an acknowledgment entry from every other replica, the VOB replica is unlocked and new operations are permitted to be performed on it.

In proof that this algorithm restores all of the missing operations to the restored replica, consider the operation possessed by any replica with the highest virtual timestamp that originated from the restored replica. The restored replica is required to import an acknowledgment from this replica before unlocking the restored replica. Such an acknowledgment is only created by the other replica in response to importing the special entry from the restored replica. The acknowledgment is added to the end of the log (i.e. after the latest operation from the restored replica), and is therefore considered by MultiSite to be potentially dependent on the last operation. According to the earlier results, the acknowledgment cannot be imported by any replica unless the replica has already imported the last operation from the restored replica. According to the corollary, the last operation from the restored replica cannot be imported unless all operations (that originated at the restored replica) with lower virtual timestamps have also been imported.

update pattern and rate). No check is performed to determine if the entry might still need to be sent to another replica.

More sophisticated algorithms exist for determining when an entry can safely be deleted from a log (i.e. when it will never need to be sent to another replica) [10]. However, such algorithms are based on knowledge of the replica backups that are performed. Such information is not available to MultiSite because VOB replica databases are just regular files that are backed-up as part of the normal filesystem. As a result, MultiSite cannot use these algorithms.

MultiSite *does* detect when needed entries have been purged from a log, and prevents potentially inconsistent updates from being made. Because successive operations originating at a replica are assigned virtual timestamps that differ by one, MultiSite can detect operation gaps between the last known state of a replica, and the actual operations written to an update packet for that replica. MultiSite verifies that the operations written to an update packet have virtual timestamps beginning with values exactly one larger than the timestamps in the table row for the destination replica. If this is not the case, then the destination replica must import the missing changes from some other replica or the replica must be recreated from a more up-to-date replica.

5.5 Recovery from Backup

When a VOB replica is restored from backup tape, it is not possible to immediately permit users to access the replica without risking the consistency of the VOB family. Other replicas in the VOB family may have imported operations that originated at the restored replica before its failure, but that were made after the backup (and not therefore recovered by the restored replica).[1] Any new operations originated at the restored replica therefore risk reusing the same virtual timestamps as those used by other operations already imported by other replicas, thereby breaking the synchronization mechanism.

MultiSite takes a roll-forward approach to dealing with this problem by requiring the restored replica to re-import any operations it originated (and that are possessed by other replicas) before permitting users to perform new operations on the replica. The recovery algorithm piggybacks on the normal synchronization mechanism and is similar in principle to an echo algorithm [11]. The basic idea behind the recovery algorithm is to cause all replicas to reset their virtual timestamp table row for the restored replica to reflect the restored state of that replica. Subsequent updates generated from the replicas will therefore carry any missing operations — that is, any operations with higher virtual timestamps — to the restored replica (Figure 8). Once all of these operations are imported by the restored replica, new operations can safely be performed without reusing any virtual timestamps already possessed by VOB family members.

Actually, it is only necessary that the restored replica import a recovery update from the last replica that it updated prior to the failure. Because updates always consist of an entire suffix of the sender's log, this other replica is guaranteed to have imported all of the desired operations that have been imported by any other replica. Unfortunately, there is not any way for MultiSite to determine from the restored VOB replica the identity of this last replica updated prior to the failure, so recovery updates are required to be imported (either directly or indirectly) from all other replicas.

---

1. In this sense, VOB replicas act as incremental backups of one another.

5.7 Re-recoveries

A real timestamp (clock time) is also added to the special log entry created by the restored replica to handle the case where the restored replica is re-restored from backup tape before completing its recovery. It is only necessary for the other replicas to acknowledge the latest recovery phase of the restored replica. The other replicas therefore only reset their virtual timestamp tables in response to a special log entry with a real timestamp later than any previously seen.

6 A MultiSite Usage Example

This section attempts to give a fairly realistic example of how MultiSite might be used to support distributed software development in a moderate-size organization. In this example, an organization does its primary development of a software product at a plant in Evanston, Illinois in the USA; it is just about to start work on a new release, V3.0. The new release will include functional enhancements, bug fixes, and will also be ported to a new workstation and localized to the Japanese language. The company decides that the porting work should be done by a subsidiary in Paris, France, and that the localization should be done by a subcontractor in Osaka, Japan.

The company uses a common ClearCase software development methodology:

- Individual subprojects, and often individual developers, work on separate subbranches.

- The *main* branch is reserved for integration of subprojects. To prepare for an internal baselevel or an external release, engineers first merge selected development subbranches back into the *main* branch.

- The ClearCase "views" used by developers ordinarily isolate them from changes occurring on the integration mainline by selecting versions from the most recent baselevel. When necessary, developers "merge out" changes from the main branch to their subbranches, in order to bring themselves up to date with changes occurring on the integration mainline.

- Periodically, a baselevel of the product is built on the main branch, is tested, and is made available for internal use. The versions used in the baselevel are labelled, both for ease of identification and so that developers can instruct their "views" to select those versions.

With MultiSite, the organization can continue to use this accustomed methodology. The Evanston office will be the master of the *main* branch — the only site allowed to make modifications on the integration branch. A porting integration branch, named *paris_port,* will be mastered at the Paris office, as will any additional subbranches of *paris_port* that may be needed to organize the work there. And, a localization integration branch, named *osaka_locale,* will be mastered at the Osaka subcontractor's office, as well as any subbranches of *osaka_locale* that may be needed there. The Evanston office will periodically merge changes from the *paris_port* branch back into the *main* branch, to keep the two sites from diverging; however, localization changes from Osaka will only be merged back into the main branch after V3.0 of the product ships, because they are expected to be too disruptive.

To support the porting and localization efforts, the project management decides that both the Paris and Osaka offices need to see changes from Evanston on a daily basis; and, for convenience, that it is useful for the Osaka and Evanston offices to see Paris' changes on a daily basis also. However, they decide that it is only useful for Osaka to update Evanston once a month, and that Osaka never needs to update Paris directly (MultiSite automatically ensures that Paris will receive Osaka's updates indirectly via Evanston). A wide-area network with the topology shown in Figure 9 is already in place among the three sites.

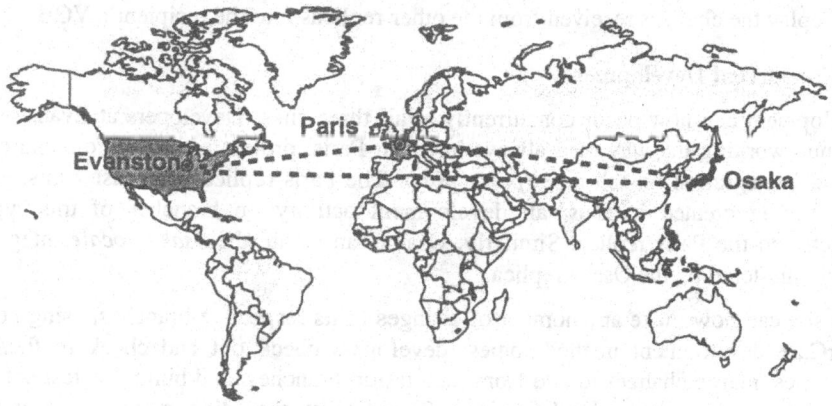

Fig. 9. Parallel Development in a Wide-Area Network

Figure 10 summarizes the direction and frequency of updates among the three replicas:

from/to	Evanston	Paris	Osaka
Evanston	—	Daily	Daily
Paris	Daily	—	Daily
Osaka	Monthly	Never	—

Fig. 10. Replica Update Frequency

6.1 Replica Creation and Configuration

Assume that the VOB to be replicated originally resides in Evanston. Then, the initial replica setup is a two-step process:

1. The administrator at Evanston runs a MultiSite command which dumps (*exports*) the contents of the VOB, in a machine-independent format, into one or more *data packets* for transmission to the remote sites. During this export step only, the VOB must be locked against changes. The administrator then arranges for these packets to be sent, via network or magnetic tape, to both Paris and Osaka.

2. The administrators at Paris and Osaka execute a MultiSite command to *import* the replica-creation packets. Once the import commands are complete, the VOB replicas are available for use by developers at the Paris and Osaka sites.

Once the replicas have been created, the administrators at each site must configure the periodic updates among the sites. For controlling periodic operations, MultiSite uses the UNIX *cron* facility. So, this configuration consists of creating entries in *cron*'s scheduler table to:

- run the MultiSite commands that package up the changes to each replica's VOB
- transport the change packets to the other replicas
- replay the changes received from the other replicas into the recipient's VOB

6.2 Concurrent Development

Development can now occur concurrently at all three sites. Developers at Evanston can continue working the way they always have. In Paris, project administrators can create the local integration branch type (*paris_port*). The Paris replica will master this branch type, having created it; thus, all development activity on branches of this type is restricted to the Paris replica. Similarly, Osaka can create the *osaka_locale* integration branch, mastered by the Osaka replica.

Each site can now make any number of changes to its respective branches, using normal ClearCase development methodologies: developers check out and check in files and directories, merge changes to and from integration branches, and build and test software using the versions selected by their views. Periodically, according to the update schedule configured using *cron*, the replicas automatically exchange update packets containing the sequence of changes made to each replica; these update packets are automatically applied to each replica in the proper order by MultiSite, allowing the developers at each site to see their colleagues' work from other sites.

6.3 Building a Release

The organization can integrate branch development and produce a release using almost the same procedure it used in the pre-MultiSite era. The only significant change is that the merges of the subprojects' branches are interspersed with synchronization updates where necessary. Rather than waiting for the periodic updates run by *cron*, at times it may be more convenient for the project administrators to manually force an update to be sent; this is easily accomplished by running the relevant MultiSite update commands by hand. A typical baselevel build procedure might include steps like these:

1. When development on the *main* branch reaches a stable point, Evanston labels the latest versions on the *main* branch, establishing a baselevel.

2. The *main* branch is locked, so that a consistent set of versions can be sent to Paris.

3. Evanston generates a synchronization update and sends it to Paris, to ensure that the *main* branch is up-to-date at Paris. The commands are the same as those used in the periodic update procedure set up using *cron*.

4. Paris developers merge changes on the *main* branch out to the *paris_port* branch. They build and test the application, then *checkin* a stable set of versions on the *paris_port* branch. As in Step #1, another baselevel is established by attaching labels to this set of versions. Then, the *paris_port* branch is locked in advance of generating an update.

5. Paris sends a synchronization update to Evanston, propagating the revisions to the *paris_port* branches.

6. Evanston developers merge the *paris_port* changes back into the *main* branch.
(This should be a trivial merge.) Then, they build, test, and wrap up the release,
labeling its versions appropriately.

This merge strategy puts the potentially-difficult work of resolving merge conflicts in the
hands of the Paris developers, who know more about their own changes.

6.4 Using Two Replicas of the Same VOB at One Site

As the organization grows, the load on a single VOB replica may become too large to be
handled by a single server machine. One possibility might be to upgrade the hardware,
but MultiSite offers another alternative: the possibility of splitting the load by creating
another replica of the VOB at the same site, and moving some of the developers over to
the newly-created replica. In the example described here, management might decide to
split the Evanston replica into two — one for new development and bug fixing, and the
other for build-intensive release-time integration work.

This task is easily accomplished, again by using the MultiSite command to create a new
replica, dumping the existing replica's contents and then importing the replica-creation
packets to form the new replica. Knowledge of the new replica's existence is
automatically propagated by MultiSite to the remaining replicas. Then, the
administrators will want to reconsider the patterns and frequency of updates among the
replicas. For replicas at a single site connected by a high-bandwidth local area network,
it may be appropriate to exchange updates more frequently — perhaps three or four
times per day. This is practical because each update only includes the *changes* made
since the previous update, so that adding extra updates only imposes a small additional
fixed cost per update (of computing the changes to be sent, and of setting up and tearing
down the network connection).

7 Experiences from Actual Usage

As a way of measuring the impact of MultiSite on our usage of ClearCase, we examined
the main VOB in use by our development organization. It contains the main source for
ClearCase, comprising approximately 190Mb of source files and 470Mb of database.
After five months of use of MultiSite on our VOB, we accumulated approximately 13Mb
of log information data. This is the main space overhead associated with the presence of
MultiSite. When compared with the total size of the database, this is a small percentage
overhead (2.7%).

Currently, we're using two replicas for development. Another measure of activity is the
amount of data shipped from replica to replica as part of day-to-day operation. At the
time of writing, there is approximately 400-1200Kb of data shipped from each replica to
the other. The day-to-day amount varies substantially, depending on details of work in
progress. For example, on weekends there is usually no data to transfer. The time to read
out log information and generate a packet for shipment is short, taking 1-2 minutes of
elapsed time and 10-20 seconds of CPU time. The time to replay log information against
a receiving replica is also usually 1-2 minutes elapsed with 10-40 seconds of CPU time.
Occasionally the elapsed time is longer, due to the fact that some operations require
proportionally more updating of the database. For example, one particular transfer took

17 minutes elapsed; this was due to the fact that version labelling on replay has not yet been optimized (as it has been done for ClearCase's original "make label" operation).

8 Future Directions

A new way to use MultiSite is for online backup. ClearCase requires that a VOB be locked for the duration of a backup, so that the database and filesystem objects are captured consistently. After creating a second replica in a local area network, it is possible to perform backups against the second replica, thereby avoiding locking the VOB. This is increasingly important as the developer work and nightly rebuilding combine to increase the busy time of a VOB to around-the-clock, making it inconvenient to lock VOBs.

Another possible use of MultiSite would be for software distribution. New software would be made available by adding it to a replicated VOB. As part of the normal process of updating other replicas, those replicas would receive the new software, which could then be used at the other locations.

One area where MultiSite could be improved would be the addition of facilities to allow portions of VOB information to be eliminated from the information being exchanged between replicas. One variation would be to mark elements as being private to a particular replica. This would have the effect of disabling operation logging for all operations performed on the element. Another variation would be "filtering", whereby a filter would be defined that would limit replication, probably by specifying an inclusive list of objects to be replicated. A number of problems appear when adding filtering. For example, what happens when only partial information is propagated and later the filter is widened, allowing previously excluded information? If portions of a version tree are propagated, what rules need to be added to deal with operations on non-propagated versions? What operations need to work even when complete information is not present? For these reasons, the area of filtering will require further investigation.

9 Conclusions

This paper has described an extension to the ClearCase software configuration management system that supports geographically-distributed development by replication of Versioned Object Bases. A combination of loosely-synchronized replicas with fine-grained object mastership prevents conflicting changes from occurring at different replicas. This enables automatic synchronization, with no need for manual intervention to resolve conflicts.

Our experience so far has validated our design choices. The MultiSite product is currently in use by about 1800 developers at 35 sites around the world, with remarkably few problems reported to date.

One of MultiSite's biggest design strengths is its unobtrusiveness. In most respects, developers in a distributed organization see little or no change in their development environment or development policies when MultiSite is introduced. Even for administrators, MultiSite imposes few additional administrative tasks, once the initial setup and configuration of replicas have been completed.

Software configuration management demands planning; geographically-distributed software development requires even more careful planning on the part of project leaders and development teams. ClearCase and MultiSite provide a framework for organizing the software development process, and a rich set of tools for enforcing and monitoring it across many sites. They cannot, however, eliminate the need for a development policy that spans the organization.

10 References

1. B. Walker, G. Popek, R. English, C. Kline, and G. Thiel. "The LOCUS Distributed Operating System" *Proceedings of the Ninth ACM Symposium on Operating Systems Principles* ACM, October 1983.

2. A. Birrell, R. Levin, R. Needham, and M. Schroeder. "Grapevine: An Exercise in Distributed Computing" *Communications of the ACM* vol. 25, No. 4 (April 1982).

3. D. Gifford. "Weighted Voting for Replicated Data" *Proceedings of the Seventh Symposium on Operating Systems Principles* ACM, December 1979.

4. J. Gray. "Notes on Database Operating Systems" *Lecture Notes in Computer Science* vol. 60, Springer Verlag, Berlin, 1978

5. J. Howard, M. Kazar, S. Menees, D. Nichols, M. Satyanarayanan, R. Sidebotham, and M. West. "Scale and Performance in a Distributed File System" *ACM Transactions on Computer Systems* 6(1):51-81, February 1988

6. B. Liskov and R. Ladin "Highly Available Distributed Services and Fault-Tolerant Distributed Garbage Collection" *Proceedings of the Fifth ACM Symposium on Principles of Distributed Computing* (August 1986).

7. R. Ladin, B. Liskov, L. Shrira, and S. Ghemawat. "Providing High Availability Using Lazy Replication" *ACM Transactions on Computer Systems* vol. 10, no. 4 (November 1992).

8. K. Birman, A. Schiper, and P. Stephenson. "Lightweight Causal and Atomic Group Multicast" *ACM Transactions on Computer Systems*, vol. 9, no. 3 (August 1991).

9. L. Lamport. "Time, Clocks, and the Ordering of Events in a Distributed System" *Communications of the ACM*, vol. 21, no. 7 (July 1978).

10. R. Strom and S. Yemini. "Optimistic Recovery in Distributed Systems" *ACM Transactions on Computer Systems*, vol. 3, no. 3 (August 1985).

11. E. Chang. "Echo Algorithms: Depth Parallel Operations on General Graphs" *IEEE Transactions on Software Engineering*, vol. 8, no. 4 (July 1982).

SCM Systems Session

Michel Lacroix & Jacky Estublier

The three systems presented in the session, support different facets of configuration management, and appeared in the discussion to be to some extent complementary.

The ODIN system, which has gone through a long process of refinements and maturation is probably the most versatile build facility available today. Its key features include a powerful derived object manager and support for variant builds.

The PROTEUS system is the result of significant research efforts on system modelling (a.k.a. modelling of configuration structures). PROTEUS models configurations and their structural variability with an object-oriented language; the build expressions are also specified in this language. The modelling of both the historical and "true" variability with the same mechanism was addressed in the discussion. The possibility of using ODIN as a build engine for PROTEUS has also been identified as worth being explored.

Finally, the STORE system proposes solutions to a problem which is usually not well addressed both by commercial and research SCM systems, viz. the administration of third- party applications in a heterogeneous LAN environment.

This session is a complement to the model session. Odin is one of the best examples of a rebuild modelling system, while Proteus did a very interesting job in looking for better system modelling, and from this point of view is the successor of works on Modules Interconnection Languages and system models.

The discussion, during this session, focused on why doing really better than Make is so difficult; Geoff provided some interesting clues on this topic, mentioning different systems which integrated Odin.

About Proteus, an interesting issue is that such powerful and detailed modelling provides the system with a deep knowledge of the system structure, and thus opens many possibilities for advanced support in software engineering, rebuilding, reverse engineering and so on. Conversely, modelling itself is very time consuming. It was felt unclear, by part of the attendance, what is the ratio cost/benefit of such modelling. Clearly this kind of experiment is one of the best way of providing better modelling; real size applications, and their experience report will be expected with interest.

Modelling Systems with Variability using the PROTEUS Configuration Language

Eirik Tryggeseth, Bjørn Gulla and Reidar Conradi

Department of Computer Systems and Telematics
Norwegian Institute of Technology (NTH)
N-7034 Trondheim, Norway
{eirik|bjorngu|conradi}@idt.unit.no

Abstract. To respond to environmental changes and customer specific requirements, industrial software systems must often incorporate many sources of variability. Developers use a diverse range of representations and techniques to achieve this, including structural variability, component version selection, conditional inclusion, and varying derivation processes.

This paper advocates specifying *all* potential variability within a system using a single formalism. PCL, the configuration language defined in the PROTEUS[1] project, provides uniform facilities for expressing and controlling variability in all aspects of a system and its manufacturing process. PCL is supported by a comprehensive tool set and is integrated with several design methods. The paper uses a simple example throughout to illustrate the facilities of PCL and how these are supported by the tool set.

Keywords: Configuration language, software evolution, software configuration management.

1 Introduction

The objective of the PROTEUS project is to provide support for system evolution. The project name is inspired by the mythological Greek sea-god who was capable of changing his shape at will to adapt to prevailing circumstances. The project has developed methods and tools for (1) domain analysis, (2) adapting existing design methods (SDL, HOOD, MD) to support evolving systems, and (3) modelling system structure and manufacture. This paper deals with the last issue. PROTEUS is an application driven project - four industrial companies operate as "users", i.e. state requirements, validate specifications and evaluate developed methods and tools in operational divisions. PROTEUS is nearing completion, and we are now in the process of evaluating tool and methodological support.

PCL, the PROTEUS Configuration Language, is a formalism for system mod-

---

1. PROTEUS is project no. 8086 in the European research programme ESPRIT III. PROTEUS started in May 1992 for a period of three years and has a budget of 9,6 MECUs. Participants are CAP Gemini Innovation (F), Matra Marconi Space (F), CAP debis SSP (D), SINTEF (N), Lancaster University (UK), Intecs (I), CAP Sesa Telecom(F), and Hewlett Packard (F). NTH is a subcontractor to SINTEF.

elling, configuration definition and system manufacture. As systems evolve, large numbers of system and component versions with slightly different properties are created. The objective of PCL is to support product management in a broad sense throughout the complete system lifetime: manage components and sub-systems, their interconnections, their variability, their evolution and their potential derivation processes. PCL covers both software, hardware and documentation parts of products. We will in this paper focus on aspects of software management.

The paper is organized as follows. Section 2 gives a compressed state of the art review of work on which PCL is partly based. Section 3 presents the PCL language constructs for system modelling with emphasis on how to express variability. A working example is used throughout the section. Section 4 provides an overview of tool support for the PCL language and the current status of the implementation. Section 5 reports some experiences gained so far in the project, while Section 6 offers some conclusions. Finally, the full PCL source for the example used in this article is listed in an Appendix.

2 State of the Art

A system model is a description of the items of a system and the relationships between them. For such a model to support configuration management, it must uniquely identify the comprising components, their static structure and derivation processes. It is a principle in configuration management that the system model must be explicit, unambiguous, and be managed as the system evolves [17].

Module Interconnection Languages, MILs, is a common approach for expressing system models. Sommerville and Dean [13] give an overview of existing module interconnection languages and compare these with the capabilities of PCL. System models are also employed by current SCM systems, although the model is usually embedded in a tool or in a database. We have extended the comparison in [13] with more fine-grained criteria and replaced the description of some MILs with characterization of three SCM systems. Table I presents a summary of the comparison, which is to some degree influenced by the concrete requirements expressed by the application partners in PROTEUS. The requirements assessed in the table can be summarized as

- **Integrated system modelling:** Modelling all aspects of the product in one formalism, i.e. incorporate descriptions of and interrelationships between software, hardware and documentation elements.
- **Multiple structural viewpoints:** Be able to express and show several viewpoints of the same system, e.g. its interface, its logical composition and its run-time structure.
- **Structural variability**: The ability to define variability in the logical composition of a system, in interfaces and in relationships in which an entity participates.
- **Component variability**: The ability to represent variability in the concrete system (e.g. revisions and variants of source files), and to allow intensional version selection. Versions should be logically characterized, related to the system model.

TABLE I Support offered by MILs and SCM systems for PROTEUS requirements

	MIL75 [3]	Cooprider's MIL [2]	INTERCOL [15]	Jasmine [10]	SySL [14]	ClearCase [8]	Adele [5]	PCL [12]
Integrated system modelling	None	None	None	None	Good	None	None	Good
Multiple structural viewpoints	Limited	None	None	None	None	None	Limited	Good
Structural variability	None	None	None	None	Limited	Limited	Good	Good
Component variability	None	Limited	Limited	None	None	Good	Good	Good
Flexible manufacture support	None	None	Limited	Limited	None	Good	Good	Good
Object-oriented modelling	None	Limited	Limited	Good	None	None	Good	Good
User tailorability	None	None	None	Limited	None	Good	Good	Good

- **Flexible manufacture support:** The details of the system manufacture process must be controlled from the system model. Definition of generic yet instrumentable manufacture tasks should be supported. The aggregation of such tasks into a manufacture process should be computed from the system model.
- **Object-oriented modelling:** The extent to which the language uses the concepts provided in object-oriented formalisms, such as classification, inheritance and encapsulation.
- **User tailorability:** Ability to provide an extensible, multi-dimensional classification scheme and offer integration with a range of different design methods. User-defined relations to tailor the modelling capabilities should be supported.

The only two formalisms offering direct support for integrated system modelling are SySL and PCL. In large-scale system evolution it is essential to capture the dependency relationships to enable successful change management. Incorporating non-software items is also necessary for proper modelling of distributed applications and embedded systems.

Although MIL75, the original module interconnection language, offered virtually no support for most of our requirements, it did offer limited support for multiple structural viewpoints. Future work largely ignored this early insight and still only provided limited support. PCL is the first language to provide good facilities to model a range of these different structural viewpoints.

Narayanaswamy identified the need for structural variability [11], although the proposed NuMIL does not contain constructs for expressing it. In SySL some variability may be expressed using cardinality on the composition relation. Clear-Case supports limited structural variability by allowing directories to be versioned. PCL allows structural variability to be explicitly declared, i.e. stating which parts of the system are stable and which parts vary by using conditional expressions in the system model. It also recognizes that variance can occur within any of the structural viewpoints, and supports reconciliation across a complete model.

Cooprider was the first to incorporate component variability into the MIL framework. INTERCOL allows structuring this information within the notion of a family, and supports version selection, i.e. allowing the system to determine which version to use in a configuration. More advanced SCM systems offer intensional configuration descriptions, consisting of a product part and a version part. Such descriptions serve as partially bound system descriptions, and must be expanded into fully bound configurations (extensional lists) by exploiting stored product and versioning information. The sequence of product and version binding varies. MILs usually first perform product elaboration into relevant product families, and then version binding for each atomic family. In Adele, an intertwined binding process over the product is used, exploiting preferences and constraint rules. Yet other systems, such as ClearCase and EPOS [9], first perform version binding, allowing transparent access to a uni-version view.

Automated support for system manufacture was introduced by Feldman [6] with the Make system. ClearCase provides more accurate and optimized re-generation by managing 'configuration records' for derived objects. In Adele manufacture support may be implemented by triggers. PCL advocates user control of re-compilation, using automatically generated makefiles tailored to the selected product configuration.

Object-oriented modelling has recently gained popularity in the software engineering community. Some of the principles behind the object-oriented paradigm, such as information hiding and grouping have been supported in previous languages. Only SySL, Adele and PCL offer extensive object-oriented facilities in their modelling languages.

User tailorability is an important requirement for enabling seamless integration with a diverse set of design methods. Different design methods often need specific types and relations for expressing their architectures, and rather than trying to include all possible ones in one language, an extensible framework should be offered. PCL does just that. Adele allows user-defined object and relationship types, and roles of these.

3   System Modelling and Variability

The aim of PCL is to provide a notation in which all aspects of a system family may be modelled. This includes software, hardware, documentation, possible configurations, how these configurations are instantiated into a system, and finally how the software parts of an instantiated system are processed into executable programs.

PCL [12] defines six distinct entity types for modelling families of systems, as defined in Table II. An entity description is organized in sections, each con-

TABLE II PCL entity types and sections

Entity type	Sections
family	classification, attributes, interface, parts, physical, relationships
version description	attributes, parts
tool	inputs, outputs, attributes, scripts
relation	domain, range
class	physical, tool
attribute type	enumeration

sisting of a sequence of named slots. These entity types are related to each other by a set of language-defined relations as shown in Figure 1. The remainder of this section explains how these concepts and relations are used to support comprehensive modelling of system families.

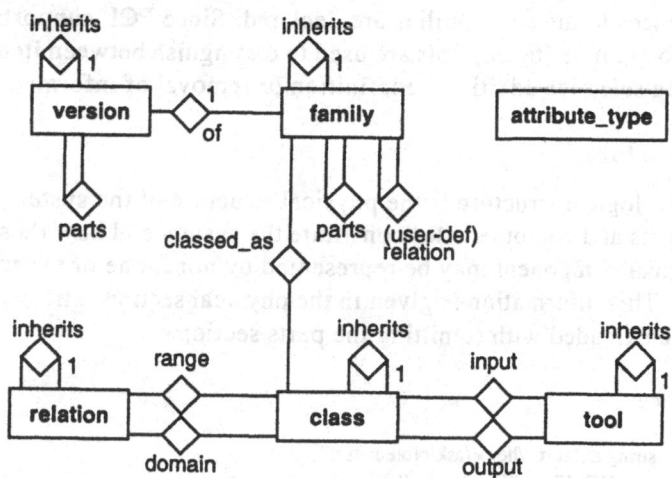

Fig. 1. Language-defined relations

3.1 Composition Structure

The basic assumption of PCL is that a system can be organized as a layered composition structure at the logical level. This means that one component may be a part of another component, and may itself have sub-components.

The family entity is the core entity in PCL. All logical components and their structure are defined by a set of family entities.

Logical Structure

In the remainder of the paper we will use a calculator program as a small, but yet complete example for exemplifying the constructs in PCL. The complete PCL source for the example is given in an Appendix. The basic composition structure in the calculator program can graphically be illustrated as in Figure 2. In PCL this logical system structure is expressed as:

(i)
```
family CalcProg
    parts
        calc => Calculator;
        math => mathlib;
    end
end

family Calculator
end

family mathlib
end
```

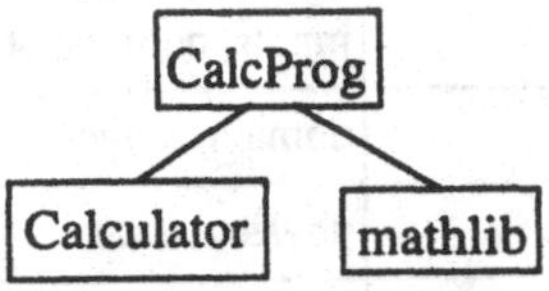

Fig. 2. Logical structure of the calculator program

The logical composition structure of a system is specified in the parts section. Note the use of *slots* (named 'calc' and 'math' in the parts section) in which the actual references to the sub-families are declared. Since PCL supports entity refinement through inheritance, slots are used to distinguish between items in a section, allowing selective addition, redefinition or removal of information.

Physical Structure

Parallel to the logical structure is the physical structure of the system, i.e. which tangible objects and computer files constitute the system and how these are organized. A logical component may be represented by none, one or several physical components. This information is given in the physical section. The calculator example can be extended with (omitting the parts section):

(ii)
```
family CalcProg
    attributes
        HOME : string default "/home/ask/proteus/test";
        workspace := HOME ++ "/calc/src/"; // string concatenation
        repository := "calc/";
    end
    physical
        main => "main.C";
        defs => "defs.h";
        exe => "calc.x" attributes workspace := HOME ++ "/calc/bin"; end
                classifications status := standard.derived; end; // This is not a primary object
    end
end
```

```
family Calculator
   attributes
      workspace := 'workspace ++ "Calculator/";
      repository := 'repository ++ "Calculator/";
   end
   physical
      calc => ("Calculator.C", "Calculator.h");
      expr => ("expr.C", "expr.h");
   end
end

family mathlib
   attributes
      workspace := 'workspace ++ "mathlib/";
      repository := 'repository ++ "mathlib/";
   end
   physical
      files => (
         "math_plus.c",
         "math_minus.c",
         "math_mult.c",
         "math_div.c",
         "math_sqrt.c",
         "mathlib.h");
      lib => "libmath.a" classifications status := standard.derived; end;
   end
end
```

For software a physical object is a file in a certain directory on the user's disk. The directory where a file is located is called the workspace for the file. Typically the files associated with one logical component tend to have the same workspace. Because of this PCL has defined a special attribute *workspace* which can be set in the attributes section of a PCL entity. The value of this will by default be the workspace of all files defined in the physical section. It is possible to override this, e.g. as for "calc.x" in CalcProg.

PCL allows propagation of attribute values along the composition hierarchy to achieve compact and easily manageable models. This is convenient for example when an application is moved from one directory to another. In mathlib we see that the workspace attribute is extended with the string "mathlib/" compared to the CalcProg's value. The notation '<attribute_name> means to use the value of this attribute closest above in the composition hierarchy.

3.2   Entity Attributes

PCL supports annotation of entities with attributes of two different kinds, *information attributes* to provide stable information about an entity, and *variability control attributes* which are determined during system instantiation. Syntactically they are distinguished by using the '=' assignment operator for entity attributes, while ':=' (or no assignment) is used for variability control attributes.

Entity Information Attributes

Entities may be annotated with a number of attributes of type string, integer, or user-defined enumerations. There is a pre-defined enumeration type, boolean, whose members are true and false. We can elaborate the calculator example with attributes for the CalcProg entity:

(iii)
```
family CalcProg
  attributes
    created_by = "Marius Kintel";
    created : string = "94/08/12";
    contract_no: integer = 1643256;
  end
end
```

Since string is the default attribute type, including the attribute type string is not necessary (e.g. for created_by).

Variability Control Attributes

A family in principle represents a set of potential logical components. The differences between the individual members of the family is declared by the use of *variability control attributes*. A specific member is produced by binding values to these.

On the logical or architectural level, the breakdown of functionality may be different according to what situation the entity is used in, and at the physical level, the mapping from logical structure to files may differ, and finally each file may exist in different versions. An example of a variability control attribute is the 'status' attribute in the example below.

(iv)
```
family CalcProg
  attributes
    ...
    status: status_type exported default initiated;
  end
end
```

The 'status' attribute is of an enumeration type. An enumerated attribute type can be declared as:

(v)
```
attribute_type status_type
  enumeration initiated, module-tested, system-tested end
end
```

This attribute is not assigned a value as the other attributes in the example, but is rather given a *default value*. The default value may be overridden by a new value, taken from a *version description*, during system instantiation. See Section 3.7 for an explanation of the 'exported' qualifier.

3.3 Expressing Variability

The parts section in a family entity defines what parts the entity consists of. Each subpart in a family is declared in a slot which syntactically is on the form:

```
<slot>  =>  <family-entity>
     |   <conditional-expr> // eventually referencing family-entities
```

The types of variability we want to show here are (1) variability in the logical composition structure of a system family, (2) variability in the mapping from the logical composition to the physical objects, and (3) variability in attribute assignments.

Structural Variability

Variability in the logical composition structure of a system family is expressed by associating a conditional expression to the assignment of a parts slot. Consider again the calculator example. We will extend the example to optionally include a graphical user interface. The original structure of the program is shown in Figure 2. Figure 3 illustrates the modified structure of the CalcProg entity:

(vi)
```
family CalcProg
   attributes
      ...
      xgui : boolean default false;
   end
   parts
      ui => if xgui = true then XGUI endif;
      calc => Calculator;
      math => mathlib;
   end
end
```

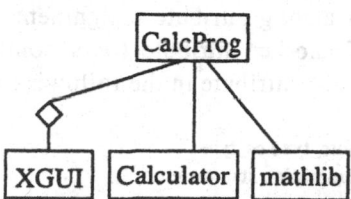

Fig. 3. Extending the structure of the calculator program

PCL also features entity refinement through inheritance. Inheritance might also be used for expressing variability between family entities. Inheritance is however mainly used for achieving economy of description by allowing extraction of common information for a set of family entities. This information can then be declared once in a generic family from which the other families inherit.

Providing these two constructs for expressing variability on the structural level allows declaring variability at different levels as needed.

Variability in Mapping

In (iii) we defined the Calculator entity to have four files, where two are related to expression parsing ("expr.c" and "expr.h"). PCL can express that the mapping from the logical component Calculator into files contains variability. This is expressed by introducing conditions on the slot assignment in the physical section. In the following example we express that the binding of files to the expression slot is dependent on the 'expression' attribute. In this case we want to distinguish between infix and reverse polish notation expression parsing.

(vii)
```
family Calculator
  attributes
      ...
    expression : expr_type default infix;
  end
  physical
    calc => ("Calculator.C", "Calculator.h");
    expr => if expression = infix then
            ("expr.C", "expr.h")
          elsif expression = reverse_polish then
            ("rpn_expr.C", "rpn_expr.h")
          endif;
  end
end
```

This allows straight forward and elegant treatment of collapsing, splitting, deleting, and moving files during system evolution. Many traditional configuration management systems have problems with handling this properly.

Attribute Assignment Variability (Constraints)

The last form of variability we present here may be used to represent simple constraints among attribute assignments. I.e. an attribute may take a special value only if another attribute (or a combination) takes a particular value like the CCFLAGS attribute in the following example:

(viii)
```
attribute_type os_type
  enumeration sun, vax end
end
family CalcProg
  attributes
      ...
    expression : expr_type default infix;
    debug : boolean default false;
    os: os_type;
    DEBUG := if debug = true then "-g -Ddebug " endif;
    INCL : string := "";
    CCFLAGS : string :=
      if os = sun then
        if expression = infix then DEBUG ++ "-Dsun4 "
        elsif expression = reverse_polish then DEBUG ++ "-O2 "
        endif
      elsif os = vax then DEBUG ++ "-C -Dvax "
      endif;
  end
end
```

3.4   System Instantiation

A system family described using PCL defines a set of possible system instances. System instantiation is the process of removing all (1) structural variability, and

(2) physical mapping variability, and assigning correct attribute values to the attributes throughout the instantiated system. We call this process *binding*.

A system is bound in an iterative way, in which the three following activities are performed interleaved: (a) Application of a version description on a family entity. (b) Evaluation of attribute expressions. (c) Propagation of attribute values along the composition hierarchy.

A variability control attribute may have its value propagated from another entity in the composition structure. This is a feature which is particular convenient for resolving logical and physical variability to build a consistent configuration. We declare an attribute to take its value from *the nearest entity above* in the logical composition hierarchy which has a value assigned for the particular attribute name. We may extend the Calculator entity with the attributes:

(ix)
```
attributes
   status : status_type := 'status;
   number : integer := 'X + 3 default 10;
end
```

Since declarations of the first form are used in most occasions, we allow the shorthand declaration below to mean the same.

(x)
```
attributes
   status : status_type;
end
```

The specification of version descriptors in PCL is intensional, i.e. defined in terms of the desired properties of the final system rather than explicitly enumerating the particular instances for each component. An example illustrates this:

(xi)
```
version my-version of CalcProg
   attributes
      os := sun;
      xgui := true;
   end
end
```

When this version descriptor is applied to the family entity CalcProg in (viii), the following happens during Bind:

- Most attributes are bound to their default values, e.g. expression is bound to 'infix'.
- The os and xgui attributes are bound to sun and to true.
- The expressions for the DEBUG and CCFLAGS attributes are evaluated to "" and to "-Dsun4 ".
- The structural variability on the ui slot assignment is resolved, so the CalcProg entity in (vi) is composed of the XGUI, Calculator and mathlib parts.

Thus the CalcProg entity, after instantiation by applying the my-version version description, looks like:

(xii)
```
family CalcProg
```

```
    attributes
      HOME : string := "/home/ask/proteus/test";
      workspace : string := "/home/ask/proteus/test/calc/src/";
      repository : string := "calc/";
      created_by : string = "Marius Kintel";
      created : string = "94/08/12";
      contract_no: integer = 1643256;
      status: status_type exported := initiated;
      xgui : boolean := true;
      expression : expr_type := infix;
      debug : boolean := false;
      os: os_type := sun;
      DEBUG : string := "";
      INCL : string := "";
      CCFLAGS : string := "-Dsun4 ";
    end
    parts
      ui => XGUI
      calc => Calculator;
      math => mathlib;
    end
  end
```

Assume that both XGUI, Calculator and mathlib declare the attribute INCL :=
'INCL;. By default, the value assigned to the INCL attribute in this case is the
value of the attribute in the nearest ancestor in the composition structure. Now,
for some reason, during system instantiation, it is discovered that the INCL attribute needs to have a different value for the XGUI entity. This is achieved by
declaring a "sub" version descriptor specifying the particular bindings for XGUI.
Figure 4 shows how this is visualized in the PCL tool set.

(xiii)
```
    version my-version of CalcProg
      attributes
        os := sun;
        xgui := true;
      end
      parts
        ui => ui-version;
      end
    end

    version ui-version of XGUI
      attributes
        INCL := "-I/local/X11R5/include ";
      end
    end
```

Now, when the bind operation is fixing the attribute values for the XGUI entity,
it uses the values applied on the entity from the ui-version version descriptor. This
has higher priority than the values propagated along the composition hierarchy,
which are used e.g. for Calculator and mathlib.

To assist the system instantiation process for large configurations, the PCL
tools provide:

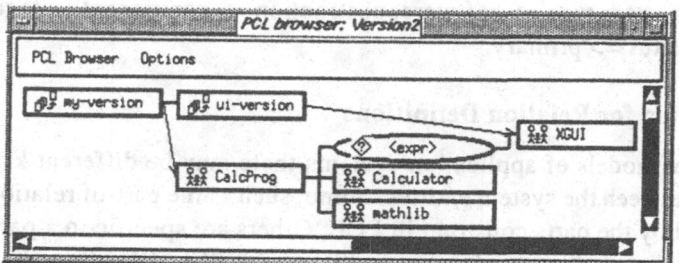

Fig. 4. Visual presentation of a composite version descriptor

- *Partial binding* to iteratively remove parts of the variability in a system model. This is useful for scrutinizing a model covering only a limited set of all possible system configurations.
- *Interactive binding* to aid the process by allowing the user to interactively choose between possible attribute bindings whenever Bind cannot compute a value. This is convenient for large and unfamiliar models, where it might be hard to know which attributes exist and which may or must be assigned a value. Automatic constructions of correct composite version descriptors is provided by the PCL tools to be able to re-instantiate the particular instance made during an interactive bind session.

3.5 Entity Classification

PCL provides a framework for classifying family entities and physical objects. Classifications are also used for defining the domain and range for user-defined relations. Requirements from the partners in the PROTEUS project have shown that entity classification is a complex task. Therefore PCL provides an extensible framework from which users can define their own classification hierarchies. PCL basically allows classification along four different dimensions, distinguished by different slot names:

- **abstraction:** Used to classify the entity according to its level of abstraction. The possible abstractions are *system, process* and *component*.
- **type:** Used to classify the entity as either *hardware, software* or an *amalgam (platform)*. *Processor* is a sub-class of hardware, used for entities which can execute software processes. *Platform* is used for entities which are logically considered as a single entity and which include one or more processors and associated software. Application software is installed on a platform.
- **category:** Used to specify whether the entity is a documentation or a representation produced during the system development process. Possible categories are *document* and *program*.
- **status:** Used to specify whether the entity can be automatically derived. Possible status assignments are *primary* or *derived*.

In addition the user may define new classification dimensions, or introduce subclasses of the pre-defined classes. Default values for classification assignment for family entities are type => software, abstraction => component, category => program and status => primary.

Classification for Relation Definitions

In structural models of application systems there may be different kinds of relationships between the system entities. Some, such as the part-of relation, is directly provided by the parts construct in PCL. Others are specific to a particular system or a design method used in conjunction with PCL. We allow these relationships to be documented by offering users mechanisms to define binary relationships between family entities in a model. Relationships may be restricted to connect only certain types of entities by declaring the legal domain and range in the relation definition. Only entities defined with classifications matching the classifications specified as domain and range may participate.

Some relations are pre-defined in PCL, such as 'requires', 'implemented-by' and 'installed-on'.

Classification for System Manufacture

Classifications are particularly important for system building, as this process is basically to find a relationship between a physical object and a tool that is able to transform the physical object into a new form.

In the calculator example we have

(xiv)
```
physical
    files => ("Calculator.C", "Calculator.h");
end
```

To be able to find a tool that may compile the file "Calculator.C", we must be sure that the file and the input expected by the tool is of the same type.

For the calculator example, a number of sub-classes of software are defined.

(xv)
```
class text inherits standard.software
end

class source-code inherits text
end

class cpp-source inherits source-code
    tools CC end
    physical
        name ++ ".C";
    end
end
```

From this example, we see that the file "Calculator.C" matches the classification 'cpp-source'. Figure 5 shows a part of the full classification hierarchy.

The next paragraph explains how we use this classification information to support system manufacture.

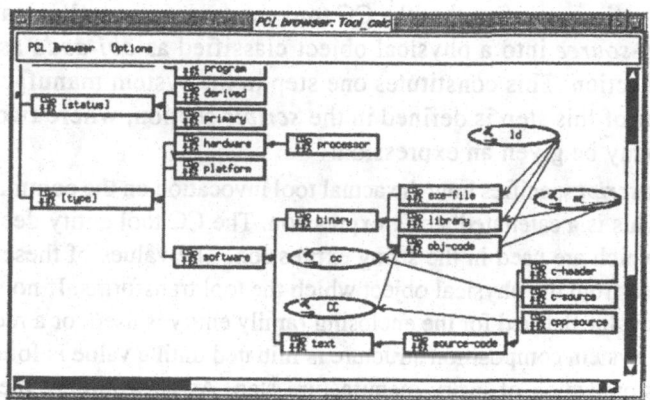

Fig. 5. Extract from the PCL classification hierarchy

3.6 System Manufacture (Building)

Borison [1] defines software manufacture to be the process by which a software product is derived, through an often complex sequence of steps, from the primitive components of a system. PCL provides constructs to define customizable tasks in software system manufacturing. The PCL tools use such descriptions to find the correct steps needed in a particular system manufacture process to build e.g. an executable program.

Section 3.4 describes how variability is removed in a PCL model. This step identifies the system configuration as a set of family members at the logical level. Variability is also removed as physical objects are mapped to file version groups and further to specific versions as described in Section 3.7. The configuration is then completely defined, with all variability removed.

From such a configuration description the system manufacture process may begin. The *tool* entity in PCL defines the signature and behavior of software tools which can transform a representation from one form to another, or more generally, transform a set of input representations to a set of output representations. A C++ compiler may be modelled in the following way using the tool entity:

(xvi)
```
tool CC
  inputs
    InSrc => cpp-source;
  end
  outputs
    OutObj => obj-code;
  end
  attributes
    CC : string default "CC ";
    CCFLAGS : string default "-c ";
    INCL: string default "";
  end
  scripts
    build := CC ++ CCFLAGS ++ INCL ++ "-o " ++ OutObj ++ "-c " ++ InSrc;
  end
end
```

The *inputs* section specifies that the CC tool can transform a physical object classified as *cpp-source* into a physical object classified as *obj-code* as specified in the *outputs* section. This constitutes one step in the system manufacture process. The behavior of this step is defined in the *scripts* section, where two pre-defined script slots may be given an expression.

1. The *build script* specifies how the actual tool invocation on the command line is formatted. This is a catenated string expression. The CC tool entity declares three attributes which are used in the string expression. The values of these attributes are propagated from the physical object which the tool transforms. If no value is found there, the value defined for the enclosing family entity is used, or a recursive search along the system composition structure is initiated until a value is found. This facilitates customization of every manufacture step. As an example, the file Calculator.C, if the enclosing family is bound with the version descriptor in (xiii), is transformed by the following command line:

> CC -Dsun4 -o Calculator.o -c Calculator.C

Since attribute INCL in entity XGUI is bound to another value, the C++ file in that entity would be derived with

> CC -Dsun4 -I/local/X11R5/include -o ui.o -c ui.C

2. The *depend script*, not used in the CC tool description, specifies the command line for (source-level) dependency extraction for the tool. The form of this script is similar to the build script.

As physical objects are transformed to new representations, which again may be further transformed, the system derivation graph is built. This information is emitted to a makefile which can be utilized by the Make program [6]. The makefile generation process can be customized in different ways, as shown in Figure 6.

Rules:	Depend-Policy:	Partitioning-Policy:
■ build	◇ None	◆ None
■ phony	◆ Depend-script	◇ By family
☐ ci	◇ KEEP_STATE	◇ By workspace
☐ co	☐ Requires	◇ By process
■ clean		
Naming-Policy:	**Path-Policy:**	**Filenames in makefile:**
◇ makefile	◆ Current directory	◆ Absolute
◇ Makefile	◇ Try to find workspace	◇ Relative to makefile-path
◆ systemname.makefile		
Checkin-Policy:	**Checkout-Policy:**	**User Interface:**
◆ Changed files	◆ Fixed	■ Derivation graph
◇ All files locked	◇ Newest	☐ Dependency graph
◇ all files in workspace		☐ Incremental during MakeGen

Fig. 6. Menu for customizing makefile generation.

The system derivation graph for the calc program is shown in Figure 7.

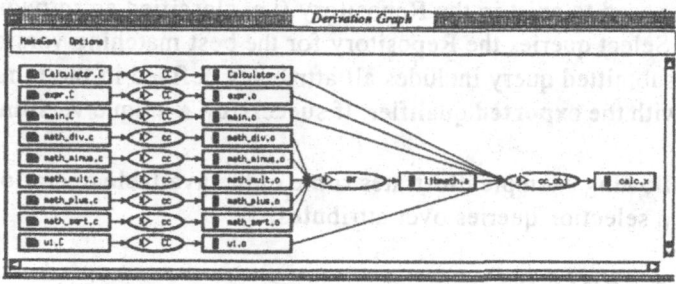

Fig. 7. Derivation graph for the calc example

3.7   Repository Management

A PCL model refers ultimately to a set of physical objects. For elements classified as software, a physical object corresponds to a *file*. These files are typically versioned, since they evolve over time and may exist in several variants. Real systems contain a large number of files, and over time there will be a vast number of file versions with subtle differences. If all file versions and their particular characteristics were represented inside the PCL model, the model would soon become impractically large. In PROTEUS we have therefore chosen a two-tier approach, in which file versions and their properties are managed by a special component library called the Repository.

Version selection is the process of determining a consistent set of versions for all elements in a configuration. Basically, this process consists of finding a unique version identifier for each element, so that the resulting configuration is consistent and possesses the desired properties. PCL supports intensional version selection, adopted from the Adele system [4].

Version selection is done by the *Select* operation. It transforms a bound PCL model to a selected model by adding explicit version identifiers to the description of each physical object stored in the Repository. For example, the following PCL fragment:

(xvii)
```
family CalcProg
  physical
    main => "main.C";
    defs => "defs.h";
    ...
```

might be transformed into:

(xviii)
```
family CalcProg
  physical
    main => "main.C" attributes repository_version := "5.14.2.4"; end;
    defs => "defs.h" attributes repository_version := "4.22"; end;
    ...
```

The intensional, attribute-based version selection works as follows. For each physical object referenced in the model, the classifications are used to determine if it is supposed to exist in the Repository (i.e. classified as *software* and *primary*). If so, Select queries the Repository for the best matching version for the object. The submitted query includes all attributes defined in the family which are declared with the **exported** qualifier. If successful, a unique version identifiers is returned.

The following example illustrates some of the available operations when stating version selection queries over attributes:

(xix)
```
version Calc_test of CalcProg
    attributes
        status >= module-tested;
        time := max; // The latest version
        author <> "bj.*"; // Note the use of regular expression
        // The time and author attributes are automatically inserted
        // for any version when checking it into the Repository.
    end
end
```

This descriptor will select the latest file versions which has reached at least status module-tested and are not entered by a user having a name starting with "bj". The Repository resolves such queries by investigating the properties of all versions of a component. Version properties are expressed as attributes, i.e. user-defined name-value pairs. A user typically associates attributes to characterize a version when checking it into the Repository, or after having tested configurations in which the version occurs. It is the responsibility of the user to choose appropriate attributes which discriminate between versions.

Upon a successful Select, the resulting selected PCL model may be further used to check out the configuration from the Repository and possibly build the configuration. A selected PCL model ensures reproducibility, i.e. it uniquely defines a system instance which may be re-created.

To summarize, the following Repository operations are available for a PCL model:

- Select: invoke intensional version selection.
- Check In: check in all changed files of a configuration, and optionally attach a set of attributes to each new version.
- Check Out: establish or update a workspace by checking out all files of a specific configuration.

4   Tool Support

A comprehensive tool set to support the creation and use of PCL models has been developed. It includes a graphical structural editor for entering and browsing PCL models, an interactive PCL compiler, and a graphical browser for inspecting and manipulating the contents of the Repository. PCL models are organized in libraries with explicit prefixing for inter-library entity referencing. The PCL compiler supports parsing of textual PCL descriptions, binding of models, version selection, and makefile generation. Figure 8 presents an overview of the core PCL tool set. In addition comes a simple reverse engineering tool for constructing a rudi-

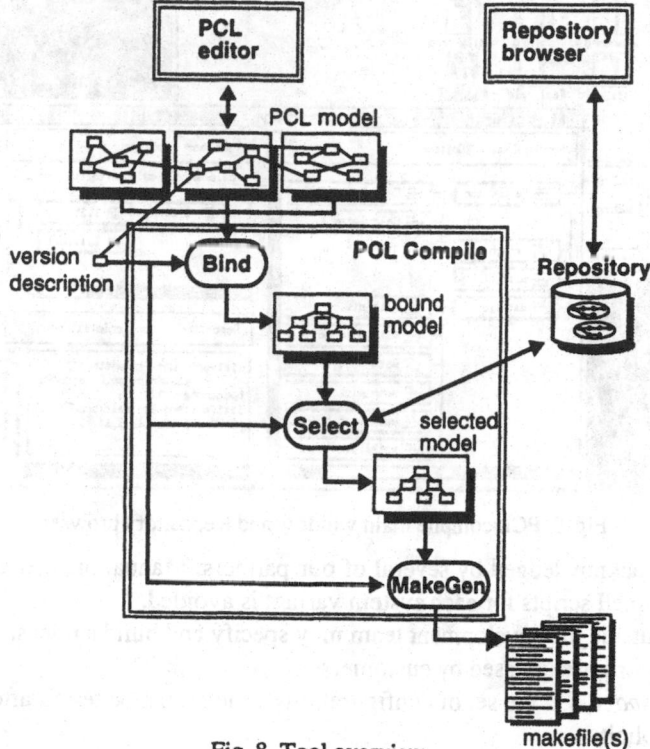

Fig. 8. Tool overview

mentary PCL description for existing software products. Figure 9 shows the user interface for the PCL compiler and the Repository browser.

The tool set is implemented in C++ using X11 and the OSF/Motif™ toolkit. The core tool set is about 60 KLOC. It is currently available for Sun and HP workstations. BMS, a selective multicast package provided by CAP Gemini, is used for tool integration, both of the PCL tool set itself and for integration with external design tools. The Repository is currently implemented on top of RCS [16].

5 Preliminary Experiences

PCL and its tool set is currently being validated at four different partners in the PROTEUS project, on applications ranging from telecommunications software to system development tools. Reported benefits include (see also [7]):

- Increased system *visibility*, i.e. recording and formalizing knowledge previously distributed and unavailable (person dependent). This system documentation is essential for controlling the system evolution (impact analysis of changes), but has in addition proved valuable for internal communication and training.
- Integrating the system manufacture process into the system configuration support

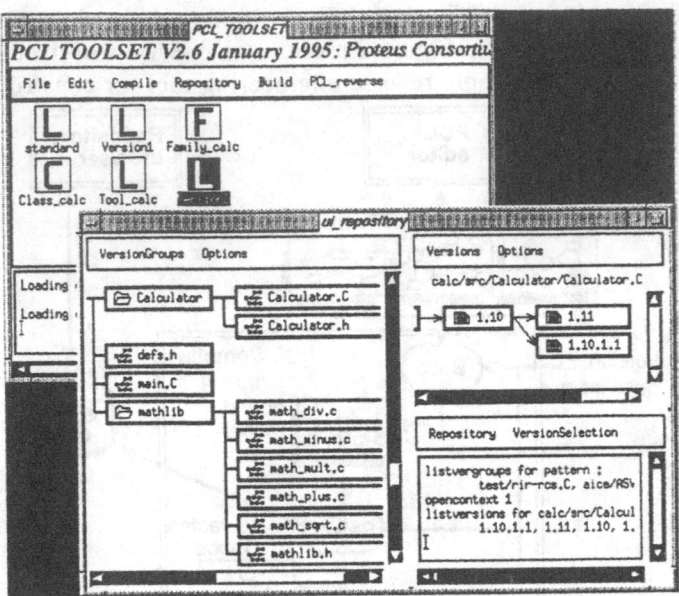

Fig. 9. PCL compile main window and Repository browser.

has been acknowledged by several of our partners. Manual maintenance of make-files and shell scripts for each system variant is avoided.

- People outside the development team may specify and build a release, based on desired properties expressed by customers.
- The *test space*, i.e. the set of configurations which must be tested after changes, is made explicit.

As a system evolves, structural changes need to be reflected in the PCL model. In order to ease the creation and maintenance of PCL system models, different strategies have been chosen. For one partner, a CASE tool has been tightly integrated with the PCL tool set, providing automatic propagation of changes. For file-base software systems, the PCL Reverse tool is able to both generate an initial PCL model and to check consistency between a system model and an actual system version in a workspace.

6 Conclusions

In this paper we have presented the PROTEUS Configuration Language and its supporting tool set. PCL supports comprehensive system modelling and provides expression of variability in the logical system model, in the mapping from the logical model to files, in the version selection, and finally in the system manufacture process. Intensional system configuration using attribute assignment accommodates configuration binding and system building in a concise and reproducible manner.

We have illustrated the important concepts in PCL on a small, but complete example. The example has been illustrated with screen dumps from the PCL tools.

Experience shows that it requires some effort to build a comprehensive system model, especially if trying to incorporate all potential variability in an industrial product. However, the benefits in terms of improved system visibility and automation are significant.

The PCL tool set will be made available by the PROTEUS consortium. Further information about the PROTEUS project, PCL and its tool set is available at http://www.comp.lancs.ac.uk/computing/research/soft_eng/projects/PROTEUS/.

Acknowledgment

We would like to thank the anonymous reviewers, Richard Sanders and Joe Gorman (SINTEF) for their constructive comments on earlier versions of this paper.

The work reported has been supported by the European Commission's ESPRIT programme. We would like to acknowledge the other members of the PCL development and tools implementation teams, namely Ian Sommerville, Graham Dean (Lancaster University), Björn Grönquist, Ariane Suisse, Gilbert Rondeau, Sergio Calabretta (Cap Gemini Innovation, Grenoble).

References

1. E. Borison: A Model of Software Manufacture. In Reidar Conradi et.al., editors, *Proceedings of the International Workshop on Advanced Programming Environments*, Trondheim, Norway, June 16-18, 1986, *LNCS no. 244, Springer-Verlag, Berlin*, pp. 197-220.
2. L. W. Cooprider: The Representation of Families of Software Systems. PhD thesis, *Carnegie-Mellon University, Computer Science Department*, April 1979.
3. F. DeRemer and H. H. Kron: Programming-in-the-large Versus Programming-in-the-small, *IEEE Transactions on Software Engineering*, SE-2(2), June 1976, pp. 80-86.
4. J. Estublier: A configuration manager: The Adele data base of programs. In *Workshop on Software Engineering Environments for Programming-in-the-Large*, Harwichport, Massachusetts, June 1985, pp. 140-147.
5. J. Estublier and R. Casallas: The Adele Configuration Manager. In W. F. Tichy, *Configuration Management*, John Wiley & Sons Ltd., Chichester, 1994, ISBN 0-471-94245-6, pp. 99-133.
6. S. I. Feldman: Make, a Program for Maintaining Computer Programs, *Software - Practice and Experience*, 9(4), April 1979, pp. 255-265.
7. B. Gulla and J. Gorman: Supporting evolution with a configuration language: industrial experience, 11 pages. Submitted for publication.
8. D. L. Leblang: The CM Challenge: Configuration Management that Works. In W. F. Tichy, *Configuration Management*, John Wiley & Sons Ltd., Chichester, 1994, ISBN 0-471-94245-6, pp. 1-37.

9. A. Lie, R. Conradi, T. M. Didriksen, E.-A. Karlsson, S. O. Hallsteinsen and P. Holager: Change Oriented Versioning in a Software Engineering Database. In W. F. Tichy, editor, *Proceedings of the Second International Workshop on Software Configuration Management*, pp. 56-65, Princeton, NJ, October 25-27, 1989. ACM SIGSOFT Software Engineering Notes 17(7), November 1989.

10. K. Marzullo and D. Wiebe: Jasmine: A Software System Modelling Facility. In P. B. Henderson, *Proceedings of the 2nd ACM SIGSOFT/SIGPLAN Software Engineering Symposium on Practical Software Development Environments*, Palo Alto, CA, December 9-11, 1986. *ACM SIGPLAN Notices*, 22(1), January 1987, pp. 121-130.

11. K. Narayanaswamy and W. Scacchi: Maintaining Configurations of Evolving Software Systems, *IEEE Transactions on Software Engineering*, SE-13(3), March 1987, pp. 324-334.

12. PROTEUS consortium: PCL-V2 Reference Manual, Technical Report P-DEL-3.4.D-1.9, September 1994, 85 pages.

13. I. Sommerville and G. Dean: PCL: A configuration language for modelling evolving system architectures, 21 pages. Submitted for publication.

14. R. Thomson and I. Sommerville: An Approach to the Support of Software Evolution, *Computer Journal*, 32(5), October 1989, pp. 386-396.

15. W. F. Tichy: Software Development Control Based on Module Interconnection. In *Proceedings of the 4th International Conference on Software Engineering*, IEEE, September 1979, pp. 29-41.

16. W. F. Tichy: RCS - A System for Version Control, *Software - Practice and Experience*, 15(7), July 1985, pp. 637-654.

17. D. Whitgift: Methods and Tools for Software Configuration Management, *John Wiley & Sons Ltd., Chichester*, 1991. ISBN 0-471-92940-9

Appendix: The Calculator Example

Below follows the complete PCL description for calculator example. Note that the latter half of this description is independent of the actual example system, allowing it to be shared among different models.

```
version my-version of CalcProg
    attributes os := sun;
            xgui := true;
    end
    parts   ui => ui-version; end
end

version ui-version of XGUI
    attributes INCL := "-I/local/X11R5/include "; end
end

family CalcProg
    attributes created_by= "Marius Kintel";
            created : string = "94/08/12";
            contract_no: integer = 1643256;
```

```
              HOME : string default "/home/ask/proteus/test";
              workspace := HOME ++ "/calc/src/";
              repository := "calc/";
              status  : status_type exported default initiated;
              xgui    : boolean default false;
              expression : expr_type default infix;
              debug   : boolean default false;
              os      : os_type;
              DEBUG := if debug = true then "-g -Ddebug " endif;
              INCL   : string := "";
              CCFLAGS : string :=
                if os = sun then
                    if expression = infix then DEBUG ++ "-c -Dsun4 "
                    elsif expression = reverse_polish then DEBUG++"-c -O2"
                    endif
                  elsif os = vax then DEBUG ++ "-C -c -Dvax "
                  endif;
      end
      parts   ui => if xgui = true then XGUI endif;
              calc => Calculator;
              math => mathlib;
      end
      physical  main => "main.C";
              defs => "defs.h";
              exe => "calc.x" attributes workspace := HOME ++ "/calc/bin"; end
                          classifications status => standard.derived; end;
      end
end

family XGUI
  attributes INC := 'INCL; end
  physical   files => "ui.C"; end
end

family Calculator
  attributes workspace := 'workspace ++ "Calculator/";
             repository := 'repository ++ "Calculator/";
             expression : expr_type := 'expression default infix;
             status : status_type := 'status;
             INCL := 'INCL;
  end
  physical   calc => ("Calculator.C", "Calculator.h");
             expr => if expression = infix then
                     ("expr.C", "expr.h")
                     elsif expression = reverse_polish then
                     ("rpn_expr.C", "rpn_expr.h")
                     endif;
  end
end

family mathlib
  attributes workspace := 'workspace ++ "mathlib/";
             repository := 'repository ++ "mathlib/";
             INCL := 'INCL;
```

239

```
      end
   physical  files => ( "math_plus.c", "math_minus.c", "math_mult.c", "math_div.c", "math_sqrt.c",
                     "mathlib.h");
              lib=> "libmath.a" classifications status => standard.derived; end;
   end
end

attribute_type status_type
   enumeration initiated, module-tested, system-tested end
end

attribute_type os_type
   enumeration sun, vax end
end

attribute_type expr_type
   enumeration infix, reverse_polish end
end

tool CC
   attributes CC : string default "CC ";
             CCFLAGS : string default " ";
             INCL: string default "";
   end
   inputs    InSrc => cpp-source; end
   outputs   OutObj => obj-code; end
   scripts   build := CC ++ CCFLAGS ++ INCL ++ "-o " ++ OutObj ++ "-c " ++ InSrc; end
end

tool cc
   attributes cc : string default "cc ";
             CFLAGS : string default " ";
             INCL : string default " ";
   end
   inputs    InSrc => c-source; end
   outputs   OutObj => obj-code; end
   scripts   build := cc ++ CFLAGS ++ INCL ++ " -o " ++ OutObj ++ "-c " ++ InSrc; end
end

tool ar
   attributes AR : string default "ar ";
             ARFLAGS : string default "rv ";
             RANLIB : string default "ranlib ";
   end
   inputs    InObj : multi => obj-code; end
   outputs   OutLib => library; end
   scripts   build := AR ++ ARFLAGS ++ OutLib ++ " " ++ InObj ++ "\n" ++ RANLIB ++ OutLib;
   end
end

tool ld
   attributes LD : string default "CC ";
             LDFLAGS : string default " ";
             LIBS : string default "-lm "; end
```

```
    inputs     InObj : multi => obj-code;
               InLib : multi => library; end
    outputs    OutExe => exe-file; end
    scripts    build := LD ++ LDFLAGS ++ " -o " ++ OutExe ++ " " ++ InObj ++ " " ++ "'fixlib "
               ++ InLib ++ "' " ++ LIBS; end
end

class text inherits standard.software end
class source-code inherits text end
class binary inherits standard.software end

class cpp-source inherits source-code
    tools CC end
    physical name ++ ".C"; end
end

class c-header inherits source-code
    physical name ++ ".h"; end
end

class c-source inherits source-code
    tools cc end
    physical name ++ ".c"; end
end

class library inherits binary
    tools ld end
    physical "lib" ++ name ++ ".a"; end
end

class obj-code inherits binary
    tools ar, ld end
    physical name ++ ".o"; end
end

class exe-file inherits binary
    physical name ++ ".x"; end
end
```

The Odin System

Geoffrey M. Clemm

geoff@cs.colorado.edu

Abstract. The Odin System is a simpler, more powerful, and more reliable replacement for Make. It computes complete dependency information automatically, making the build scripts shorter and easier to manage. Odin gains efficiency by parallel builds on remote machines, by eliminating most of the file system status queries required by Make, and by sharing from a cache of previously computed derived files.

1 Introduction

1.1 Derived Object Managers

A software environment can be simplified if the user's attention is focused on the information provided by the environment rather than the tools that create this information. A *derived object manager* provides this focus by automating the process of tool invocation. A derived object manager responds to a request for a piece of computed information, or *derived object*, by invoking the minimal number of tools necessary to produce that object. If previously computed objects are automatically stored by the object manager for later re-use, significant improvements in response time can be achieved.

In an extensible environment, the kinds of information potentially provided are extended by adding new tools that manipulate and generate new kinds of information. A few examples of the kind of information in a software environment are program source text, test data, modification histories, attributed syntax trees, compiled object code, data flow analysis, and results of symbolic execution.

A derived object manager must provide a language with which a user or a tool can name any desired object, and a specification language for describing the kinds of objects to be managed and the tools that produce them. In the Odin system, derived objects are named by *odin-expressions*, and the specification language is an extended production system called a *derivation graph* in which each tool is described by a single declaration.

1.2   Odin Objects

Each Odin object is either a *file*, a *string*, or a *list* (an ordered sequence of objects). An example of a file is a file containing source code, an executable binary file, or an output file from a test run. An example of a string is a command flag. An example of a list is the source files of a program or the arguments to a command.

Source and Derived Objects Source objects are files that can be created or modified directly by the user. They can be regular files, directories, or symbolic links. Source objects cannot be automatically recreated by the Odin system, but are the basic building blocks from which the Odin system creates all other objects. Every source object is given a type by the Odin system based on its host filename, and this type determines what derived objects can be produced from the source object. Derived objects are objects that can be produced from source objects and other derived objects through the invocation of one or more tools. Tools are invoked only as needed to create a specified derived object. The Odin system automatically saves objects from previous requests, so a given object might already exist and therefore be available immediately. Derived objects are created and modified only by the Odin system itself, not by users. Examples of objects that can be derived from source code are a cross reference listing, executable binary code, or the list of files referenced by #include statements.

The Derived Object Cache In the Odin system, all derived objects are stored in a directory called the *derived object cache*, or simply the *cache*. The cache also contains the database that stores the *depends* relationship between the output and input files of a tool run, and the *contains* relationship between a list and its elements.
All host files other than those in the cache are source objects. A derived object can be copied from the cache into a source directory, but this does *not* make the file in the source directory a derived object – it just creates a source object that happens to have the same contents as the derived object.
The default location for the cache is a directory named .ODIN in the user's home directory. A non-default cache location can be specified in the $ODIN environment variable, or with the -c option to the odin host-command. The main reasons for specifying a non-default location for the cache are to share a common cache with other users, or to locate the cache on a local disk for more efficient access to derived files.

2 The Odinfile

2.1 Targets

A build *target* in a directory is a source file whose value is computed by the derived object manager. Just as Make uses a file named `Makefile` to specify targets for a directory, Odin uses a file named `Odinfile`. When the host-command:

```
odin prog
```

is executed, Odin checks to see if `prog` is a target in `./Odinfile`. If it is a target, but is not up-to-date, Odin invokes whatever tools are necessary to bring it up-to-date. Odin automatically looks in all directories that contain the input files for these tools, and if there is an `Odinfile` that contains a target for an input file, Odin ensures that the input file is up-to-date before using it.

A target definition in an `Odinfile` consists of a filename followed by two equal-signs and an *odin-expression*. For example, the `Odinfile` entry:

```
prog == prog.c +debug :exe
```

declares that the value of the source file `prog` should always be equal to the value of the file specified by the odin-expression `prog.c+debug:exe`.

2.2 Odin-Expressions

Just as any source file can be named with a source filename, any derived file can be named with an *odin-expression*. An odin-expression is just like a source filename, except that in addition to the slash operator used in source filenames for selecting elements of directories, there is a plus-sign operator for adding parameters to an object and a colon operator for selecting a derivation from an object. For example, in the odin-expression:

```
src/prog.c+debug:exe
```

`prog.c` is selected from the `src` directory, the parameter `+debug` is associated with `src/prog.c`, and the `:exe` (i.e. executable binary) derivation is selected from `src/prog.c+debug`.

244

Selection Expressions A selection expression, indicated by the slash operator, selects a file from a directory. The argument to the slash operator is the *key* of the desired file. For example, the odin-expression:

    src/prog.c

selects `prog.c` from the directory `src`. (The careful reader will note that an odin-expression composed entirely of selection expressions bears an uncanny resemblance to a standard Unix filename.)

Derivation Expressions A derivation expression, indicated by the colon operator, is used to specify a derived object. The argument to the colon operator is an *object type* that has been declared in one of the tool packages (see Section 4.3). For example, the odin-expression:

    prog.c :fmt

names a formatted version of `prog.c`, and the odin-expression:

    prog.c :fmt :exe

names the result of compiling and linking the formatted version of `prog.c`. A derived object can be a directory, in which case it is called a *derived directory*. Elements of a derived directory are selected with the same slash operator used to select elements of source directories. For example, if `src/prog.c:output` is a derived directory containing the output files from a test run of `prog.c`, and this directory contains three files named `DATA`, `source.listing`, and `source.errors`, then these three files are named by the odin-expressions:

    src/prog.c:output/DATA
    src/prog.c:output/source.listing
    src/prog.c:output/source.errors

Parameterization Expressions A parameterization expression, indicated by the plus-sign operator, extends an object with additional information that affects the derived objects produced from that object. The argument to the plus-sign operator is a *parameter type* (see Section 4.4), optionally followed by an equal-sign operator and a sequence of one or more identifiers and parenthesized object-expressions. The identifiers name strings and the object-expressions name objects. For example, in the odin-expression:

```
prog.c +lib=(support.c.sm +debug :a) +lib=termcap
```

the value of the first +lib parameter is the object support.c.sm+debug:a and the value of the second +lib parameter is the string termcap. Parameters of a list object are inherited by all the elements of the list. For example, if the odin-expression:

```
prog.c.sm :list
```

names a list whose elements are main.c and subrs.c, then the odin-expression:

```
prog.c.sm :list +debug
```

associates the +debug parameter with main.c and subrs.c.

2.3 Virtual Targets

In addition to targets, an Odinfile can contain *virtual targets* that define a set of *virtual files*. A virtual target is like a target, except that the value is not copied into a host file, but is simply associated with the specified virtual filename. Virtual files provide a mechanism for specifying aliases for complicated odin-expressions, and a mechanism for specifying build-support files without cluttering host directories.

A virtual target definition is the same as a target definition (see Section 2.1), except that the filename begins with a percent-sign. For example, the Odinfile entry:

```
%prog == prog.c +debug :exe
```

binds the odin-expression `prog.c+debug:exe` to the virtual filename `prog`. The syntax for selecting a virtual file from an `Odinfile` is identical to that for selecting a file from a directory, except that a percent-sign is used instead of a slash. For example, the odin-expression:

```
src/Odinfile%prog
```

selects the virtual file prog from `src/Odinfile`.

2.4   Text Targets

The value of a target can be specified directly as lines of text (a *here document*), instead of as an odin-expression. In this case, the value declaration consists of two left-angle-brackets optionally followed by an arbitrary tag identifier. For example, the `Odinfile` entry:

```
prog.c.sm == << END
    main.c
    routines.c
END
```

declares `prog.c.sm` to be a text target. The value of `prog.c.sm` is then a file containing the text:

```
    main.c
    routines.c
```

2.5   Executable Targets

A target is an *executable target* if an exclamation-point is specified following the filename. For example, the `Odinfile` entry:

```
prog ! == prog.c.sm +debug :exe
```

specifies prog to be an executable target.

Normally, when a filename is specified as an argument to the odin host-command, Odin simply ensures that the value of the filename is up-to-date. If the filename is an executable target, Odin also executes the file after it is made up-to-date. For example, with the preceding target definition for prog, the host-command:

```
odin prog
```

makes sure prog is up-to-date with respect to prog.c.sm+debug:exe, and then executes it.

3   Using Odin

To get started using Odin, go to a directory containing your favorite "hello world" program.

```
1% cd /u/fred
2% cat hello.c

main()
{ printf("Hello World.\n"); return 0; }
```

Then create an Odinfile containing the line hello==hello.c:exe.

```
3% ls
Odinfile   hello.c
4% cat Odinfile

hello == hello.c :exe
```

You are now ready to build hello. Just say:

```
5% odin hello
```

By default, Odin issues a message every time it invokes a tool, for example:

```
scan_for_includes hello.c
cc -c hello.c
cc hello.o
** Copying up-to-date value into /u/fred/hello
```

The first tool scanned the source file for includes; the second generated object code; the third generated an executable; and the fourth copied the executable into the file named /u/fred/hello.

You have now built your first executable with Odin. Now to test it:

```
%6 hello
Hello World.
```

3.1 Systems with Several Files

Interesting systems will usually consist of more than one file. In Odin, you list the source files that make up the system in a file called a *system model*. The files named in #include statements should not be listed in the system model – Odin will discover them by running a tool that scans the source files looking for #include statements.

Modify hello.c so that it calls a print() routine in the file print.c.

```
7% ls
Odinfile    hello    hello.c    print.c
8% cat hello.c

main()
   { print("Hello "); print("World.\n"); return 0; }

9% cat print.c

print(s) char *s;
   { printf(s); }
```

Now you need to create a system model, hello.c.sm, for the new hello system. The system model can be a regular file, but it can equally well be specifed as a *virtual file* in the Odinfile.

```
10% cat Odinfile

hello == %hello.c.sm :exe

%hello.c.sm == << EOF
   hello.c; print.c
EOF
```

The new version of hello can now be built:

```
11% odin hello
```

You will notice although the file hello has changed, no new files have appeared in the source directory.

```
12% ls
Odinfile    hello    hello.c    print.c
```

This is because all derived files are stored in the derived file cache directory ($HOME/.ODIN by default – a non-default location can be specified in the $ODIN environment variable).
But the derived files are available for re-use. For example, if you to add a comment to the print() routine:

```
13% cat print.c

/* print the string s to standard output */
print(s) char *s;
  { printf(s); }
```

and then ask Odin for hello again:

```
14% odin hello
```

you will notice a couple of things. First, the previous results of scanning hello.c for includes and compiling it are both re-used, as you would expect. Somewhat more surprising may be that Odin notices that the compilation of the modified print.c produced the same object code. Odin then skips the link phase since the old executable is still valid.

3.2   Files in Other Directories

The files in a system model can be in any directory, using either absolute or relative pathnames. Odin knows that /u/fred/print.c is potentially different from /u/jane/print.c so will not be confused if you switch from one to the other in your system model.

```
15% cat ../jane/print.c

print(s) char *s;
  { printf("*%s*", s); }
%16 cat Odinfile

hello == %hello.c.sm :exe

%hello.c.sm == << EOF
    hello.c; ../jane/print.c
EOF

%17 odin hello
```

3.3 Recursive Odin Calls

Suppose that /u/jane/print.c is modified to include a y.tab.h file generated by the yacc tool from a file named print.y. The fact that y.tab.h is generated from print.y is indicated in /u/jane/Odinfile.

```
18% ls ../jane
Odinfile   print.c     print.y
19% cat ../jane/print.c

#include "y.tab.h"
print(s) char *s;
  { printf("*%s*", s); }

20% cat ../jane/Odinfile

y.tab.h == print.y :h
```

If you were using make, you would have to somehow get make ../jane invoked before you tried to make hello. In Odin, all these dependencies are computed for you, so a simple odin hello is sufficient.

```
21% odin hello
```

3.4   Debugging Your Program

Odin uses parameters instead of tool flags to modify the behavior of tools. In particular, +debug adds debugging information. Either the entry for hello in the Odinfile can be modified, or as is done below, a second entry such as test-hello can be added.

```
22% cat Odinfile

hello == %hello.c.sm :exe

test-hello == %hello.c.sm +debug :exe

%hello.c.sm == << EOF
   hello.c; print.c
EOF
```

At this point, you can build test-hello and run the debugger.

```
23% odin test-hello

24% dbx test-hello
```

These two steps can be combined by adding an executable %dbx entry into the Odinfile.

```
25% cat Odinfile

hello == %hello.c.sm :exe

test-hello == %hello.c.sm +debug :exe

%dbx ! == %hello.c.sm +debug :dbx

%hello.c.sm == << EOF
   hello.c; print.c
EOF
```

Then the host-command:

```
26% odin %dbx
```

would build an up-to-date executable from %hello.c.sm, build a script
for executing dbx on this executable, and then because %dbx is an executable target, execute the script.

4 Tool Package Libraries

In the Odin system, all information about tools, object types, and parameter types is specified in special directories called *tool package libraries*.
Tool package libraries are commonly located in /usr/local/lib and are
shared by all Odin users. The Odin distribution includes a tool package
library containing tool packages for most of the common Unix tools, so
most Odin users never have to look at or understand tool packages.

When a cache (see Section 1.2) is created, *tool packages* from the tool
package libraries are installed in the cache. A tool package is just a sub-
directory of a tool package library, where the name of the package is
the name of the sub-directory. The list of tool packages and the order
in which they should be loaded is specified in a file named PKGLST (one
package name per line) in the tool package library directory.

4.1 Tool Packages

A tool package is a directory that contains a *derivation graph* file and any
support files that implement the tools declared in the derivation graph.
If pkgx is the name of the tool package, then pkgx.dg is the name of the
derivation graph file.

A derivation graph consists of a sequence of source, object type, parameter type, and tool declarations. A source declaration associates a filename pattern with an object type. An object type declaration associates
an object type with a set of supertypes. A parameter type declaration
associates a parameter type with an object type that is applied to the
parameter values. A tool declaration specifies the inputs and outputs
of the tool, where the inputs are object types, parameter types, odin-
expressions, and strings, and where the outputs are object types.

4.2 Source Declarations

A source declaration specifies the type for a host file based on the filename of the host file. It consists of a *filename expression*, a right arrow
(composed from an equal-sign and a right-angle-bracket), and the name

of a declared object type. A filename expression consists either of a string
followed by an asterisk (i.e. all filenames that begin with that string), an
asterisk followed by a string (i.e. all filenames that end with that string),
or just an asterisk (i.e. all filenames). For example, the derivation graph
entries:

```
*.c    => :c;
*.c.c => :cplusplus;
s.*    => :sccs;
*      => :FILE;
```

declare that the object type of a filename ending with .c is :c, the object
type of a filename ending with .c.c is :cplusplus, the object type of a
filename beginning with s. is :sccs, and the object type of any filename
is :FILE.

4.3   Object Type Declarations

An object type declaration consists of the object type being declared,
a *help string*, a right arrow, and the *direct supertypes* of the type being
declared. For example, the derivation graph entries:

```
:source 'source code' => :FILE;
:fmt 'formatted source code' => :FILE;
:c 'C source code' => :source;
```

declare that the direct supertype of :source is :FILE, the direct supertype of :fmt is :FILE, and the direct supertype of :c is :source. The
help string is used by the Odin help system to generate messages about
the installed types.
An object type can be declared with multiple direct supertypes, either in
a single declaration or in separate declarations. For example, the derivation graph entry:

```
:fmt.c 'formatted version of C code' => :c :fmt;
```

declares :c and :fmt to be direct supertypes of :fmt.c.
The *supertypes* of an object type are the transitive closure of the direct
supertypes (i.e. the supertypes are the direct supertypes and all supertypes of the direct supertypes). For example, from the preceding object

type declarations, the supertypes of :fmt.c are :c, :fmt, :source, and :FILE. The supertypes of an object type help determine what objects can be derived from an object of that type. In particular, if the type of the object obj is :objtyp, then the odin-expression obj:deriv is valid if :deriv is a supertype of :objtyp, if :deriv is the output of a tool whose inputs can be derived from :obj, or if :deriv is a supertype of an object that can be derived from :objtyp.

4.4 Parameter Type Declarations

A parameter type declaration consists of the parameter type being declared, a help string, a right arrow, and an object type. When a parameter type is used as the input to a tool, the list of values for that parameter type is first derived to the specified object type. For example, the derivation graph entries:

```
+define 'a macro definition'       => :cat;
+lib     'an object code library' => :ls;
+debug  'debug flag'               => :first;
```

declare a +define parameter type whose values are :cat'ed, a +lib parameter type whose values are :ls'ed, and a +debug parameter type whose first value is selected.

4.5 Tool Declarations

A tool declaration consists of a tool name, the tool inputs, a right arrow, and the tool outputs. The tool name is either EXEC, COLLECT, or READ-LIST. A tool output is an object type in parentheses. A tool input is a string or a parenthesized *input-expression*. An *input-expression* is just like an odin-expression, except that a *derived input* or a *parameter input* can appear wherever a source filename can appear in an odin-expression. A *derived input* consists of a declared object type (e.g. :obj), while a *parameter input* consists of a declared parameter type (e.g. +debug). For example, the derivation graph entry:

```
EXEC (/bin/yacc) -dv (:y) => (:y.tab.c) (:y.tab.h) (:y.output);
```

declares an EXEC tool that has inputs (/bin/yacc), -dv, and (:y), and that has outputs: (:y.tab.c), (:y.tab.h), and (:y.output).

EXEC Tool The EXEC tool passes its inputs to the Unix `execl()` system call and expects its outputs to be placed in current working directory. For example, the derivation graph entry:

```
EXEC (/bin/ld) -o exe (:obj) => (:exe);
```

declares that a file named **exe** is produced in the current working directory by executing the C statement:

```
status = execl("/bin/ld", "/bin/ld", "-o", "exe", "/xxx/filename.o");
```

where **/xxx/filename.o** is the name of a file with type `:obj`. When the `execl()` completes, Odin moves all output files into the cache.

An input-expression is passed to the `execl()` as an absolute pathname of the file named by the input-expression. The value of a derived or parameter input in the input-expression depends on the input object to which the tool is being applied. For example, in the odin-expression:

```
prog.c +debug :exe
```

the input object to the `:exe` derivation is **prog.c+debug**.

Each derived input is replaced by a file that is the result of applying the derived input object type to the input object. For example, when the `:exe` object is being computed for **prog.c+debug:exe**, the `:obj` derived input is replaced by the file **prog.c+debug:obj**.

Each parameter input is replaced by the object resulting from applying the object type specified in the parameter declaration for that parameter type, to the list of values of all parameters of that type associated with the input object. As a special case, if no parameters of that type are associated with the input object, the parameter input is replaced by the empty string.

Each `execl()` is invoked in an empty directory provided by Odin, and the tool is expected to put its output files in that directory. The name of an output file should be the same as the type-name of the output. For example, the result of the `execl()` call for the output (:exe) should be an output file named **exe**.

In addition to the declared outputs, there are two standard output files named ERRORS and WARNINGS. Fatal errors should be written to ERRORS, while recoverable errors should be written to WARNINGS. The ERRORS and WARNINGS files are used by Odin to determine if error or warning status should be set for the output of the tool.

If the exit status of the execl() call is non-zero, Odin ignores the results of the execl(), and aborts the current odin-command. Non-zero exit status should therefore only be used to indicate transient failures (such as memory or disk errors). This means that most standard Unix tools must be wrapped in shell scripts, so that normal error messages are sent to the file ERRORS and only transient errors cause a non-zero exit status.

COLLECT Tool The COLLECT tool produces a list whose elements are the input objects. For example, the derivation graph entry:

```
COLLECT (:c_inc) (:c_inc :apply=:all_c_inc) => (:all_c_inc) ;
```

declares that :all_c_inc is a list that contains :c_inc and the result of applying :all_c_inc to each element of :c_inc.

READ-LIST Tool The READ-LIST tool produces a list whose elements are the objects named by the odin-expressions in the input file. For example, the derivation graph entry:

```
READ-LIST (:c.sm) => (:c.sm.list) ;
```

declares that :c.sm.list is the list specified by the contents of a file of type :c.sm.

5 Why Not Just Use Make?

The most ubiquitous build manager is Stu Feldman's Make program[3], with its many descendents[2][6][5][4]. Although ideal for small projects, Make has two major problems when used for large or complex projects: inaccurate dependency information and poor support for variant builds (such as builds for different architectures or builds with different levels of compiler optimization). Inaccurate dependency information leads to inefficient builds when unnecessary recomputations are performed and, more seriously, incorrect builds when necessary recomputations are not performed. Poor support for variant builds consists primarily of problems with specifying the variants and with storing the intermediate files for the variants. An indication of the difficulty of specifying a complex build variant is that often the only way to find out what a given build description means is to run Make and see what kind of commands it executes.

5.1 Dependency Information

Inaccurate dependency information results from a variety of causes. If the user maintains the dependency information by hand, it is virtually guaranteed to be incorrect. A "make-depend" tool can automate the production of dependency information, but because of the expense of running such a tool on an entire system, it is usually not automatically invoked before each build, again leading to builds based on incorrect dependency information. If a separate dependency file is created for each source file to allow incremental dependency computation, it becomes feasible to automatically compute dependency information before each build. Unfortunately, the source directories then become cluttered with dependency information files, and the overhead of opening and reading all the dependency information files becomes excessive.

In Odin, tools that automatically gather dependency information are as easy to describe as standard tools like compilers, and Odin takes care of running them incrementally when they are needed. The results of these tools are stored in a persistent database rather than in the user's Makefiles, so that this information can be retrieved efficiently and does not clutter up source directories.

Other dependency problems stem from Make's use of file modification time ordering to determine whether a file is up-to-date. Network clock inconsistencies and the use of tools that restore files with their original modification dates can result in changed sources files whose modification dates are less than those of derived files that depend on them. In Odin, this problem is avoided by storing the date stamps of the inputs to a build step in the dependency database, so that any change to the modification time of a file (either earlier or later) triggers a re-build.

The use of file modification time ordering can also result in inefficient builds when a change to a source file does not result in a corresponding change to an intermediate derived file. For example, adding a comment to a source file will usually not change the result of compiling that file, which means that there is no reason to relink the unchanged object code to form a new executable. Odin avoids this inefficiency by re-running a tool only if the *value* of one of its inputs has changed. In particular, this allows Odin to build directly from an RCS xxx,v or an SCCS s.xxx file, without first checking out a version into a source directory (the check-out operation is just a tool like any other tool). This is not feasible in Make because every time a new version is added to the version control file, it would assume everything derived from *any* version of that file must be recomputed.

5.2 Specifying Build Variants

In Make, a derived file variant is specified by changing the values of the appropriate Make variables. For example, the CC variable can be changed to build with a different C compiler, and the CCFLAGS variable can be changed to build with different C compiler flags. Unfortunately, the scope of a variable is the entire Makefile, while a build variant often involves different variable values for different intermediate files (for example, most of the files are to be compiled with debugging on, except for certain files containing time critical routines which are to be compiled with optimization on). To work around this problem, in Make you have to introduce a special build rule for each intermediate file build variant.

In Odin, a filename can be extended by an arbitrary number of build *parameters*, that are then used by Odin to customize the way that file is processed in any build step that refers to it. For example,

```
prog.c +debug
```

indicates that the debug flag should be set whenever prog.c is used in a build step, while

```
io.c +optimize=2
```

indicates that optimization level 2 should be set whenever io.c is used in a build step. If the parameterized filename refers to a list of other files, the parameters are inherited by each of the referenced files. Because of the controlled scoping provided by Odin parameters and the expressive power of Odin implicit build rules, explicit build rules are hardly ever needed in an Odinfile.

5.3 Storing Derived File Variants

Make usually stores a derived file in the directory containing the source file from which it is derived, since this allows other builds that reference the source file to reuse that derived file. The main disadvantage of this approach is that only one variant of a given derived file can exist at a given time. The build manager can easily mistake which version is currently in the directory, leading to an incorrect build. Other disadvantages are that a user must have write permission to the source directories in order to re-build derived files, a user can mistakenly delete a source file thinking it is a derived file, and a user can mistakenly edit a derived file thinking it is a source file.

The usual approach to this problem is to have the user explicitly allocate different directories to contain the results of different variant builds. Unfortunately, this makes it difficult for build sharing to take place, and unless the version of Make has been extended to write out the variable values used for the builds in a given directory, it is easy to get incorrect builds if different variable values are used for builds in the same directory. Another approach to this problem used in ClearMake[1] consists of introducing a a proprietary *multi-version file system*. Every file opened for reading during the build and every variable value is tracked by the system, and if the same set of files with the same variables are present in a later build request, the previously computed results of the build are re-used. Even this approach, though, requires that the user explicitly manage variant derived file locations if concurrent variant builds of files local to a view are desired.

The alternative approach used by Odin that does not require replacing the native Unix file system is to use a derived file cache. In effect, the file namespace is extended to provide names for every derived file variant. For example,

    /usr/src/prog.c :exe

is the executable computed by compiling and linking /usr/src/prog.c,

    /usr/src/prog.c +debug :exe

is the executable with debugging information, and

    /usr/src/prog.c +optimize=2 :exe

is the executable compiled with level-2 optimization. These extended names are parsed by the Odin interpreter, which either maps the name to a source file or to the correct derived file in the derived file cache.

5.4 Parallel Builds

Odin provides concurrent parallel builds on local and remote hosts. You just specify a list of build hosts and the maximum number of parallel builds.

5.5 Help

Odin provides a powerful help system that uses its knowledge of the currently installed set of implicit rules (including those added by the local site administrator and an individual user). In particular, it can tell you what kinds of file extensions are currently recognized, what kinds of files can be derived from a specific type of file, and what parameters can be specified to produce a variant of a given derived file.

5.6 Errors

Odin maintains a persistent database of all error and warning messages associated with each build step. You can request a summary report of all errors and/or warnings associated with all the build steps of a particular derived object. For derived object variants, any valid error information from other variants is reused from the database rather than recomputed.

5.7 Disk Space Management

The user can specify how much total disk space a derived file cache can use. If this space is exceeded, Odin automatically deletes the least recently used derived files until this space quota is no longer exceeded. The disk space quota of a given cache can be changed at any time, either to free up disk space for other uses or because more disk space is available.

5.8 Operations on Lists

Enhanced versions of Make each provide their own idiosyncratic set of operations for manipulating filenames and lists of filenames. In Odin, these operations are performed by arbitrary Unix tools – this is feasible because Odin caches the results of these tools in the dependency database.

5.9 Editing while Building

You can edit files that are currently being used for one or more builds, and Odin will automatically recognize the changes and redo the parts of the builds that are affected by the changes, before letting the builds complete.

5.10 Recursive Implicit Rules

Odin allows you to recursively chain implicit rules, so for example, you can specify that the files included by a file are the files directly included by the file plus the files included by the files included by the file. Even enhanced versions of Make that do support chaining of implicit rules do not allow recursive chaining.

5.11 Circular Dependencies

Odin allows a file to depend on itself. This may seem unreasonable until you start writing tools that generate code, and you find that it would be very useful to have the tool generate part of itself. In this situation, Odin will terminate the computation when the tool produces a file that is identical to the one used as input to the computation (i.e., when the computation reaches a *fixed-point*).

5.12 Efficient Dependency Computation

In very large systems, even when a desired derived file is up-to-date, simply `fstat()`'ing all the source files upon which it depends can take Make several minutes. Since Odin can broadcast file change information in its dependency database, dependency computation can be made proportional to the number of file dependencies that have *changed* rather than the total number of file dependencies.

5.13 Tool Dependencies

Build steps automatically depend on the tools and scripts that produce them, so if you change a tool, Odin will recompute anything produced by that tool the next time you request a build. If the tool change did not affect a particular run of that tool, the recomputation is short-circuited, and the rest of the derived files that depend on that output of the tool are marked as still being valid.

5.14   Availability

Finally, Odin is portable, free, and available in source form. It can be retrieved via anonymous ftp from the compressed tar formatted file pub/cs/distribs/odin/odin.tar.Z at ftp.cs.colorado.edu.

References

1. *ClearCase Reference Manual.* Atria Software, 1993.
2. B. Erickson and J.F. Pellegrin. Build - a software construction tool. *ATT Bell Labs Technical Journal*, 63:1049–1059, 1984.
3. S. I. Feldman. MAKE - a program for maintaining computer programs. *Software - Practice and Experience*, 9:255–265, 1979.
4. G. Fowler. A case for make. *Software - Practice and Experience*, 20:35–46, June 1990.
5. A. G. Hume. MK: a successor to make. In *USENIX Summer Conference Proceedings*, pages 445–457, 1987.
6. Richard M. Stallman and Roland McGrath. *GNU Make: A Program for Directing Recompilation.* Free Software Foundation, 1993.

Store — a System for Handling Third-Party Applications in a Heterogeneous Computer Environment

Anders Christensen* and Tor Egge**

University of Trondheim

Abstract. This paper presents the Store system administration tool suite, which helps administering third party applications in a heterogeneous Unix environment, giving better overview, more consistency, and less manual work. The problems targeted by Store are listed; the basic functionality of Store is described, and experiences from constructing and maintaining the system are presented.

1 The Problem

From experiences, we have found that a number of problems arise in the area of administering computer systems. These problems are often caused by the local, strategic organization of the computers, including heterogeneous hardware, multiple software versions, deviating user needs, multiple system administrators, geographical distribution, duplication of data, and organizational structure.

These give rise to a number of specific problems, where the more common ones are listed below:

Traceability. As the complexity of a computer system rises, the knowledge of "who-did-what" becomes more important, as does the "why-did-they-do-it-like-that" information. However, activities like logging, documenting, and registering are often ignored during particularly hectic periods in the daily system administering. A lot of self-discipline is required to maintain these activities in a highly result-oriented trade.

Affinity. In a traditional /usr/local file system, a large number of files are mixed fairly unorderly together. Files are somewhat grouped into applications, but it is often not obvious who maintains which applications. Typically, which files belong to which applications, and which applications consist of which files, are matters of uncertainty and vagueness.

Architecture dependency. Since different hardware architectures require different binary programs, system management tend to administer different hardware platforms separately. This adds unnecessarily to the costs; most applications are identical across platforms except from the differing binaries.

---

* SINTEF RUNIT (email: *anders.christensen@runit.sintef.no*)
** Division of Computer Science and Telematics (email: *tegge@idt.unit.no*)

Bit rot. There is no good explanation for it, but it is a well-known observation that unattended applications tend to stop working after some time, generally due to of changes in the surrounding environment. Therefore, users slowly move over to the "safe" computers; the computers that contain software being used. This speeds up the process of bit rot on the less used computers.

Source code. System administration does not involve program development, except for installation, bug-fixing, and local customization. The changes to program source code for these areas are often lost over time, as source code is often considered disk space overhead and deleted. This often results in minor differences between versions and installations on different architectures. For the users, these differences can be very annoying.

2 The Domain of Store

Store is a system administration utility that attempts to handle the problems listed in the previous section.

Store limits its scope to handling third party applications. That is, any group of programs and data files that form a logical unit and can be isolated from the operating system. Two main sources of third party software are downloadable freeware from international networks and packages from commercial vendors.

Furthermore, Store limits its operations on these third party applications to the installation, operation, maintenance, bug finding and -fixing parts of their life cycles.

That is, areas outside the domain of Store are: program development; user and network administration; OS maintenance, configuration, and surveillance.

Currently, Store is also limited to Unix systems. Initial testing is being performed for one-user, personal computers; specifically PCs running MS-DOS.

3 Requirements

The main requirements we have placed on Store are:

No OS modifications. No changes to the operating system should be necessary in order to run Store. Neither new device drivers, kernel modifications nor permanent daemons.

OS-supplied mapping. The operating system should provide the mechanism to map from the view (linktree) to the repository (store). A space-efficient such mapping for most Unix systems is soft-links.

Source code availability. The source code for the system should be available to the users.

Portability. The system should be able to run on any system that follows the POSIX.1 standard and has symbolic links.

Versioned binary files. The system should handle the existence of several versions of binary executables available in the repository, choosing the right one to become visible in the linktree.

4 Other Existing SCM Systems

Most existing SCM systems does not meet our specified requirements. To a large extent they target *programming* environments, instead of *installation* environments. Also, many of them can only manage textual files, are commercial products (available only for a subset of the platforms), or require changes in the operating system.

Two other existing SCM systems that meet our requirements are "Depot"[1] and "Lude"[3].

The problems described above have been targeted by several other systems. The initial implementation of Store (spring/summer 1991) was heavily influenced by "Depot" . However, no implementation of "Depot" was available and the local implementation turned out to be different from the original in many ways, so another name was given.

Other systems that target the problems in a similar ways are Ericsson [2]; and "Lude" .

In addition, Pleasant and Lear [4] describes "Track", which is a basically a transport mechanism, and how it has been put into use in order to solve the same problems as Store.

Many university CM systems target configuration management of source code. However, for a system administrator, the one-time effort of compiling an application is often manageable and trivial compared to the continued effort that has to be put into continued, on-going administration of a complex system involving a large number of applications, organizations, architectures, and users.

Furthermore, most large Unix operating systems have a system for distributing software packages. But unfortunately, most of these commercial products are available only for a single OS and few offer more than insufficient, elementary support for the system administrators. Generally, they only offer support for loading software into the machine, a crude inventory list, and perhaps support for unloading.

5 The Concepts

The main concepts of Store are:

Separability. Everything related to a single application, including all versions and support for various hardware platforms, are isolated at one location in the computer file system. This "master location" of the application can be institution-wide; it can also span multiple cooperating institutions.

Consistency. An installation of an application should be consistent throughout the institution. If incorrect or buggy, the application should be consistently incorrect everywhere. Only then is there a fair chance of the problem being corrected; else users move over to computers that work, allowing the faults to continue and to accumulate.

Automation. Any kind of manually performed routine work will eventually be skipped or performed incorrectly. Thus, such work should be automated as much as possible.

Documentation. Locally written documentation should be as scarce as possible, and preferably be limited to: a) "gluing" together documentation accompanying the applications; b) documenting local conventions and deviations; and c) filling in fatal gaps in accompanying documentation. Locally written documentation tends to get outdated quickly, so the lesser there is to maintain, and the more automated is maintenance, the better.

Standardization. The more need a system administration tool has for specific and non-standard support, the more difficult and troublesome it is to port it to new architectures and organizations. Thus, when implementing solutions, standardization, portability, and robustness is more important than simplicity and elegance.

Strategy-less mechanisms. In constructing Store, the mechanism has been attempted isolated from the strategies that it implements. Thus, the Store transport mechanisms can be employed for various security schemes and to mimic various intra- and inter-organization relations.

6   Technical Description

Store separates applications from each other, in a two-level system: at the top there are one or more stores, or "store servers". At the lower level there are one or more applications. Multiple stores enable distributing the files in Store among several machines and organizations, e.g. duplication to counter slow or temporarily broken networks.

The directory tree shown in figure 1 indicates the directory structure for a Store system containing two servers and nine applications. The node named "/store/" is the top directory. Thus, path names for the locations of the applications are /store/store/storlind/zip, /store/store/khym/tex, etc.

The store names ("storlind" and "khym") can be identical to the names of the host on which they are located, but this is not a requirement. However, we have found this naming scheme to be fairly practical. One machine can host multiple stores.

Now we shift the focus to a single application. The structure of a small application is depicted in figure 2. For such a package there are one or more "version" directories, zero or more "src-" directories, and a file called "registration". The root of the tree shown in figure 2 is /store/store/khym/shar, if the application is "shar", and it is stored on the store "khym".

The "src-" directories contain the source code for the application. The original, official source code is stored in directories named "src-*version*" where *version* refers to the release number. In directories named "src-*version-architecture*", a link-tree (of symlinks) is used to contain modifications specific to that architecture; this linktree is said to be a "shadow" of the original linktree. The linktrees

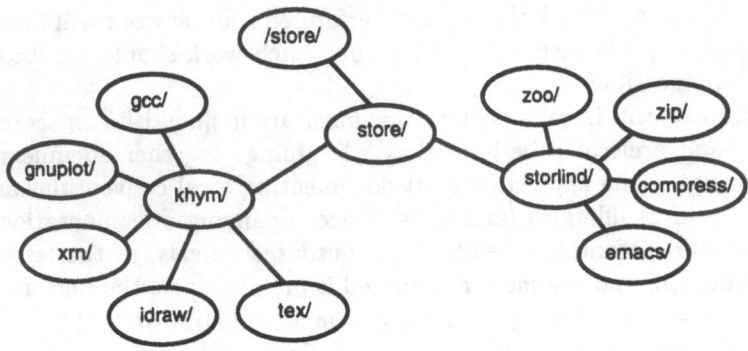

Fig. 1. Structure of Stores

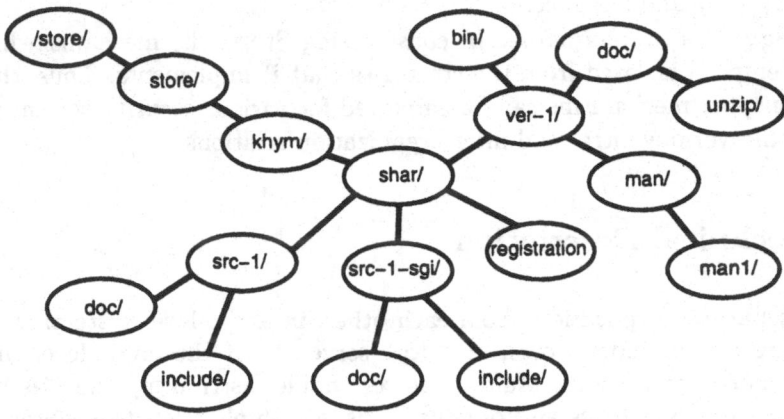

Fig. 2. Structure of Applications

can be configured in a way suitable for the application. For instance, a linktree can be a shadow of another linktree shadow.

In figure 3, a common situation is shown. One directory contains the official source; another contains local "hacks" and configurations, which shadows the official source; and several directories, each containing architecture-specific configuration changes, which shadows the local "shadow". The arrows in figure 3 refers to linktree-inheritance, i.e. shadowing.

Each "ver-" directory contains possibly multiple hardware-variants of one version of the application. Below the "ver-" directory, the structure of subdirectories is similar to the structures usually found in /usr/local and /usr. Figure 4 shows in detail the structure under a "ver-" tree.

In order to simultaneously handle support for multiple architectures, one need a method for distinguishing between hardware variants of a file in the file system name space. This is done by adding an identifier suffix to the filenames. For instance, the binary file `shar` becomes `shar@sun4os4` and `shar@hp700ux9` for SunOS 4 on Sparc and HP/UX 9.xx on HP-PA, respectively. In Store this is

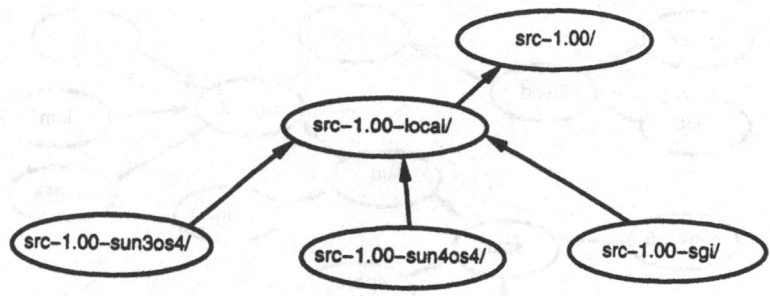

Fig. 3. Interrelationship of Source Directories

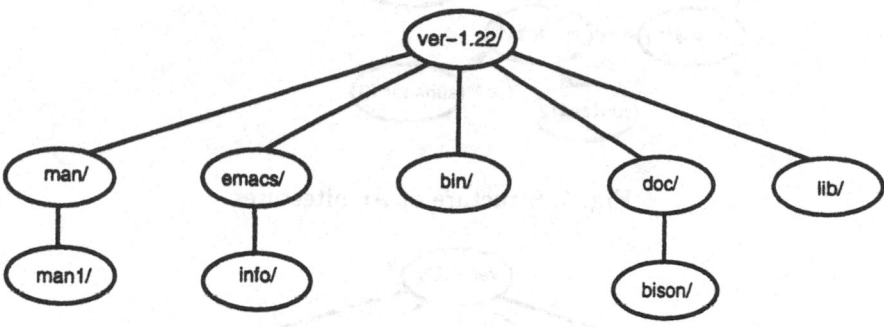

Fig. 4. Structure of a "ver-" Tree

perhaps a bit inelegant, but fairly simple and very portable and standard.

The names of the architectures are defined hierarchically, as shown in figure 5. Although most systems only need the name of the OS, some need to be related to the exact OS release level, or even to the specific configuration of a kernel. Normally, only files are given a file name suffix, but Store also supports suffixes for directories, in which case all files in that directory subtree implicitly inherit the directory.

The implementation of Store does not distinguish between OS-architectures and hardware architectures. Although these are two different dimensions (one OS can run on several hardware platforms, and each hardware platform can run many OSes), we have found it advantageous to collapse these two dimensions into one. The reason is that very few files for one OS are common for multiple hardware platforms; likewise for files specific for one hardware platform but common for multiple OSes. We might have implemented this differently if our target had been operating system software rather than third party applications.

We can now add filenames to the figure showing the subtree of a "ver-" directory (figure 4). Ovals denote directories, filenames are listed below the directory in which they are located. The new, expanded figure is shown in figure 6. Files containing the "@" character and a suffix, are architecture dependent files.

The last component in the application directory is the `registration` file. It

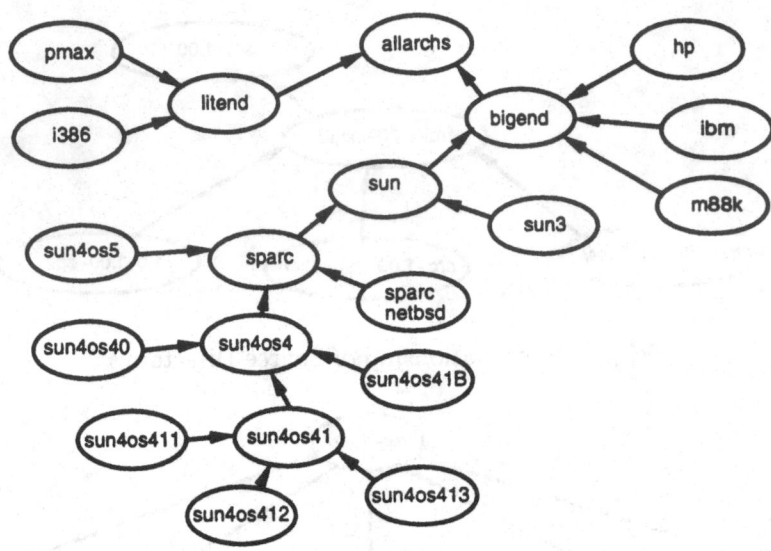

Fig. 5. Structure of Architectures

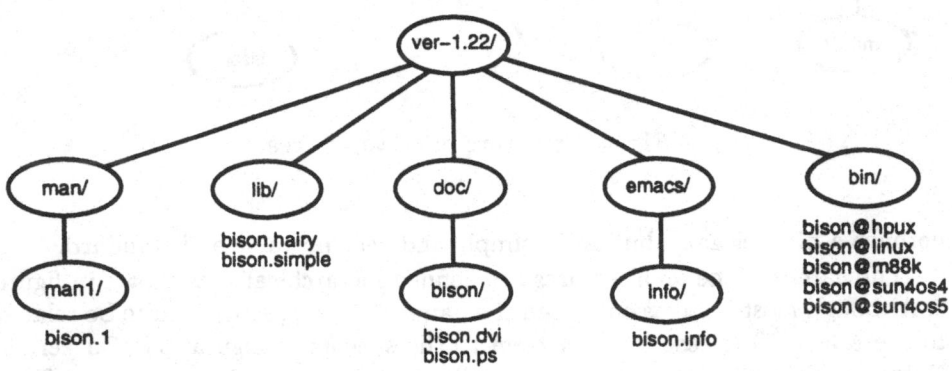

Fig. 6. Extended structure of a "ver-" Tree

contains information about the application, such as the name of the application, the source, the compilation history, who is responsible for local maintenance, which versions that are available and their stability, etc. It can be considered a configuration file for that application.

The system as it has been described so far is not very useful, since the files are distributed widely in a large number of directories. Therefore, the second part of Store automatically creates a linktree under /store, generated from all applications on all store servers. Effectively, it creates a directory hierarchy, which name space is the union of all name spaces in the "ver-" trees for all applications. However, there are some exceptions: if there are multiple versions of an application, only one version is used (e.g. the newest); if there are multiple variants of a file (for several architectures), only the file most relevant to the

```
/store/bin/bison              ->/store/store/khym/bison/ver-1.22/bin/bison@hpux
/store/lib/bison.hairy        ->/store/store/khym/bison/ver-1.22/lib/bison.hairy
/store/lib/bison.simple       ->/store/store/khym/bison/ver-1.22/lib/bison.simple
/store/man/man1/bison.1       ->/store/store/khym/bison/ver-1.22/man/man1/bison.1
/store/doc/bison/bison.dvi   ->/store/store/khym/bison/ver-1.22/bison/bison.dvi
/store/doc/bison/bison.ps    ->/store/store/khym/bison/ver-1.22/bison/bison.ps
/store/emacs/info/bison.info->/store/store/khym/bison/ver-1.22/emacs/info/bison.info
```

Fig. 7. Symlinks Generated for Application in Figure 6 (HP)

linktree is used, and the suffix part is removed from the links in the /store name space. The linktree is a view into the file repository under /store/store. For the filenames that are listed in figure 6, the corresponding symlinks generated are listed in figure 7.

Our next concerns are consistency and access time. Consistency requires that an application is only stored at one place in order to avoid two diverging copies. Access time requires that many copies are distributed among the computers in a network, in order to minimize access time and to ensure continuous access to the application even if parts of the network are inaccessible.

In order to satisfy these two requirements, Store implements "slave store servers". They are normal stores, except that applications stored on a slave store are automatically copied from the normal store (a.k.a. "master store"). The master store holds a repository of application code, the slave stores contains replicas of it, and the linktrees provides a view in to the repositories and replicas. Thus, consistency is ensured by uniqueness. Every piece of information should be stored at only one location. If further copies are required, they are generated from the master copy and repeatedly synchronized later.

All maintenance is performed at the master server. The main function of a slave store is mostly to cache applications from the master server in order to serve local linktrees. Calling it "master" and "slave" servers is a bit imprecise. Stores are either masters or slaves on a per-application basis: Given two servers and two applications, the first server can be a master store for the first application and a slave store for the second, and vice versa for the second store.

A simple directory naming convention notes the difference between slaves and masters. The directory /store/store/khym/tgrind is the master copy, while /store/store/storlind/.tgrind is a replica, due to the name starting with a dot. This convention also ensures that the replica directories stay out of sight in normal ls-listings.

Each linktree under /store will pick an application from a master or slave store for that application, and it points its symlinks towards it. Which server it chooses depends on which machine is closest measured in a distance metric, a metric that can be configured separately for each /store linktree.

Store slave servers only copy the files that they need, i.e. source code is not copied, are architecture-dependent files for hardware that none of the linktrees connecting to that server can ever use.

7 A Full-Scale Example

To flesh out the description given in the previous section, we here show a full-scale example, involving two stores, one application, four linktrees, and four architectures.

The application in question is "mpage", which consists of a binary file **mpage** (architecture dependent), and a manual page **mpage.1** (architecture independent). Figure 8 shows part of the file system on four machines: khym and storlind are servers, master and slave respectively; dekk and chur are linktree-only machines. In this figure, dotted, pointed lines indicate NFS-mounts; solid, pointed lines indicate symlinks; fat lines indicate directory structure; and thin lines group directories and files physically belonging on one machine.

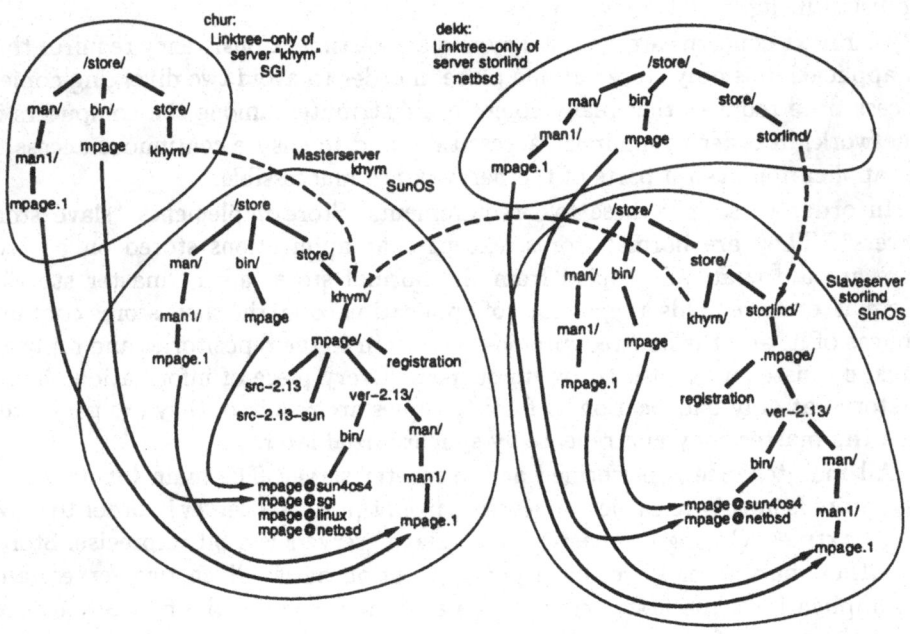

Fig. 8. Full-Scale Example of Store System

The figure shows that the slave server only copies the files for "sun4os4" and 386 "netbsd", the two architectures it serves. Names ending with a "/"-character refer to directories. The linktrees generated for the four machines are shown in figure 9.

Compared with a traditional /usr/local directory structure, there are several practical advantages of this scheme: Given a file in Store, one can determine which application and version it belongs to merely by looking at what the symbolic link expands to. By following the symbolic link, we can find any and all

```
                       For master store khym
/store/bin/mpage          ->/store/store/khym/mpage/ver-2.13/bin/mpage@sun4os4
/store/man/man1/mpage.1->/store/store/khym/mpage/ver-2.13/man/man1/mpage.1
```

```
                       For linktree chur
/store/bin/mpage          ->/store/store/khym/mpage/ver-2.13/bin/mpage@sgi
/store/man/man1/mpage.1->/store/store/khym/mpage/ver-2.13/man/man1/mpage.1
```

```
                       For slave store storlind
/store/bin/mpage          ->/store/store/storlind/.mpage/ver-2.13/bin/mpage@sun4os4
/store/man/man1/mpage.1->/store/store/khym/mpage/ver-2.13/man/man1/mpage.1
```

```
                       For linktree dckk
/store/bin/mpage          ->/store/store/storlind/.mpage/ver-2.13/bin/mpage@netbsd
/store/man/man1/mpage.1->/store/store/khym/mpage/ver-2.13/man/man1/mpage.1
```

Fig. 9. Symlinks Generated for Figure 8

other files related to that particular version of the application.

Users get their traditional /usr/local directory structure (although as symlinks), while system administrators get each application separated from the other applications. This means better overview and easier system maintenance. It also helps automatic generation of user documentation.

Each linktree may be configured to comply with various policies for updating to new versions. "Progressive" linktrees upgrade to the newest version of any application, even if it marked as alpha-test software. "Coward" linktrees only use versions marked as stable. Between these, several other policies exist. In addition policies may include the application's origin, i.e. which stores the linktree trusts.

Store is maintained by a number of Perl scripts. The scripts perform the majority of the tasks needed, except for most of the compilation process, which have proved difficult to automate on a general basis.

8 Where is it Being Used?

Currently, Store is being used at the University of Trondheim, where 10-20 of its departments and faculties cooperate in administering third-party applications through a common Store installation. A total of 300 Unix machines employ Store, that is approximately half the number of Unix machines at the University.

More than 400 applications are installed in Store. The degree to which hardware platforms are covered varies. However, most of the common Unix platforms (around 10) are reasonably covered. When checked, approximately one half to two thirds of the most frequently used user-commands at a typical workstation were loaded from Store. The remaining commands typically were shells (should always reside under /bin) and standard Unix commands.

Initial installations on institutions outside the University of Trondheim is being done, although none of these are yet of the same size as the installation at the University of Trondheim.

9 Experiences

We have learned many lessons while working with Store.

Higher competence. While Store decreased the amount of system work required, it increased the need for those fewer persons to have better skills regarding the applications they manage.

Prevalence. As soon as we reached a threshold (i.e. a large number of applications and a fair number of hardware platforms), new faculties and departments joining the Store-team got most of what they ever needed of freeware and third-party applications. Since their only cost was the price of extra disk space, this service tended to become very popular.

Vulnerability. After having used Store for a while, we have experienced higher vulnerability to incorrect installations. We are so to speak putting all the eggs into one basket; if someone introduces a fault into an application it is spread throughout the university within the next day. To counter this, much work has been put into authorization and configuration mechanisms. Also, Store makes it equally easy to correct faults throughout the university within a day.

A method for reducing this problem is to have an empiric form of quality assurance: No automatic updating of the slave stores, and only manually initiated updating of specific applications on the slave store servers.

Number of architectures. During the first period of Store, we experienced a strong trend towards standardization on a small number of OSes supported by Store. Lately, we have experienced a trend the other way; all it takes is one OS-bigot willing to recompile all Store-applications for "her" OS, and that OS is supported throughout the university on the same basis as major OSes.

Consistency. Using Store as a framework for installing applications ensures that one application is installed the same way, independent of hardware, ownership, and disk-sharing strategies. Only the first person installing a new application decides the strategy for where to put the files. Other persons, recompiling for new hardware architectures or upgrading versions, can simply follow the initial setup. This often implies less work, and the work remaining contains fewer decisions.

Symlinks. Store depends on symlinks, and that has posed some problems, although not as many as feared beforehand. For instance, the maximum number of links allowed by Unix (normally 8, although some OSes have more) has proven too small in some circumstances. When using the automounter, /store is itself a symlink, which increase the problem quite a bit. In addition, if the linktree is given a partition by itself, it might require an increased number of inodes, because of the large number of small files.

More disk usage. A side effect of using Store is an increased use of disk space. But this extra cost is small compared to the perceived reduction of system administration cost. To compute the overhead introduced by Store, assume a system consisting of 2 master stores serving 4 slave stores each, four architectures, 10 linktrees (one for each server), 200 applications. Per application, assume 3 architecture dependent files of an average size of 100 Kb and 12 architecture independent files of an average size of 20 Kb. The extra overhead in the linktrees is 10 servers × 14 symlinks × 200 applications, giving 24,000 symlinks. If each symlink occupies 512 bytes, this means a systemwide overhead of 12 Mb plus some extra, minimal space for directories. The files in a /usr/local tree would be 10 servers × 200 applications × [for each application 12 files of 20 Kb and 3 files of 100 Kb], resulting in a total of 1080 Mb. The extra files in Store which are not directly used are 2 servers × 200 applications × 3 variants × 3 files × 100 Kb, giving 360 Mb. This means a 33% disk-space overhead for this configuration.

Continued maintenance. Continued maintenance is important. We receive a daily mail, reporting the status of the Store installation. The output is adjustable. The reports may also be centralized if one support staff handles multiple Store installations.

Reduced Installation time. When a new computer lab with 10 machines was installed, it took only 20 minutes to link up all applications in Store that supported the given architecture. This is very fast, compared with the alternative situation: recompilation of all those applications.

The final decision is made locally. It is possible to *freeze* a replica, inhibiting further automatic updates for applications considered critically important. If a department wants to use a specific version of an application, they are free to do so. They can even set up their own master for that application. The /usr/local/bin directory can be placed in the PATH environment variable before /store/bin, in order to let locally installed applications take precedence over Store-applications.

Better interdepartmental cooperation. Departments using Store are implicitly encouraged to cooperate. This has resulted in positive side-effects at this university: a) university-wide documentation, b) sharing of human resources, and c) the quality per application is maximized.

Less duplication of work. Store has resulted in a reduced workload, mainly due to less duplication of work because of interdepartmental cooperation.

File name space mangling. The technique of mangling the attributes into the file system name space have proved sufficiently strong. In addition, it is simple, portable, and the limit of 255 characters in file names does not pose a problem. It is even precedented, as compilers use the "file type" to decide the type of contents of a file.

Name space dimensions. Store only uses two dimensions: architecture and domain. However, we envision at least five such dimensions: hardware, operating system, geographic location, organizational affiliation, and release type (alpha, beta, etc). Store uses one dimension (architecture) for the two first; and another (domain) the the two next. The last dimension is put into the configuration file for the application, as all files of a version in an application are considered to be of the same release type.

10 Further Developments

Possible future developments include:

Alternative transport mechanisms. Currently, NFS is the only supported transport mechanism. In the future, support for other mechanisms will be included: ftp, the alex file system, world wide web, etc. Also, support for transport to other systems than Store will be implemented.

Non-Unix platforms. Some initial experiments have been performed with PCs under DOS, using PC-NFS as the transport mechanism. PC-NFS handles symlinks, and technically it worked fairly well. However, some major conceptual problems turned up: most freeware applications are either Unix-only or DOS-only. Thus, the advantage of maintaining a multi-platform configuration of packages disappears.

Another problem is that site-specific-configuration and user-specific-configuration are often mixed together in the same configuration file under DOS; under Unix these are generally more separated.

Furthermore, under DOS and Windows, programs performing certain tasks during program installation that Unix typically performs during program startup, e.g. mail programs under DOS typically set the user name during installation, while under Unix the programs read the user name during startup. Thus, DOS-applications are often single-user applications that are difficult to incorporate into a system like Store.

Automatic documentation for the end-user. We have plans for a WWW gateway to semi-automatically generated hypertext documentation about the applications in Store, where the user can navigate between information about applications, the persons that installed those applications, the category of an application (e.g. image processing, games), the licensing conditions, the manual pages, info pages, examples, release notes, local diffs, and so on. Added to this, some search forms should also be present, so that the end user can easily find the program needed given some keywords about what the user wants to do. This would give one Web "home-page" per application, through which all information about the system is accessible.

Improved feedback. Feedback information should go directly by electronic mail to the person that installed an application, not just to a support team.

Availability monitor. NFS, although stateless, is very vulnerable to a situation where the server for a mounted file system becomes unavailable. If the server does not come up again, programs accessing those mount points will hang, causing the client machine to become rather unusable. Neither Sun's "automounter" nor "amd" provide the needed functionality to switch to a different server on-the-fly. By having identical stores with application replicas only, and an extra level of indirection, one can switch to a server that is available when the previous one becomes unavailable. Note that this is also possible with the traditional approach, just let /usr/local be a symlink to e.g. /usr/locals/*machine*.

Virtual stores. Currently, stores are located below `/store/store`. However, by adding an extra level of indirection, the level specifying the location of the store can be removed. If `/store/store/idt` is a virtual store, then it can dynamically be replaced by any of a set of identical stores. To become effective, this feature needs the availability monitor. However, for two stores to be identical, they cannot be master stores for any application.

Conflict handling. When conflicts between applications occur, they can be resolved, based upon metrics describing the importance of the application and the source of an application (i.e. which master store, who installed the application).

11   More Information

More information about the Store system can be found at the anonymous ftp site ftp.pvv.unit.no, in the directory "/pub/store", and through World Wide Web from http://www.pvv.unit.no/~arnej/store/storedoc.html.

12   Conclusion

We think that Store provides a suitable environment for installing third-party applications, and eases the the daily tasks of the computer systems administration staffs. The main effects are better overview; the automation of repetitive and trivial tasks; ensured consistency; the considering of many computers as one system.

   We have got positive experiences from installing Store at various installations at the University of Trondheim, where currently, around half the Unix-computers use Store. The feedback from users have been generally pleasant, although most users are not aware of Store, even though most of their tools are installed in Store.

References

1. Stephen N. Clark Kenneth Manheimer, Barry A. Warsaw and Walter Rowe. The depot: A framework for sharing software installation across organizational and unix platform boundaries. Proceedings of the Fourth Large Installation Systems Administration IV. Colorado Springs, Colorado, October 1990.
2. Thomas A. Lundgren. A file server directory tree hierachy. Technical Report ETX/TX/DD-91:110, Ericsson Telecom, January 1992.
3. S. Boucher, M. Dagenais, R. Gérin-Lajoie, P. Laplante, and P. Mailhot. LUDE: A Distributed Software Library. University of Montreal, June 1993.
4. Melvin J. Pleasant Jr. and Eliot Lear. Transcending administrative domains by automating system management tasks in a large heterogeneous environment. USENIX Workshop Proceedings. New Orleans, Louisiana, April 1989.

Evaluation Session

Jacky Estublier

This session is very symptomatic of the mood of many software industry professionals, and it was very intense. The controversial title of the first paper by C. Adams "Why can't I buy an SCM Tool" is in itself the program of this session. Why (some) customers think the vendors offer is still inadequate. The discussion, in this session was around the dilemma "Buy versus Build".

Until now, the "build" option was the major one. Very many attempts have been done starting from RCS, Make and shell scripts. The second paper by R. Ray "Experience with a Script-Based Software Configuration Management System", is significant of this approach.

At least some opinions look to be accepted by most attendants. In the short term, building a custom system seems cheaper, but experience constantly showed that an home made SCM system finally turns to be very expensive, difficult to maintain, inflexible and worse it becomes a limiting factor for further evolution.

However, the question remains: why professionals are (may be) unhappy with commercial, off the shelf tools. The session was largely devoted to identifying these aspects that make professionals uncomfortable, and discussing the vendor answers to these criticisms.

The main criticisms against buying a commercial SCM tool have been that (1) it has a pretty high initial cost, (2) plus an important initial cost for adapting to tool to local needs, (3) plus the cost in personal education; with (4) still a risk it does not really fit the company evolving needs and expectations.

Some attendants justified their "build" option by the fact an actual state of the art SCM system is very big and expensive. When they started their SCM system, they required only the most basic SCM functions (versioning + ..). Thus they decided to start with basic free tools. Later, when more functions were needed, it was cheaper to add few scripts shell... and after a few years, yet another inadequate home made SCM system was born.

The discussion turned to ask vendors to provide SCM system with incremental functionalities, and incremental prices. Customers with "low" needs should buy an advanced SCM system, limited to these functionalities it needs. Advanced functionalities should be released at customer demand only.

It was a clear customer demand to have state of the art SCM system but with incremental functionalities (and incremental cost), with very low introduction cost (both in application transfer and personal education), with more evidence of return on investment.

Vendors answer was that it is not always technically feasible to package the functionalities into independent components, and that they are working hard to reduce the technology transfer cost.

Why Can't I Buy an SCM Tool?

Chris Adams

Consulting Software Engineer
Medtronic, Inc.
7000 Central Avenue NE, T418
Minneapolis, MN 55432 USA
E-mail: c.adams@medtronic.com

Abstract. An organization that is evolving its software engineering environment needs an SCM tool that can evolve with the environment. SCM tools are available that can meet the long term needs of such organizations, but those tools are generally packaged in a way that, because of financial and managerial risks, makes them unacceptable for department level computing. SCM vendors are consequently excluded from a significant part of the SCM market, and users are forced to build custom SCM systems. The build-versus-buy dilemma could be resolved by a vendor-supplied SCM tool that is designed for incremental sale, delivery, and operation, where later increments are differentiated by functionality beyond that of earlier increments. Such a tool might be composed of separate, interoperable tool-sets.

1 The Dilemma of Build Versus Buy

Software Configuration Management (SCM) is central to any software engineering environment, whether that environment is cobbled together with informal procedures and various software utilities, or is more highly automated with a CASE framework. Though SCM is sometimes a component of larger, corporate-wide, systems configuration management, an SCM tool is more often procured or developed within the context of a given software engineering environment, which in turn spans a small to medium sized organization (20 to 100 people within, say, a single department of a large corporation). An unscientific assessment of the author's experience suggests department level systems outnumber corporate level systems by at least 4-to-1. The evolution of a software engineering environment is characterized by increased precision and accuracy of procedures, covering an increasing number of steps in the software development cycle with increasing levels of automation. An evolving environment is also characterized by increasing numbers and types of users, beginning with software engineers and continuing with testers, quality assurance engineers, and project and middle-to-upper level managers. Departments with evolving environments eventually recognize their need for evolvable SCM tools. These organizations want to leverage the work of others by buying rather than building SCM functionality. Indeed, commercial, off-the-shelf tools that meet the long term needs of these organizations are now available. Unfortunately, most of these tools are not buyable by most of the organizations that could use them. The market for department level SCM tools is not particularly limited by need, so much as by the financial and managerial risks posed by the available tools. A tool that can meet the long term needs of an evolving software engineering environment incorporates a broad perspective of SCM:

- Version control, with history tracking
- Configuration management, with history tracking
- Dependency tracking and build automation
- Change management, with integrated problem tracking and version control
- Software inventory (asset) administration
- Release management
- Workspace management
- Process automation and management

However, an organization interested in such a tool currently faces the prospect of buying all this functionality as a unit, or perhaps as two units (typically, a version control component and a defect tracking component) from the same vendor or from different vendors. Such a purchase is problematic for six reasons.

1.1 Problem 1

Any projection of the future needs of the software engineering environment is at best an educated guess. Both the timing and direction of the environment's evolution are questionable. For example, the champions of the tool may foresee significant gains from process management facilities, but may not be able to predict when such functionality could or would be used.

1.2 Problem 2

Financing the purchase is difficult.

1. The price can make the tool a major purchase for the organization or even a richer parent organization, not only in the year of the purchase but also in succeeding years.
2. The high price usually dictates that authority for the purchase is held by higher level management, above the department level. Much more effort is needed to get sponsorship from such levels, often more effort than the champions realize or are able to exert.
3. The return on investment must be projected further into the future, increasing the likely error in the projection.

1.3 Problem 3

More cajoling is needed to get buy-in. Managers must be convinced in advance that they, and not just the engineers, will benefit. A full-featured SCM tool is as much a management tool as it is a software tool, a perception not appreciated by many software managers. Software engineers themselves often need convincing. The most distinguished software engineers in a successful company are often successful because of their impressive understanding of the company's mission, markets, and customers, and not because of the engineers' application of advanced software engineering technologies.

1.4 Problem 4

Training users is more complicated and expensive. The initial training for the tool must be reduced to only cover the features of the tool to be initially used. The training must then evolve as the tool's use evolves.

1.5 Problem 5

Administering the tool is more difficult. Administration is comparable to the administration of large databases and database management systems. Network administration is complicated by the infancy (read unstable) or even lack of client-server architectures. System and file administration is sometimes further complicated by needed customizations to kernels and file systems. System administrators are particularly wary of network solutions that might affect the security of their networks, and of system patches that are part of a tool's design.

1.6 Problem 6

Customizations needed before the tool can be deployed often take substantial time. Often, customization is sufficiently complicated to require that it initially be done by consultants provided by the vendor (at extra expense).

1.7 Consequence

Very often, departments determine that although building is expensive, the problems listed above make buying also expensive, as well as risky and difficult. The build-versus-buy dilemma is resolved by starting with a version control tool and perhaps a database management system, and incrementally building a custom SCM system, even though the long term cost of such a system could be an order of magnitude greater than if it had been purchased from an SCM vendor.

2 How SCM Vendors Could Resolve the Dilemma

An SCM vendor could resolve the build-versus-buy dilemma with a tool architecture designed for incremental sale and delivery of SCM functionality. Such an architecture is envisioned as a suite of tool-sets. The tool-sets would be layered, with higher level tool-sets built upon the lower level sets (upper layers can call lower layers but not vice versa). The tool-sets would be purchased from the bottom-up, as more functionality is needed, and configured into the operational suite on-site. As illustration, a suite of SCM tool-sets might include:

- SCM object repository
- Version control for source code
- Configuration control
- Document control
- Binary/library version control
- Tool version control
- Workspace management
- Problem (issue) tracking
- Change control (state machines for SCM objects)
- Change control integrated with problem tracking
- Process management
- Platform-dependent server layers
- Platform-dependent client layers
- Network-dependent layers
- Graphical user interfaces

Each tool-set might consist of some combination of database management system, schema definitions, executables and application program interface libraries, and configuration definition files. The developer of such an architecture would have to determine a feasible decomposition. The overall price to a buyer of all the features would be the same as for tools now available but would be stretched out over several years. Where an organization might now spend US$100,000 in a single year for, say, twenty software licenses, and another US$100,000 for consulting and customizations, that user might instead spend one-fifth that in each of five years. An evolutionary suite of tool-sets would minimize the building of SCM functionality in favor of incrementally buying that functionality. SCM vendors would be able to sell more software because they would have more customers. Users would buy more SCM tools because the risk and effort of doing so would be reduced.

Experiences With a Script-Based Software Configuration Management System

Randy J. Ray

U S WEST Communications, Software Configuration Management

rjray@lookout.ecte.uswc.uswest.com

Abstract. As software systems grow in size and complexity, the need for a software configuration management tool to control problems such as sharing code and version control also grows. Such tools are also subject to issues of complexity and maintainability. If a configuration management tool can be designed with a certain degree of simplicity, while still providing generous functionality, then the task of supporting larger software systems with the tool becomes simpler. This paper describes the design, implementation, and evolution of a script-based software configuration management system.

1 Introduction

The area of software configuration management is gaining a foothold in the field of software engineering, in both concept and application. Software projects are often faced with at least one common requirement: reproducible results. On the surface, this appears to be a minor requirement, but in reality there are a lot of dynamics that contribute to the ease or difficulty of creating trackable, reproducible results. Matters such as hardware upgrades to development or deployment platforms, multiple platforms to be simultaneously supported, upgrades to development tools and environments, and many more can complicate configuration management. Occurrences as minor as the replacement of a faulty disk drive with a different make of drive can also contribute to problems of configuration.

The Software Configuration Management team at U S WEST Communications is tasked with providing service to development teams. These services are, by charter, restricted to issues of software, so hardware configuration issues will not be discussed here. The responsibilities assumed by the SCM team include:

- Assist in setting up project structure and environment and determining what resources will be required for daily support of the project.
- Produce complete builds of the project software, independent of the development team, delivered to the system test team.
- Provide complete reports of changes to be delivered and files effected. This is called the *audit* of the build.
- Provide a report on the completed build, showing what changes were delivered, what other elements (databases, external libraries) were incorporated, and what problems were encountered during the course of the build of the software.

In order to be accepted as a viable approach, a tool has to offer a varying degree of assistance for all of these duties. The variance would range from areas such as project setup, where there would be more paperwork and decision-making, to the actual build and delivery processes, where most decisions were already made, and had to be enforced by actions taken by the tool.

2 Design Issues

The approach taken at U S WEST for the development of a configuration management system was governed by two primary factors. The first was that a configuration management system must conform to and support a set of U S WEST Communications rules which govern aspects of project management, often referred to as the "Fifteen Audit Principles."[1] The second consideration was that a configuration management system must be developed in such a way as to support as many diverse UNIX[2] architectures as possible. In the current software development market, it is no longer sufficient to support only one platform. In many cases, even three or four separate platforms are not sufficient.

It was the second issue, support of diverse UNIX architectures, that prompted a script-based solution. While there are plentiful development packages available that simplify multi-platform development in high-level languages such as C or C++, it was judged that such an approach would not be cost-effective given the number of platforms that would have to be supported. Rather, an interpreted language that behaved consistently on all platforms would be used. This solution would then be developed in such a fashion as to satisfy the other requirement. Requirements that were taken into consideration included:

- Must be capable of supporting more than one system for tracking and managing change/bug reports. These systems are generally referred to as *Change Management Systems* (CMS), and at present there are two completely different systems in use.
- Should have the capacity to support more than one *version control system* (VCS). While RCS (Revision Control System) is currently the standard tool, the flexibility must be there for expansion, in the event of the advent or discovery of another suitable tool.
- Should incorporate a mechanism for supporting cross-platform development.
- Must not dictate a particular development environment to the project team being supported.

---

1. Their wording and application has less to do with the physical configuration and management of machine resources than with project management practice and procedure. They are not delved into with any detail in this paper, except where there is a direct relevance to a decision in design or implementation.
2. UNIX is a registered trademark of the UNIX Systems Organization of the Novell Corporation

And, very importantly:

- Satisfy the requirement of reproducible builds.
- Be readily run on new, even drastically different UNIX systems.

Clearly, not all of these goals could be realized immediately, and this led to a significant additional requirement: the system had to be developed in a fashion that promoted modularization of the parts of the software build process, with minimal interdependency.

Implementing modularity took the route of dividing the software build process into a series of phases, each with a clearly-defined scope and sequence:

In the **Build Setup** phase, the builder confirms that adequate resources are available on the host machine, and sets up an operating environment tailored to the particular project and release that he or she is tasked to build. Following that, in the **Pre-Audit** phase the project's configuration file is marked with the proper revision, the source code base is "baselined" (a process in which it is noted which versions of the files were used for the most recent build, to eliminate redundant processing), and a list of change requests scheduled for delivery in the build is generated.

The **Audit** phase performs a detailed analysis of the source code base to determine what files have undergone change since the last build, and which of these changes should in fact be used in the build about to take place. Thanks to the baseline applied earlier in the Pre-Audit phase, the search of revision-controlled files can be pruned to the point where the last build was performed, as all versions prior to the baseline would have been audited in previous builds. The audit phase will inform the builder of files that appear to be in development, of files added or deleted[1] and, most importantly, files with changes not associated with a valid change request. Also reported will be the special case when an invalid change request is sandwiched between two change requests scheduled for release. This phase cannot be considered completed until all the problems have been resolved with project personnel.

In the **Delivery** phase, the changes deemed valid are accepted for delivery. Files that have changed have the build symbol moved from the revision used in the previous (baseline) build to the revision selected for delivery in the current build. Following this is the **Build** phase, in which the commands are executed to compile and link binaries, shuffle files into the desired structure for delivery, and set security parameters such as ownership and access permissions.

---

1. Files are not actually deleted from the source base, as that would impede the reproduction of an earlier build that used said file. Rather, they are marked with a special symbol that inhibits their use in the build.

In the **Archive** phase, the completed product is transferred to the format requested by the project test personnel.

Finally, in the **Release** phase, the release notes for the build are generated, noting any problems encountered, providing a list of all changes delivered, providing a list of changes not yet delivered, and a transcript of the builder's session.

Once the final phase is reached, the completed build is passed to the hands of the test team, and the builder turns to other tasks. Personnel on the SCM team at U S WEST often support in excess of three projects per person, and some as many as five or more.

The definition and ordering of these phases was designed such that in the event of an error, the builder should not have to back up further than one phase. This greatly helps in narrowing down the areas in which errors can occur. The abstraction and modularity of the phases reduces the likelihood that an error is due to a problem several phases prior, and allows the search for solutions to be more focused. In practice, most errors or interruptions are in fact identified and dispatched within the scope of the "current" phase.

3 Initial Development

To begin the development of the configuration system, it was necessary to select a development platform that would meet the requirement of portability, then determine the impact that accommodating the aforementioned "audit principles" would have on development.

Based on the earlier decision to adopt a scripting language, the initial prototype was developed primarily in the C-Shell (*csh*) and Korn Shell (*ksh*) languages. These were chosen for their universal availability on UNIX machines, and the fact that such a set of scripts would conceivably execute consistently across different platforms. While these assumptions were in fact true, *csh* and *ksh* suffered from poor speed performance and limitations in functionality. As it had already been decided to use interpretive languages, these shortcomings were tolerated for the time being in favor of increased platform-independence.

Using the concept of phases, an approach was formulated that relied on the UNIX tool model. Tools would be designed in such a way that each performed only one task or a very few. They could then be chained together in sequence to effect more complex tasks. Scripts were broken down and divided by their function with respect to the set of phases previously defined. Each phase was sufficiently independent from the others that tool development on a per-phase basis was possible (with the exception of the Deliver phase, which exhibited some coupling to the Audit phase). As development of an initial toolset progressed, the function and scope of the phases were refined. While this initial tool set was effective, the limitations imposed by the shell languages soon became impossible to overcome, and it was clear that a replacement was needed.

4 Further Development

A solution to the limitations was found in the form of the Perl programming language. Perl combined the functionality of several UNIX tools including *csh*, *awk* and *sed* into a single scripting language. The nature and design of Perl offered many improvements over the shell languages, in areas of speed, maintainability, and flexibility. Existing scripts were re-written in Perl, providing an immediate increase in performance.

The benefits of switching to Perl were not limited to increases in speed of execution. As a very high level language, Perl offered dynamic resolution, and complete access to all features of the UNIX operating system. The rich basic functionality of the language itself allowed for improved text manipulation, modularization of tasks and solutions, run-time evaluation of constructs to trap error conditions, and efficient interaction with both the user and the operating system. Most importantly, Perl came in a publicly-available package, supporting all different architectures in use at U S WEST at the time[1]. Adopting Perl as the tool to implement the software configuration management solution allowed for more capability than was possible previously, without a significant decrease in system performance.

5 Growth and Enhancement

The potential for greater functionality lead to the requirement for greater functionality. While more abilities were being added to the tools, a parallel effort was undertaken to stabilize the existing scripts in terms of structure and consistency. Common functionality between tools (and phases) was identified and abstracted into a series of libraries. An error and status logging package was developed to not only standardize the means by which output to the user was managed, but to increase the flexibility of the output logging and re-direction. With this addition, it was possible to control the output streams of all the tools by using a single configuration file.

Other enhancements followed in logical order. Gradually, some UNIX tools such as *find* were replaced by libraries. Some functionality previously provided by toolset scripts was replaced by libraries of subroutines. The run-time environment could be managed by a few configuration files on a project-by-project basis, and was extensible. Importantly, the system could be applied to support a development project with minimal impact on project structure. Projects ranging from 1-2 developers to teams of 30 or more personnel could apply the same solution to their configuration management needs.

6 Tools and Combinations

At present, the toolset consists of:

- 77 executable command scripts
- 22 run-time-loaded libraries

---

1. Since the initial adoption of Perl, U S WEST has also adopted several new development platforms, all of which were supportable with Perl.

- 102 UNIX-style "man" pages
- 46 configuration/support files

While on the surface this appears to describe a very complex system, it is an easy system to learn. Several of the command scripts are in fact *encapsulators*, running one or more other commands with automatically-crafted command lines based on the original command line options passed to the encapsulator. This aids in grouping together related sequences of commands, or crafting high-level interfaces to lower-level tools.

The concept of the tool encapsulator is based on the phase model described earlier: A phase is broken down into a series of steps, each step being represented by a tool. Those steps that lend themselves to further modularization are represented by encapsulation of the sub-steps into a controlling tool. Further encapsulation can be implemented when necessary.

7 Addressing the Requirements and Phases in Detail

Now that the evolution of the tools has been covered to some degree, a return to the requirements and the stated concept of the process phases can include more detail on exactly what takes place and how issues were directly addressed.

Addressing the requirements, the tools:

- Support the interface to project-selectable change management systems and version control systems through dynamic libraries (a feature available in Perl)
- Support development on multiple platforms simultaneously
- Give the developers freedom to use whatever favorite tools and environment they choose

And covering the two critical requirements, the tools:

- Mark the project files in such a way as to insure reproducibility of builds
- Can be applied to any UNIX platform that Perl runs on

In the case of addressing the phases, the tool-to-phase mapping in an average configuration has the builder executing twelve tools, and a small number of basic UNIX commands. The small number of tools actually utilized by someone performing a build makes the build process easy to learn and apply.

8 Conclusions and Future Plans

The solution described here meets operation requirements U S WEST. Currently, over thirty active or completed projects are being or have been supported by the SCM tools. Even as new projects are adopted, bringing with them newer, more complex requirements, the design of the toolset and the nature of the Perl programming language allow for quick response to the new requirements. Future development plans for the tools include expanded parallel development and a graphical user interface. The key to the development of this software configuration system has been the flexibility of design, the flexibility of the language used, and dedication to the UNIX model of a tool.

Experience Session

Michel Lacroix & Jacky Estublier

Karen Parker reported on her experience of customizing CaseWare/CM for supporting the development of embedded software system in ADA (40 developers). Significant efforts were invested in customizing the system for supporting the development lifecycle, especially with component states and state transition rules. One ironic conclusion worth reporting, is that although the system was instrumental in the on-schedule delivery of the project, CM does not appear to be really recognized as a critical success factor by management.

Anita Persson reported on the introduction and use of ADELE for the development of telecom software. The system proved very flexible and easy enough for modelling the methods of the company. On the negative side, it seems that the complexity of some data models in ADELE may be a problem for some end-users. Both presentations triggered short discussions on the role of SCM system in the support of development processes. Although some consensus was reached on the need for improving further the customizability of SCM systems, it was felt that process modelling itself remains a challenge in most organizations.

This session is to compare with the SCM evaluation session. Here the experience was from companies who decided to build their "own" SCM system, but not from scratch, as traditionally done, but from modern SCM systems. To some extent the experience is similar. Building a specific SCM system is still a challenging task. The effort is significant. Karen mentioned that 2 full time persons were employed during the whole project duration, essentially in defining and maintaining the processes. Anita mentioned only 2 man month for implementing their solution, but after 2 years of experience with the system.

Both speakers agreed in the following conclusion:

- Process support is a mandatory aspect for the SCM system. This aspect was bar far the most time consuming in both experiences. Both speakers think this support is currently too primitive, and process definition too time consuming.
- Both insisted on the fact that this approach (starting from commercial system) was the key success factor to produce a stable are (relatively) easy to maintain system, that exactly fit the company needs.

This session was very active; most attendants being very interested in the experience report. Their was a general feeling that this is the direction to go, but that the current technology is still weak in the most critical dimensions: customizability and process support.

Customization of a Commercial CM System to Provide Better Management Mechanisms

Karen Parker
Summit Design
9305 SW Gemini Drive
Beaverton, OR 97008
email: parker@sd.com)

ABSTRACT

Consider the question often asked in software development: Whyproduct 10 times faster than one engineer? Effort and schedule arerelationship. What function is the additional effort serving ifThis extra effort is generally referred to as overhead. The primarycomplexity of developing many pieces concurrently and integrating

Assuming software schedules will not become less demanding, theon minimizing the overhead associated with adding more people.

The overhead can be minimized by using a development process modelnication and tracking capabilities as well as configurationnisms during the initial and rework phases of a project.

Such a model was defined and implemented by our company by addingmanagement, communication and integration mechanisms to thetion Management) 3.0 and CaseWare/PT (Problem Tracking) 3.0model was used and improved on several projects and contributedof the projects.

1 Introduction

The purpose of this paper is to describe briefly our experience ofmodel that supports methods for productively managing theteams. A related paper [1] describes this model in much moreauthor of this paper.

The implementation of the model integrated a database, aagement system. It was iteratively developed over a two year periodand then improved based on users' feedback.

2 The Overhead Problem

The overhead which this model reduces is related to the additionalrently develop the parts and integrate the software. There areoverhead effort to grow non-linearly as more people are added to

The first major contributor is the communication required among theessential in order to develop correct interfaces and identifyreduce this overhead source is to make the communication awhich supply automatic documentation and notification of changesoverhead.

A second significant contributor is the added difficulty ofsimultaneously. One way to reduce this overhead is to provideand accurately track the progress of the development. Tools which-tus information can provide management with this capability.

The iterative nature of the software development process is anothercost. This iterative process makes the maturity of the softwarewhich are considered to be completed often require rework. Thiseffectively, since a clear picture of the remaining work is noting of the rework tasks provide management with the capability todifficult schedules.

Unlike the assembly of hardware, the integration of software is notdevelopment cycle. The software implementation must be repeatedlylifecycle to validate the correctness of the components'internal implementation and interfaces. Because the integration process is performed repeatedly, the overhead of thisproject overhead. More efficient methods for performing thetotal overhead costs.

Because the effect of these factors is multiplied as the number ofoverhead be reduced to allow for teams of any size to work

3 A Model for Reducing Overhead

Our company is primarily a hardware manufacturing company in theage of our market is in the aerospace industry. Since the airplanedors to provide integrated systems which contain both hardware andthe critical path in meeting our product development schedule.

In order to meet aggressive schedules, it was determined that aadded to the projects. The overhead resulting from the additionalopment process model was needed that would provide bettering the initial and rework phases of a project to reduce theto provide the configuration identification and baseliningperforming integration.

It was decided that the CaseWare/CM 3.0 (Configuration Management)Tracking) [2] products would be used as the foundation of ourconfiguration management platform to reduce the integrationtomize the environment to provide the stronger project managementrequired.

Since the model source code is delivered with the CaseWareble. The customizations that we implemented included:

- Additional component states and state transition rules were addedwork product (or component version) is a accurate indication ofstates were added to the work product groups (or assemblies) forintegration and baselining process.

- E-mail notifications on state transitions were added in order todevelopers. For example, e-mail notification is sent to thereview. Notification is sent to subscribers when a new version of ation. The software lead can choose to be notified when reviews are

- Extensive customizations of CaseWare/PT was done to provide a tasking are some of the customizations included:

  1 Added revised estimate for task completion date and effort.

  2 Added estimates for task review effort and completion date inplanning and tracking of verification work.

  3 Added a "task_deferred" state and "reactivate" date to(Sometimes part of a solution is implemented while some is

  4 Added a task verification state and review attributes to tasks toand findings of a review.

  5 Implemented auto-calculation of task review planned completionmentation planned dates.

  6 Added a replanning capability allowing the lead role to reassigncompletion dates and effort.

  7Added task views for each task state as well as a task replanning

4 The Implementation Effort

Since there was no commercial product which met all our needs, weuse a commercial product as is and settle for solving only some ofcustomize a commercial product.

The implementation of our development process model from scratchour relatively small company. The model provided by CaseWare gavedeploy a system containing parts of our model relatively quickly.our ability to customize it allowed for an environment to applyWare product allowed us to build on a solid CM platform and providegrated software development environment.

One of the difficulties we encountered with customizing awhich were not part of the original design. Some of thedesign, but others were not, and therefore are less intuitive and

The total customizations represented over 3 person-years of effort.extensive and will require a significant effort to integrate ourproduct (Continuus 4.0). However, as the commercial product evolvesour customizations may become unnecessary.

The deployment of this tool on several projects was verytaken at our company was completed on schedule. We attribute muchassured more consistency in the process and allowed much betterIncreasing the size of the team to accelerate the schedule wasapply the resources efficiently. The combination of strongallowed the team members to work productively together.

5 Conclusion

The success of medium to large size projects depends on minimizingdevelopment. The keys to reducing this overhead are betterment of the resources. Controlling the development with adation for building these mechanisms. Our experience shows that aexcellent basis for building a more complete and customized

6 References

[1]: Parker, Karen, "Reducing Software Schedules with a Processstem" 1995

[2]: CaseWare, Inc., "CaseWare User's Guide", Part Number

7 Acknowledgments

I would like to thank Brandon Masterson and Tim Fujita-Yuhas for their multiple reviews of this paper.

Experiences of Customization and Introduction of a CM Model

Annita Persson
Ericsson Microwave Systems AB
S-431 84 MÖLNDAL
SWEDEN
Telephone:+46 31 67 10 00
Direct:+46 31 67 19 00
Telefax:+46 31 67 35 92
E-mail:emwapn@emw.ericsson.se

ABSTRACT. This document describes the experiences of the first stage of customizing and introducing Adele and Adele MMI Builder at a department of Ericsson Microwave Systems AB in Mölndal, Sweden. The document lists positive as well as negative experiences and also provides a short discussion of unsolved problems.

1 SUMMARY

Introduction of a CM tool in a development organization is time-consuming and can be difficult. The more confident the people are in their own established CM methods, the more difficult it is to get acceptance for new methods and tools. In a more chaotic environment, the benefits of a CM tool are more obvious. Thus, the introduction of a CM tool must be supported and coordinated from the top, with management decisions from all management levels.

During the customization of the CM tool it is important to have frequent co-operation with end-users to get confidence and a good usability as well as relevant functionality in the product. Representatives from different staff groups should form a reference group together with the customization team.

Adele works well as a highly customizable CM tool. However some functionality, which is essential for using the CM tool as a general tool for the entire organization, is missing.

2 INTRODUCTION

Ericsson is an international leader in telecommunications, recognized for its advanced systems and products for wired and mobile communication in public and private networks. Ericsson is also a leading supplier of electronic defence systems. Ericsson has 70,000 employees and activities in 100 countries.

Ericsson Microwave Systems is responsible for defence electronics and microwave communications within Ericsson. The product range includes ground-based, naval and airborne radar systems, defence communications, electro-optics and airborne EW systems. The company is active in civil telecommunications, being a world leader in the supply of radio links, and is also the Ericsson R&D centre for very high speed electronics.

Ericsson Microwave Systems make active use of the technical synergy between defence electronics and civil telecommunications

The company, with sites in Mölndal, Kista and Borås in Sweden, employs 3,000 people, and has a turnover of more than SEK 3,000 million.

2.1 CM WITHIN ERICSSON

As one of the leading telecommunications manufacturers of the world, Ericsson has a long experience of the development of complex and technically advanced products. A prerequisite of the success is a long tradition of CM in the sense of item identification, version handling and change control.

Products and documents are central in the Ericsson CM nomenclature. A product may consist of subproducts and/or documents.

2.1.1 Product Identification

Products are classified in what is called the *ABC classification system*. Each version of a product is identified by means of a product number and an *R-state* (Release state). If the product is stored while in production, an indication of the processing stage is also included. How a product identity is built is shown in the figure below. The product

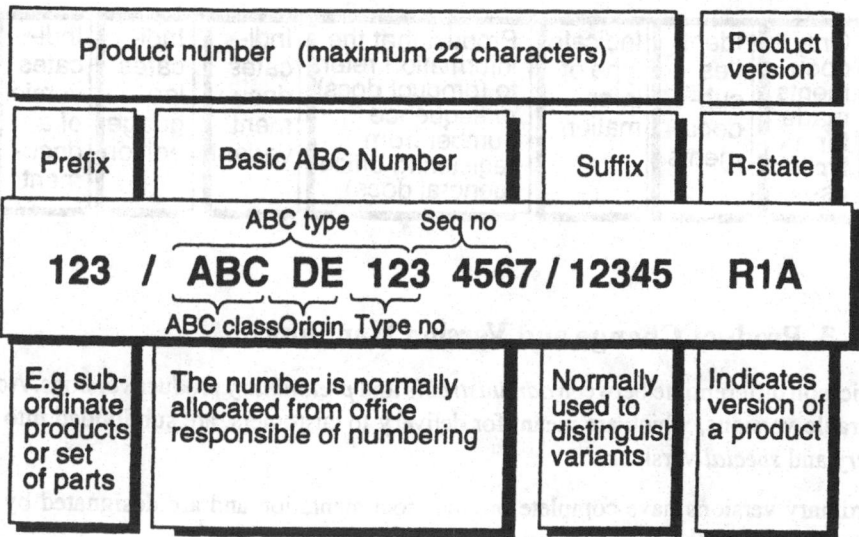

version is defined by the set of documents that is related to it. The R-state is used to distinguish between sets of documents, and the mapping between R-states and document sets is found in the DSU (Document Survey) for the product. In general terms, the DSU is a kind of VDD (Version Description Document).

2.1.2 Document Identification

Each document is identified by its document number, its version called *Rev-state* (Revision state), and the language in which it is written. Usually language code is not included when a document is referred to, because editions in different language contain the same information. Document that require updating are registered with *registration notation* and can be product documents or general documents. Documents that do not require updating are registered (locally) with *reference notation* and can be office documents or personal documents. How the document identity is built for a document with registration notation is shown in the figure below.

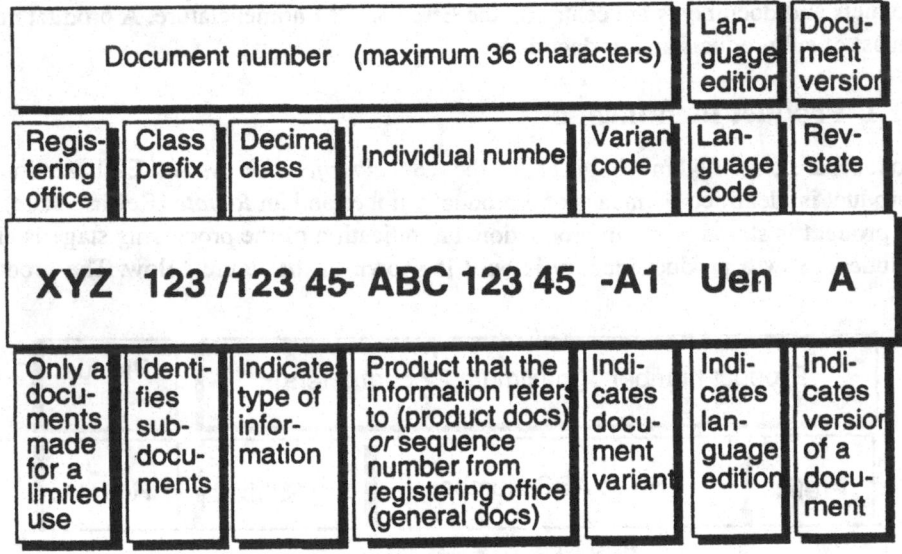

2.1.3 Product Change and Version Handling

Ericsson differentiate between *administrable* and *preliminary* product versions. Administrable versions, which are meant for delivery to customers, are subdivided into *ordinary* and *special* versions.

Ordinary versions have complete product documentation and are designated by ordinary R-states of the following types:

- **R1** Interchangeability is stated in the documents, usually in the Product Revision Information, PRI.
  (limited interchangeability)
- **R1A** Interchangeability is indicated by the R-state.
  (regulated interchangeability)
- **RA** The latest version replaces all earlier ones.
  (simplified R-state)

Preliminary version is used during the development process to identify different versions of a product. Interchangeability does not exist between preliminary R-states. The type of version is identified in the R-state of the product, illustrated in next figure.

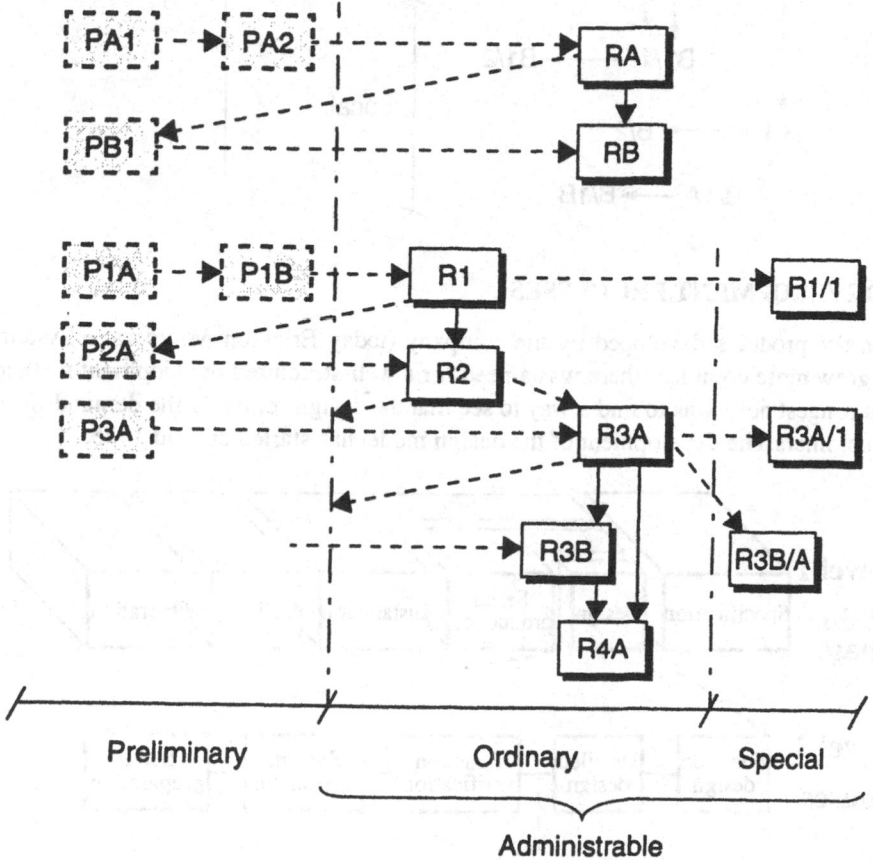

2.1.4 Document Change and Version Handling

Ericsson differentiate between *administrable* and *preliminary* document versions by means of the Rev-state. Administrable versions are meant to be registered, filed, stored and distributed to subscribers. A document that is to be corrected even though a new version of it has been registered is called a *special version*. The *local version* is used when document versions are adapted to local Ericsson requirements. The type of version is identified in the Rev-state of the document according to following figure.

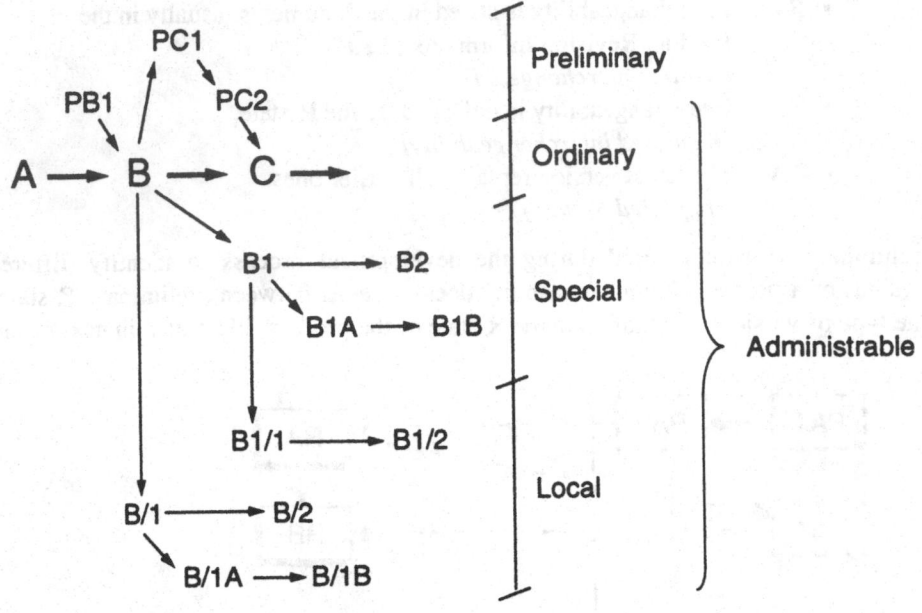

2.2 DEVELOPMENT PROCESSES

When the products developed by the company (today Ericsson Microwave Systems AB) grew more complex, there was a need for a well-structured development method. The strongest need was to find a way to see that the design followed the demands from the customers. The development of the design model has started around 1975.

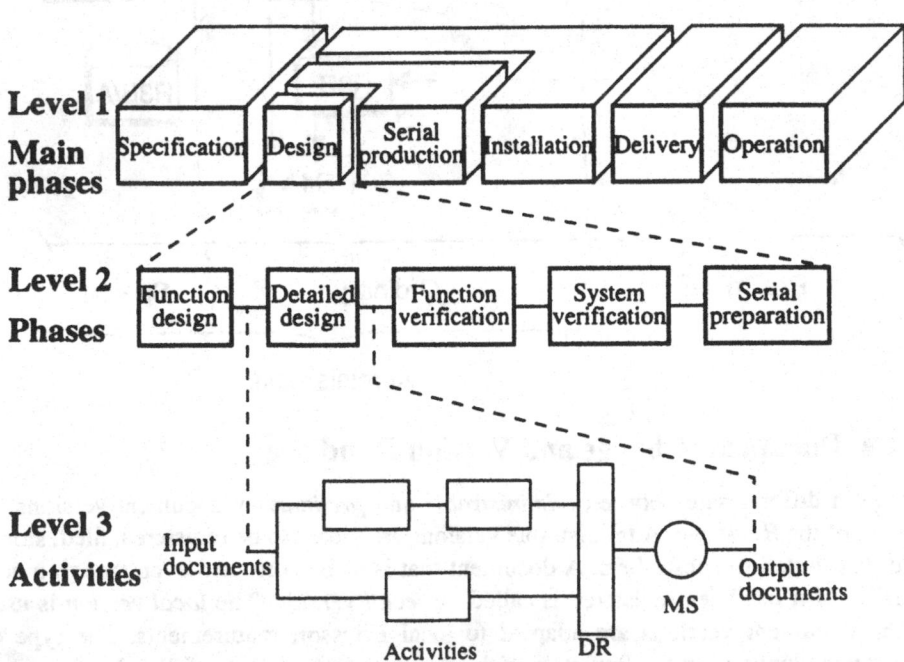

The used design model is defined on company level. The current model is not a water-fall model although this is a common misunderstanding. The iterations and the concurrent engineering are not drawn in the picture because it would make the picture too messy.

An alternative, possibly better, way to illustrate the model is the V-shape shown in next figure.

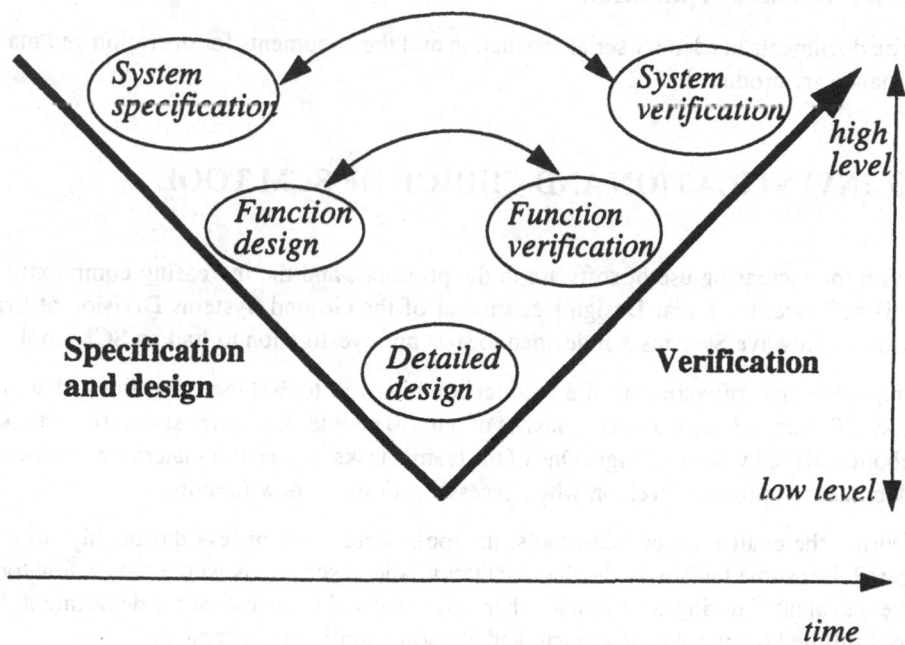

The main phase Design is the one which is important for design of software and hardware. The phase is divided into five sub-phases, explained below.

2.2.1 Function Design

Function design is also known as top-down design, which means drawing block diagrams of the system, showing the functions of different parts, not how they are implemented.

2.2.2 Detailed Design

During detailed design the hardware and software processes are different. Software design includes design specifications, implementation and verification. The hardware design includes design specification and realization of hardware requirements.

2.2.3 Function Verification

During this phase the design is checked to match the function design.

2.2.4 System Verification

The system is verified before serial production to match the system specification.

2.2.5 Serial Preparation

The documents needed for serial production and the documents for operation and maintenance are produced.

3 INVESTIGATION AND CHOICE OF SCM TOOL

With the increasing use of software in the products, and the increasing complexity of this software, the Radar Design Department of the Ground Systems Division at Ericsson Microwave Systems AB decided to start an investigation to find an SCM tool.

In general the software part of a product contains 150 to 300 thousand lines of source code. The design team usually consists of 5 to 40 people. A general software part takes about 100 man years to design. One of the team's tasks is to re-use material on software, document or product level, or, when necessary, design a new function.

During the evaluation of SCM tools, the tools were more or less thoroughly investigated. For some tools only the documentation and descriptions were read. A few tools were evaluated during courses and other investigated during tests at the department. No tool fulfilled the product, document and version handling requirement.

When the investigation was complete, the choice of an SCM tool was Adele and Adele MMI Builder. The main reason for this choice was that the tool appeared to be easily customizable to fit the company-specific methodology, for easy and efficient use.

3.1 CONCLUSIONS

The main important thing before starting the investigation, is to have a SCM requirement specification with priority-ranked requirements. To get confidence during investigation, the requirements need to be approved from the whole organization.

During the investigation it is very important to have participants from the different parts of the organization to get a well established acceptance of the chosen SCM tool.

To have the very best acceptance of introducing a SCM tool in an organization with their own CM, take your time.

4 CUSTOMIZATION

4.1 INTENTION OF CUSTOMIZATION

A basic requirement was to use the SCM tool both as a product and project archive. This implies no need of double data storage.

One requirement from the end-users was to have an MMI (Man Machine Interface, GUI Graphical User Interface) and not just a command line interface.

Another requirement was to have a familiar data model with the company- specific notation, for example Ericsson version management and handling of products and documents, and also a familiar presentation in the MMI.

There was also a requirement of handling different roles and a status machine in the system. The status machine controls the life-cycle of a document.

During design there are different roles in a project, which the tool had to support. The roles design responsible, release responsible, document responsible, preparer and reader was required to be supported. The document responsible is the one who performs approving of documents.

4.2 END-USERS

For the first version of the customization, the main group of the end-users were software designers. Their tasks included writing design documents, designing code, testing and verification.

4.3 CUSTOMIZATION PROCESS

Before starting up the customization of the tool, there was a need of having a reference group with participants from the end-users, from the department office and the customization team. The participant from the end-users was a software designer with long experience of Ericsson CM handling and software design. The participant from the department office was the department expert of Ericsson CM methods.

The reference group had a three day brain-storming meeting to define the requirements on the customization. During this work the data model was designed and documented. The layout of the MMI views was designed and documented as well. A scenario description was written to document the work-flow in the CM tool. Before starting the design phase, all the documents were approved by the pilot project (the end-users).

The customization was estimated to take a team of two people a period of two months. To secure the time schedule, a consultant from the vendor was introduced in the task and was involved in the design for one week.

Every week a follow-up meeting with the managers and the reference group was held, to discuss customization status according to time schedule, planned work, finished work and remaining work and risks.

During the customization the team had highest priority on design comparing to other problems in the area. The team was placed together in the same room for highest efficiency.

4.4 POSITIVE EXPERIENCES

As we have expected, the data model can easily be tailored to fit company-specific work methodology and development processes as described in chapter 2.1 on page 3. Since the data model was documented in detail, the implementation phase was short and secure.

Creating customized commands is easy and gives good performance results compared to shell scripts.

The workspace support, configuration management, process engine and version management works very well for the company requirements.

The history manager works well for including new versions of objects in the database.

There is a powerful language for building customized views and dialogue boxes in the MMI. The language is easy to understand and use.

During the customization we got a quick and helpful support from the vendor. This is essential for a fast and successful customization result.

To have all requirements well-documented, together with the reference group, before starting the implementation shortens the implementation phase and provides better acceptance from the end-users.

4.5 NEGATIVE EXPERIENCES

The data model concept is complex and can be difficult, but often necessary, for end-users to understand.

Process modelling is time-consuming and difficult for end-users to implement. Only the system administrator has the capability to implement processes. The process modelling must have a more common easy-to-use availability.

4.6 CONCLUSIONS

Since the Ericsson internal CM is quite different from what most SCM tools offer, the need of an easy customizable tool is obvious. Before starting the customization of a tool, the following questions must be answered:

- How many requirements on the tool are an absolute "must"?

- How much do we want to invest in building new features?

- Is it a requirement to use the process modelling in the tool, or is it more efficient to buy a specific process tool and integrate the two systems?

To get confidence during customization a reference group is required. The participants must be selected carefully with different categories of people like internal CM expert, CM tool expert, participants from the pilot project, quality management and a project manager for the customization project being authorized to decide about money and resources. The participants need to be accepted in the organization as the right representatives. The group should still be quite small.

5 EXPERIENCES OF INTRODUCTION

5.1 POSITIVE EXPERIENCES

End-users involved in the requirement, design and implement phase provide a high acceptance. The pilot project provides a feed-back of usability.

A well-documented customization documentation shortens the time schedule.

5.2 NEGATIVE EXPERIENCES

It is difficult to know if the tool follows standards like ISO 9001, MIL-STD-973. This is a requirement from our customers.

CM is a complex technique which takes time to fully understand. This is one reason why there are problems for the organization to understand the positive effects on introducing SCM tool. It is even more troublesome to introduce a CM tool in a company with its own well-established CM procedures.

Estimating the pay-back of a SCM tool is very hard. There is no evidence of cut costs or improved revenues. The company managers and controllers have low understanding of this type of investment.

5.3 CONCLUSIONS

To get full acceptance for the SCM tool, confidence from top-management during introduction is essential.

SCM tool vendors have to document what standards their tool complies with, and according to what standards it was developed.

6 UNSOLVED PROBLEMS

There is no standardized interface for interaction with other tools. There are conflicts with other tools with closed databases and their own version handling.

The history manager handles only comments for creation of objects, not for removal. This is a requirement for having Adele as a product archive.

Handling of configuration items smaller than a file, like for IETMs. An IETM is built of a presentation equipment, an MMI and a database with information. The information is created only once, stored only once and is presented when necessary. This implies the manual to be built of many small information blocks. A normal project has a database containing thousands of information blocks which implies a need of configuration management. An information block, configuration item, must be smaller than a file and contains for example a figure, a chapter in a document, a sentence. Every configuration item is SGML (Standard Generalized Markup Language) tagged. One configuration item can be reused in several customer projects.

There is no easy handling of directory structures produced by CASE, CAD and CAE tools. The directory contents normally need to be consistent.

Coupling between source files and change requests (CR, request for corrective action etc.) is necessary for a complete change control.

7 TERMINOLOGY

CR   Change Request
DR   Design Review
DSU   Document Survey
      A document connecting the R-state of an Ericsson product to the Rev-states of the belonging documents
EW   Electronic Warfare
GUI   Graphical User Interface
IETM   Interactive Electronic Technical Manuals
MMI   Man Machine Interface
MS   Mile Stone
      A point of time in the activity when a phase is completed (EMW development model); an event which denotes measurable progress
SGML   Standard Generalized Markup Language
VDD   Version Description Document
      A form identifying the version of a composite item by listing the versions of the components

8 ABOUT THE AUTHOR

Annita Persson received her B.Sc. in Mathematics from Göteborg Univesity in 1983. After graduation, she spent two years of teaching and postgraduate studies in Numerical Analysis at the Department of Computing Science, Göteborg University and Chalmers University of Technology.

In 1985, she joined Ericsson and worked for eight years as a software designer in several projects. Since November 1992 she has been CM coordinator and project leader of the customization and introduction of a CM tool at the Radar Design Department of the Ground Systems Division, Ericsson Microwave Systems AB.

Future Session

Jacky Estublier

A single paper in this session, from Colorado University, called "Does Configuration Management research have a future", but which in itself covers the whole session.
Quoting the authors: "SCM have come a long way since SCCS and Make. Second generation CM systems have raised the level of sophistication dramatically creating greater challenges... and raising new questions. Configuration system architecture, product representation, product software architecture, and extended application domains are just a few areas that should keep researchers busy for the next several years".

In the discussion, other topics came to be discussed, and notably the process support challenge, the dynamics of application, the very fast evolution of the context in which applications are developed and maintained, the wild distribution of our world (10^6 Work Stations, 10^7 PCs, 10^8 lap top), both for development and distribution; the fact there is no longer central control, the need for controlling multimedia data, the need for better models, the need to support cooperative work....

Not to mention the fact that SCM systems should be simpler tools, easier to learn, easier to customize, easier to make evolve, easier to integrate in wider environments, and... cheaper (customer point of view).
There was a very clear feeling from the attendants that progress has been impressive, but that SCM have still many conceptual, methodological and technical challenging issues.

Does Configuration Management Research Have a Future?

André van der Hoek, Dennis Heimbigner, and Alexander L. Wolf

Department of Computer Science, CB 430
University of Colorado
Boulder, Colorado 80309 USA
{andre,dennis,alw}@cs.colorado.edu

Abstract. In this position paper we raise the question of whether Configuration Management (CM) research has a future. The new standard in CM systems—typified by commercial products such as Adele, ADC, ClearCase, Continuus/CM, and CCC/Harvest—largely satisfies the CM functionality requirements posed by Dart. This implies that research in the area of CM is either unnecessary or that we must find new challenges in CM on which to focus. We believe that these challenges indeed exist. Here we present some areas that we feel are good opportunities for new or continued CM research, and therefore conclude that CM research *does* have a future.

Introduction

Numerous attempts have been made to lay out the overall functionality requirements for CM systems. Dart [1, 2] defines eight areas.

- **Component**: identifies, classifies, and accesses the components of the software product.
- **Structure**: represents the system model of the product.
- **Construction**: supports the construction of the product and its artifacts.
- **Auditing**: keeps an audit trail of the product and its process.
- **Accounting**: gathers statistics about the product and the process.
- **Controlling**: controls how and when changes are made.
- **Process**: supports the management of how the product evolves.
- **Team**: enables a project team to develop and maintain a family of products.

The first generation of widely-used CM systems—namely SCCS, RCS, Build, and Make—clearly do not meet these requirements. After a decade of research, a second generation has emerged as the new standard in CM systems. Commercial products such as Adele, ADC, ClearCase, Continuus/CM, and CCC/Harvest,

This material is based upon work sponsored by the Air Force Material Command, Rome Laboratory, and the Advanced Research Projects Agency under Contract Number F30602-94-C-0253. The content of the information does not necessarily reflect the position or the policy of the Government and no official endorsement should be inferred.

which represent a coalescing and distillation of many research and commercial prototypes, largely satisfy the CM functionality requirements posed by Dart.

Of course, each of the second-generation CM systems mentioned above has its strengths and weaknesses. All can still be expected to improve over time. But their general coverage of Dart's eight functionality requirements raises the important question of whether there is a future to CM *research* as opposed to CM *engineering*. The answer is certainly "no" if research continues to stay focused on the eight areas. While there are engineering improvements to be made in those areas, research must turn its attention to new challenges.

In the following sections we propose some areas that we believe are the future of CM research. Exploration of these areas should eventually lead to new capabilities, and a new generation, of CM systems.

CM System Architecture

The second generation of CM systems is based on a three-level model: a low level that provides data storage, a middle level that provides basic CM services or mechanisms, and a high level that consists of processes or policies for using the mechanisms in the middle level.

At this point, CM systems allow some restricted flexibility at the low level (e.g., one can choose to use RCS, the file system, or a DBMS), and even less flexibility at the middle level (e.g., the naming and locking mechanisms are usually fixed). At the high level of process, second-generation CM systems either provide no explicit support for expressing policies or they provide particular processes for a specific task, such as change control. (Adele is a notable exception to this.)

Two important research questions arise. First, is it possible to provide more flexibility at the various levels and, second, is there even a better CM system architecture than the three-level model that might, for example, allow for this greater flexibility? The three-level model implies that the primitives of CM are data storage, basic mechanisms, and specific policies. An alternative view is a set of cooperating services, such as general relationship maintenance, dependency reasoning, and artifact access brokering, as well as process specification, monitoring, and control. Such alternative architectural views might lead to novel solutions in other areas of CM.

Another much needed topic of research is interoperability among CM systems. More and more, companies are starting to jointly develop products. Clearly, the need arises for companies to share CM artifacts. Yet each company will continue to use its own CM system to preserve its investment (of money, training, and trust) in that system. Therefore, it must become possible to form (temporary) alliances among different CM systems. This is a problem at all levels of the CM system architecture, from sharing of data to integration of processes. Notice that security issues arise as well in this context: it can be assumed that companies will not be willing to share all their CM artifacts. Again, an interesting question is whether the three-level model helps or hinders in solving the interoperability problem or whether there is an alternative architecture that is better suited to the solution.

Product Representation

As a rule, current CM systems represent the relationship among product versions through a directed acyclic graph (DAG), where the nodes are the version objects and the edges represent the *is-version-of* relationship. Implicitly, the edges also represent the deltas among versions. An interesting question is whether there are additional graphs—or, more generally, views of the available information—that might be useful.

The change set approach (as found in ADC, for example) provides an alternative view over similar information. A product is represented by an initial instance of a product combined with a constellation of change sets, which are sets of deltas to be applied to the product as a whole. Using change sets, one is able to do such things as apply a single bug fix to multiple branches. This is not possible, strictly speaking, with the traditional DAG model, and therefore the change set notion clearly adds useful functionality.

Software process provides examples of relationships that would be useful in an extended CM system. A software product actually consists of a rich web of related artifacts such as requirements, designs, and test cases, as well as the standard code artifacts. A CM system should be able to model relationships among related versions of these varied artifacts. In addition, it should be possible to tag relationships with process activities. For example, if a new version of some code has been created, then it is possible that the corresponding test cases also need to have new versions. A CM system should be able to traverse links to locate those test cases and interact with a process execution system to put the creation of new versions of test cases into a task agenda.

Product Software Architecture

The relationship between software architecture and CM systems has not been explored in any depth. However, knowledge of a product's architecture might have very interesting implications for a CM system. To date, the system model is the closest that CM systems come to representing product architectures. But system models primarily deal with the *building* of executable object modules, including the selection of versions. They do not represent other important architectural information, such as data or control flow connections among the modules.

Giving CM systems greater knowledge about the architecture of the software that they are managing would allow them to provide useful capabilities. For example, a geographically distributed effort to develop a certain product might apportion responsibility for different architectural pieces of the system to different sites in order to allow for parallel development. With the current generation of CM technology, each site must be assigned its own development branch. This implies that later in the development process an extensive, and possibly error-prone merge must take place to give the various sites consistent views of the entire system. In contrast, by using knowledge of a product's architecture, a CM system can make decisions about distributing artifacts based on, for example, module interconnections.

Domain Extensions

The capabilities provided by sophisticated CM systems should be applicable to domains outside of software development. Systems engineering is an example of such a domain. Systems engineering is concerned with products that are combinations of both software and hardware. Conceptually, second-generation CM systems already should be capable of maintaining hardware configurations. Of course, there is the problem of controlling and monitoring changes to hardware, which is not an issue for software (i.e., since software is intrinsically on the computer, unlike hardware, changes are immediately evident to the CM system). But ignoring that problem, there is still a serious question about how to represent and version the relationships *among* hardware and software.

The post-deployment phase for software provides another interesting domain ripe for configuration management research. There is a wide variety of problems involved in distributing software into the field and then maintaining it once there. Dynamically reconfigurable systems provide an example. For such systems, only part of a product may need to be upgraded, while the rest of the product should continue running. Suppose the installation of a product consists of a collection of client and server programs, where a certain client or server needs to be replaced by a new version. The CM system should offer support to decide whether the new client or server is compatible with the other clients and servers in the environment. Also, the CM system should indicate which clients and which servers are dependent on each other. This can determine the extent to which part of the whole product needs to be brought down in order to let the upgrade succeed.

Conclusion

Configuration management systems have come a long way since SCCS and Make. Second-generation CM systems have raised the level of sophistication dramatically, creating much greater challenges to CM researchers. Many problems and opportunities remain and, indeed, the second-generation systems themselves raise new questions. Configuration system architecture, product representation, product software architecture, and extended application domains are just a few of the areas that should keep researchers busy for the next several years.

References

1. S. Dart. Spectrum of Functionality in Configuration Management Systems. Technical Report SEI-90-TR-11, Software Engineering Institute, Pittsburgh, Pennsylvania, December 1990.
2. S. Dart. Concepts in Configuration Management Systems. In *Proceedings of the Third International Workshop on Software Configuration Management*, pages 1–18. ACM SIGSOFT, 1991.

Author Index

Lecture Notes in Computer Science

For information about Vols. 1–926

please contact your bookseller or Springer-Verlag